D1539724

Immigration and Religion in America

Immigration and Religion in America

Comparative and Historical Perspectives

EDITED BY

Richard Alba, Albert J. Raboteau, and Josh DeWind

A PROJECT ORGANIZED BY
THE SOCIAL SCIENCE RESEARCH COUNCIL

New York University Press

NEW YORK AND LONDON

NEW YORK UNIVERSITY PRESS
New York and London
www.nyupress.org
© 2009 by New York University
All rights reserved

Library of Congress Cataloging-in-Publication Data
Immigration and religion in America : comparative and historical
perspectives / edited by Richard Alba, Albert J. Raboteau,
and Josh DeWind.
p. cm.
"A project organized by the Social Science Research Council."
Includes bibliographical references (p.   ) and index.
ISBN-13: 978-0-8147-0504-9 (cl : alk. paper)
ISBN-10: 0-8147-0504-9 (cl : alk. paper)
ISBN-13: 978-0-8147-0505-6 (pbk : alk. paper)
ISBN-10: 0-8147-0505-7 (pbk : alk. paper)
1. Immigrants—Religious life—United States. 2. United States—Religion.
3. United States—Emigration and immigration.   I. Alba, Richard D. II.
Raboteau, Albert J. III. DeWind, Josh.
BL2525.I46 2008
200.86'9120973—dc22   2008030904

New York University Press books are printed on acid-free paper, and their
binding materials are chosen for strength and durability.

Manufactured in the United States of America

C 10 9 8 7 6 5 4 3 2 1
P 10 9 8 7 6 5 4 3 2 1

Contents

Introduction: Comparisons of Migrants and   1
Their Religions, Past and Present
    Richard Alba, Albert J. Raboteau, and Josh DeWind

PART I : INTEGRATION OF ITALIAN AND   25
    MEXICAN IMMIGRANTS INTO
    AN AMERICAN RELIGION

1. Passages in Piety: Generational Transitions and the   32
    Social and Religious Incorporation of Italian Americans
    Richard Alba and Robert Orsi

2. Migration and Mexican American Religious Life,   56
    1848–2000
    Roberto Lint Sagarena

3. Whither the Flock? The Catholic Church and the   71
    Success of Mexicans in America
    David Lopez

PART II : RELIGIOUS CONVERSION AMONG   99
    JAPANESE AND KOREAN IMMIGRANTS

4. Japanese and Korean Migrations: Buddhist and   106
    Christian Communities in America, 1885–1945
    Lori Pierce, Paul Spickard, and David Yoo

5. Critical Faith: Japanese Americans and the   135
    Birth of a New Civil Religion
    Jane Naomi Iwamura

6.   Buddhism, Rhetoric, and the Korean American   166
     Community: The Adjustment of Korean Buddhist
     Immigrants to the United States
     Sharon A. Suh

PART III : INCORPORATION OF NEW RELIGIONS   191
           INTO AMERICAN SOCIETY BY
           EUROPEAN JEWS AND ARAB MUSLIMS

7.   Immigration and the Transformation of American Jews: 198
     Assimilation, Distinctiveness, and Community
     Calvin Goldscheider

8.   Choosing Chosenness in America: 224
     The Changing Faces of Judaism
     Arnold Eisen

9.   The Shaping of Arab and Muslim Identity   246
     in the United States
     Yvonne Yazbeck Haddad

10. Muslim, Arab, and American: The Adaptation of   277
     Muslim Arab Immigrants to American Society
     Ann Chih Lin

PART IV : RELIGIOUS DIVERSIFICATION AMONG   297
          AFRICAN AMERICAN AND
          HAITIAN MIGRANTS

11. Black Migration, Religion, and Civic Life   304
     James Grossman and Albert Raboteau

12. Catholic, Vodou, and Protestant: Being Haitian,   319
     Becoming American—Religious Pluralism,
     Immigrant Incorporation, and Transnationalism
     Elizabeth McAlister and Karen Richman

     Integrated Bibliography   353
     Contributors   381
     Index   383

Introduction
Comparisons of Migrants and Their Religions, Past and Present

Richard Alba, Albert J. Raboteau, and Josh DeWind

The importance of religion for the incorporation of immigrants and their children into American society was a truism for those who attempted to understand the aftermath of the mass immigration of Europeans and East Asians of a century ago. The scholars and laypersons who studied and reflected on immigrant groups in the America of the first half of the 20th century took for granted that the institutions and meaning systems that religion provided shaped the immigrants' experiences in profound ways and could help or hinder the adjustment to the new setting. They understood also that the "religious factor," to borrow the title from one famous sociological study of the early 1960s, was not a given but evolved for each group in response to the challenges of living in a new environment. These points were all the more consequential because the immigrants formed not only ethnic minorities in the U.S. society of the time but also religious ones. Heavily Catholic and Jewish, they had entered a society that defined itself not simply as Christian but as Protestant and which regarded the immigrants of the time with suspicion and even xenophobia. Largely forgotten today is that Catholics and Jews were targets of Ku Klux Klan venom and that, during the 1920s, the Klan was a powerful organization in many of the northern cities where immigrants concentrated (Jackson, 1967).

The most famous reflection on these issues was Will Herberg's *Protestant-Catholic-Jew* (1960 [1955]), but their traces are evident almost everywhere one looks in the literature of 1900–65: for instance, in W. I. Thomas and Florian Znaniecki's classic work *The Polish Peasant in Europe and America* (1918–20). Remarkably, religion was initially a minor theme in the scholarship on the "new," post-1965 immigration. Among sociologists and economists, the predominant emphasis was for a time on the socioeconomic insertion of immigrants and their children. From this perspective, the omission of the religious aspects of immigrant incorporation is perhaps understandable: scholars no longer credited religion with as much economic significance as they did when they were still under the spell of Max Weber's *The Protestant Ethic and the Spirit of Capitalism* (1958 [1904–5]).

But it was a major omission, nevertheless. As in the early 20th century, immigration today is fueling the development of minority religious groups, such as Korean and Chinese Buddhists, Indian Sikhs, and Arab and South Asian Muslims, thereby expanding the range of religious diversity. More than in the mass immigration of a century ago, however, many new immigrants belong to religions that are well established on the American landscape, such as Mexican Catholics and Korean Presbyterians, though often immigrants set up their own congregations rather then join existing ones. In any case, religion has not lost any of its power to shape the incorporation of immigrants as an institution where immigrants can seek some shelter from the stresses they face in the U.S. environment, share knowledge about jobs and business opportunities, and introduce their children to the ethnic community; indeed, religion has become a cultural scheme that they can use to interpret their experiences and guide their actions.

Religion of necessity is gradually being restored to its rightful place of importance in inquiry into the immigrant and second-generation experience. While scholars of religion did little for a number of years to tackle descriptively or theoretically the complex nexus of religion and immigration (with the exception, most notably, of Jay Dolan, Robert Orsi, and Karen McCarthy Brown), the signs of change are increasingly evident. Diana Eck's Religious Pluralism Project at Harvard University recognized and began to describe the stunning variety of religious groups brought to the United States largely as a result of the new immigration. Her book, *A New Religious America* (2001), synthesized the results and brought them to the attention of a wide audience. Meanwhile, the New Ethnic and Immigrant Congregations Project, under the leadership of sociologist Stephen Warner, supported investigations into a variety of new immigrant groups and religions, resulting in a volume of essays, Warner and Judith Wittner's *Gatherings in Diaspora: Religious Communities and the New Immigration* (1998). On an even more ambitious scale, Pew Charitable Trusts supported research on the role of religion in the lives of new immigrants based in seven immigrant "gateway cities." The project has produced several major published studies, including *Religion and the New Immigrants: Continuities and Adaptation in Immigrant Congregations* (2000) and *Religion across Borders: Transnational Religious Networks* (2002), both edited by Helen Rose Ebaugh and Janet Saltzman Chafetz.

To impart additional momentum in this rediscovered direction, the Pew Charitable Trusts provided funding to the Social Science Research Council's International Migration Program to organize a project that would support research and convene scholars to examine relations between Religion, Migration, and Civic Life. Led by Josh DeWind, this program convened a series of meetings involving both social scientists and scholars of religion interested in immigration, with the purpose of creating a working group that would lay out the terrain of inquiry for the field and point in some fruitful directions. After a number of preliminary meetings, a group emerged with Richard Alba and Albert Raboteau as its co-chairs and defined an agenda for a first round of intellectual surveying. Sixteen scholars would be invited to prepare papers on the religion(s) of a particular immigrant group from a doubly comparative perspective. One comparison would be historical, pairing a new immigrant group with an older one to ascertain what is distinctive about the new immigration and what remains continuous with the patterns of the old. The other comparison would pair scholars from different disciplinary areas, social-scientific and religious studies, to see what new insights such collaborative exchanges might spark. In short, the basic motivation for the working group was to help shape the burgeoning field of immigration studies by bringing together perspectives from religious studies and those of immigration studies to enrich our understanding of the institutions by which immigrant communities organize themselves and the systems of meaning by which they "map" their lives. The current volume results from this group's efforts.

Religion as Institution—Religion as System of Meaning

Two approaches—religion as institution, religion as system of meaning—strike us as essential to any investigation of the ramifications of religion for the incorporation of immigrants and subsequent generations. No single scholar needs to give equal weight to both, and most of the authors in this volume devote more attention to one than to the other. But the scholarship on the immigration-religion nexus must deploy these approaches in a balanced way. For as institutions, religious organizations have acted as social service agencies, materially aiding immigrants through such "secular" concerns as economic opportunity, political activity, and the promotion of educational achievement. Descriptions of the institutional forms and activities of religion tend to deploy sociological categories and to emphasize the socioeconomic and political effects of religious activity (e.g., Hirschman, 2004; Foley and Hoge, 2007; Foner and Alba, 2008). As a meaning system, religion has furnished immigrant communities with symbolic interpretation of the experience of immigration, ritual reinforcement of identity, and the moral support of self-esteem. Descriptions of the meaning-making function of religion use the categories of religious studies and focus on beliefs, values, worship practices, and devotional piety (e.g., Orsi, 1985).

These two aspects of religion, while analytically separable, are not separate but cohere, even if imperfectly. When, for example, a particular religion fails to fulfill desired socioeconomic functions, practitioners may adopt another religion that does, thus demonstrating the greater efficacy and plausibility of the new religion's meaning system, as do, for example, Latino and Haitian Catholics who convert to evangelical forms of Protestantism. They may even adopt another religion while continuing to embrace the system of meaning of the previous one for certain occasions or particular purposes.

Four themes weave throughout the chapters and engage both aspects of immigrant religion, those of institutional structures and systems of meaning. All the themes can be viewed in terms of the most basic dilemma that confronts any immigrant group: How do its members cope with their status as outsiders? The question itself is Janus-faced. One face looks outward from the group to its place in the receiving society; this aspect is concerned with the barriers to inclusion. The other face looks inward and is concerned with the vulnerability of the group and its members in the new environment.

One theme, then, that emerges prominently from the substantive chapters is religion as a site for the articulation of the relationship to the host society. From the perspective of civic life, religious institutions of immigrant populations and their leaders have frequently played an important role in representing the group's interests to nonethnic audiences and making claims on its behalf (Foley and Hoge, 2007). The interests involved may be religious—for instance, the right of Muslim female students to dress in distinctive ways and to participate in required school activities, such as physical education, without having to compromise religious and moral injunctions. But, even more frequently, they involve overtly secular concerns, such as the legal and political rights of immigrants. Thus, the Roman Catholic Church, nominally the religious home of millions of Hispanic immigrants, the largest portion of the contemporary immigration stream, has taken strong positions on numerous questions touching on the rights of these immigrants. The Catholic Bishops' Conference, for instance, condemned Proposition 187 in California, which would have deprived illegal immigrants and their children of many public services, and the Catholic Church worked against its passage and subsequently joined lawsuits to block its implementation.

For many of the groups studied in this volume, systems of meaning also seem to shift in the American environment to address the concerns about outsider status. One manifestation, our first theme, is the rise of theological discourses to assert the compatibility of the group's values with those of U.S. society. Sometimes these take quite remarkable forms, assertions that, despite the superficial appearance of difference, the group is, at bottom, ultra-American, more American in some respects than native-born Americans themselves. Sharon Suh's discussion of Korean Buddhists (chapter 6) provides an example: her respondents insist that Buddhist teachings, with their emphasis on self-reliance, are more consistent with the American ethos of individualism than are the theologies and orientations of the Christian churches with which most Korean immigrants affiliate.

A second theme invokes the involvement of religious institutions in ethnic community building. Historically, this was a pivotal role that churches and synagogues played for European immigrant groups in the United States. As numerous observers have noted, one of the first activities of immigrants who settled in compact concentrations in American cities in the early 20th century was to collect funds to erect a religious center and to recruit the clergy to lead it (Orsi, 1985). In the case of Catholic immigrants, churches serving different ethnic and language groups were often erected within sight of each other, since the American Catholic Church recognized the critical need for national parishes (parishes whose membership was based on common ethnicity, language, and national origin instead of geographical proximity). These religious institutions, within which the mother tongue was the secular language of communication between clergy and laity, served as visible representations of the establishment of an ethnic community and sometimes of its material success. They provided spaces where this community qua community could congregate and recognize itself beyond the individual needs and mundane activities that dominated workaday life.

In one respect, the need for such institutions is perhaps even greater today than it was during the previous high point of immigration. True, the immigrants of the turn of the 20th century tended to cluster in the lowest rungs of American society and were probably placed generally in a more powerless position than is the case today. Yet many contemporary immigrant groups are more spatially dispersed than those of a century ago: advances in transportation and the affluence and professional standing of some groups, such as Indians, have led to this outcome (Kurien, 1998; Portes and Rumbaut, 2006). Therefore, they have at least as much need as the impoverished southern and eastern Europeans for spaces to come together as a community—for reasons of respite from the pressures of living in a strange society; maintaining connections to and sharing experiences with others from the same places and homelands; and introducing children, the second generation, into the ethnic community. Quite famously, Korean Christian churches fulfill these functions for the immigrant generation, though less so for the second generation (Min and Kim, 2005).

This is not simply a need met on the institutional level. The strains of the immigration experience are difficult: some individuals are placed in extremis. Religious systems of meaning can be invoked to provide guidance and significance for such persons. At times, they produce answers that border on the nationalistic, proclaiming the superiority of the immigrants to the surrounding society. Thus, it is not uncommon to find theological answers to immigrant dilemmas that declare the mission of the group as one of "saving" American society from its impending moral fall. In reflecting on why Jews and Muslims find themselves in American society, theological discourse in both groups has identified a salvific role they can play; and Korean Christians have sometimes cast themselves in a similar role, as revitalizers and purifiers of American Christianity.

Closely associated with the communal aspects of immigrant religion is the third theme, the theme of connection to the homeland. Sometimes such a connection is built indissolubly into a religion, such as when the homeland is recognized as its sacred center or the seat of religious authority. The latter was the case for Italian Catholics and, during the period of Protestant proselytizing, added to the intensity of the struggle for their loyalties, since they were defined as the "Pope's people." But even when the connection does not have this essential nature, it arises generally out of a straightforward institutional logic, since, for instance, the recruitment of clerics who speak the mother tongue requires it. Likewise, the circulation of sacred objects between the parent religious body in the homeland and its satellites abroad creates connections. In these senses, religions are, by their natures, transnational institutions that link places separated by great distances on the earth's surface in fraternal embrace (Smith, 2006; Levitt, 2007). Indeed, the re-creation of important religious sites establishes immigrant holy sites as translocative. As Elizabeth McAlister and Karen Richman demonstrate here (chapter 12), the Madonna of 115th Street in East Harlem became the translocated site of pilgrimage to the Haitian *lwa* Ezili Danto (Our Lady of Mt. Carmel) for Haitian immigrants in New York.

The relationship of the immigrants to the homeland also is frequently taken up by systems of religious meaning. A case discussed at length by Richman and McAlister is that of Haitian immigrants whose connection to an ancestral plot of land represents a spiritual and moral tie to family and kin relationships that is reaffirmed in economic responsibilities sanctioned by Vodou. For some immigrants, these responsibilities become such a drag on their economic and social advance in the new environment that they seek to jettison them by converting to evangelical Protestantism.

The final, fourth, theme of broad significance arises from the plural religious environment of the United States, which has varied ramifications for religions and for immigrants. Many religious groups come to the United States from homelands where they were the dominant presence, the religion of the majority, while others, such as eastern European Jews, had survived in hostile surroundings where group members were segregated in separate communities and conversion to the religion of the majority was a possibility rarely taken. They find themselves in the United States in a society where many religious groups exist and are free to compete for members. After a long period of being able to take the loyalty of their members for granted, they find themselves in a religious marketplace, an agora, where their members may be tempted by the wares of other denominations; and the new setting may thus provoke innovations. National parishes for Catholic immigrants at the turn of the 20th century served, in part, as the American hierarchy's response to the unexpected success of Protestant proselytizers, who made inroads among Italian and other immigrants. Eastern European Jews, too, recognized the need to attend to religious loyalty in an open society where anti-Semitism was not strong enough to wall Jews into a sort of ghetto. As Calvin Goldscheider describes (chapter 7), mid-20th-century Jews drew a line at intermarriage; but the rapid rise of outmarriage by Jews during the last quarter of the last century has led to other strategies for preserving a demographic core.

For the immigrants themselves, the availability of many more religious options than they previously were familiar with can have profound consequences. For African American migrants from the South, the greater religious spectrum in the black communities of the North provided novel ways of translating the basic problems of racial inequality into religious terms. Thus, the immigrant who might have been a Baptist or Methodist in rural Georgia might become attached to the Garveyite group in the North as one strategy for laying claim to greater rights; or she might become a devotee of Father Divine, implying another strategy for attaining material and social well-being.

For some groups, the relative openness and tolerance of American society provides acute theological challenges, to which different generations have responded in different ways. This phenomenon is elegantly presented in Arnold Eisen's discussion of Judaism (chapter 8). Eisen demonstrates that, for many, the notion of Jews as God's chosen people required revision in the United States; here, within the frame of a pluralist democracy where anti-Semitism abated, that notion resonated with a sense of superiority that produced discomfort. Even the meaning of being Jewish shifted for many Jews in the less oppressive atmosphere of American society, leading to such widespread variants as self-identified Jews who maintain cultural and social attachments to the ethnic group but do not practice the religion.

Entrance to the agora was fraught with difficulties for non-Protestant immigrants during the 19th century and for much of the 20th as well, due to the legally unestablished but socially pervasive hegemony of evangelical Protestantism, which viewed Catholics and Jews as inimical to the ideals of a Christian "redeemer nation," chosen by God for a special salvific role among the nations of the world. Matched with a xenophobic "Anglo-Saxonism," periodic outbreaks of religious bigotry led to the organization of various societies to protect America from subversion by foreigners within, who held allegiance to foreign powers, such as the papacy, or to international secret cabals, "exposed" by propaganda like the "Protocols of the Elders of Zion." Old stereotypes died hard and were dusted off and reused during periods of perceived threat such as the presidential campaign of the Roman Catholic, Al Smith, in 1928 and even that of John F. Kennedy in 1960.

Despite these hurdles, religious minorities, as Smith and Kennedy illustrate, have successfully used the free exercise clause of the First Amendment, the universalistic rhetoric of the Declaration of Independence, and their own upward social and economic mobility to achieve gradual acceptance, often begrudging at first, into the public square of religious tolerance, thus expanding and realizing the national ideal of pluralism. Ongoing tensions about the extent of admission to the agora still trouble newer immigrants such as Hindus, Sikhs, Jains, and especially Muslims in post-9/11 America, as Yvonne Haddad's essay argues (chapter 9).

Design of the Study

In our conception, the study had a natural 2 × 2 design. One twosome originated with disciplinary affiliation: pairing a social scientist who could speak to the demographic and institutional aspects of an immigrant religion with a religious scholar who attended to meaning and symbolic aspects. This pairing also had to cover two different bodies of knowledge in another way: one scholar, in our view, should have an understanding of the immigration and incorporation history of the group; the other, its religious affiliations.

The other twosome was implied by the comparative nature of the investigation. Our conceit was to compare the religious aspects of incorporation of groups from the classical and contemporary periods of immigration that have similarities in their location within the immigration spectrum and also in their religious location. Thus, the Italians and Mexicans were chosen because they are both examples of large, low-wage labor immigrations—indeed, each epitomizes this phenomenon for its respective era (Perlmann and Waldinger, 1997; Perlmann, 2005)—and they are overwhelmingly Catholic groups with homeland histories of low rates of observance and of a fusion of Catholicism with folk practices. As the subsequent comparisons reveal, however, one can never declare a faithful parallelism to exist between two groups with two distinct experiences. The Italian-Mexican comparison is imperfect in some important respects, as are each of the others. The fruitfulness of the comparison comes through, nevertheless, because it sheds new light on the institutional discrimination confronting Mexicans in the West and Southwest through much of the 20th century. Briefly put, Catholicism did not help Mexicans nearly as much as it helped Italians to advance in American society.

The 2 × 2 design led us to the notion of each comparison as staffed by a quartet of scholars, like a bridge table. In fact (and with some difficulty), we commissioned scholars to fill these roles at each table. While we initially imagined that each scholar would write a separate paper from his or her particular vantage point and from this four-way conversation a larger story would unfold, for a variety of reasons various scholars teamed up to write joint papers. In the end, only the comparison of eastern European Jews and middle-eastern Muslims lived up to the original, four-paper plan.

In many ways, the most difficult part of the plan was arriving at a suitable set of comparisons, and even far into the process, participants were raising questions about the precise comparisons we chose. In conceiving of the comparisons, we attempted to lay out a theoretically designed set of boxes, one for each comparison. Given the religious history and constitution of the United States, it seemed appropriate to use the comparisons to understand the incorporation of the following:

> 1. Immigrant groups whose religion is already well established in the United States (Italian and Mexican Catholics). Abstractly, it would seem as if religious and social incorporation could proceed according to a set of preexisting templates that eventually bring members of the group, perhaps especially of the second and third generation, into multiethnic congregations and hence increasing integration into communities beyond those of the immigrant group. This is an old idea and was the core of the hypothesis of the Triple Melting Pot, formulated by sociologist Ruby Jo Reeves Kennedy in the 1940s and 1950s. According to the hypothesis, the descendants of European immigrants were being absorbed into multiethnic communities defined along religious lines, exemplified in patterns of intermarriage that took place between individuals of different ethnicities but common religions (Kennedy, 1944, 1952).
>
> 2. Immigrants whose religion is related to, but not one of, the "charter" religions of American society (eastern European Jews and Arab Muslims). The charter religions are those that, because of historical "agreements," have become identified with the American mainstream.

Today, these religions include the major Protestant denominations, Catholicism, and Judaism, and their charter role is represented by the common description of the United States as a "Judeo-Christian society." Moreover, these religions and their observances have become institutionalized in the everyday realities of the mainstream society in a way that sets them above the situations of other religious groups, which are faced with difficult struggles to have, for example, their claim on holiday exemptions recognized. This is indisputable in the case of the Christian denominations, given the society-wide exemptions from normal quotidian responsibilities observed during their two major holidays, Easter and Christmas.

The definition of the charter religions can change over time. Groups once defined as outsiders can succeed in making their way into the inner circle. This is exemplified by Judaism. When eastern European Jews arrived en masse in the late 19th and early 20th centuries, they found a society that resolutely defined itself as Christian, even Protestant, and identified them as outsiders. Yet, during the second half of the 20th century, Judaism gradually achieved a charter status, at least in the regions of the country where many Jews are settled and where, today, many school systems close down for the holidays of Rosh Hashanah and Yom Kippur. A reasonable question is whether Muslims can achieve the same feat, and in fact (and ironically) Muslims often take Jews as the model to be emulated, as Yvonne Haddad points out (chapter 9).

3. Immigrants who bring religions unrelated to any of the charter religions (Japanese and Korean Buddhists). Many observers of the contemporary immigration scene have noted its religious diversity, some going as far as to predict the end of Christian hegemony in the foreseeable future. Muslims, Buddhists, Sikhs, and others have increased in number and, in some cases, planted their initial congregations in the United States as a result of contemporary immigration. Much of this diversity is associated with Asian immigrants. Yet this is not the first time that religions entirely outside the Judeo-Christian family of faiths have arrived on American shores, for they were brought also by the sizable streams of immigrants from Japan and China that were part of the classical era. Thus, we can hope to learn something about contemporary religious incorporation by examining how religion was implicated in the incorporation of these earlier groups.

The comparison between Japanese and Koreans focuses on groups coming from countries where Buddhist traditions are predominant in the religious faiths of the majority but where Christianity had made inroads before the onset of immigration and conversions to Christianity among the immigrants were frequent.

4. The previous comparison involves groups that are racially different from the largely white mainstream. Before the legal and institutional changes brought about by the civil rights movement, which led to the radical elimination of racial bars to immigration in the Immigration and Nationality Act of 1965, the ability of members of the Asian groups to enter the mainstream was almost nil due to institutionalized racism, which, for instance, until 1952 prevented Asian foreign-born residents from naturalizing as citizens of the United States. How much the changes of the civil rights period and the more tolerant climate ushered in by them and by the resurgence of immigration have reduced the impact of racism on Asian groups is the subject of debate.

The continuing impact of racism on individuals of African ancestry is not open to debate, however. Research on contemporary Afro-Caribbean immigrants, exemplified by Mary Waters's acclaimed *Black Identities* (1999), has established unambiguously that these immigrants—and, even more, their children—are treated on numerous occasions as members of an undifferentiated black group and that their life chances in consequential domains, such as residence, are hemmed in by race. Moreover, a long-established literature has demonstrated the significance of churches as sites for the contestation of race and racial oppression by African Americans. Hence, the interaction between race and religion has a special significance for African-ancestry migrants. There could also be similarities in this respect between black immigrants, who cross a national boundary, and migrants, who move within the territory of the United States.

The comparison for this conceptual cell involves contemporary Haitian immigrants, on the one hand, and the southern African Americans who moved north during the era of the Great Migration.

What Do We Learn from the Comparisons?

With such a varied set of comparisons, it is not clear, at first, what conclusions might be extracted from the quartet of comparisons as a whole. Before we can address this question, though, we need to examine the results of each of the comparisons in turn. Needless to say, there is much that must be regarded as tentative because our effort has been exploratory, covering terrain that has been overlooked by many scholars of contemporary immigration. To an important extent, also, the studies in this volume specify the questions that subsequent research should address.

The Italian-Mexican comparison was conceived as one where religion, especially in its social and institutional dimensions, might be thought to provide long-run advantages for an immigrant group, one belonging to an established, mainstream religion, which already has many American adherents. This initial hunch, however, has not panned out. Instead, the comparison of the study of Italian Americans by Richard Alba and Robert Orsi (chapter 1) to those of Mexicans by Roberto Lint Sagarena (chapter 2) and David Lopez (chapter 3) seems to reveal a previously unrecognized aspect of the exclusion of Mexican Americans from the mainstream.

What made this comparison particularly appealing were some sociological similarities that have led some scholars to see the Mexicans as potentially the Italians of today. The two groups represent the great low-wage labor migrations of their times. In both cases, too, mainstream Americans have doubted the assimilability of the immigrants and their children. These sociological similarities are bolstered by religious ones: both groups brought a syncretic Catholicism mixed with folk practices that distinguished the immigrant religious practice and belief from those of mainstream American Catholics. The groups are alike also in that the weak attachments of many group members to the Catholic Church have engendered relatively high rates of conversion to Protestantism.

The most intriguing aspect of the comparison is that, for the most part, the Italians have entered the American mainstream. Indeed, as the chapter by Alba and Orsi reveals, the Italians exemplify as well as any other European group the paradigm of generation-by-generation progression into the mainstream that has traditionally dominated thinking about the incorporation of immigrant groups. Not only was their social ascent paralleled by transitions in their Catholicism, but also the options for religious inclusion within the church were implicated in their rise up the social ladder. The point of immigrant inclusion was typically an Italian parish located in an area of immigrant settlement. As upward movement occurred, in the second or the third generations, outward movement (migration away from urban ethnic enclaves) typically did as well. In the geography of post–World War II America, this migration often led Italian Americans into suburban settings where parishes were multiethnic and set the stage for further intermarriage.

Paralleling this movement were changes in piety and in the relationship to Catholic schools. Italian immigrant piety, with its emphasis on relationships to saints, exemplified in *festas*, and its casual norms about church attendance, especially for men, was quite distant from the American—or perhaps more accurately, Irish American—understanding of religiosity. But over generations, Italian American Catholics appear to have grown much closer to American Catholic norms. The same was true for the parochial school system. Italians were well known during their first decades in the United States for keeping their distance from parochial schools and sending their children to the public system. However, as they rose socioeconomically, they became more likely to send their children to Catholic schools; in this respect, Catholic education, which for many provided the initial entrée to the university world, became a mark of success and inclusion.

This could have been the storyline for Mexican Americans, but it has not been, at least up to this point. The chapters by Lopez and Lint Sagarena tell a story in counterpoint to the Italian one. For much of the 20th century, the Mexicans, who had become a largely immigrant, rather than indigenous, group by then, were not regarded as an integral part of the European American Catholicism that was developing in the West and Southwest, especially in California. Indeed, the American Catholic Church was not as ethnically anchored in the western United States as it was on the East Coast, because it was largely dependent on migrants from the East and Midwest, who in many cases were cutting their ties to their ethnic communities of origin through migration. As Lint Sagarena describes, the church was attempting to gain acceptance as an American religion, and thus its western leaders drew distinctions between European American Catholics and Mexican American ones. They thereby shared with Anglo Protestants a set of demeaning attitudes toward Mexican American Catholics, seeing their practices, for instance, as involving folk superstitions.

The Catholic Church did not provide Mexican Americans with the avenues leading to the mainstream in the way that it did for European American ethnics. In the West, Mexican Americans kept their distance from the Euro-American-dominated church—for instance, worshipping at home altars and preserving their veneration of the Virgin of Guadalupe, which was maintained more by lay devotional societies than by parish clergy. The church's investment in Catholic educational institutions, which provide alternatives for families in poor neighborhoods where the quality of public education may be low, was heavily concentrated in the areas of European immigrant settlement. Thus, Mexicans have not had the helping hand of Catholic schools and colleges to assist them in breaking through educationally to the same degree that Italians and Poles have.

The comparison between eastern European Jews and Arab Muslims also reveals a thought-provoking blend of similarities and differences. When immigrant Jews arrived in large numbers in the early decades of the 20th century, there seemed to be little reason to expect that their descendants would be seen as part of the mainstream. American society, while not nearly as oppressive as Russia and other parts of eastern Europe, was still anti-Semitic. Yet, as the essays by Eisen (chapter 8) and Goldscheider (chapter 9) indicate in different ways, America turned out to be open to an extraordinary upward mobility by many Jewish families; and Judaism itself, which has come to be identified as a mainstream religion, is the only non-Christian one so far. Ironically, then, many Muslim Americans, seeing their religion under attack, look to Jews and Judaism for a model of how to gain acceptance and influence.

These may seem hopeless goals in light of the scrutiny and suspicion that have fallen on Muslims since 9/11. However, one does well to remember that other ethnic and religious groups have prospered after enduring similar periods of trial. The paramount example is that of Japanese Americans, who had recovered socioeconomically and dispersed throughout society within two decades of the disaster wrought on them by World War II internment. The blinding light of suspicion was cast on Jews, too, during the McCarthy period, but not long afterward their intermarriage rates had begun a sharp upward climb. Thus, it is too early to draw strong conclusions on whether the tensions and suspicions of the present will exclude Muslims from the mainstream.

These two groups are alike, moreover, in the close relationship of their faiths to Christianity; indeed, all three—Jew, Muslim, Christian—are now acknowledged as kindred branches of the Abrahamic tree. Their mono-theism has common roots, and they share prophetic traditions, along with some of their texts and spiritual forebears. Of course, such commonali-ties are related also to historic entanglings that have left behind memories of hostility and battle. Nevertheless, they also place Islam, like Judaism, in a fundamentally different position with respect to the Christian ma-jority than is the case for religions like Buddhism that are unrelated to Christianity.

The similarities do not end there. As Ann Shih Lin observes in the es-say on Detroit Arabs (chapter 10), "Islam is a noninstitutional faith: like Judaism, the rituals of faith are lived through daily life and personal prac-tice." The absence of hierarchy and the lack of attachment of the majority of Muslims to mosques suggest the possible evolution of the religious ob-servances of many Muslims in directions that are compatible with a high degree of social intermixing with non-Muslims. The same evolution oc-curred in the case of eastern European Jews, although, as Goldscheider reminds us, many of the immigrants were secular to begin with. There is also an enormous difference, however. Jews were coming from European societies in which they were ghettoized minorities, suffering from oppres-sive strictures on their educational possibilities and economic activities, as well as from occasional murderous assaults. For the most part, Muslims are coming from societies in which their religion is dominant, although in some cases they belong to branches of the faith or ethnic groups that are discriminated against.

The American environment has created major challenges for the self-understandings of both religions, and the Jewish case suggests that they can provoke theological evolution in the direction of the mainstream. Eisen brilliantly dissects the dilemmas of Jews' self-understanding as the "chosen people," which was appropriate for group survival in the face of Christian exclusion in Europe but unsuited to the more tolerant, democratic envi-ronment of America. Thus began an intellectual quest for an answer to the question of what it means to be a Jew in America. According to both Eisen and Goldscheider, most American Jews have arrived at a position that al-lows them to be fully integrated into society while they maintain some degree of ethnic and religious distinctiveness. One catches sight of a simi-lar process of self-examination in the case of Muslims, who, in Haddad's depiction, struggle with the question of whether they reside in *dar al-harb* (the abode of war), rather than *dar al-Islam* (the abode of the faith). For the most part, they arrive at hopeful answers, which recognize the freedom that America offers to the practice of their faith, and thus avoid this fundamental dichotomy in the Muslim worldview. Whether the evolution in their understandings of their place in American society will follow the trajectory already blazed by American Jews, it is too early to say.

The Japanese-Korean comparison was initially conceived by us as a way of investigating the incorporation of groups that come from countries dominated by religions outside of the Judeo-Christian mainstream of American society. In this case, too, the comparison when fleshed out moved in directions that we did not anticipate initially. For one thing, it demonstrates the slipperiness of the notion that non-European immigrant groups bring nonwestern traditions that are altered in the American context by the intense pressures of adaptation. For while the Japanese and Koreans came from societies in which variants of Buddhism were dominant, by the time of outmigration the religious landscapes of both had been altered by the efforts of Protestant missionaries. It seems likely that migration was selective of those who had already converted to Christianity—they were and are overrepresented in the migration streams, compared with their percentage of the population.

In addition, many other immigrants were probably familiar with Christian ideas before immigration and readily converted to Christianity within a short period after arriving—this happened in both cases, as Lori Pierce, Paul Spickard, and David Yoo observe (chapter 4), though it has undoubtedly been more common among Koreans, some 40 percent of whom are estimated to have converted to Christianity in the United States. Nevertheless, as Pierce et al. document, this similarity between the groups has not produced similar religious configurations in the United States. Buddhism was characteristic of the Japanese during the migration period, while Christianity, especially of an evangelical kind, has been typical of the Koreans.

The chapters also suggest the impact of race on the forms that religious incorporation took. Indeed, the overrepresentation of Christians among the Japanese and Korean immigrants by itself hints at this impact, for it seems to indicate that many nonwhite immigrants, recognizing the constraints that race might impose on their opportunities, sought to minimize other differences from the American mainstream. Certainly, during the first half of the twentieth century, this strategy did not help the Japanese very much; whether they were Buddhist or Christian, they were still the targets of institutionalized discrimination, such as California's Alien Land Acts, which sought to impair the success of Japanese American farmers.

However, this strategy may have greater chances for success in post-1960s America, and this is one of the questions these chapters pose for future scholars.

In any event, the sense of being vulnerable strangers, subject not only to the liabilities associated with immigrant status—for example, standing out because of an accent or lack of proficiency in English—but also to possible racial discrimination, has probably heightened the protective role of religious institutions for both groups. This theme of religious institutions as refuge and as sites of community building emerges very prominently in the chapters on the Japanese and Koreans. As Pierce, Spickard, and Yoo argue for the Japanese, Buddhist "churches," especially those associated with the Nishi Hongwanji sect, fulfilled these roles in the pre–World War II period.

In the competitive religious agora of the United States, the strategies that non-Christian religions have taken have affected their success. Suh's chapter on Korean Buddhists brings this point into sharp relief. The Korean Buddhist congregation that she studied has not attempted to meet the practical needs of immigrants during the initial phases of adapting to the United States. Indeed, it has taken a reserved stance with respect to the immigrants, in effect serving as a presence for those who want it, while ignoring the many who have been courted successfully by Christian congregations. The result has been a massive streaming of the immigrants and, even more so, the second generation in the direction of Christianity. One question that needs to be addressed, however, is whether this Christianity always takes the form of one that is circumscribed by ethnicity and race. That the first generation adheres overwhelmingly to Korean Christian churches, where they can socialize with other Koreans and speak Korean, is well known. That the second generation is frequently uncomfortable in this immigrant environment and seeks out other Christian churches is also well known. What is not known is whether the churches attended by the U.S.-born tend mainly to be Asian American congregations, which have arisen in some parts of the country, or ones that are more ethnically heterogeneous.

One must not lose sight here of the multiple orientations of these ethnic congregations of the immigrants. While they have been to some degree inward-looking, protective carapaces for the immigrants, they have also looked outward, but in two directions—one way toward the homeland and the other way toward American society. The homeland orientation of the Japanese Christian churches is remarkable, given that conversion to

Christianity presumably marked a step of Americanization, of acceptance of the dominant religion of the receiving society. Nonetheless, in the pre–World War II period, Japanese immigrant Christians were exhorted by some of their pastors and co-ethnics to conceive of their Christianity as in service to Japan and to their fellow Japanese. As Pierce et al. describe, the Japanese American Protestant churches attempted to meld Japanese nationalism with American cultural values.

At the same time, religious institutions became the places where immigrants could formulate claims for inclusion in the society in which they were now located. These seem to be one aspect of the Japanese American civil religion, centered on the travails of the group's experience, that Jane Iwamura identifies (chapter 5). At other moments, such claims have taken the extreme form of assertions of ultra-Americanness, of being more American in some ways than native-born white Americans. Thus, we find Japanese Christians claiming in the prewar period that Japanese Christianity was superior to the American versions: that it was more faithful to the model that Jesus provided. As Suh shows, a similar claim is asserted by contemporary Korean immigrant Buddhists, who argue that Buddhism is more consonant than Christianity with the core American values of self-reliance and individualism.

The comparison of Haitians and African Americans is exceptional, for it is the only case in this volume in which international and national migrants are compared. Our decision to compare the Haitian immigration to U.S. cities such as Miami and New York with African American migration from the rural South to the urban North was premised on the common origin of both groups in the forced migration of their African ancestors to the Americas in the Atlantic slave trade and a common legacy of racial discrimination that oppressed both groups long after slavery's demise. We surmised that the long-term effects of slavery and racism created, at least in part, the conditions that led African Americans to migrate in the early 20th century and Haitians to immigrate later. It seemed that the two groups also matched our comparative grid of "old" and "new" (im)migration. As the chapters demonstrate, the common history of slavery and racism took different trajectories in Haiti and the United States, however, resulting in interesting similarities and divergences (and surprising interactions) between the two groups and the roles of religion in their migrations.

For both African Americans and Haitians, religion served to blunt the internal and external effects of racism, but their experiences and hence their strategies were different. African Americans took the Christianity of their masters and used its narratives and moral logic to powerfully counter the oppression from which they suffered. Thus, the narrative of Exodus with its optimistic motif of escape from slavery and entrance into the Promised Land served as a means of group valorization and a moral argument against racial discrimination. Exodus as a symbolic map of meaning enabled African Americans to counter racist stereotypes of themselves and to project a hopeful future of social justice and equality.

For Haitians, the Revolution of 1791–1804, the only successful overthrow of a slave society in the Western Hemisphere, severed their experience from that of African Americans. Haitian independence led to an alternative black identity distinct in language, religion, culture, and history from the pejorative qualities of blackness ascribed to African Americans. This departure from the black experience in North American slavery was strongly marked in the sphere of religion, where Vodou preserved a manifest link to the religious traditions of the west African societies from which the slaves had been brought. Religion, Roman Catholicism as well as Vodou, thus served as a marker of their transnational identity as Haitians and a rejection of being placed in the subordinate category of "African American."

Given this very different experience, one might ask: How would Haitian immigrants to the United States, facing the prospect of a racialized incorporation, locate themselves religiously? Would they, like African Americans, look to religion both as a shelter from the racism beyond the sanctuary walls and as a site for forging discourses and symbols to combat it? Or would they, like many other contemporary Roman Catholic immigrants, see in conversion to evangelical Protestant sects principally an opportunity for trying out the possibilities of assimilation, by putting on the cloak of an American identity?

The questions turn out to be too simply formulated, in part because American versions of Protestantism, especially Pentecostalism, had already infiltrated Haiti before immigration ever became substantial. We find both similarity and divergence in the ways that religion has figured in the postmigration experiences of the two groups. In the process of resettling, both have explored new religious options in their new environments and adopted a diversity of elements from them, in part or whole, as seemed instrumentally adaptive and useful in the new context. At the same time, a key divergence lies in the religious transnationalism of many Haitian immigrants.

James Grossman and Albert J. Raboteau (chapter 11) take up the religious ramifications of the Great Migration of African Americans, which began in the early 20th century, when unprecedented numbers of black laborers and their families left the land for the cities and the South for the North and West. The double process of migration and urbanization recast both the physical and social landscape for the migrants, creating new opportunities while presenting new challenges. Yet the reliance on religious ideas—on those of Christianity, in particular—carried over into the Great Migration. In the North, too, religion was central to African Americans' attempts to forge positive identities for themselves, which could be linked to moral schemes that made white racism comprehensible and provided strategies for undermining it. In addition, the pluralism of the urban religious marketplace in the North helped in the establishment of surrogate public spaces for civic activity, which would ultimately constitute the basis for the development and growth of black political organization.

Liza McAllister and Karen Richman (chapter 12) present evidence that transnational Haitians living in the United States have created a religious landscape that is at once American and diasporic. For Haitians in Haiti and in North America, the religious landscape consists of overlapping fields: (1) the indigenous Afro-Haitian religion called Vodou, (2) Haitian Roman Catholicism, and (3) the evangelical Protestant denominations such as Baptist and Pentecostal. Each of these religious fields is separate from, yet overlaps with, the others. Their religious frameworks and religious practices span transnational social spaces, interacting in complex and various ways with processes of migration. Each sphere is the site of a different dynamic of imagining, and entering into, American culture. The religious choices that immigrant Haitians make correlate with a variety of social and economic agendas that seem likely to enhance their chances of success in the American setting.

One of the striking discoveries to emerge from this comparison is migration as a source of religious pluralism and exchange. Haitian Pentecostalism derives from a Pentecostal movement in Los Angeles in 1906, which involved African Americans from its outset. Pentecostalism, as many observers have noted, has had the "unintended consequence" of facilitating upward mobility among several generations of African American migrants. Indeed, a new "gospel of wealth" has been articulated by a current group of black Pentecostal televangelists to large audiences. What institutional ecclesial relationships have and will develop between Haitian and African American Pentecostals remains to be studied. Similarly,

Roman Catholicism has a long, if statistically small, presence among African Americans. What relationships exist or will emerge between these communities remains to be discovered.

Conversely, Haitian Vodou has contributed to the reawakened interest of African Americans in the traditional religions of Africa, as has Cuban Santería. African Americans have converted to these religious communities; the scale and significance of such conversions remain to be studied, as does the impact of the migration of independent African churches from Nigeria, Ghana, and elsewhere. But the Haitian migration has clearly added new possibilities to the already rich religious palette in African American communities.

Final Thoughts

What the studies in this volume establish beyond any doubt is that research on immigration ignores the religious aspects of incorporation at its peril and, likewise, that scholars of religion must pay attention to the profound impacts of immigration on the spiritual landscape of the United States and on specific religious bodies, their institutions, and beliefs.

Religion, as Jose Casanova and others have observed before us, is the one truly valid form of expressing ethnic difference in the United States (Casanova, 1994). A comparison with language is instructive, for the United States is known as a graveyard of mother tongues (Portes and Rumbaut, 2006). Even in the contemporary, globalized era, when communications of many sorts between immigrant communities and their homelands have been facilitated by technological advances, English still prevails over mother tongues in the second and, even more, the third generations (Alba et al., 2002). But religious distinctiveness is sanctioned by mainstream America, which places great emphasis on the value of religious observance, and, consequently, it is not eroded to the same degree, even if immigrant religions do undergo significant changes in the American environment.

The services of religious congregations are undoubtedly the most regular and widely observed of the manifestations of immigrant and ethnic communities. We can think of no other institution that provides so frequently the sites and occasions for the members of these communities to come together, recognize each other, engage in a variety of communications and transactions, and give meaning, both transcendental and secular, to their experiences. Immigrant congregations are thus social spaces where an overloaded palette of purposes and needs is served: these can be instrumental, sociocultural, or psychological and spiritual. Thus, congregations enable immigrants to keep abreast of events in the community and in the homeland and to learn about occupational, educational, residential, and other opportunities for their own advancement in the receiving society. They also provide an array of services for persons in need, whether these needs arise from, say, the stresses of overwork in the typical immigrant jobs or the centrifugal forces frequently tearing at immigrant families (Hirschman, 2004). They are sites where the second generation can be introduced to the wider immigrant and ethnic community, learn its rituals, and appreciate the significance of its culture (Kurien, 1998). Finally, through religious systems of meaning and the interpretive efforts of pastors and laypersons, congregations offer the possibility of lifting the personal travails experienced by immigrants onto a higher plane, infusing them with moral purpose and transcendent value.

Any institution capable of serving such a dizzying array of purposes for a large number of people deserves more attention than it has received so far in the literature on immigrant incorporation. In addition, as some of the chapters in this volume demonstrate convincingly, immigrants are not simply the passive beneficiaries of religious institutions but work out their personal strategies of incorporation in and through them. For this reason, students of religion cannot afford to ignore the impact of immigration on religions, their institutions, and their practices and beliefs.

The religions of immigrant groups usually find that they must change in the American environment to meet an unexpected set of novel needs or risk losing their adherents. The Korean Buddhist congregation described by Suh exemplifies the latter possibility, while the change of Islamic imams from prayer leaders to pastors of American-style congregations, as described by Haddad, exemplifies the former. But even the beliefs and values of religions may undergo shifts, in emphasis at least, to face the challenges of the American context and its agora of religions. This certainly has been the case for American Jews' interpretation of the doctrine of chosenness.

Some of the largest changes lie in the future as a result of the continuing flow of immigrants into established religions. In this respect, the most momentous are likely to be seen in the American Catholic Church because of the enormous inflow of Latin Americans, especially Mexicans. Even though evangelical Protestant churches have made inroads in the

Latino population, the great majority of Latinos are Catholics. The cliché is that many are nominal Catholics. However, a consistent pattern to be observed in incorporation into American society is that immigrant groups, especially in their native-born generations, tend to become more religious over time. If that pattern holds for Latino Catholics, and we see no reason it will not, and if the projections of a rapid growth in the Latino population in coming decades hold, and we think this likely, then two conclusions seem obvious: the proportion of Catholics in the U.S. population, currently around 25 percent, will grow appreciably; and Latinos will make up a larger and larger fraction of American Catholics, perhaps as many as half by mid-century. What will the consequences be for the Catholic Church itself and for the place of the church and the people it serves within American society? We do not know, but we are certain that these questions demand consideration.

It seems appropriate that we end this introduction with questions because the study of the interaction of contemporary immigration and religion is not far enough along that we should allow ourselves the conceit of presenting firm conclusions. But, then, difficult questions have always been the purview of religion.

Part I

Integration of Italian and Mexican Immigrants into an American Religion

The Italian-Mexican comparison occupies an essential cell in any theoretical design for understanding the incorporation of immigrant-ethnic groups. These two groups represent the great low-wage labor migrations of their time, dominated by immigrants with little or no schooling who were funneled by the U.S. labor market into manual jobs involving minimal skill (Perlmann, 2005). In both cases, mainstream Americans doubted the assimilability of the immigrants and their children, given the very low educational levels of the newcomers and the apparent ethnic distance separating them from white Americans, distances that were conceptualized in terms of "color," though not with the rigidity of the black-white color line (e.g., Guglielmo, 2003; Jacobson, 1998; Lopez and Stanton-Salazar, 2001).

The comparison also has a salient religious dimension that gives it an additional point of leverage—it speaks to what happens when the members of an immigrant group are largely adherents, at least nominally, of an already established religion. Moreover, this comparison has a number of appealing features, although, like most comparisons across different historical settings, there are also differences that must not be overlooked. Perhaps the most obvious of these is that Mexicans have been entering the territory of a state with which they stand in a long historical relationship, troubled by a heavy burden of colonialism and territorial usurpation (Acuña, 2006; Sánchez, 1993). No such history existed for the Italians. Nevertheless, as the two huge Catholic immigrations of the late 19th and the 20th centuries, the Italians and Mexicans presented and present a series of similar challenges to the largest religious denomination of the United States.

The most tantalizing aspect of the comparison is that, for the most part, the Italians have entered the American mainstream, those parts of the society and culture that are home to its dominant ethnic and racial groups (Alba and Nee, 2003). When the southern Italian immigrants arrived at the turn of the 20th century, the dominant groups could be equated with native white Protestants, who then were overwhelmingly of northern European descent; today, they are constituted by whites with ancestries from anywhere on the European continent. The integration of the Italians into the mainstream is a major strand in the story of this transformation. In marked contrast with the situations of their immigrant and second-generation ancestors during the first half of the 20th century, the socioeconomic attainments of Italian Americans today, as reflected in the average situations of the members of the group born after 1950, are no less, and probably slightly higher, than the averages for other white Americans. Further, their rates of marriage with Americans of other ethnic origins, especially European, are very high by any absolute standard—70–75 percent of Italians of the third and later generations marry out (Alba, 1985, 1995).

The successful incorporation of Italians into the mainstream prompts the following questions: Will the second and third generations arising from contemporary Mexican immigration undergo a similar trajectory of incorporation? Is their entry into the mainstream simply a matter of generational time? These questions, which have already surfaced into the literature in the form of analogies between the Mexicans of today and the Italians of yesterday, are difficult, perhaps impossible, to answer with authority. Penetrating even slightly below the surface, one finds similarities but also differences that are hard to disentangle from the problem at hand.

On one side of the ledger, the immigrants' conceptions of their goals appear to have important similarities. As is well known, the Italian immigration was initially a sojourner one, whose earliest arrivals were men who intended to amass small amounts of capital and return home to their families in the Mezzogiorno, the south of Italy. It is apparent that the rate of return during the early years of the Italian immigration was quite high—perhaps as many as 50 percent of the Italian immigrants went back, though how many subsequently may have entered the United States for a second or a third time remains shrouded in mystery (Cinel, 1991). Except that return and reentry were more difficult for the Italians because of distance, similar patterns can be observed in the Mexican immigration. Thus, a single migrant generally is the pioneer within a family, though this person is not always a man. A process of settlement sets in after a few cycles of entry and return, and settled immigrants help to bring other relatives to the United States (Massey, Durand, and Malone, 2003). Yet one enormous difference separates the Italian patterns from the Mexican ones: many of the pioneer Mexican immigrants cross the border outside of official avenues of entry and thus join the so-called undocumented population, whereas the status of illegal migrant was largely irrelevant to the Italian immigration, since the United States had few laws restricting the entry of Europeans in a substantial way until the second decade of the 20th century (Ngai, 2004).

On the other side we find additional differences. The Italian immigration was mainly a short but intense burst of some 15 years duration. About 60 percent of all Italian immigrants in the history of the United States came in the 1900–1914 period. This concentration in time meant that Italian communities were not regularly renewed by immigrant inflow; consequently, for the most part, they have undergone a gradual decline. Also, the concentration of the Italian immigration in time implies a strong correlation between age and generational distance from immigration, and this, in turn, has contributed to an assimilatory dynamic (Alba, 1988). By contrast, the Mexican presence in the Southwest and California predates these regions' attachment to the United States. Anglo attitudes toward Mexicans were initially formed during a process of wresting sovereignty over a territory and effective control over its resources. Even immigration as such has a long history, commencing with the late 19th and early 20th centuries and continuing at greater and lesser intensities ever since (Massey et al., 2003).

The incorporation of Mexicans has suffered from a racism far more severe than any the Italians encountered. The most salient emblem of this discrimination is the mass deportations of Mexicans during the 1930s, which apparently included some who were American citizens. In parts of the Southwest, and especially in Texas, Mexican children attended segregated schools into the second half of the 20th century. Moreover, because of the degree of *mestizidad* (mixture of European and indigenous ancestry) in the Mexican American population, they are recognizably different through somatic cues in the eyes of white Americans. As David Lopez and Ricardo Stanton-Salazar put the racial distinction in a recent essay:

> Those who fit the mestizo/Indian phenotype, who "look Mexican," cannot escape racial stereotyping any more than African Americans, though the stigma is not usually so severe. The sizable minority that looks essentially Euro-American has at least the potential to pass as individuals, but to the degree that they continue to be identified as Mexicans, they are subject to

much the same treatment as their darker brothers and sisters. (2001: 72; see also Murguia and Telles, 1996)

This racism thwarted among Mexicans a generational dynamic that came very much to the benefit of the Italians. As Richard Alba and Robert Orsi attest (chapter 1), the Italians exemplify as well as any other European group the paradigm of generation-by-generation progression into the mainstream that has conventionally dominated thinking about the incorporation of immigrant groups. Beginning as a group that was concentrated on the lowest rungs of the socioeconomic ladder—"rag picker" and "ditch digger" were common descriptions of Italian workers in the early 20th century (Kessner, 1977)—by the third generation, Italians had for the most part entered the mainstream, as evidenced by educational attainment, occupational position, and entry into suburban, multiethnic Catholic parishes. This process failed among the descendants of the Mexican immigrants who arrived during the early 20th century for reasons that are clear only in an abstract sense. Certainly, like the Italians, the Mexican second generation made a substantial advance over the first; but the situation of the third generation appears to have been not much better than that of the second (Bean et al., 1994; Wojtkiewicz and Donato, 1995; cf. Smith, 2003).

What does a consideration of religion add to this picture? For the Italians, an examination of the largely neglected aspects of religious incorporation reveals how crucial they were for entry into the mainstream. For one thing, Italian immigrants were like contemporary Hispanic groups in being susceptible to conversion to Protestantism, a form of religious mobility that was undoubtedly connected to aspirations for social advancement and assimilation (Form, 2000). These conversions reflected, in the first place, the weak attachment of many of the southern Italian immigrants to the Catholic Church and, in the second, the cold reception they initially received from parishes dominated by other ethnic groups, especially the Irish (Orsi, 1985). The loss of a significant number of Italian Catholics was a major concern ("the Italian problem") for the American Catholic Church of the early 20th century, all the more so because the immigrants were coming from the nation that was the seat of Catholicism and thus were seen as the "Pope's people." The problem was eased by the establishment of numerous Italian-language parishes, and, in the end, the great majority of the immigrants remained loyal to the Catholic Church.

For them, the institutions of the Catholic Church abetted their entry into the mainstream. This is not to say that the immigrants and the Catholic Church were easily reconciled; many appeared in the pews only to mark significant life events, such as marriages and baptisms, and sent their children to public schools. Indeed, the distance between Italian Catholics and the parochial schools was a notable feature of the American Catholic landscape of the mid-20th century (Greeley and Rossi, 1966: 37). Yet the role of Catholic educational institutions, especially colleges and universities, in providing a protected route of social mobility for the second and third generations was notable, as the prominent second-generation examples of Mario Cuomo (who went from New York City public schools to St. John's University) and Geraldine Ferraro (alumna of Marymount College) suggest.

Moreover, social and spatial mobility generally brought Italian American families closer to Catholic institutions. Across generations, their religious practices increasingly resembled those of other American Catholics (Russo, 1969), even as some of their most cherished practices, such as the feasts in honor of hometown saints (e.g., New York's famed San Gennaro festival) were influencing the public and private culture of American Catholicism. Socioeconomic success, moreover, was often registered by placing the children in Catholic schools. And the move to middle-class neighborhoods, often located in suburbs, brought families into ethnically mixed parishes, increasing their contacts across ethnic lines. The first intermarriages were typically with Catholics of other ethnic backgrounds, with the result that Irish is the ancestry most commonly found in mixtures with Italian. In the first half of the 20th century, these and similar intrareligious marriages gave rise to the notion of an emerging Triple Melting Pot, which broke down ethnic dividing lines but reinforced religious ones (Kennedy, 1944, 1952).

That the surge of intermarriages by Italians eventually swept across religious lines, leading to substantial losses once again for the Catholic Church, this time in the third and fourth generations, is a novel finding of the Alba and Orsi analysis. But it does not negate the generally positive role played by the Catholic Church in assisting Italians into the mainstream, a role that was consistent with its mission in the American context of representing the various immigrant and ethnic peoples in its ranks. Why has it not also been able to play the same role for Mexicans? More pointedly, why have they not been able, like the southern Italians, to draw advantage from their attachment to an established religion?

Roberto Lint Sagarena (chapter 2) and David Lopez (chapter 3) sketch out an answer, one that deepens our understanding of the barriers that have impeded the entry of non-Europeans into the American mainstream. Lint Sagarena's portrayal of the American Catholic Church in the Southwest and California reveals that, for most of the late 19th and the 20th centuries, its vision of itself was of a church welcoming the Euro-American Catholics who were coming from the East and arriving as migrants rather than immigrants. Indeed, its initial problem was to distinguish itself from the Mexican Catholic Church by substituting the central authority of the early Euro-American bishops for the lay initiative on which it had been dependent in Mexico's northern regions. This process produced conflict with Spanish-speaking clerics, and Mexicans were subsequently neglected by the Catholic leadership when they were not being patronized for their folk brand of Catholicism, seen by Euro-American clergy as uncivilized. While in this last respect, one can see a parallel with the disparaging view of the southern Italian immigrants, there was not in the Mexicans' case the same commitment to bring them into the mainstream of the church. Thus, at least until the civil rights era, if not later, Mexicans remained on its margins and therefore receptive to the appeal of evangelical Protestantism. Their religiosity was frequently maintained and expressed by lay societies, especially those devoted to the Virgin of Guadalupe; and they were subject, beginning in the 1950s, to an Americanization campaign within the church, which was based on the assumption that they needed to be "elevated" to join mainstream Catholicism.

Lopez's comprehensive essay adds vital institutional dimensions to this picture, revealing some of the mechanisms by which Mexican social advancement remained blocked. Drawing on research conducted in the late 1960s, he argues that a gulf existed between parish clergy, who were often Irish American, and immigrant Mexicans, who were not being recruited even into the lowest of the sacral roles, that of altar boy, to say nothing of the priesthood. The gulf was bridged to some degree by the reforms of Vatican II, which led to a much greater use of Spanish in the mass. But the more important institutional argument Lopez presents concerns the Catholic educational system, which, he demonstrates, substantially underserves Mexican American youth. The regions in which Mexican Americans are concentrated were never areas for heavy investment in the Catholic educational system, which has been most developed in the Northeast and Midwest, where Catholic immigrants from Europe settled. Even in its temporal trajectory, the Catholic school system seems most adapted to the mobility needs of Euro-American Catholics. As Lopez points out, the system was at its largest in the 1940–65 period, just as the second and third generations issuing from the Irish, Italian, Polish, and other European Catholic immigrations were attending school (see also Steinfels, 2003). It has slumped since then, even as the immigrations from Latin America have swelled. Even though a smaller parochial school system continues to provide educational opportunities for some children of upwardly striving inner-city families, it has generally failed to erect a viable alternative to the underfunded public school systems that many Mexican American students in the Southwest and California attend. The protected avenue of educational advance the Catholic schools provided for Italians during their period of vulnerability has not existed to the same extent for Mexicans.

Are these observations the end of the story? For one thing, the mid-20th century, the most critical period in the chapters by Lint Sagarena and Lopez, is not the beginning of the 21st. The legal-institutional environment within which groups are incorporated is quite different today than it was even half a century ago. The crude institutional discrimination from which Mexicans suffered in the pre–civil rights era is much less likely to occur, and, on an individual level, white Americans are more accepting of racial and ethnic diversity than they were in the past. Moreover, the American Catholic Church is being forced to recognize that its future depends on bringing Hispanic groups fully into its mainstream. As Lopez notes in his chapter, young Latinos amount to roughly one-half of the current cohort of Catholic young people, and population projections, which indicate rapid growth of the Hispanic population in coming decades as a result of immigration and higher fertility, suggest that this fraction will only increase (Pew Hispanic Center, 2007). The Catholic Church will face an even graver crisis than that created by the sexual abuses of some of its priests if it fails to bring Hispanics in from the margins. As the chapters here note, this need has been recognized in Cardinal Roger Mahoney's Los Angeles cathedral project. But more than welcoming architecture will be needed to overcome the barriers that have until now prevented Mexican Americans from using their Catholic affiliation as a means to advance their integration into American society.

Passages in Piety

Generational Transitions and the Social and Religious Incorporation of Italian Americans

Richard Alba and Robert Orsi

The Italians have achieved a paradigmatic status for the American story of incorporation and eventual assimilation that few other immigrant groups can match (Perlmann, 2005). One of the largest of the European immigrations, the Italians came mostly during a very short burst of emigration that brought 3 million arrivals to American shores within a 15-year period at the beginning of the 20th century. These immigrants were departing largely from the heavily agricultural southern part of the country, the Mezzogiorno, and possessed little education and few industrial skills. In the cities where they concentrated, mostly in the northeastern United States, the immigrants took up, and sometimes took over, manual jobs that typically involved little more than muscle power and occupied the bottom of the labor market.

At the time of their immigration, the Italians from the Mezzogiorno seemed to pose an insurmountable challenge to the assimilatory mechanisms of American society. For one thing, they were racially "in-between," to use the characterization of historians James Barrett and David Roediger (1997). The questions about their status as "whites" were epitomized by a common epithet for them—"guinea"—with its reference to Africa and roots in American slavery (Roediger, 2005: 37). For another, they were viewed by native-born Americans as a source of disturbing social problems, which ranged from their alleged proclivity to criminality to the frequently troubled relationships between the immigrant families and American schools (Covello, 1972; Gambino, 1974; Higham, 1970; Perlmann, 1988).

Yet, for the most part, their grandchildren, the third generation, and their great grandchildren, the fourth, have unquestionably entered the American mainstream. The socioeconomic profile of these generations looks no different from that of other white Americans, and intermarriage is the experience of their majority (Alba, 1990, 1995; Lieberson and Waters, 1988; Waters, 1990). The general outlines of the story by which this assimilation occurred are increasingly known: the generation-by-generation ascent it involved was strongly linked to individual social mobility, both upward on the socioeconomic ladder and outward from Italian ethnic enclaves to middle-class and ethnically mixed areas (Alba and Nee, 2003). These processes took hold especially in the several decades after World War II, propelled by the overall expansion of the middle class and of higher education and by the exodus to the suburbs, creating opportunities for social advancement for ethnic and working-class whites (Alba, 1985; Gans, 1982 [1962]; Vecoli, 1978). In addition, the Italians benefited from a cultural shift associated with the mainstream interpretation of the World War II experience, which highlighted the contributions of white ethnic Americans to American victory (Alba, 1985).

Yet religion has been a missing aspect of this story, which has been told mostly by secular social scientists who view religion's role as overshadowed by the fundamental mechanisms located in the labor market and other socioeconomic institutions. This contemporary emphasis has not only lost sight of the importance accorded religious institutions and worldviews by observers closer in time to the period of immigration and initial settlement, such as Oscar Handlin, Will Herberg, and Ruby Jo Reeves Kennedy, but also it overlooks the potential significance of the Catholic Church in particular. A multiethnic institution, in contrast to many Protestant denominations, the church encompasses diverse possibilities for integration and advancement: for example, the social intermingling produced in multiethnic, territorially based parishes or the educational mobility available in the protected world of Catholic colleges and universities. In this chapter, we attempt to better link the storyline of socioeconomic assimilation to the role of religion, in the hope of illuminating mechanisms that might apply also to more contemporary Catholic immigrant groups, such as Mexicans. We follow a generation-by-generation outline because of its fidelity to the way in which the Italian story has unfolded.

The First Generation

Immigration Setting

Perhaps it should be said that there were several first generations. Richard Juliani (1998) has demonstrated for Philadelphia that the foundations for what later became the large immigrant settlements of the early 20th century were set in place by small numbers of Italians who arrived in the pre-1880 period, settling in the neighborhoods that later became Italian and establishing some of the institutions that received the immigrants. These early immigrants were of very different regional and social origins than were those who constituted the huge, later waves. In contrast to the southern Italian origins of the great majority of those who came in the early decades of the 20th century, for example, the earliest immigrants came from northern Italy—in the case of Philadelphia, from the region around Genoa, in northwestern Italy. Even among the post-1880 immigrants, a substantial minority came from the north, the portion of the boot from Rome northward. The well-known regional differences in Italy, supported by data published by a congressional committee in 1911 about literacy and other differences between northern and southern Italian immigrants, indicate that the human-capital levels of immigrants from the north were generally higher. The role of regional differences in the intergenerational trajectories of Italians remains unknown. By far the largest portion of the Italian immigration, especially during its zenith in the 1900–1914 period, came from the Italian south, the Mezzogiorno.

Many, if not most, of this wave were sojourners. The initial immigrants were males who, it appears, intended to return home after earning a target amount of money. Levels of remittance were high, as were rates of return (Caroli, 1973; Cinel, 1991; Foner, 2000). One of the huge unanswered questions is who returned, but a potential answer is necessary to understand more fully the characteristics of what eventually became the settled Italian population. For example, some, after returning, reimmigrated to the United States; in this group were seasonal migrants, who came to the United States to work for part of the year and spent the remainder in their Italian home towns. Family reunification occurred in many cases relatively late in the immigration era.

Given the low levels of human capital in the southern Italian immigrant population, their place in the U.S. labor market was humble. By and large, the immigrants were coming from small towns and agricultural backgrounds; they lacked industrial experience. Some, however, had acquired construction-related skills (e.g., masonry) before leaving Italy. Yet many initially took jobs as unskilled laborers in the United States (Kessner, 1977; Yans-McLaughlin, 1977). Given current accounts of the differences between the contemporary and past immigration eras, an underappreciated question is how many Italian immigrants took jobs in the manufacturing sectors, as opposed to the construction and service sectors (Waldinger, 2007). There was also a substantial small-business class, from which some large enterprises (e.g., construction firms) eventually emerged. Family incomes were frequently supplemented by home work by women; common was the boarding of other immigrants or the home manufacture of artificial flowers or clothing (Bose, 1984). Historical studies appear to indicate that the first generation experienced some upward mobility in the United States, but the definitive account has yet to appear (Kessner, 1977).

Regional origins played a central role in the settlement patterns and communal life of the immigrants. Given the key part played by migration chains in bringing immigrants to particular places, it is perhaps unsurprising to find residential concentrations on specific U.S. streets of immigrants from the same Italian towns (Gabaccia, 1984). But it is well known that the organizational life of the immigrants was also centered on commonalities derived from town and regional origins (Nelli, 1983). This *campanilismo* (parochialism), as it is known in Italian, had analogues among other groups (e.g., the *landsmanschaften* of Jewish immigrants; these are societies for individuals who originated from the same town) and began to wane during the 1920s, as group-wide organizations came into ascendance (Luconi, 2001).

At least by the evidence of the behavior and views of communal leaders, the first generation retained, or developed, considerable loyalty to Italy and the Italian state. (Most commentators believe that the immigrants from the Mezzogiorno had little or no cognizance of the Italian nation-state when they arrived, so that these sentiments then developed in the United States.) During the 1920s and 1930s, communal celebrations of Italian events and holidays, such as the king's birthday, were common (Luconi, 2001). The attempts of the prominent and wealthy leaders of Italian American society of the first generation to affect U.S. policy toward fascist Italy persevered until the eve of World War II.

Immigrant Religious World

Religiously, southern Italians were also a group apart. The kind of Catholicism they brought, characterized by irregular church attendance, an emphasis on close personal relationships between individuals (and households) and particular saints, and a skeptical and often enough mistrusting attitude toward the clergy, was viewed by the mainstream Catholic Church as exotic and worse (Gambino, 1974; Orsi, 1985). The former pastor of one of New York City's largest Italian churches, looking back on his time as a young priest in one of the city's major Italian settlements, recalled that officials in the New York church "thought we were Africans," suggesting that cultural tensions within American Catholicism were exacerbated by the peculiar dynamics of American racial categorization.

The arrival of millions of Italian Catholics threatened to render the status of the American Catholic Church in the wider culture even more insecure than it already was, and so it was with a mixture of embarrassment, apprehension, and a sense of responsibility that longer-established Irish Catholics looked on the newcomers. In many areas, Italians were initially accommodated in the basements of churches, until they were able to establish separate nationality parishes. In areas with large Italian settlements, such as South Philadelphia, there were numerous Italian parishes. When there were sufficient numbers of immigrants from a single Italian village or region to do so, these churches were specialized in terms of the regional origins of parishioners (Luconi, 2001). When this was not possible, immigrants from a particular region would gather together to purchase a statue of the patron saint of their hometown to put in their church, alongside the patron saints of other immigrants from other regions. In this way, Catholic churches became one of the first sites of an emerging Italian American identity, beyond *campanilismo*.

The church building was not necessarily the primary site of Italian religious life and worship in this first generation, however. Italian immigrants in the first generation practiced a home-centered Catholicism. Critics who commented that Italians did not attend mass regularly, as had become the American Catholic norm (but only recently), recognized that Italians appeared in church on occasions important to their families, such as weddings, baptisms, and funerals. At the center of their domestic piety were Italian women, who tended the home shrines (which were often set up in bedrooms), said the family's necessary prayers (for the dead, for example, or for the ailing), and generally presided over the religious and moral world of their homes. Women also went to church much more regularly and in greater numbers than men in Italian American communities did, a pattern of church attendance that was generally true throughout late-19th and early-20th-century Europe. Little groups of men clustered outside churches, smoking and talking together, and waiting for their wives and children to come out after mass, were a familiar sight in Italian neighborhoods. In times of family crisis, however, women might prevail on men to go to church with them.

Italian women also brought with them a rich vernacular healing tradition, which drew on both Catholic and pre-Christian sources. Unfortunately, very little research has been done on women's healing idioms in the first-generation communities. But Italians had a well-documented fear of hospitals. Mostly unfamiliar with institutional care in Italy, the immigrants entered the United States at a time of tremendous growth in the number of hospitals and in the professionalization of American medicine. The newer hospitals were being built outside urban residential areas, moreover. So going to the hospital meant that immigrants had to leave their familiar sense worlds—the comforting and orienting smells, sounds, and tastes of home and neighborhood and the proximity of kin—for an impersonal, distant environment of strangers. It is no wonder, then, that many in the first generation believed that going to the hospital was a sure indication that all hope was lost for them and that they were dying. Unsurprisingly, its members preferred to be healed at home.

Italian neighborhoods each had a number of older immigrant women who had well-established reputations as healers. Most specialized in minor aches and pains, treating the many stresses of immigration (especially among the earliest arrivals, men on their own, who missed the ministrations of their mothers and wives) with old-world remedies that involved a mixture of herbs and water or alcohol, the manipulation of objects, and prayer. A common ailment brought to these local healers was headaches, which they treated with string, oil, and water. The women healers were also called on to help with sorrows of the heart, and some of them had particular reputations for offering protection against the plans of badly intentioned neighbors. Healing techniques were often passed on from mother to daughter. Such practices seem to have largely disappeared between the second and third generations.

Perhaps the most familiar religious expression of immigrants from southern Italy was the street festival, held on the occasion of the feast day of the various patronal saints of the towns from which different groups of immigrants had come. Every town in southern Italy had a protector saint. Local narratives about the origins of a saint's relationship with a particular village usually stressed the supernatural nature of this association (Gambino, 1974). Two towns may have been vying for the relics of a saint, for example, when some unexpected event erupted that was interpreted as the saint's expression of a preference for one town over the other, or a saint's statue may have been suddenly discovered, perhaps during a local crisis, after lying hidden for a long time. Once established as a town's special protectors, these saints were then called on in times of local distress—famine, war, disease—and in return for their ongoing protection, the town honored them with an annual celebration on their feast days.

Immigrants from southern Italy brought this custom with them to the United States, much to the dismay of longer-established American Catholics. One of the first things immigrants from a particular area would do soon after their arrival in an American city would be to send back to Italy for a representation of their patronal saint; sometimes they brought these images and statues with them on the journey over. The responsibility for organizing celebrations in the United States was in the hands of devotional societies of men and women from the same Italian villages; each Italian neighborhood in the United States had many such organizations, which combined the functions of a devotional sodality with those of a mutual aid society. The various societies each sponsored a separate annual celebration, called a *festa,* in honor of their patronal saints—which meant that every year in Italian neighborhoods there would be many such public celebrations of regional pride and local devotion.

In the very early years of the migration from southern Italy, the *feste* were simple affairs: men and women (or most often the men who had come alone) from a particular village gathered on their saint's feast day for prayers and a shared meal. But these events quickly evolved into major public neighborhood occasions. A procession through the neighborhood, in which members of the *festa* society marched with friends and family behind a statue or banner of their saint, was often accompanied by a street festival in front of the society's headquarters or the local church, with food, fireworks, games of chance, and entertainment of various sorts (depending on the resources of the society and community). These *festa* societies were in complicated relationships with local Catholic churches. Some of them stood in open competition with the neighborhood parish; the societies sometimes had their own little buildings, which included a chapel where the saint's statue was kept during the year. Others entered into uneasy alliances with local pastors.

During the height of the immigration from southern and eastern Europe, the American Catholic hierarchy committed itself to a policy of organizing the newcomers into "national parishes," parochial districts organized not on the traditional grounds of residence (which meant that all people from a particular area went to the same church) but by ethnic group. (This meant, in practice, that the churches of different ethnic groups stood quite close to each other, which often enough resulted in conflict, tension, competition, and battles among the children of the various communities, until they were old enough to marry each other, much to their parents' horror.) The priests assigned to Italian parishes, whether Italian themselves (e.g., members of religious orders, such as the Scalabrini Fathers, with special missions to care for Italian immigrants) or American secular clergy (i.e., priests attached to the diocese and under the authority of the local bishop) necessarily had to contend with the *festa* societies. Some responded by trying to destroy the societies, either by prohibiting their activities and refusing to say mass during the annual celebration (a very serious matter) or by bringing them into the church and under clerical authority. Even in the latter case, however, tensions persisted. Although Italian immigrants had the reputation of not contributing to the church (accustomed, as they were, to state-supported churches), they were quite willing to contribute to the *festa* societies, which made the latter important potential sources of revenue for financially strapped clergy. Bitterness between *festa* societies and parish clergy in many cases lasted for decades, occasionally flaring into open, embarrassing hostility and mutual recrimination.

The annual *feste* in honor of the regional saints of southern Italy played an important role in the lives of first-generation immigrants. In the days when the migration was composed primarily of men traveling on their own, support for and participation in the celebrations was a way of demonstrating their enduring honor and respect for the traditions of their childhoods—customs that were associated with the women from whom they were now separated. The *feste* offered welcome respites from the grind and discipline of industrial labor, under the supervision of hostile foremen from other ethnic communities and paced according to the new disciplines and regimens of time just then being adopted by management. The *feste* re-created the sense worlds of the immigrants' villages—on these days, they could smell in the streets familiar cooking odors, they moved among their compatriots, their beloved saint was in the streets with them. Among other things, the *feste* were one way that Italian immigrants openly declared their presence on the American landscape, in their own distinctive way.

For this same reason, however, the *feste* were a source of tremendous embarrassment to American Catholic leaders. The *feste* were completely public occasions. Already by the 1890s, visiting such religious celebrations in Italian neighborhoods had become a popular feature of city tourism. Middle-class residents of West Harlem, for instance, strolled east to Italian Harlem (until World War II the largest Italian American neighborhood in the United States) to watch the goings on at the annual celebration of Our Lady of Mount Carmel, which had been introduced by immigrants from the town of Polla in the early 1880s. The police paid particular attention to the celebrations, which operated just on the edges of legality under the new codes that urban reformers instituted as a means precisely of controlling the behaviors of immigrants on city streets. (Later, in the time of the second generation, when Italian communities wielded more local power, special arrangements could be made with police for the festivals.)

Not surprisingly, then, the American church could be harshly critical of such celebrations; local prelates often took what steps they could to restrict or prohibit the celebrations or particular features of them. It is still remembered with considerable rancor in East Harlem that at one point in the 1940s, the New York archdiocese failed to grant the community the dispensation it had requested from the stricture on eating meat on Fridays in a year when the feast of Mount Carmel, which by this time had become a huge neighborhoodwide event, fell on a Friday (despite the chancery's generosity in such matters, it is always pointed out, when St. Patrick's day happened to come on a fast day). But the celebrations persisted in the first generation and, in many cases, grew significantly in the next generation.

Another custom among Italian immigrants that rankled American Catholic leaders was that of building family chapels on privately owned property in gratitude or as request for the intervention of God or the saints in a family crisis. These family chapels were completely independent of local religious authority. Sometimes the family involved could prevail on the priests of their neighborhood church to say mass in the chapel on commemorative occasions, but if local priests were not willing to do so, the family might privately locate and pay a priest to come anyway.

Occasionally these chapels were the center of an annual *festa;* more often, *feste* societies in the neighborhood would make a point of stopping at the chapel during their annual celebrations to pause before its doors, kept open on such occasions. Such public recognition of these independent religious sites was a further cause of distress to neighborhood clergy. Most of these chapels have since disappeared: in some cases, they were given into the care of local churches by members of the second and third generations, who were themselves participating members of the neighborhood parish and whose attitudes toward the clergy were significantly different from those of their parents and grandparents; in other cases, the chapels were simply torn down as the neighborhood changed.

There were two important exceptions to southern Italian mistrust of clergy: the priests and brothers of religious orders, and women religious. A number of men's religious communities played important roles in caring for immigrants during the peak years of immigration, such as the Pious Society of St. Charles (also known as the Scalabrini Fathers after the order's founder, Giovanni Battista Scalabrini), the Franciscans, and the Servites. Two priests, Luigi Giambastini, O.S.M., a Servite, and Aurelio Palmieri, O.S.A., an Augustinian, became prominent advocates for the Italian community in the United States. Women religious staffed schools, hospitals, and industrial schools and offered immigrants services ranging from child care to nutritional guidance and help finding work. One of the best-known women religious to work among Italian immigrants was St. Frances Xavier Cabrini, founder of the Missionary Sisters of the Sacred Heart of Jesus, who came to the United States in 1889. Mother Cabrini's sisters were a familiar sight in Italian American neighborhoods: they opened schools and orphanages in New York and in other American cities, visited immigrants in their homes, undertook a prison ministry, and sponsored devotional societies for adolescents. The Missionary Sisters provided heroic service in New Orleans during two epidemics of yellow fever. Mother Cabrini advocated a moderate form of bilingual education in her schools: primary instruction was in English, but teachers spent some time each day speaking to students in Italian about the history and heritage of Italy.

Other Italians did not feel at home in the American Catholic Church; exposed to the numerous religious alternatives available in the United States, they converted to Protestantism (which for some represented an introduction to the idioms and manners of the American middle class; see Form, 2000). Although the loss of Italians in this way was probably not very high as a percentage of the immigrant group, the phenomenon was disturbing enough to be named the "Italian problem" and to provoke countervailing efforts on the part of the American church. Italians entered the United States at a time of considerable ferment and creativity in American Protestantism. Protestant churches responded to what was widely seen as the crisis and challenge of the cities by refurbishing old urban congregations as centers of social service, education, employment services, and recreation, as well as worship, and these proved attractive to immigrants, even if they had no intention of converting. Denominations sponsored home missionary outreach programs that sent "friendly visitors" into immigrant neighborhoods and homes. Finally, Pentecostalism, a new religious movement emphasizing a direct, emotional encounter with Jesus that empowered practitioners to speak in tongues and to heal, was proving powerfully attractive to rural and urban workers of all ethnic groups. A number of Italian immigrants were attracted to this new way of being religious already at the turn of the century; later, in the 1960s, Italian Americans would show a real interest in the Catholic charismatic movement, which was inspired by Pentecostalism.

One of the most intimate and familiar ways that Italians in the first generation encountered American culture and values was in the presence of young women who, for various motivations, took on the responsibility of social service among the immigrants. Some of these women worked in settlement houses; among the most famous of these was Hull House, founded by Jane Addams on Chicago's Halstead Street in 1889. Settlement workers were committed to sharing the lives and circumstances of the communities they assisted. Addams and her fellow workers settled among Chicago's Italian population; they conducted careful studies of conditions in immigrant quarters, providing valuable data for progressive reform campaigns, and offered the immigrants a number of necessary services. Other women worked as visitors for Protestant home missionary societies or institutional churches, and some were sent into immigrant neighborhoods by charity organizations.

Whatever brought these women into Italian neighborhoods, all shared the determination to introduce the immigrants to American middle-class customs and norms: they set out to change how immigrants prepared food, decorated their homes (some friendly visitors protested, for example, that Catholic artifacts collected germs and warned immigrants against them), cared for their sick (visitors objected in particular to the

Italian custom of giving the ailing red wine), nurtured their infants (Italian women's practice of keeping their babies tightly swaddled was seen as particularly dangerous, as was the immigrants' preference for closed windows), and raised their children. The immigrants themselves had decidedly mixed feelings about these various service providers: while they valued the many practical benefits offered, they resented the assault on their ways of doing things. As a result, in most cases, the immigrants took what they needed, but otherwise circumvented the visitors' normative agendas.

In sum, the prospects of the Italian group, as judged by the situation of the first generation, seemed not far from those described by the present-day notion of "segmented" assimilation as applied to Mexicans and other non-European, low-human-capital immigrant groups. Dominated by the largely agricultural and illiterate immigrants from the Mezzogiorno, the Italian group was subject to prejudices as harsh as those experienced by any other European group. The "whiteness" literature describes the Italians, like the Irish and Jews, as one of the "in-between" groups, not clearly white but also not on the same plane as the non-Europeans (e.g., Barrett and Roediger, 1997; Jacobson, 1998; Roediger, 2005). This seems a fair description, and in point of fact color words, such as "guinea," have long been used as epithets for Italians. The Italians were set apart in other ways—for instance, they worshipped in their own Catholic parishes, which thus provided no opportunity for integration with other Catholic ethnic groups. Indeed, most Italian Catholic parents even kept their children out of Catholic schools. However, the Italians were never subject to the severe forms of legal and institutionalized discrimination—including the denials of citizenship or of its rights—that afflicted non-European immigrants, such as Mexicans and the Chinese.

The Second Generation

Social Context

The birth of the second generation was spread across a wide swath of time, despite the temporal concentration of the arrival of the immigrants. The second generation grew rapidly between 1900 and 1930, but it continued to grow until after World War II (Alba, 1985: 48). Over time, the second generation was more and more composed of the offspring of immigrants who had married native-born individuals, suggesting that the immigrant parents were in many cases members of the 1.5 generation. Thus, it became more and more a 2.5, rather than a second, generation (Perlmann, 2005).

The second generation, at least through the World War II period, was raised mostly in Italian settlements in cities, large and small, throughout the Northeast and, to a lesser extent, the Midwest. John Logan's (2001) analysis of New York residential data in the early decades of the 20th century reveals a residential segregation as extreme as that of blacks; however, segregation in the Italian case declined rather steadily from this point on. As mid-century approached, a significant part of the second generation must have been raised outside of heavily Italian enclaves (see also Lieberson, 1963, 1980).

Thus, the heterogeneity within the Italian group increases markedly with the arrival of the second generation. This is signaled in the well-known study of Boston's North End in the 1930s, *Street-Corner Society* (Whyte, 1955 [1943]; see also Gans, 1982 [1962]). While Whyte's focus falls mainly on the group of unemployed young men around a central figure, Doc, he describes a second group of men as well—these are the college bound. It seems likely that the socioeconomic trajectories of the second generation thus diversified with the passage of time, and this supposition is supported by Stanley Lieberson's research in *A Piece of the Pie* (1980), which demonstrates that the college-educated and professional portions of the second-generation group increased robustly across birth cohorts.

At the same time, we know that the overall educational attainment of the second generation was below average (compared with other whites). During the period of immigration, the intention of many Italian immigrants to return eventually to Italy led to abbreviated educations for their children: one estimate is that as many as 10 percent of the children of Italian immigrants in New York were kept out of school altogether. Italian parents were well known for their cultural conflicts with schools, especially public schools; and many Italian children were removed from school as soon as the law allowed (if not sooner) and sent into the labor force (e.g., Perlmann, 1988). During the 1930s and 1940s, when the Italian American educator Leonard Covello was conducting research, the rates of truancy and dropout for Italian American high school students were several times higher than for other students (Covello, 1972).

Second-generation Italians benefited from the revision of the national sense of mission and of some public policies that occurred during and shortly after World War II. They, along with other Europeans, were conspicuous in the consciously cultivated vision of national solidarity in the prosecution of the war itself. Afterward, the GI Bill to sponsor the educational careers of veterans and VA-insured mortgages to assist their home purchases contributed to some social and spatial mobility in this generation (Katznelson, 2005); these effects were obviously concentrated among those who came of age during the 1940s and later.

Religious Situation

From what we know, religious changes appear to reflect the acculturation of the second generation and, for some of its members, their social and spatial mobility. A question is whether religion also promoted their further assimilation. These statements, however, rest on a slender body of evidence, which appears to show, for instance, that the religious practices of Italians in the second generation began to shift in the direction of those prevalent in the American Catholic Church, as defined by Irish Americans (Russo, 1969). Second-generation parents were more likely to send their children to Catholic schools than their parents had been, and this was almost certainly more common as one moved up the socioeconomic ladder. Departure from Italian American enclaves, while perhaps a minority phenomenon, was associated with participation in multiethnic Catholic parishes or those dominated by Irish Americans. Intermarriage also increased noticeably in the second generation and, for the most part, was confined to the other ethnic groups among Catholics. Given the presence of large Irish populations in the metropolitan areas where Italians were most concentrated, Irish-Italian combinations were initially very common.

Vocations to the religious life developed among members of the second generation. Young Italian American men and women developed positive attitudes toward priests and nuns as role models in their schools, churches, and playgrounds. Responding to the needs of the immigrants and their children, the church sponsored numerous programs for young people, including neighborhood dances at parish halls (where youngsters from different ethnic communities met each other, regardless of their parents' prejudices), sports (boxing was particularly popular among Italian American boys) and clubs, and outings to the country. The Catholic Youth Organization, founded in 1931 by Father Bernard Sheil, provided athletic and recreational opportunities for the immigrants' children and grandchildren. Catholic publishers offered magazines and books especially geared to youngsters that depicted the church and religious life in the most positive, indeed heroic, terms. Second-generation men and women entered religious orders and the diocesan clergy; when possible, they returned to serve their neighborhoods as priests and nuns.

The movement of the second generation into religious life was not untroubled, however. Not all southern Italian parents were pleased by their children's vocations, and the latter's decisions to leave home for seminary or convent caused tensions in these households. Italian American women who chose communities not primarily Italian often encountered prejudice in their convents. (Italian American pastors responsible for founding new churches and schools in these years, as the population of the second generation grew, were determined to staff their schools only with Italian American nuns. A Capuchin Franciscan who opened a school in the north Bronx in the 1950s, for example, made it clear to his congregation that he would protect their children from what he considered the negative attitudes of Irish sisters toward Italian Americans.) Italian American priests labored under the authority of Irish American superiors; an Italian American bishop was not appointed until the 1960s.

The place of the second generation at Italian street *feste* was complicated as well. Already in the early years of the 20th century, the street festivals had become sites of some tension between generations, and this intensified as the second generation developed. Younger Italian Americans, both those born in Italy but taken to the United States as very young children and those born here, were more familiar with American ways and styles. The immigrant generation had not known the age category "adolescent": one was either a child, under the protection and authority of one's parents and kin, or an adult, working for the family and shouldering appropriate responsibilities. But in the first years of the 20th century, various factors converged to pose serious challenges to the established arrangements of Italian American families.

Progressive legislation extended the period of mandatory schooling. The number of youngsters going to high schools increased significantly in the first two decades of the 20th century. High school students constituted a new peer group, more independent than ever before from parental supervision; a young person's peers, with whom he or she now spent the greater portion of the day, became the primary source for information, styles, and values. Moreover, the nascent American advertising industry specifically targeted young people in this age group, further intensifying the sense of generational identity and separation. This was an *embodied* difference, moreover: Italian American adolescents looked and sounded different, wore distinctive clothes and hairstyles, and carried their bodies differently. The result of all this was tension within the immigrant household.

Intergenerational tensions were reflected and performed at the *feste* and even exacerbated during the days of the festivals. Street celebrations were a privileged site for introducing the second generation to the ways and expectations of Italian culture, as this culture was reconstructed and performed by their parents and grandparents in the streets of their communities. The older, Italian-born generation was itself in an uneasy relationship to memory and to the norms and values of the old country; its members found themselves in the middle decades of the 20th century becoming Americans by attrition. One response to this confusing situation was to insist ever more strenuously on youngsters' submission to ways of being that the older folks themselves no longer adhered to, to demand that youngsters fulfill roles of family responsibility during the days of the celebrations and that on these days they carry themselves as "Italians," a fluid and unstable designation by this time. Young people responded by resisting the *feste,* keeping away when they could, and by making the celebrations into their own events. They arranged to meet and hang out with their friends in the chaos on the streets, they flirted with each other, commented derisively on the funny ways of the "greenhorns" and old-timers, and evaded parental supervision.

There was another level to the complexity of street festivals in these years. The name given various urban Italian neighborhoods—"little Italy," "Italian Harlem," and so on—masks the reality that these were never ethnically homogenous worlds. Even when Italian Harlem was most Italian— for example, in the late 1930s and 1940s—"Italian Americans" (a relatively recent identity itself, cobbled together out of the many regional differences in the immigrant population and inflected by American stereotypes and expectations) lived beside people from more than 40 other ethnic groups. The designation "little Italy," in other words, belies a more complex social reality.

In this context, *feste* became an important vehicle for announcing and mapping Italian presence and prominence in the neighborhoods. The processions made their way up and down areas most heavily populated with Italian families, marking out exactly where the Italians lived. Moreover, during the days of the celebration, however ethnically diverse an area was, it looked and smelled Italian; the *feste* were thus not simply expressions of Italian presence but the claiming of it, along with the occlusion of others. This became particularly clear in the late 1930s and 1940s in eastern cities when newly arriving Puerto Ricans who were moving into Italian American neighborhoods—and who shared the same Catholic faith with the immigrants and their children—were excluded from the *feste*.

As Italian political power solidified in the cities of the North and Midwest in the 1930s and 1940s, the *feste* also became displays of achievement. Youngsters marched behind the patronal figure in their new (and relatively expensive) first communion outfits. Prominent local and citywide politicians paraded at the front of the line; arrangements were made with local police departments for special concessions (suspension of parking rules, for instance). The processions often stopped in front of the homes of important and successful members of the community, who came out to greet the patronal figure and make an especially large, and very public, contribution to the festival society. (The statues commonly made their way through the streets bedecked with ribbons on which men and women pinned dollar bills in thanksgiving for or anticipation of a special favor to be bestowed by the saints.) Mid-century *feste*, then, became public displays of Italian American arrival on the American scene.

The Third Generation

Social Setting

The third generation is, with rare exceptions, a post–World War II phenomenon, and the majority of its members have been raised in the post-1960 atmosphere, a period when American Catholics closed the socioeconomic gap between themselves and white Protestants and en masse broke through into the mainstream. In addition, the civil rights movement, which attained the zenith of its influence in the first half of the 1960s, helped to stigmatize prejudices of various kinds.

Concomitantly, the third generation of Italian Americans appears to have achieved socioeconomic parity with the white American mainstream. This means that such probabilities as those of going to college, finishing college, and attaining a professional or managerial occupation are very similar for the Italian third generation and other whites. Parity does not imply that there is no longer an Italian American working class, for there is also a working class among other whites. But the socioeconomic distribution of Italians, which widened with the second generation, shifted its center of gravity upward with the third. (The transition from the second to the third generations is very critical for the Italian-Mexican comparison, in that the Mexican third generation does not appear so far to have advanced beyond the position of the second, a sharp contrast to the trajectory exhibited by the Italians [Bean et al., 1994].)

The residential distribution of Italians also continued to change with the third generation. The exodus from ethnic enclaves continued, and third-generation households were about as likely as those of other whites to be found in the suburbs (Alba, Logan, and Crowder, 1997). This has produced a very distinct generational profile for the remaining Italian residential enclaves, which disproportionately house the members of the first and second generations (the modest but nontrivial post–World War II immigration replaced some of the losses produced by suburbanization and other departures). This generational profile makes the enclaves increasingly vulnerable, for as these older generations die off, there is nobody to replace them. Italian Bensonhurst, for example, is receding rapidly as new immigrant groups, such as the Chinese, arrive in south Brooklyn (Berger, 2002). (The Bronx's Belmont is yet another example.)

Religious Change

Just as the socioeconomic and residential diversity of Italians have increased in the third generation, so, too, have the forms of their religiosity. Probably the characteristic mode is that of integration into multiethnic but heavily white parishes, located mostly in suburbs. It is likely that, on average, the Catholicism of this part of the third generation, in belief and practice, is scarcely different from that of its fellow parishioners. This implies, of course, a great shift from the Catholicism brought by southern Italian immigrants. Yet, at the same time, some of the devotional practice of the immigrant culture survives, carried on, to be sure, by a minority of the group. It is reflected in the saints' *feste* that are annually celebrated in some historically Italian parishes; what is unclear is whether the celebrants are drawn largely from the residents of Italian enclaves or include suburbanites who seek to maintain an Italian ethnic identity.

At the other end of the spectrum, however, the "Italian problem" of the first generation, which had largely disappeared in the second, has returned in a quieter form. As a result of high rates of intermarriage, which includes substantial intermarriage across religious lines, a significant fraction of the third generation is involved in Catholic-Protestant marriages and some of these individuals have joined Protestant congregations with their spouses (whether or not they have undergone formal conversions). It appears that about 20 percent of the third generation identifies as Protestant and another 10 percent has no religious affiliation at all (these and other statistical data come from our analysis of the NORC General Social Survey [Davis, Smith, and Marsden, 2003]).[1] The latter is a relatively high figure for an American ethnic group and may reflect a particularly Italian American adaptation: a falling way from the Catholic Church, to which the attachment was weak from the start, but yet with sufficient residual identification with it to prevent entry into another denomination. Approximately two-thirds of the third generation retains a Catholic identification, a noticeable drop-off from the 80 percent level of the second.

In the postwar years, Italian American Catholics participated actively in the vibrant devotional and popular culture of the American church—in the novenas, First Friday devotions, block rosaries, and so on—and in the thrilling imaginative world of the supernatural that characterized American popular culture in these years. In the 1940s, the Virgin Mary was said to have appeared to an Italian American boy living in the north Bronx, and so for a while it looked like the community would have its own Bernadette and its own Lourdes, although this event, widely covered in Catholic newspapers at the time, soon faded. Italian American children in the baby boom generation filled the classrooms of Catholic schools to overflowing. Vocations to the religious life peaked in the early postwar years and then declined sharply after the Second Vatican Council.

Italian American neighborhoods in the old industrial cities of the Northeast and Midwest were changing rapidly in these years, and among the ways that members of the third generation responded to these transitions was in the familiar practices of religious devotion. Although the process of suburbanization had begun before the war, it accelerated after it; the children and grandchildren of the immigrant generation left the old inner-city neighborhoods in ever greater numbers. In a community that defined moral quality in terms of family loyalty and the expectation that one would live close by one's kin, this proved to be a traumatic time. The distress of moving away from the familiar environment and older relatives was so great that Italian Americans in these years often told themselves and others that they had not chosen to move but, instead, had been forced out by the arrival of African Americans, Puerto Ricans, and other new populations. It was true that the racial demographics of the industrial cities were changing in this period, but many third-generation Italian

Americans moved away from the old neighborhoods because they could finally do so, having securely now entered into the middle class.

Racial tensions were high in these years. Moreover, because the housing stock in old Italian neighborhoods was often among the worst in a city, and because Italian Americans did not have adequate clout in many city governments to prevent this (or because their representatives cynically ignored them), these areas were among the first to be targeted by urban renewal, which became another source of neighborhood upheaval and dispersal (Gans, 1982 [1962]). A familiar image of the 1960s was that of the desperate, terrified Italian American homeowners protesting the imminent demolition of their homes to make way for a housing project or highway. Italian American neighborhoods in Brooklyn, the Bronx, Chicago, St. Louis, and other cities were devastated in this period; churches, stores, and meeting halls were destroyed in the path of bulldozers. Although the causes of all this were complicated, never as simple as people believed, this was a time of real grief and loss in Italian American neighborhoods around the country.

Religious responses to these circumstances took various forms. Third-generation children returned from the suburbs to their old neighborhoods to attend *feste*. (In some cases, familiar festivals were re-created in suburban settings.) The processions during street festivals now made their way under highway overpasses and across empty lots, mapping out neighborhoods that no longer existed, or did not exist in the same way as a decade before, and declaring an enduring Italian presence even as this was disappearing. On the days and nights of these *feste*, the old neighborhoods came back again, if only in imagination. In Williamsburg, Brooklyn, for instance, *feste* processions knitted together two pieces of an Italian neighborhood that had been separated by a highway (Sciorra, 1999). The warm ties between grandparents and grandchildren were often articulated in the idioms of devotionalism, with youngsters sharing the grandparents' love of certain saints (and eventually inheriting the older people's statues and holy cards when they died).

Italian American cemeteries became elaborate expressions of enduring family ties across generations and across the new distances that separated them. Italian American cemetery customs developed an idiomatic richness, even extravagance, in these years. More Italian Americans now sought to bury their dead out of the ground, in new mausoleums. Customs related to the dead proliferated: Italian Americans at St. Raymond's cemetery in the Bronx, for example, in an area of third-generation settlement (many residents of this neighborhood are the descendants of people who lived elsewhere in the Bronx or East Harlem, who were themselves descendents of residents of the Lower East Side), leave greeting cards addressed to the dead taped to mausoleum walls, lay out holiday items throughout the year (baskets at Easter, for instance; little wrapped presents at Christmas time), and put toys on the graves of young children. This culture of the dead, while rooted in southern Italian ritual customs, developed in this transitional period as Italian Americans struggled to cope with morally and spiritually disorienting upheavals in their everyday lives.

There is no indication that Italian Americans resisted more than any other group the changes in church ritual and practice that followed the Second Vatican Council, and, indeed, although there is little research on this, it may be that Italian Americans embraced many of the changes with greater enthusiasm than others (although some third-generation Italian Americans may be found among conservative and restorationist Catholic groups). Certainly, many in this generation valued the new opportunities to take more extensive responsibility for the life and work of their parishes. Italian Americans also involved themselves in the charismatic movement, enthusiastically embracing the warmer, more personal experience of Jesus available in Catholic Pentecostalism, which reflected the kinds of intense bonds their parents and grandparents had forged with the saints. Also important to Italian Americans in this generation was the Cursillo ("litle course") movement, a means of personal and communal spiritual revival introduced into American Catholic culture after World War II, at first in Mexican American communities in the Southwest. Cursillo weekends became a site where Italians and Mexican Americans encountered each other in the post-conciliar church.

The Fourth Generation

Social and Religious Situations

The fourth generation is still quite young, though its leading edge has entered young adult ages. There is no reason to think that the great majority of its members will not be fully integrated into the mainstream. Indeed, most members have mixed ethnic ancestry, and many may not be externally recognizable as Italian because of their names, their appearance, and their class and community origins. The fourth generation is, in fact, the first where individuals of mixed ancestry substantially outnumber those who have Italian backgrounds on both sides. According to the data of the General Social Survey, the latter make up only one-quarter of the generation; another one-third, though of mixed ancestry, identify more strongly with the Italian element in their backgrounds than with any other. The remainder, less than one-half, have another ethnic identity or don't think of themselves in such ethnic terms. Thus, while there is a minority in the fourth generation that may have been raised in ethnic Italian conditions, it is dwarfed by those for whom this is not true.

The religious affiliations of this generation have undergone another significant shift away from the equation between Italian origins and Catholicism that characterized the first and second generations. To begin, only 60 percent of the fourth generation was raised in the Catholic faith; most of the rest was raised in one or another Protestant denomination. Because of a strong pattern of interreligious marriage, there has been further movement away from Catholicism between childhood and adult years. As a consequence, the fourth generation is evenly divided between Catholics (47 percent) and others. However, since it also contains an unusually large proportion (18 percent) of individuals who declare themselves to have no religious affiliation, a phenomenon that may be especially concentrated among its many young adults, Catholicism may make a modest rebound as family formation and aging bring some of the currently unaffiliated back to church (or some other house of worship, but the number of Jews and other non-Christians is very small).

Among the Catholics, religious behavior seems to have settled into patterns that, while not distant from those among later-generation European American Catholics, still retain a distinctive Italian accent. Thus, about one-quarter (26 percent) of the fourth-generation Italian Catholics report that they attend mass approximately on a weekly basis or more frequently; the figure is marginally higher (30 percent) among non-Italian Catholics of the same generation.[2] However, the Italians seem to pray less frequently than other Catholics do—nearly 60 percent of the non-Italian Catholics pray at least several times a week, compared with 45 percent of the fourth-generation Italian Catholics. This difference, which does not admittedly seem large, hints that at least some in the fourth generation have been influenced by Italian American family cultures that have downplayed intense religiosity.

Conclusions

The view of the Italian case as paradigmatic for the model of generational progression into the mainstream seems sustained by this examination. In comparison with Mexicans, a non-European immigration that is tantalizingly similar in some respects but quite distinctive in others, the critical transition lies between the second and third generations. For both groups, the socioeconomic advance of the second generation over the first is indisputable but not determinative. It is, in any event, predictable for groups whose immigrants have very limited schooling and skills, an almost unavoidable consequence of entry into a society with universal education. The divergence of the Italians from the Mexicans in the third generation is probably related to a variety of factors. But central are the greater legal and social liabilities from which the Mexican group suffered, epitomized in the difficulties they confronted in attempting to gain full recognition of their citizenship rights. Thus, there was no equivalent for the Italians of the mass deportations of the 1930s, and the Italians were not excluded from local political power in the way that Mexicans were. Whether this divergence, which appears among the grandchildren of Italian and Mexican immigrants who arrived in the pre-1930 period, will also characterize the third generation to emerge from the post-1950 Mexican immigration should be regarded as an open question. For the legal and institutional context governing the latter's incorporation is very different.

The religion of Italian immigrants has reflected this generational trajectory but also contributed to it. Although, initially, Italians were kept apart from the bulk of American Catholics by the nationality-parish form and because of the "exotic" nature of their Catholicism, social and spatial mobility inevitably brought them into closer contact with other Catholics and apparently led to a faith closer in practice and spirit to that of their co-religionists. Not only did this shift lead to an important form of acculturation, but also it helped set the stage for large-scale intermarriage with members of the other ethnic groups within the Catholic fold. The fact that the most common ethnicity found in combination with Italian is Irish suggests the critical role that this intermarriage played in the overall social assimilation of the group. Arguably, the same pathway of integration *through* church institutions was not as available to the Mexicans because the Catholic Church in the Southwest and California was less interested in their inclusion.

To judge by the contemporary fourth generation, the assimilation into the American Catholic Church, more or less complete by the third generation, set the stage for a dispersion of Italians across the religious spectrum of the American mainstream. As has happened to many other European American Catholics, this dispersion is associated with acculturation, socioeconomic and spatial mobility, and intermarriage. A group that was almost entirely Catholic (at least nominally) upon arrival in the United States lacks, in the fourth generation, an unambiguous Catholic majority. Catholics remain the plurality, but Protestants belonging to various denominations are not far behind in second place.

More important than the mere shift away from the exclusive Catholicism of the immigrants is the absence of any simple equation between Italian origins and characteristic forms of religious expression and piety. Later-generation Italian Americans dot virtually all parts of the religious landscape, from those Catholics who seek a restoration of pre–Vatican II forms of worship to those who participate enthusiastically in the new movements in Catholicism, to mainstream Protestants, to unchurched agnostics. This dispersion reflects the on-going assimilation of a group that entered the United States a century ago at the bottom of the social and economic ladder and, at least in its early decades, seemed unlikely to climb it very far.

NOTES

We are grateful to Dalia Abdel-Hady for her assistance in the preparation of this chapter.

1.   Our analysis is based on a cumulative file of Italian Americans ($N = 1,885$, when those who cannot be generationally identified are excluded), drawn from the surveys between 1972 and 2000.

2.   Since most Italians in the fourth generation have not reached middle age and age affects religious behavior, both groups in this and the subsequent comparison have been restricted to those not older than 40.

2

||||||||||||||||||||||||||||||||||||||||||||||||||||||||

Migration and Mexican American Religious Life, 1848–2000

Roberto Lint Sagarena

In 1969, a coalition of students, lay women, and Immaculate Heart nuns calling themselves "Católicos por la Raza" organized as a group with the principal goal of making Catholic clergy more accessible and engaged with the religious and social concerns of America's growing ethnic Mexican communities. In December of that year, the group began to voice its concerns through public demonstrations held outside of St. Basil's Cathedral in Los Angeles. Hundreds picketed the church in a series of protests that culminated in a protest on Christmas Eve, resulting in the arrests of 21 Católicos. This, in turn, inspired larger demonstrations, hunger strikes, and, most dramatically, the public burning of baptism certificates.

These protests would eventually spark a series of reforms and changes within the church hierarchy. But the hostile reaction of church officials to the demonstrations laid bare the long-standing rift between Mexican-origin Catholics and the American Catholic Church. The divide was a result of more than a century of ethnic and religious conflicts that marginalized Latinos within the institutional church. While other Catholic immigrant groups such as Germans, Poles, and Italians developed ethnic branches within the church, this was not the case for Mexican-origin peoples. Viewed historically, this exclusion both maintained and fostered new forms of folk religious practices among Mexican-origin laity (Dolan, 1997). And, in time, through the work of groups like Católicos por la Raza and as the largely Catholic Mexican-origin population skyrocketed in the late 20th century, their religious cultures have come to greatly influence the mainstream Catholic Church.

Birth of Southwest and Mexican Religious Life

Mexican migrants to the United States have had a distinctive experience in that the principal points of entry and intended destinations are in a region (the southwestern United States) that was taken from their home country by military force. This conquest has largely been naturalized within American national history, often being treated as little more than a brief prelude to the Civil War in historical narratives (but see Eisenhower, 2000; Johannsen, 1988). Still, the historical memory of the loss of nearly one-half of the nation's territory to the United States remains strong for Mexicans. Further, the presence of Mexican communities dating before the war, the prevalence of Spanish-language place names, and the geographic proximity of Mexico itself all provide close links to Mexican culture that have contributed to their unique immigrant experience.

During both the Spanish colonial and Mexican periods, Catholic clergy were sparse in the region that would become the Southwest. This paucity resulted in the creation of long-lasting lay religious traditions, many of which remained well into the American period and some of which are still extant today. Alta California's mission chain housed the most significant body of priests in the region. But, after Mexican independence in 1821, support for the missions dwindled. In New Mexico, Mexican priests were vastly outnumbered by lay Catholics. Seminaries were established in both Santa Barbara and Taos in an attempt to foster the creation of a local clergy; however, this project was interrupted by the war with the United States and a subsequent importation of foreign-born clergy. Ultimately, the maintenance of religious belief among Mexican-origin people in the region remained in the hands of lay practitioners for much of the 19th and into the 20th centuries (Weber, 1994).

The U.S.–Mexico War (1846–48) precipitated massive demographic and social changes as Mexico's northern territories changed hands and became the southwestern United States. While the war had many secular causes—the expansion of slavery and popularization of the idea that spanning the continent was America's manifest destiny, as well as the relatively undefended condition of Mexico's northern frontier—it was often perceived as a religious and cultural conflict. Many on both sides understood the war as a dispute arising from a fundamental opposition between Anglo Protestantism and Latin American Catholicism.

In the decades before the war, the arrival of large numbers of Irish Catholics to the United States sparked a period of fierce anti-Catholic nativism (for the classic treatments of nativism, see Billington, 1938; Higham, 1970). As the immigration of the Irish rose sharply, they were increasingly demonized for allegedly importing crime and disease, stealing jobs, and practicing a long list of imagined moral depravities. The rites of the Catholic Church were often cast as dangerous and sinister. Catholic rituals and iconography were caricatured as sensuous earthly distractions that weakened the will, ultimately working to erode America's moral fabric and invite catastrophe. For many Protestant nativists, Catholicism represented all of the evils of the old world and functioned as a political network controlled by the pope. Popular writers and public intellectuals such as Lyman Beecher and Samuel Morse portrayed Catholicism itself as antithetical and a direct threat to American democracy. These sentiments peaked in popularity mid-century, just at the time of the war with Catholic Mexico.

For American Catholics faced with these prejudices, the war with Mexico presented an opportunity to prove their patriotism and loyalty to their Protestant neighbors. As a result, it was generally quite popular with American Catholics, although there were noteworthy exceptions (the most notable of which was the St. Patrick's Battalion [Miller, 1989]). In time, many American Catholics would themselves come to perpetuate some nativist concerns as other ethnic and religious groups arrived after them.

For Mexicans, the first half of the nineteenth century was a time of great transition in the northern frontier. It began the century under Spanish colonial rule, went through a quarter century of Mexican control, and by 1848 was a territory of the United States. In fewer than 50 years, New Mexicans went from being subjects of Spain, to citizens of the Mexican republic, and, finally, to citizens of the United States. The cultural transformation of the region began to accelerate considerably in 1821, the year that the Mexican government announced it was opening its northern border to international commerce. Under Spanish rule, commerce with foreign merchants from the United States was strictly prohibited. For example, the monopolistic policies of the Spanish crown obliged New Mexicans to purchase their manufactured goods in Chihuahua so that profits could accrue directly to the Spanish Empire.

The opening of trade along the Santa Fe Trail marked the beginning of an era of unaccustomed prosperity for New Mexicans. The trail quickly became a major international thoroughfare for commerce and intercultural contact. And, as time passed, Americans arriving with the freight caravans began to settle in Mexican Santa Fe. During this period of Mexican rule, migration ran toward Mexico, as considerable numbers of Americans also moved into the territories of Tejas and Alta California (the latter corresponds roughly with the territory that ceded to the United States after 1848). Many of these American immigrants became Mexican citizens, sometimes marrying into prominent Mexican families and converting to Catholicism—their offspring being the first generations of Mexican Americans.

Mexican rule also brought great religious transformations. Most significantly, many missions in the territory began to be secularized (Chavez, 1974: 208). Many Franciscan missionaries of Spanish origin had been vocal monarchists during the Mexican War of Independence. And after the war, the Mexican victors took their revenge. In 1827, the Mexican government issued a decree banning all Peninsulores (Spaniards born on the Iberian peninsula) from civil, military, and ecclesiastical offices. While the order was not strictly followed, the Spanish Franciscans were slowly replaced with the first generation of native priests. The order was most successful in New Mexico, where by the end of the period of Mexican rule there were between 10 and 15 priests in the territory and most of these had been born in the region (Hazen-Hammond, 1988: 80–81; Weigle, 1976: 22–23).

A related religious and social change that occurred during the Mexican period was the growth of the influence of the Hermanidad de Penitentes in New Mexico.[1] Due to the limited number of available priests, members of penitential confraternities took the lead in New Mexican religious life. In *The American Catholic Parish,* Catholic historian Jay Dolan has written,

> Hispanic Catholics in the Southwest depended on the family, on the community, and on lay cofradias (those brotherhoods that simultaneously sought to fulfill the people's religious needs and to help them maintain a sense of cultural identity). In New Mexico and Southern Colorado, the people participated in public rituals under the leadership of the *penitentes*. (1987: 208)

The ecclesiastical capital of the territory of New Mexico was in Durango, Mexico, 1,500 miles away, and when Bishop Zubria of Durango made his first visit to the region in 1833, he was shocked by the zealous mortifications of the flesh practiced in many New Mexican confraternities. The bishop banned the brotherhoods' practice of crucifixion as "extreme" but allowed other forms of self-discipline, such as self-flagellation and the wearing of hair shirts (Weigle, 1976: 6–25). While the local strength of the lay organizations prevented direct conflict with Zubria's distant episcopal authority, Zubria's attempts at reform presaged religious conflicts that were to plague New Mexico in the years to come.

The tension between the authority of the universal church and the strength of local religious expression is a central one in the Catholic tradition. After the war, Mexican and American visions of Catholicism developed with different emphases on these elements. The geographic isolation of the church in New Mexico led to almost complete dependence on lay initiative. In contrast, the Catholic Church in the United States tended to stress the central authority of the episcopacy. The arrival of the American Catholic Church in New Mexico signaled the beginning of an era in which these two visions of Catholicism would collide.

When Jean Baptiste Lamy, a French Sulpecian and the first American bishop of New Mexico, arrived in Santa Fe in 1854, many Protestant missionaries were already established in the city working to convert New Mexican Catholics and shore up the faith among Anglo settlers. These missionaries were mainly Baptists, Methodists, and Presbyterians (Banker, 1993; Walker, 1991). Lamy believed firmly in the central religious authority of the church over that of the laity, and he quickly came into conflict with the penitential Hermanidades (brotherhoods) that were used to near total autonomy from the authority of the clergy.

One of the most interesting consequences of Lamy's conflict with the Penitentes was that it created fertile inroads for these Protestant missionaries among New Mexican Catholics. In fact, several prominent Penitentes became Presbyterian converts, and Presbyterian schools became popular with Penitente groups. The Penitentes of the village of Embudo, for example, spilt in two over the issue of Presbyterian schooling for their children. The group refusing to bow to Catholic pressure to take their children out of Presbyterian schools became known as "Penitentes Presbyterianos."

Serious conflicts arose between the bishop and the New Mexican clergy as well. Throughout the 1850s, ecclesiastical conflicts grew more volatile as relations between the bishop and the New Mexican priests deteriorated. This was particularly true of Lamy's relationship with one of New Mexico's most prominent priests, Father Antonio José Martínez. Lamy and Martínez engaged in a public debate over the tithe in the pages of the *Gaceta de Santa Fe,* and what had begun as an internal ecclesiastical affair was placed before the public eye. In a steady series of articles, Martínez cited both canon law and the U.S. Constitution in his argument against what he considered to be Lamy's perverse use of episcopal authority. Martínez maintained that the payment of stole fees (payments to clergy for services such as baptisms, weddings, and funerals) and episcopal tithes was necessarily a free and voluntary act. Martínez argued that the principle of separation of church and state protected the voluntary selection of one's own church of affiliation and particular minister. And further, that no minister, not even a bishop, had the right to enforce monetary collections of any kind. Martínez ultimately called for U.S. government intervention to publicly reprimand Lamy for overstepping the boundaries of his authority (Horgan, 2003: 240, 250; Chavez, 1981: 135, 151–54).

Their debate, pivoting around the issues of tithing, episcopal authority, and clerical prerogative continued until Bishop Lamy formally suspended Martínez in 1857 and ultimately excommunicated him. Martínez's suspension only served to fuel the conflict as many Taos residents sided with the New Mexican priest, reinforcing dissident spirit among the laity.

In the place of local clergy, members of several religious orders were brought in to run New Mexico's Catholic schools, hospitals, and orphanages. These orders included the Sisters of Loretto, the Sisters of Charity, the Sisters of Mercy, and the Jesuits. When it came time to recruit parish priests, Lamy preferred clergy from his former seminary at Montferrand, France. These recruitment campaigns began a tradition of French dominance in the region's clergy that lasted well into the 20th century. During New Mexico's territorial period (1850–1912), French clergy comprised almost two-thirds of the approximately 177 clergy who served there. The French also held an ecclesiastical dynasty as the region's first five New Mexican archbishops were Lamy's countrymen (Howlett, 1987: 365).

In California, the Gold Rush of 1849 precipitated a massive influx of immigrants from all over the world to the newly Americanized territory. Among the largest groups heeding the call of gold were miners from northern Mexico. As a result of this first wave of Mexican immigration, the Mexican-born population of California quickly became greater after the war than before it. These immigrants would create the first *barrios* (Mexican neighborhoods) in the United States. Americans would call them "Sonora-towns" after the Mexican state that most of the immigrant miners came from. The imposition of foreign miners' taxes and brutal racist violence worked to reinforce an American understanding of the

Mexican population as foreign and unwelcome in a region that had been Mexican just a few years before (Camarillo, 1979; Monroy, 1993).

As Americans came to dominate the region politically, financially, and culturally, they continued to cast Mexican and Mexican American peoples as alien to the region. For much of the 19th century, native-born Mexican people referred to themselves and were referred to by Americans as Texans (Tejanos) and Californians (Californios). But, as early as the 1880s, Americans began to claim those titles for their own native-born populations. And, it was this shift in ethnic ascription that finally marked those of Mexican origin and background as outsiders in the Southwest.

Changes in secular authority in California also resulted in changes in religious authority. In May of 1850, Joseph Sadoc Alemany, a Spanish-born priest serving in Ohio, was named bishop of the Californias. His election marked a reversal of the Mexican effort to rid the region of Spanish clergy. Unlike New Mexico where the culturally Mexican population remained relatively stable, the Gold Rush in California very quickly created a European American majority. And, as other European American clergy entered the region, they also tended to perpetuate the popular understanding of Mexicans as inassimilable foreigners and generally focused their ministerial efforts on the needs of newly arriving American Catholics (McGloin, 1966: 90).

Mexicans in America

The next rise in Mexican immigration to the United States began during the 1910s as large numbers of Mexicans were displaced by the violence of the Mexican Revolution. But it was not until the 1920s that this wave of immigration reached its peak. This postwar migration doubled the number of Mexican-born residents of the United States in a single decade, from roughly 0.75 million in 1920 to 1.45 million by 1930. And, by 1928, Los Angeles had the largest Mexican-born population of any city outside of Mexico (Meir and Ribera, 1993: 103–30). This northward migration of Mexican workers was motivated, in part, by the worsening of protracted economic hardships in Mexico and the lure of jobs in the rapidly developing American Southwest—jobs available to Mexicans as a result of new immigration restrictions on Asian and European laborers. At the time, as many as 1,000 Mexican laborers a week were recruited by agents of the Southern Pacific and Santa Fe Railroads along the U.S.–Mexico border as track hands and agricultural workers; the very same rail lines that had initially brought American settlers to southern California eventually reintroduced a large Mexican origin population as well.

Although a great number of Mexican clergy also came to the Southwest during these decades, their migration was largely a result of involuntary exile as they sought refuge from anticlerical revolutionary forces. And, generally speaking, their principal concern was a quick return to Mexico rather than the spiritual well-being of Mexican congregations in the United States. With the exception of limited Americanization campaigns and the funding of Sunday schools for Mexican children, Mexican and Mexican American communities were largely neglected by the American Catholic clergy well into the 1940s. But the neglect often went both ways—though Mexican immigrants were still nominally Catholic, the anticlerical violence of the war had left many of them unaccustomed to regular church attendance and some others had become staunchly anticlerical (Beal, 1994; Sandoval, 1990: 50).

While Mexican participation in Catholic services was low, domestic piety in the form of home altars and prayer groups maintained connections to the Catholic faith much as it had for other Catholic immigrant groups. The proximity of the Mexican border and the speed of rail travel further limited incentives to actively assimilate or convert. These factors, combined with racism and segregation, resulted in fairly insular Mexican and Mexican American communities in the early 20th century; from 1910 to 1930, only 5 to 13 percent of Mexican nationals in the United States applied for permanent residency or citizenship. And, in spite of Protestant missionary efforts and general neglect by the Catholic clergy, the rate of conversion among Mexican Catholics in southern California never exceeded 10 percent (Sanchez, 1993; see also Gamio, 1930, 1931). The social tensions created by the Great Depression set off a new era of nativism in the United States and inspired the establishment of a repatriation program designed to rid the United States of unwelcome Mexican immigrants. Because of its large population of Mexican immigrants, Los Angeles became a focal point for these repatriation efforts. Between 1931 and 1934, roughly 50,000, or about one-third, of the city's Mexican and Mexican American residents were sent to Mexico; most were sent forcibly, a few went voluntarily (Balderrama and Rodríguez, 2006). And even as repatriation efforts abated in the mid-1930s, those remaining in California faced continuing widespread anti-Mexican sentiments. By attempting to settle in the United States and with no intention of returning to Mexico, these immigrants confronted serious issues surrounding their identity; they were now more a part of *México de afuera* (external Mexico) than Mexican, and yet they faced great difficulties in integrating into American society as Mexican Americans.

Shortly after the end of American repatriation efforts, Mexican workers would again be recruited and invited into the United States. Beginning in 1942, the U.S. government initiated a bilateral labor agreement with the Mexican government to recruit poor rural Mexican workers. With the advent of World War II and the end of the depression, Mexican labor was needed again. This agreement, known as the Bracero program, brought nearly 5 million Mexicans to the United States, and more than one-half of them went to the agricultural fields of California.

Although most Braceros eventually returned to Mexico, their presence greatly increased the size of the region's Mexican American communities. The majority of Braceros came alone, but some women and families made the trip as well. Many of these women formed communities for themselves in lay Marian prayer groups where members called themselves "Guadalupanas" after their patroness, the Virgin of Guadalupe (Galarza, 1964). Ultimately, the Bracero program firmly established a virtual tidal pattern for Mexican immigration to the United States that would last through the rest of the twentieth century—during times of plenty, Mexican laborers would cross the border, and during lean times, they would return to Mexico— resulting in prolonged cultural exchanges between Mexican and nascent Mexican American cultures.

In the midst of this renewal of Mexican cultures within the United States, the American Catholic Church launched its first concerted Americanization campaigns among Mexican-origin peoples. These campaigns included English-language lessons and a catechism that encouraged forms of devotion that were alien to lay Mexican traditions. Still, some of these programs were successful. Easily the most influential Catholic outreach of the mid-20th century was the Cursillo movement. Originating in Majorca, Spain, in 1947 and arriving in the United States a decade later, the Cursillo has had a great effect on Mexican and Mexican American Catholics across the country. Participants in the Cursillo undertake three-day "retreats" for religious renewal and dedication. While the clergy often participated in organizing the retreats, the aim of the Cursillo was to stress greater responsibility among lay persons in the maintenance of the church and their own spiritual lives. The Cursillo movement also had a significant effect on the larger American culture because it fostered social activism among Mexican Catholics. The Cursillo movement can be credited with influencing Catholic leadership during the civil rights era. César Chávez of the United Farm Workers, for example, became a Cursillista.

With the advent of the civil rights movement in the 1950s, Mexican Americans witnessed African Americans' successes through demonstrations, picketing, and direct confrontations with racism. By the decade's end, they began to emulate these tactics in both the political and religious spheres. Beginning in the late 1950s, Reies Tijerina, a Pentecostal minister, began to radicalize the issue of land ownership in New Mexico. He cited the often broken provisions of the Treaty of Guadalupe Hidalgo that guaranteed the retention of lands by Mexican citizens remaining in the annexed territories. Tijerina called for the return of property that had been taken through American deception and fraud, including large tracts that were now under the management of the U.S. Forestry Service (Busto, 2005). And in 1965, César Chávez headed the first attempts by Mexican agricultural workers in California to unionize under the banner of the United Farm Workers (UFW). During Lent of 1966, members of the new union undertook a 300-mile march of "Pilgrimage, Penitence and Revolution" from Delano to Sacramento under the banner of the Virgin of Guadalupe and both Mexican and American flags.

The use of the image of Guadalupe by the UFW was in part an expression of ethnic identity and in part a strategic use of symbolism to counter accusations from the right of communist subversion. Criticism of the union helped to foster communication and dialogue between field workers and American Catholic clergy as both sides reached out to each other—union leaders seeking protection from cold war nativism and a new generation of activist clergy seeking to participate in the moral renewal of the civil rights movement. In Chavez's own words: "We had the Virgin with us. And people, see, people said no they're not communists, once they saw the church around us. That was the way we broke the red-baiting" (quoted in Rosales, 2000: 283).

As a result of the prominence given to the symbol of the Virgin of Guadalupe by the UFW, one of the most innovative and lasting legacies of unionization is the transformation of Guadalupe into more than an emblem of Mexican nationalism. In the context of the American civil rights movement, the image of Guadalupe at once became a radicalized religious symbol for popular protest and an emblem for Chicano/a nationalism.

Changes in Mexican American Catholicism

The civil rights movement allowed for the creation of some common ground for the American Catholic Church and the ethnic Mexican laity. However, the relationship remained strained well into the following decades. Among the most significant efforts to reform the church came from within. In the 1970s, a coalition of Mexican priests formed the group Padres Asociados para Derechos Religiosos, Educativos y Sociales (PADRES) (Martínez, 2005). Their principal goal was to fight discrimination against Mexican and Mexican American peoples within the Catholic Church. They petitioned for the placement of Spanish-speaking clergy in largely Mexican American dioceses and the elevation of Mexican American bishops. The work of PADRES, as well as protests such as the one St. Basil's, can be credited as sources of the political pressure that prompted the church to commission several Mexican American bishops and cardinals in the 1970s. Ultimately, the confluence of several factors in the late 1960s would change the public character of American Catholicism (especially in the Southwest).

Many reforms instituted by Vatican II, such as the vernacular mass, provided powerful new methods for outreach in ethnic parishes. In the early 1970s, Spanish-language services became increasingly popular and took inventive new forms such as the "mariachi mass" that featured Mexican musicians in the performance of the liturgy. While Mexican-origin Catholics welcomed the integration of Mexican cultural elements into services that targeted them, churches that sponsored these types of masses faced considerable criticism from many American Catholics who were wary of the rise of ethnic particularism within the larger church.

At the same historical moment that Mexican culture and Mexican-origin Catholics were making inroads into the American Catholic Church, the study of race and ethnicity was being formalized within the academy. Early ethnic studies programs fostered a politicized sense of identity for Mexican-origin peoples as Chicano/as and promoted active resistance to Americanization. Like members of the early UFW, Chicano/a nationalists often employed religious iconography—most importantly, the Virgin of Guadalupe—as emblems of ethnicity.

Chicano/a artists have reinvented Guadalupe in a variety of forms symbolizing political and cultural autonomy. While the image of Guadalupe has retained its sacredness, many artists depict the virgin in a manner that radically departs from Catholic orthodoxy; for example, Chicano/a artists often depict Guadalupe in ways that stress her connection to the Aztec goddess Tonantzin in an attempt to valorize and claim continuity with the indigenous cultures of Mexico. Further, Chicana feminists have reimagined Guadalupe in a host of forms suggestive of feminine strength and sexuality. Among a multiplicity of forms, Guadalupe has been cast as a black-belt karate practitioner, as jogger, as factory worker, as a powerful nude, and as the subject of countless tattoos (Del Castillo, McKenna, and Yarbro-Bejarano, 1991).

As Chicano/as embarked on the project of creating a culture betwixt and between Mexican and American cultures, the liberalization of American immigration laws resulted in a massive influx of Mexican-origin people. In the 1980s, large-scale immigration from Mexico became one of the most significant elements of what scholars of immigration to the United States have come to term "the new immigration." In specific consideration of Mexicans, this immigration is characterized by large-scale flow of legal and undocumented immigrants that intensified rapidly after 1980. In the 1990s, there were more legal immigrants to the United States from Mexico than from all of the countries of Europe combined.

Many of these "new" Mexican immigrants in the United States are transnational citizens rather than simple transplants. These recent arrivals are emerging as important actors in American society and civic life while still participating in Mexico's religious, economic, political, and cultural spheres. This situation is not lost on Mexican politicians: former Mexican President Vicente Fox toured the border region in December of 2000 to personally welcome back a few of the estimated 1 million Mexicans traveling south for Christmas. The popularity of Fox's dual nationality initiative, whereby Mexican immigrants becoming U.S. citizens retain a host of political rights in Mexico, suggests an emerging transnational framework for the identities of these "new" immigrants.

While contemporary immigrants have found the American Catholic Church more sympathetic than earlier generations did, Protestant denominations (especially charismatic churches) have had significant success in their conversion efforts. Many of these churches make use of transnational networks to establish satellite congregations in Mexican hometowns, thereby creating important support networks for their members and religious cultures that are American and Mexican all at once. The transnational character of the religious lives of many new Mexican immigrants has led to great innovations in Catholic devotional life in the borderlands. Among the most noteworthy is the existence of two separate cults of patron saints of undocumented Mexican immigrants, Juan Soldado and San Toribio Romo.

Although not recognized by the Catholic Church, Juan Castillo Morales, commonly known as Juan Soldado, has long been understood to be a patron saint of undocumented Mexican immigrants (Vanderwood, 2004). Morales served as a soldier in Tijuana when he was accused of the rape and murder of an 8-year-old girl, a crime for which he was executed in 1938. His hagiography claims that he was framed by a superior officer who was actually guilty of the horrible act. As he was led to his execution, he swore that his innocence would be proven when miracles were asked and granted in his name after his death. Juan Soldado's burial site has become a pilgrimage spot for the faithful to ask for intercession in issues of immigration: crossing the border safely, dealing with the border patrol, and negotiating permanent residency and citizenship. Devoted followers have built a chapel on the site of his grave that is decorated with thanksgivings in the form of photographs, letters, gifts, candles, flowers, and copies of green cards.

In 2000, Pope John Paul II canonized 24 martyrs killed in Mexico's Cristero revolt, an insurrection against a repressively anticlerical Mexican government that occurred in the late 1920s. One of these newly minted saints is Father Toribio Romo, a priest shot and killed by government forces in an ambush in Tequila, Mexico. Since canonization, Romo has gained considerable popularity among Mexican migrants and is credited with leading many lost or injured people safely across the border. While Romo's relics reside in a church in central Mexico, it is significant that all of Romo's surviving relatives have emigrated from Mexico and live in the United States.

A New Church

The Northridge earthquake of 1994 damaged Los Angeles' St. Vibiana's Cathedral badly enough to warrant its condemnation by structural engineers. However, plans for a grander cathedral were quickly drawn up, and by the following year the campaign to build a new structure was well under way. In September of 2002, the massive new cathedral of Our Lady of the Angels was dedicated and opened to the public.

Like St. Basil's, the new cathedral makes use of a simple, modern, and very controversial architectural vocabulary. However, the design of Our Lady of the Angels is radically different from that of its predecessor. In some ways, the architecture of the new cathedral can be read as a compensatory gesture by the American church to ethnic and national Catholics. Its architect and the clergy very self-consciously created the building as an emblem of a pluralistic vision of American Catholicism. The entrance to the cathedral is surmounted by a statue of Mary that, the visitor's literature tells us,

> does not wear the traditional veil. Her arms are bare, outstretched to welcome all. Her carriage is confident, and her hands are strong, the hands of a working woman. From the side can be seen a thick braid of hair down her back that summons thoughts of Native American or Latina women. Other characteristics, such as her eyes, lips and nose convey Asian, African and Caucasian features.

Below the multiracial statue of Mary are monumental cathedral doors designed by a Mexican-born artist and emblazoned with 15 distinct Marian images from around the world.

As the laity enters the cathedral, they pass a series of side chapels that are designed to house and acknowledge the important role of the diverse ethnic parishes of the city. The interior walls of the cathedral are decorated with large tapestries that depict the communion of saints: Catholic saints, revered individuals, and children of all nationalities and epochs are presented in an eclectic mix. But of these symbols of inclusivity, the one that would be most striking to the Chicano/a protesters of 1969 at St. Basil's is the full-scale replica of Our Lady of Guadalupe, placed just outside the exit of the cathedral and centrally visible to all visitors.

The tremendous array of ethnic religious emblems that adorn the new cathedral marks a dramatic change in the American Catholic Church. The church seems to have come full circle to an ethnic model, but now as a larger American church made up of many transnational ethnic parishes. Given that the cathedral's design and location (near government offices in downtown Los Angeles) promote its use as a ceremonial and public center for the city, it seems likely that the religious culture and symbols of immigrant ethnic Catholics, most notably Mexican-origin Catholics, will only come into greater prominence in American Catholic culture.

NOTES

Portions of this essay appeared in Roberto Lint Sagarena, "Porous Borders: Mexican Immigration and American Civic Culture," in *Faith in America: Changes, Challenges, New Directions,* edited by Charles Lippy (New York: Praeger, 2006), 129–40.

1.   The origins of the Penitentes are disputed; Martha Weigle (1976), lists no fewer than five competing theories for the origins of the group.

3

‖‖‖‖‖‖‖‖‖‖‖‖‖‖‖‖‖‖‖‖‖‖‖‖‖‖‖‖‖‖‖‖‖‖‖‖‖‖‖

Whither the Flock?

The Catholic Church and the Success of Mexicans in America

David Lopez

Contemporary migrants north from Mexico to the United States have much in common with the "humble masses" that came from Europe a century ago, in both the modest resources they bring with them and their initial integration into the bottom rungs of American society. For the most part, they also share the same religion, Roman Catholicism, as did the previous large groups of "labor migrants," the Irish, Italians, and Poles. Mexicans and other Latinos now constitute the single largest ethnic segment of the American Catholic population and virtually all of its growth. It is a commonplace to say that religious institutions have played a key role in the integration of immigrants into American society, though the specific mechanisms of that "integration" are often not delineated.

In the case of Latino Catholics and the American church, it is difficult to point to any important ways in which the church has facilitated their climb up the ladder of success. Indeed, it would seem that the church needs Latinos at least as much as Latinos benefit from the church: it is no secret that Catholic leaders see in them the future of the church in the United States. Simple principles of institutional self-interest predict that the American church should be doing everything possible to ensure the happiness and loyalty of Latino Catholics, and, in fact, there are a myriad of programs at the national, diocese, and parish levels aimed at Latinos. However, a review of these efforts suggests that they do little to improve the status of Latino immigrants or their children. The church may or may not be successful in its attempt to secure the loyalty of its flock, but, in contrast with the religious institutions that serve many other contemporary immigrant communities, it is contributing little to the integration and upward mobility of Mexican and other Latino immigrants in the United States.

In developing this thesis, I ground my analysis in three bodies of literature and social science theory. Above all, I approach the question of immigrant communities first from the perspective of a social scientist concerned with ethnic conflict and ethnic differences in socioeconomic attainment, including the different patterns of integration and assimilation among recent immigrant-origin ethnic groups and how present patterns compare with the last great wave of immigration a century ago. A fundamental assumption of this school of research is that group-level outcomes are a result of historical circumstances and societal prejudices and conflicts as much as they are the result of the resources that immigrants bring to America (good examples of this tradition are Gordon, 1964; Alba and Nee, 1997; Portes and Rumbaut, 2001). A second research tradition that informs this essay is the study of the "ethnic church" in America, which for the most part is the study of religious organizations in immigrant communities (e.g., Dolan, 1985: 127–293; Ebaugh and Chafetz, 2000; Kwon, Kim and Warner, 2001). I am not so much concerned with the religious and the cultural lives of these communities as I am with parsing out what contributions ethnic churches make to the integration and success, or isolation and failure, of immigrant communities. A third tradition, also borrowed from students of religion, is the "religious competition" approach to understanding how religious organizations act as institutions. "Religious competition" is the rational-choice-theory-derived approach to religious organizations that seeks to explain policies and practices of organizations on the basis of institutional self-interest and the "economics" of the supply of and demand for religious services. Anthony Gill (1998) provides a detailed application of this theory to the case of the Catholic Church's defensive actions in the face of Protestant competition in Latin America (see also Warner, 1993; Young, 1997). Both the theoretical perspective and the geographical case on which most research has been done are of particular importance to the topic at hand, since in many ways church-Latino community relations in the United States are an extension of processes south of the border.

Despite the similarities with labor immigrant groups of the past, there is troubling evidence that the Mexican immigrant-origin population may not be headed for the same eventual assimilation and upward mobility.

Of course, the path trod by Italians and Poles was no stroll in the park; social acceptance and economic equity were the result of individual and collective struggles that took place over three generations (Alba, 1985). On the other hand, Mexican communities have existed in the Southwest for hundreds of years and remain economically and socially marginal to this day. In recent times, there was a first great wave of migration from Mexico, from 1910 to 1930, that produced second and third generations only slightly later than the canonical European groups like Italians and Poles, generations that never achieved the same levels of assimilation and social mobility. And there is troubling evidence that conditions today, though different, may be no more propitious for economic integration and upward mobility. Economic opportunities for unskilled immigrants and their children seem bleaker and more dead-end in today's postindustrial economy, with its premiums on both formal education and entrepreneurship.

The renewal of large-scale migration from Mexico occurred at the same time as the sudden expansion of immigration from Asia and other parts of the world that had previously sent few settlers to the United States. Most of these groups bring with them a winning combination of educational, entrepreneurial, and other resources that allow them to achieve economic success far more rapidly than previous immigrants, and their children often achieve in school at levels that exceed those of native whites. In contrast, Mexican and Central American immigrants arrive with little formal education and few job skills. Even if the children and grandchildren of contemporary Mexican immigrants do manage to achieve and assimilate at rates approximating Poles and Italians a century ago, they will still lag behind other immigrant children. In the early 20th century there was a similar disparity between the success rates of Jewish and Catholic children of immigrants. Now as then, the reasons for these disparities are complex and often simplified into invidious comparisons. But there is one big difference between then and now: whereas Jews were the exception and the various Catholic groups were the norm, today Mexicans (and perhaps Central Americans) are the exception and the array of high-achieving Asian and Middle Eastern groups are the norm.

Do class origins, and the various "capitals" (financial, human/educational, cultural, and social) associated with these origins, really provide a complete explanation of why, on average, the children of Asian immigrants are headed for the secure middle class and the children of Mexican immigrants seem on a path toward an uncertain occupational purgatory? What role might religious institutions and practices play in the success of immigrants and their children? It is from the perspective of these questions that I approach the question of religion among Mexican immigrant communities in the United States. Clearly, religion plays an important part in the lives of Mexicans in the United States just as it did in Mexico, and Mexican Catholicism has provided important symbols of solidarity that have helped some Mexican Americans rally around collective goals. However, in this chapter, I consider religion among Mexican Americans from the limited, and perhaps rather vulgar, perspective of a secular social scientist concerned with understanding the problem of economic and social achievement. I am not concerned with the degree to which the church satisfies spiritual needs or to which people achieve their religious goals, except to the degree that the economy of these "religious ends" helps explain the outcome of competing religious institutions.

The integration of Mexicans in America centers on their economic prospects and factors that affect these prospects, such as legal status and English-language ability, and, for the children of immigrants, success in school, the essential key that unlocks economic success in today's economy. To these individual factors one might add less tangible but no less important macrolevel factors. The historically high rates of intermarriage between Mexicans and whites (Mittelbach and Moore, 1968) suggest that they do not face the same degree of interpersonal prejudice that continues to haunt African Americans. Still, residual racism against Mexicans certainly exists. The public attitude toward Mexican immigrants, particularly the poor and the undocumented, is a significant force in the public life of states like California, so it is reasonable to conclude that these attitudes may also influence successful integration. To the degree that religious institutions combat political and legal marginality, poor English skills and poor schooling, and societal prejudice, they contribute to the success of Mexicans in America. As we shall see, the church record on all these scores is modest, however well intentioned.

In this essay, I summarize the uneven history of the integration of Mexicans in America and seek to assess the ways in which the Catholic Church may have contributed to or impeded this integration. Although approximately 20 percent of Mexican Americans are Protestants and evangelical Protestantism may be playing an important minority role in Mexican American communities, I have confined my consideration of religious factors to the Catholic Church and its manifest institutions. Other research deals with the fascinating but extremely complex issue of evangelical Protestantism, which here is treated largely in relation to the success and failure of the Catholic Church.[1]

After a brief historical overview of the formation of Mexican American communities and the place of U.S. Latinos in the Catholic Church, I turn to an analysis of the actual impact of the church on the education and economic lives of Latinos. I have already suggested that I see little in these materials to warrant the conclusion that the church plays much of a role. Anticipating my conclusions, the modesty of the church contribution seems to derive above all from the organization and culture of the church itself: in contrast to the congregationally controlled (and usually Protestant) ethnic churches of other immigrant groups that seem to provide such important support for the education and upward mobility for immigrant children, the patriarchal, priest-centered way of doing things in the Catholic Church stifles initiative and provides little or no support for the habit of study that is so essential for the success of immigrant children today.

There is one way in which the church might make an enormous contribution: through the austere but effective mechanism of Catholic schools, which are so superior to inner-city public schooling today. However Latino youth, even though they constitute one-half or more of all young Catholics in America, are grossly underserved by Catholic schools, and there is little hope that this will change in the future.

In chapter 1, Richard Alba and Robert Orsi provide a valuable framework for comparing and contrasting the Italian and Mexican cases of immigration, which they characterize as the two "great low-wage labor migrations of their times." I touch on comparative issues throughout this essay, but at the outset I want to underline two points they make. First, Mexicans preceded Anglos in California and the Southwest: their first great wave of large-scale migration came just after the Italian influx (1910–25, compared with 1900–1914), and migration from Mexico ebbed and trickled until the 1960s, when it began to flow again with a vengeance. But Mexican Americans who trace their origins to this earlier immigration have yet to attain equity with whites and Asians in the United States. Alba and Orsi are able to tell a clear story of upward mobility from generation to generation; to the degree that one can identify generations among Mexican Americans, the story is much less uplifting.

Second, despite four generations of acculturation and assimilation, if not equality, and despite the fact that in California and the Southwest the dioceses of the Catholic Church were originally part of the Mexican

Catholic Church, in many ways the U.S. Catholic Church has still not come to terms with and provided equality to Mexican Catholics in the United States. Italians initially provided a challenge to the Catholic Church in America, but by the third generation, Italian Americans were well represented in the hierarchy of the church and a majority have maintained their Catholic identity even as the salience of their national origin declines. In contrast, Mexicans are underrepresented in the hierarchy, from the priesthood all the way down to enrollment in parish schools. There is a "Secretariat of Hispanic Affairs" within the U.S. Conference of Catholic Bishops, but its Pastoral Plan, dating from 1987, reads like a missionary plan to evangelize some exotic tribe, not the largest and oldest ethnic group in the American Catholic Church.

Migration from Mexico, New and Old

The very roots of California and the Southwest are Mexican, and Mexicans have continuously inhabited the region for hundreds of years. But most Mexicans in America trace their origins to migration north either early in the 20th century or in the past few decades. Tiny traditional Mexican/Hispanic populations were overwhelmed by emigration from wartorn Mexico between 1910 and 1930. The Great Depression drastically reduced migration north and led to forced repatriation. There was a gradual resumption of migration during the war years and the 1950s, but as late as 1960 the typical Mexican American could still trace her origins back to the migration of the early decades of the century. First, second, and third generations corresponded roughly to age cohorts, much as they did for Italians or Japanese. Today's Latino population is actually an overlay of two quite different groups: a numerically predominant recent and continuing immigrant population, which provides most of the workers and most of the schoolchildren, and an aging population whose immigrant origins trace back 80 years into the past. The first wave is demographically comparable with groups like Italian Americans, perhaps 10 to 20 years delayed. The current wave is also demographically comparable with Italian Americans, as they appeared about 1910.

Migration from Mexico has always been determined more by economic forces and social networks than by laws and regulations (McWilliams, 1968 [1948]; Massey et al., 1987), though there is evidence that recent legal changes intended to reduce undocumented immigration have had the opposite effect (see below). Even today, the border is notoriously porous, and early in the 20th century it existed hardly at all. Back then, what is today called "illegal" immigration was probably the norm. Certainly, prewar official immigration statistics from the U.S.–Mexico border are meaningless. Of course, as the surprises emanating from the 2000 U.S. Census demonstrate, undocumented immigration from Mexico continues to be the way that a very large proportion of Mexicans (and Central Americans) arrive. Most Mexican American families in the United States contain undocumented current members or forefathers and mothers. This sets off the Mexican and Central American experience from virtually all other immigrations to the United States, past or present. Douglas Massey and his associates (Massey and Bartley, 2002; Massey, Durand, and Malone, 2003) have argued that the Immigration Reform and Control Act of 1986 and subsequent legal changes in the United States have vastly increased the undocumented population in the United States, as well as the exploitation and disadvantage of illegal status. Laws and fences may not have impeded migration north, but the consequent status of being illegal affects Mexicans far more profoundly than other immigrant groups, both yesterday and today.

Even by the imperfect metric of the 2000 census, we know not only that Mexican immigration in recent decades has been larger than other migration streams but also that it has had transforming effects on parts of American society. Three-quarters of California's population growth throughout the 1990s is attributable to Mexican immigration, either directly or indirectly in terms of the growing population of children of immigrants (the rest, one-quarter, is due to other immigration from Latin America and Asia). Nearly one-half the state's schoolchildren are Latino, presaging what is certain to be a Latino majority in the state within two or three decades. California is by far the state most affected by Mexican immigration, but the real news of the 2000 census is the degree to which Mexican immigrants and their families are colonizing virtually all states of the union. Demographically, the most obvious sign of Mexican dispersion is in school enrollments; the spread of Mexican immigrants across America comes as no surprise to school superintendents from Oregon to Maine and Georgia. This all adds up: according to preliminary 2000 census figures, 42 percent of *all* the nation's population growth since 1990 is attributable to Latino immigration or natural increase. Latinos in the United States outnumber African Americans today, in census counts if not in the national consciousness (U.S. Bureau of the Census, 2001).

Dispersion throughout the United States is the new story in Mexican immigration, but the effects are still felt most in California, where anti-immigrant politics rise and fall according to economic conditions. During the economic slowdown of the early 1990s, tight state and municipal budgets led to the success of Proposition 187, which literally targeted the undocumented but was, in fact, a vote against the immigration of poor Latinos generally. The disastrous political consequences of Proposition 187 for the state Republican Party, along with economic recovery, marginalized the anti-immigrant movement, but, with the current fiscal crisis of the state, there are signs that it is moving back into the public forum. If it does, it will be interesting to see if the church is able to play a prominent role as protector and advocate for Latino immigrants. Moral arguments aside, the logic of religious competition suggests that the church must play this role.

Throughout the 20th century, the upward mobility and social acceptance of Mexicans in America ebbed and flowed. There was never a period of genuinely rapid progress, but there was a time, about 30 years ago, when it appeared that Mexicans were embarked on a slow but steady incorporation not dissimilar to what Italians had experienced a few decades before. To be sure, this was a much-contested analysis: in contrast to the "like Italians but slower" model, progressive social critics in the 1960s offered the "internal colony" theory—or, rather, metaphor, as it never really made much sense as applied to a population with recent immigrant origins. And yet if Mexicans appeared to be just slow Italians, there were clear indications that they faced persistent structural barriers. In Texas, Mexicans struggled against a heritage of discrimination similar to if not as severe as that faced by African Americans. Even in more enlightened parts of the nation, like California, social, residential, and occupational segregation was common, perhaps even enforced by the state. Mexican workers were not as well situated to take advantage of structural changes in the economy as Italians had from 1930 to 1960. And their children were not as able to ride the wave to the expansion of mass education and the growth of higher education. But by 1960, structural change was lifting even Mexican boats.

However, the evidence is clear that the first Mexican American third generation did not reach the same stage of "optional ethnicity" that was apparently the norm for Italians and other Euro ethnics. Research over the past 40 years has demonstrated conclusively that these children and grandchildren of Mexican immigrants have not joined the American mainstream to the same degree as Euro ethnics but, instead, hover somewhere between the poles of white and black America (Blau and Duncan, 1967; Grebler, Moore, and Guzman, 1970; Ortiz, 1996; Grogger and Trejo, 2002).

Latin American Context

From the point of view of the church, the challenge of keeping the faith among Mexicans in the United States is part of a broader effort to regain ground among its single most important constituency, Latin American Catholics. The Second Vatican Council (Vatican II; 1962–65) created a plan for confronting what it saw as its two principal competitors worldwide, and most especially in Latin America: the secular left and Protestant evangelism. To its credit, instead of simply condemning its opponents as sinful, the core of the Vatican II strategy was to recognize the legitimacy and appeal of both, then to devise plans of action within the church to offer Catholic alternatives. In Latin America, the principal result was the support of Liberation Theology, the nascent movement among the left within the church to build a social program that was frankly anticapitalist and on the side of the poor. A secondary but also important outcome was tolerance and even support for "charismatic" and participatory worship, consistent with the shift from Latin to vernacular mass.

For the last four decades, the history of the Catholic Church in Latin America has largely been the history of its struggle with these two competing forces. Initially, the great threats were communism and secular socialism, but gradually they were displaced by evangelical Protestantism, which made massive inroads, particularly in Brazil and Central America. The institutional weakness of the church (especially the low ratio of priests to population) set the stage for its vulnerability. Pope John Paul II's withdrawal of support for the "people's church" inspired by Liberation Theology reforms deprived the church of its most effective defensive tool. But it has been the grassroots appeal of evangelical Protestantism that most threatens the church's previous monopoly over religious services in Latin America. The majority of Latin Americans still identify as Catholic, and even in regions with rapid change (Central America, southern Mexico, Brazil) the Protestant proportion rarely exceeds one-quarter. But the rate of apostasy and the numbers involved in some regions are enormous and explain why the ailing pope visited Mexico and Guatemala yet again in 2002, to curry favor, however ineffectively, with the region's indigenous population that has been so especially vulnerable to the Protestant appeal (Stoll, 1990; Burdick, 1993; Gill, 1998).

Appeals to Latino Catholics in the United States have to be seen in the broader framework of the church's competition for the souls of its all-important Latin American flock. Critics have noted that many of the efforts emanating from the upper reaches of the hierarchy (the Secretariat of Hispanic Affairs, as well as Cardinal Roger Mahoney's $200 million cathedral in Los Angeles) have many of the same authoritarian failings of Catholicism's efforts to combat Protestantism in Latin America, suggesting that they, too, may be doomed to failure. The ultimate outcome of this momentous struggle is impossible to predict. Gill (1998) points out that the Catholic Church is holding its own in many countries of the region, and the contest for the loyalty of Latino Catholics in the United States may well decide the outcome.

According to the most recent data, 71 percent of U.S. Latinos identify as Catholics, 22 percent identify as Protestants, and the rest, 7 percent, indicate no particular religious identity. At least one-half or more of the 22 percent are evangelicals and, apparently, recent converts, suggesting significant Protestant inroads into the Catholic population (Espinosa, Elizondo, and Miranda, 2003). On the other hand, these proportions are roughly the same as those in many Latin American countries, and they approximate the religious loyalties of Italian Americans and other "Catholic" ethnic groups in the United States (Alba and Orsi, chapter 1 in this volume). The actual rate of Protestant conversion and its duration are hotly contested in both Latin America and the United States; it is hoped that ongoing research will provide better guidance than published studies.

Mexicans and the Catholic Church in America

As Anglo America spread across the continent, it encountered several important regions of Latin Catholic society: French Louisiana, the Spanish Southwest, and California. The initial incorporation of Latin Catholics, then, was the direct consequence of Yankee imperialism, not immigration. To this day, those parts of the Southwest that have a long history of continuous Hispanic settlement have as part of their well-established culture a network of parish churches and bishoprics that date back to the Mexican church. Initially neglected by the North American Catholic

Church that was still struggling to deal with the influx of southern European Catholics, these parishes were gradually absorbed into the Catholic Church in the United States before the end of the 19th century. In some New Mexican parishes, the traditions of Mexican folk Catholicism endured, despite the overlay of Irish American priests and bishops who dominated the U.S. church (Gamio, 1930: 100–115).

The transformation occurred more rapidly in California, where there was a massive demographic and institutional transformation between 1848 and 1860. In 1859, Thaddeus Amat was appointed as bishop of a large diocese of what is now southern California. Church history reports that a Father Gallagher returned to Ireland in the 1850s to bring back a colony of teaching nuns, and a group of Italian teaching brothers came to San Francisco in the early 1860s. Though it does not record the ethnicity of the students being served, they were probably largely the children of Irish and Italian immigrants to San Francisco (Burns, 1912: 168–70). Mexicans were a minority among Catholics in the San Francisco archdiocese throughout the 19th century, and in 1920 Archbishop Hanna was apparently speaking for his flock when he petitioned the government to restrict the immigration of Mexicans because they were a drain on charity coffers and their presence scared away white Catholics (Gamio, 1930: 116–20).

John Cantwell, the first bishop of the new archdiocese of Los Angeles, ruled for 30 years, until 1947, followed by Cardinals McIntyre, Manning, and Mahoney. Cantwell was no liberal, but he was sympathetic to the plight of the impoverished Mexican immigrants arriving during his first decade of leadership; he apparently understood that it was in the interest of the church to incorporate these new arrivals. In 1922, he founded 50 Spanish-speaking parishes, and throughout the 1920s, he kept to himself the true cost of the charity he bestowed on the immigrant community (Sánchez, 1993: 158–60; Roman Catholic Archdiocese of Los Angeles, 2008). During the 1930s, he encouraged religious instruction for the Mexican newcomers, whose religious knowledge he found sadly lacking. Decent and supportive though he was, many in the Mexican community found him to be condescending and insufficiently supportive of Mexican Catholic traditions such as devotion to the Virgin of Guadalupe, leading to the formation of various Mexican Catholic devotional groups that were essentially independent of the hierarchy (Sánchez, 1993: 160–67; Monroy, 1999: 50–54). These groups, while independent from the church hierarchy, were dominated by lower-middle-class family men, focused on religious processions and familial celebrations, and run so as to, as Monroy (1999: 203–6) puts it, reinforce traditional Mexican Catholic "notions of hierarchy and authority."

Even before Cantwell's action in 1922, many predominantly Mexican parishes throughout California and the Southwest were effectively Spanish speaking, even when the priest, whose principal contact with the flock was saying mass (in Latin, of course), spoke little or none of the language. Whether de facto or de jure, these "Mexican" parishes were isolated—indeed, segregated—from white Catholics, and this was reinforced by residential segregation. To the degree that parish support services were provided in Spanish, those who spoke little English must have appreciated it. But, with rare exceptions, the level of lay participation was low, even by Catholic standards of the day. Processions, particularly honoring the Virgin of Guadalupe, were the major exception and were usually organized by semi-independent Mexican lay organizations.

One tradition that continues to this day is the annual Blessing of the Animals, a core southern California Mexican American folk tradition that bishops reluctantly performed. Babies were baptized, young children catechized, marriages and funerals performed, and alms given. But for the most part, the priests and the church played little role in the family lives of Mexicans in Los Angeles. Few children went to parochial school, and only a minority were involved as altar boys or in the few youth organizations active in Latino parishes. The social gap between parishioners and priests was considerable: few of the latter were Latino, and even fewer were actually from the Mexican American community (Sandoval, 1994: 133–43; Dolan and Figueroa Deck, 1994: 442).

Even under the comparatively enlightened leadership of Cantwell, Protestant missionaries made inroads into the Los Angeles Mexican community during the 1930s. The indifferent relations between Mexican parishioners and Irish American priests, combined with the missionaries' message that to be Protestant was to be American, seduced at least some into the arms of the Methodist and Presbyterian churches, which then proceeded to segregate Mexicans as much as the Catholic Church had done (Sumner, 1970; Sánchez, 1993: 155–58). But for the Mexican Catholic majority, this appeal of Protestant "Americanization" was not successful, and in Los Angeles, missionary activities waned for a time.

Research from Texas, New Mexico, and northern California in the 1960s portrays even higher levels of alienation, if not outright hostility, between poor Mexican Americans (especially recent immigrants) and local parish authorities. Manuel Servin (1970 [1965]: 148) argued that the traditional church hierarchy's support for the old Spanish-speaking elite and indifference to the concerns of immigrants throughout the Old Southwest was a major factor contributing to the conversion of many Mexican Americans to Protestantism. Nancie Gonzalez (1969), summarizing the research on "Spanish Americans" in New Mexico, noted that church neglect created a fertile ground for Protestant missionaries, who were especially successful among the small-town lower middle classes. According to her, throughout the Southwest, Latino converts associated being Protestant with progress and material success, and often with being more "American" as well. Margaret Sumner (1970) reported similar processes and understandings in the San Francisco area. She noted that, in comparison with the Southwest, Mexicans were less segregated and stigmatized in California. Nevertheless, Mexicans were generally not welcome in established Catholic parishes, which were usually predominantly Italian, and were instead segregated in separate "Spanish-speaking" parishes. But she was unimpressed by the quality of religious and social services in these "national" parishes, and she, too, noted a tendency for Mexicans to succumb to Protestant evangelical appeals.

In the post–Vatican Council II (1962–65) international environment, many U.S. Catholic leaders were among the most progressive forces in the church. The shift to the vernacular liturgy was no less popular among Latino Catholics than others, but in most parishes it was interpreted as the right to have mass said in Spanish, not English, and the hierarchy usually responded positively (Stevens-Arroyo, 1998: 167–69). Building on Hispanic ministries active in Texas, the U.S. Conference of Catholic Bishops established its Division (later Secretariat) for Hispanic Affairs in 1969. The Cursillos de Cristianidad, weekend religious study retreats typically aimed at middle-class and lower-middle-class married couples, that had proven so successful in Texas (and throughout the Spanish-speaking world), were expanded nationally, to Latinos as well as others. In the late 1980s, the secretariat issued a "National Pastoral Plan for the Hispanic Minority," now posted on its website, that spoke in terms of integrating Hispanics into the life of the church while also respecting their distinctive traditions (U.S. Conference of Catholic Bishops, 1987).

Today, according to the secretariat website, over 2,000 U.S. priests are Latino and 4,500 use Spanish in their services. But those 2,000 represent only about 3 percent of all priests in the United States, and apparently many are recent imports from Spain and Latin America, not native U.S.

Latinos. The higher number who "use Spanish" underlines the continuing problem that the vast majority of priests ministering to Latinos, and even the majority of those doing so in Spanish, are not themselves Latino. Priests of any sort are in short supply in the United States, as they are in Latin America. And the church is, after all, universal.

But in an earlier era, when the U.S. church maintained explicit support for "national" churches that served specific ethnic minority groups, it tried to match priest to parishioners. Certainly the modest presence of Latinos among priests (3 percent, in contrast to their 40 percent of the entire Catholic population), and the even lower representation among the hierarchy, is sure to reduce the church's ability to retain the loyalty of Latinos. A national survey from a decade ago found that 16 percent of U.S.-born Mexicans were Protestants, compared with 8 percent of immigrants (de la Garza et al., 1992: 37–38). Preliminary figures from the recent HCAPL survey indicate that, overall, 22 percent of Mexican Americans report being Protestant, one-half of them recent evangelical converts (Espinosa et al., 2003). As in Latin America, the majority may still be Catholic, but the direction of change is clear.

Within the Catholic Church in the United States there is a variety of networks and semiofficial organizations of priests, brothers, nuns, and laity that manage to operate almost independently (at least for a time) from the hierarchy. Despite the Vatican sanctions against the "excesses" of Liberation Theology, a strong network of progressive priests and nuns continues to operate within the confines of the church, especially in the Southwest. Many spent their formative years working in Latin America, and today they work with gang members and teenage mothers in East Los Angeles or Houston. These are, by liberal standards at least, decent and even saintly individuals doing their all for Latino Catholics on either side of the border. What they are not, for the most part, is Latinos themselves. In fact, these progressive priests and nuns today tend to have names like Doyle and Callahan, just like the parish priests of a century ago.

Nowhere are the dilemmas of the church's hopes and practices better exemplified than in Los Angeles. Under the long-term leadership of Cardinal Roger Mahoney, the Los Angeles archdiocese has become in many ways a paragon of the socially liberal church. Priests are obliged to learn Spanish, and efforts are made, with meager results, to train Latino youth for the priesthood. The generally liberal Mahoney speaks out on behalf of the rights of immigrants and workers, against gouging landlords and corporate greed. He also tolerates some parish priests who are substantially more progressive, allowing them to support feisty grassroots community organizations—as long as their protests are not directed against the church or the cardinal's closer supporters. At the same time, Mahoney is resorting to the most time-honored tactic for gathering the faithful: he is building a massive cathedral.

Liberal and clever leader that he is, Mahoney has tolerated, if not enjoyed, a substantial level of criticism leveled against the cathedral project, but he has also charged ahead full-speed. Criticism from lay Catholics and renegade nuns has focused on two issues. First is the rather predictable point that the $200 million he raised for the new temple would be better spent on direct charity—a dubious proposition since the funds were raised specifically to build the cathedral, and even before the current scandals the church was having difficulty raising general monies. Their second point is more telling: they explicitly criticize the very idea of building a massive cathedral as medieval and condescending to Catholics in 21st-century America—parishoners who are well educated, secular in most aspects of their lives, and quite opposed to playing the traditional role of "sheep" in the "flocks" that make up the traditional church. In response, Mahoney has all but said that this cathedral is just what the church needs to retain Latino Catholics.

The eventual success of Mahoney's strategy, combining contemporary progressive social policy with the ancient strategy shared by both popes and Maya priests a millennium ago, will be determined only by time. But the equivalent of his social program does not seem to have worked for the church in Latin America, partly because it was undercut by the Vatican, but largely because the direct appeal of Protestantism wins out against the abstract ideals of Liberation Theology (Stoll, 1990).

The Ethnic Church in America

The extensive literature on the "ethnic church" in the United States concentrates on the earlier era of immigration and describes how Protestant, Catholic, and Jewish congregations provided a bridge for immigrants and their children, with one pillar grounded in religious and cultural traditions brought from the old country and the other planted firmly in the strange new world in which immigrants found themselves (Ebaugh and Chafetz, 2000). A review of this literature suggests that the actual effect of membership in ethnic religious congregations is rarely demonstrated or even hypothesized in terms that can be tested. I am aware of no studies that systematically compare matched immigrants with and without strong ethnic church ties. Instead, we are provided with historical sketches that emphasize the sense of "belonging" that the congregations gave to immigrants, stories of how congregations sponsor the immigration of pastors from the old country, and the gradual decline of urban churches as the second and third generations move away from the old neighborhoods into multiethnic suburbs.

Catholic parishes have had a distinct place in this story. The "new" immigration from 1880 to 1920 was predominately Catholic and settled in cities. Throughout most of this period, there was a dialectic in the church between, on the one hand, the program of "national" churches that supported the provision of ethnic-language parishes (mass was, of course, in Latin) and, on the other hand, the "universal" culture of the church, which in practice meant the domination of diocese and parish life by Irish American clergy. The distinct Mexican Catholic experience in California and the Southwest has some elements in common with the Italian Catholic story. Within the entire panoply of ethnic churches, Catholic parishes generally stand out as the least "congregational" in the sense that parishioners had the least influence over the naming of pastors or other local church business. As Alba and Orsi (chapter 1) emphasize, the ethnicity of priests was a constant issue in Italian parishes—this despite the fact that Italian priests were certainly available. Broadly speaking, Catholic parishes were less congregational than Protestant churches or Jewish synagogues, and Italian parishes were among the least congregational. As discussed here, Mexican "Spanish-language" churches of the same era were even less in charge of their own affairs and at least as alienated from the parish priests.

Clearly, ethnic churches past and present provided important social support and a sense of belonging to immigrant communities, solidifying and perhaps extending the salience of ethnic origins for millions of new Americans. To the extent that they served as a meeting ground for young people, their effect would have to be to *reduce* assimilation, in the sense that the church or synagogue served as the venue for endogamous marital matching. There is certainly nothing wrong with this, but it is difficult to see how this can be labeled as aiding "integration." Rather, it is part of the broad historical process that Milton Gordon (1964) characterized as "acculturation without social assimilation," the predominant adaptation pattern among the wave of southern European groups who arrived in the United States between 1880 and 1925.

How might ethnic churches have materially aided immigrants and their children? Perhaps the greatest material function was to serve as a venue for the ethnic networks that led to jobs and services, especially in the midwestern and eastern cities where ethnic political machines operated. Roger Waldinger (1986) provides a vivid description of the ways that these ethnic job networks functioned in New York, and it is easy to imagine ethnic parish churches playing an important role. Certainly, to the degree that parishes and congregations were ethnically homogeneous, they would have facilitated these networks. Presumably, these processes worked more smoothly, to the degree that religious leaders were of the same ethnic group; other things being equal, a priest of one's own ethnicity must have been more helpful.

What contribution might ethnic churches have made to the academic success of immigrant children? In the early 20th century, when most Americans still did not finish high school, any form of direct support for academic performance must have been rare and, for most, unimportant. The great exception, of course, is Jewish congregations in which (for boys, anyway) study was an integral part of religious training and experience. I have no interest in entering the debate about what gave Jewish youth their academic advantage over other immigrant (and most native) students. But even a structuralist like Steven Steinberg (1989: 100–103) admits that there be something to the idea that the habit of study instilled by Jewish religious training may carry over into secular learning. Whether or not there is anything to the nostalgic accounts of "love of learning" and "stress put on education," Jewish youth did clearly excel, and the socioeconomic effects of this leg up are still evident in socioeconomic statistics that indicate that Jews stand apart from and above other "whites" in educational and occupational attainment to this day (Waldinger and Lichter, 1996).

Can ethnic churches still play an important role for the adaptation and "integration" of immigrant communities in the United States? Church attendance and active religious affiliation have declined overall, but both research and anecdotal evidence suggest that ethnic churches continue to provide social support for some immigrant groups, including services that may aid in their economic adaptation. The best-known examples are the megachurches founded by Korean and other Asian immigrant groups. A large proportion of Korean immigrant families affiliate with one of the Presbyterian or other Korean churches, which provide all the traditional "ethnic church" services and more besides. Korean and many other Asian Protestant churches, and apparently some Asian Catholic parish churches as well, provide the venue for a wide variety of academically relevant activities for youth (Kwon et al., 2001). Saturday Chinese schools may provide fluency no more than the Hebrew schools of the past century did. But they do provide reinforcement of ethnic identity and family ties, as well as the habit of study. Korean and other Asian churches are also the venue for Kumon-like cram schools that have no religious or ethnic content whatsoever, unless there is some "ethnic" connection between being Korean and doing well on exams.[2]

In general, the myriad activities that these highly congregational churches provide for their members and especially their youth are simply not present on a sustained basis in the Catholic parishes that cater to Latino families. It is difficult to write about a "negative," and it would be unfair to say that nothing similar takes place in Catholic parishes. But, as argued above, what does take place is usually under the control of priests, not the result of collective actions by congregation members.

Catholic Schools: Promise Undelivered

Of course, the Catholic Church does have one enormous resource to offer Latino youth: a Catholic-school education. Both anecdotal and statistical evidence abound that Catholic elementary and secondary schooling is superior to what inner-city children are likely to find in their neighborhood public schools. Selectivity plays a part: parents who manage to maintain their children in parochial school are likely to be a cut above in financial and other resources, and the schools themselves do not tolerate disruptive children. Be that as it may, the evidence of test scores, high school completion, and college entrance demonstrates decisively that children from families of modest means tend to perform better in Catholic schools (Youniss and Convey, 2000: 87–200). Since, as argued above, improving school performance is the single most important way in which religious institutions can facilitate the "integration" of immigrant children today, it follows that the single greatest gift that the Catholic Church can give to Mexican and other Latino youth is parochial education. On the one hand, Catholic educators deserve high marks for their efforts to bring the benefits of parochial schooling to Latino children. Their record of accomplishment, on the other hand, is unimpressive and unlikely to improve.

Nationwide, about 2 million children attend Catholic elementary schools, and over 600,000 attend Catholic secondary schools. Nearly two-thirds are in the East and Great Lakes regions; only 18 percent are found in the entire "West/Far West," which includes all of California and the Southwest, where most Mexicans reside. From 1940 to 1960, the number of parochial students nearly doubled, followed by a similar expansion in the enrollments of Catholic colleges and universities. After about 1965, however, enrollments plunged precipitously, and in the past 20 years few new schools have been established. At the elementary level, parochial enrollment today is about the same as in 1940 (McLellan, 2000: 23–30). In other words, Catholic education in America thrived during the decades that the Euro-ethnic second and third generations were experiencing assimilation and upward mobility. There is no evidence that a similar expansion to meet the needs of Latino Catholics is taking place today.

Given the working-class status of Italian and other Catholic immigrant youth early in the early decades of the past century, and the low educational qualifications of most jobs open to them, it makes little sense to say that parish-level activities had any significant effect, positive or negative, on their working lives via education. As late as the 1950s, Herbert Gans (1982 [1962]: 110–15) looked at the low level of involvement and general mutual indifference between priests and Italian youth in the West End of Boston. According to him, even the minority who attended Catholic schools was little affected by the church. He reports that parents chose to send their boys and girls to parish schools primarily to teach them "respect," and most returned to public education for high school. Gans provides an image of parish schooling in which students were given the opportunity to do serious work, but most declined the opportunity. Just as Gans, by his own admission 20 years later, grossly underestimated the degree of upward mobility taking place among second- and third-generation Italian Americans (Gans, 1982 [1962]: 311–19), so he also probably underestimated the value of Catholic schooling, at least for the minority motivated and situated to take advantage of it. Alba and Orsi argue that it was the Italian American third generation that turned to Catholic schools, first as students and then more decisively as parents, part of that mid-century expansion noted above. Whether cause or consequence of upward mobility is not clear, but the two were clearly associated.

Resources certainly play a major part in the stagnation of Catholic education in recent decades. There is a shortage of both parents able to pay even the modest tuition, as well as teachers willing to work for the modest pay offered. Tuition at the primary level averages only $2,200 a year, representing 60 percent of the actual cost, yet 84 percent of students nevertheless receive some form of financial aid. Secondary tuition averages $4,300 (78 percent of the actual cost), and, according to the National Catholic Education Association (NCEA), fully 97 percent receive some sort of aid. These figures contrast sharply with the cost of independent schools ($10,000–$18,000 per year) and, as has often been noted by supporters, are also well below the costs of public schooling. The NCEA calculates that the Catholic schools save taxpayers over $18 billion a year, and, of course, they are strong supporters of programs like school vouchers and charter schools that could be run as church/public partnerships (Youniss and Convey, 2000; National Catholic Educational Association, n.d.).

Given the financial constraints under which they have to operate, it is no surprise that parochial-school service to Latino and other poor communities is not all that it might be. Nationwide, only 11 percent of the students are Latino, far below the estimated 50 percent of all Catholic children who are Latino and even below the proportion of all children 5 to 18 who are Latino (about 18 percent nationwide). African Americans are represented at approximately their proportion of the general population (8 percent of Catholic enrollment, 12 percent of the population) and well above their representation among U.S. Catholics: only about one in ten African Americans are Catholic, which means that the black enrollment in parochial school represents about 22 percent of all black Catholic youth, though apparently many black parochial students are not from Catholic families. The relatively high representation of black (and Asian) children is a reflection of the fact that in the past few decades non-Catholic parents in these communities have discovered the great bargain to be found in Catholic education. The proportion of non-Catholics enrolled in parochial schools has jumped from 3 percent in 1970 to 14 percent in 2002. Over the same time span, the total minority enrollment (Latino as well as black, Asian, Native American, and mixed) has increased from 11 percent to 26 percent; obviously, a good proportion of this "minority" growth has been among non-Catholic African and Asian Americans. Their parents should be applauded for their good sense, but this also means that the growth in "minority" enrollment is not entirely, or even largely, due to growing service to the Latino community.[3]

Catholic education is a minor factor in the upward mobility of Latinos, who are underrepresented in Catholic education by any measure. By my estimate, only 4 percent of Latino Catholic youth attend parochial school, in contrast to 26 percent of non-Latino Catholic youth. Only about 3 percent of all Latino children (including non-Catholics) attend Catholic schools, and it is a good bet that a significant proportion are middle class to begin with. Most schools are obliged to require most parents to pay one-half or more of their school fees, and middle-class Latino parents are better able to afford their children's education, just like any other middle-class parents.

The plight of parochial schools in the nation's largest Latino archdiocese provides further insight into the insignificance of Catholic schooling for Mexican and other Latino children. The archdiocese of Los Angeles is the largest Latino archdiocese in the country. The official count of the total Catholic population in the three-county area (Los Angeles, Ventura, Santa Barbara), 5 million, is below the estimated Latino Catholic population (derived by multiplying the total Latino population of the region by a low estimate of the Catholic proportion: 7.5 million × 0.71 Catholic = 5.3 million). The archdiocese contains at least 8 percent of the nation's Catholic population. But this is not reflected in its parochial enrollments, which constitute only 4 percent of Catholic K–12 enrollment in the nation. While nationally Catholic schools enroll about 6 percent of all schoolchildren, in these three counties the figure is only half that. The archdiocese does not release an ethnic breakdown of its student body, but even if the majority were Latino, it would represent only a few percent of all Latino schoolchildren in the region. The archdiocese's Office of Religious Education does brag that 95 percent of its graduates go on to college. Less encouraging is the information that only 5,000 students receive scholarships, a rate of only about 5 percent, far below the national average. Combined, these two facts suggest that Catholic education in Los Angeles is disproportionately for middle-class youth, though we have no direct evidence for this.[4]

Given the demonstrated educational effectiveness and cost-effectiveness of Catholic schooling, it is difficult to avoid the public policy conclusion that state support in the form of vouchers and both public and religious charter schools is the single most important contribution to the upward mobility of Latino youth that the state can provide. Since graduates of parochial schools presumably become more committed adult Catholics, such a step should also serve the competitive goals of the church. Poor children in Los Angeles public schools receive about $10,000 in state and federal funding per capita; Catholic schools get by on less than half that amount. Even a program limited to the most needy students could have a substantial effect, since Latino youth are such a large proportion of the needy. While there are limits on the supply side (e.g., facilities and good teachers willing to work for low wages), the undeveloped nature of parochial education in areas such as southern California suggests that there is room for at least some expansion. Alas, political opposition and continued bungling by Catholic authorities make it unlikely that tax dollars will contribute significantly to the expansion of parochial education in the United States.

Is Religion a Factor in the Success of Immigrants?

The focus of this essay is the comparison of the Mexican and Italian experiences with the Catholic Church in America and the role the church has played in their integration. The neglect and ambivalence that characterized the Italian American experience with the church were and are more the case with respect to Mexicans in America. As a venue for ethnic job contacts and as a source of disciplined parochial schooling or other educational assistance, the Catholic Church has done even less for Mexicans than it did for Italians. The essay could end here if the Italian-Mexican comparison were our only concern. Alas, like it or not, in the real world, Mexican immigrants and their children are being compared with other contemporary immigrant groups, particularly Asians, not to Italians a century ago. I close with some thoughts on this matter.

Much if not most of the occupational success of Asian immigrants compared with Latino immigrants is explicable by differences in material resources. On average, Asian immigrants are better educated, bring more financial capital and business experience, and have more useful contacts within preexisting immigrant communities (Portes and Rumbaut, 2001: 44–90). Likewise, the advantages of growing up in comfortable middle-class homes surely explains the lion's part of the difference in educational success of Asian as opposed to the largely poor Latino immigrant children (192–268). But if these ordinary socioeconomic factors adequately explain the low achievement of poor immigrant Latino children compared with whites, and much of the Latino/Asian gap, they do not explain the extraordinary academic success of Asian children, especially those from lower-middle-class, working-class, and downright poor homes, who seem to do nearly as well in school as affluent Asian youth. Whatever the reasons, the facts of Asian American academic success are indisputable. The tendency of Asian American children to outperform whites, not just other minorities—noted by Charles Hirschman and Morrison Wong (1986) more than two decades ago—has only increased with the subsequent rise in immigration. Just one example: 30 percent of California Asian American high school seniors are eligible for entry into the University of California, compared with only 3 percent of Latinos and 13 percent of whites.

Much of the otherwise admirable recent comparative research on the "new second generation" (e.g., Portes and Rumbaut, 2001) ignores or discounts the importance for success of religious beliefs or participation in religious organizations, despite their well-documented importance in several high-achieving groups. It is no surprise, then, that this research has been unable to explain Asian American hypersuccess. Many sociologists ignore the possible effects of religious participation, in part because they themselves tend to be secular in orientation and averse to explanation of anything in terms of "values," but also because of the sensitivity of the topic. Others, such as Steven Steinberg (1989), seek to explain away the apparent effect of religion with "hard" socioeconomic correlates. Subpar socioeconomic achievement is attributed, usually without evidence, to "discrimination." Above-average achievement is largely ignored, especially if it seems to be associated in some way with religion.

But what sort of religious effects are at play? Min Zhou and Carl Bankston (1998), writing about the academic success of poor (and mostly Catholic) Vietnamese children in Lousiana, argue that it is the result of Confucian ethics enforced by a strong ethnic community. Portes and Rumbaut (2001: 160–61) discount the Confucian side, arguing that since Asians represent such a variety of religions, many Western in origin, the content of beliefs cannot play a part. But they embrace the centrality of "the ethnic community," without really explaining why it is that *Asian* ethnic communities are such powerful forces for success while others are not. If the answer is not in the content of specific religions, and certainly not in anything having to do with "race," then what is left?

Koreans and Chinese are indeed a mix of Protestants, Buddhists, and Catholics, and South Asians are mostly Muslims and upper-caste Hindus. The content of Asian and South Asian religions could not vary more greatly, and a group with one of the greatest "success stories," the Vietnamese, largely shares Catholicism with Mexicans. *This suggests that, if religion bears any importance to ethnic success in America, it is not due to the specific content of beliefs but, rather, to the social organization of religious life and the social practices carried out within these organizations.* What most clearly sets off the organization of religious youth activities in most Asian immigrant communities from the organization of religious practices in most Mexican immigrant communities, or among native whites, is the degree to which they combine the traditional character of the "ethnic church" with programs designed to help children succeed in school. These are community institutions totally controlled within the ethnic community, not provided by benevolent outsiders. Identity and cultural pride are thereby reinforced, but in genuine, substantive ways, not in the superficial and usually self-defeating sense of instilling "self-esteem."

Of course, not all Asian ethnic churches take on the appearance of Kumon cram schools on Saturdays. Some of the more evangelical Asian churches put more emphasis on Bible study, and, of course, the study of sacred texts is central to Islam and upper-caste Hinduism. In fact, *what sets all of these traditions apart is not the content, religious and otherwise, of what is being studied but the very act of studying.* I am sure there must be Mexican Catholic parishes where lessons for children exist, but in a casual survey all that my respondents can recall is the dreaded catechism, the rote study of not-to-be-questioned beliefs that make Pakistani madrasas look like centers of free thinking. Catholic parishes in southern California with substantial immigrant congregations (which means most) do offer basic English classes to adult immigrants, along with a host of other social services. But these classes, like the other services, are typically delivered in the hierarchical spirit and form of Catholic charity, not institutions created and controlled by the immigrants themselves. And, importantly, priests and auxiliary teachers are typically non-Latinos who, though they have learned Spanish, are really authority figures from outside, not members of the community. Most important of all, few parish-sponsored activities directly or indirectly support academic success among children.

But what about high-achieving immigrant groups today that are also Catholic? These exceptions prove (i.e., *test*) the rule, which has nothing to do with Catholic beliefs but, instead, with the community spirit and empowerment of local congregations, along with the parentally organized and controlled use of religious venues for religious and secular study. Where parish churches do serve as venues for such activities, as in the Vietnamese or some Filipino congregations that manage to use church resources for educational ends, by all accounts the results parallel programs in congregational Asian Protestant ethnic churches (Zhou and Bankston, 1998). Korean Catholics, in particular (one-quarter of all Korean immigrants), have a tradition of lay leadership and control and operate much like Korean Protestant churches. Uniquely among U.S. Latinos, Cuban émigrés asserted control over religious and practical matters in their new parishes in Miami, making these parishes part of the "ethnic enclave" that apparently explains Cuban success (Levitt, 2002). Yes, Cuban success is largely the result of the human resources that the elites brought with them and is the nexus of the political, educational, and cultural institutions that they created in South Florida. And private bilingual academies, not parochial schools, are the basis for the limited amount of academic excellence seen among Cuban Americans (Portes and Rumbaut, 2001: 235–37). Still, it is worth noting that this comparatively successful immigrant community took control of its own churches, even if the churches did not become important factors in further success.

It is interesting that the Asian Catholic and (largely secular) Cuban educational programs have a crucial component in common with the Chinese, Korean, and other ethnic church–based Protestant educational programs: ethnic-language study and maintenance are usually at the core of their programs. In most Latino immigrant communities, day-to-day life provides strong support for the maintenance of Spanish, and resources for the formal study of Spanish are scarce. In all of Los Angeles, the only Spanish "language" school I am aware of is the Argentine School, a Saturday school set up by Latin American expatriate business families and housed at the University of Southern California. Might this be an equally important part of the puzzle? That is, the majority status of Mexican Americans (who make up three-quarters of schoolchildren in Los Angeles) deprives the group of the need to consciously preserve their culture and language, needs that are so often conscious reasons for establishing institutions like Chinese schools. Such schools may not succeed at their manifest function of maintaining Chinese-language skills, but their latent function of reinforcing habits of study is admirably served. I am not arguing that the institution of Spanish-language schools would in itself close the gap between Mexican and Asian students but, rather, that the experience of these schools, wrapped in the nexus of parents, community, and often church, is yet another advantage that Asian American children often have over Mexican Americans.

Conclusions

In sum, the Catholic Church has contributed little to the integration of Mexican immigrants and their children in the United States. Its many good works, support for immigrant rights, and charities are bestowed in

precisely that way: as charity to a needy "minority" population. It is difficult to be against charity, and I certainly am not. But the fact remains that
the church's mode of engagement with Mexican Catholics keeps them out
of the mainstreams of power within the church and does not encourage
community-based programs focused on education. The authority structure within parishes continues to be priest-centered, with all the well-
meaning but initiative-destroying and off-putting patriarchy that charac-
terizes Catholicism throughout Latin America, where it is fighting a losing
battle against the dual forces of secularism and evangelical Protestantism.
Those activities open to the Latino laity that do have a participatory quality, such as the Cursillos and charismatic forms of worship, do seem to
genuinely meet some of the spiritual needs of the Latino Catholics who
experience them. But they have no spillover into the secular educational
lives of Latino youth, which, I have argued, is the essential sphere to be
addressed in order to contribute to the integration and upward mobility
of Latino youth. The one potential exception is Catholic education, but
for the reasons reviewed above, it is available to only a tiny proportion of
Latino youth.

Let me be clear: I am not arguing that a few policy changes and the
shifting of resources from marble for cathedrals to bricks for schools
would suddenly redress all the disadvantages faced by immigrant Latino
youth. The problems are simply too great, even for a healthy institution,
and the American Catholic Church today is hardly in good shape financially or otherwise. And it is easy to overestimate the quality of parochial
education, which compares favorably with inner-city public schools but
overall is only slightly better than public schools generally. As with public
education, the best Catholic education is in the better-endowed suburban
schools; inner-city parish schools struggle with greater challenges and
fewer resources.

Still, Catholic K–12 and higher educational institutions could do a
much better job in building and maintaining a Latino middle class.
Catholic schools in the past hardly made scholars out of Irish, Polish,
and Italian immigrant children, but they did provide much of the educational foundation for the regional and national Catholic middle classes
and elites that emerged in the second and especially third generations.
But with only 4 percent of Latino Catholic youth enrolled (in contrast
to 26 percent of non-Latino Catholics), parochial schools are apparently
playing only a minor part in the maintenance of the Mexican American
middle class and little or no part in its expansion.

Catholic institutions of higher education are not doing much better. Catholic colleges and universities expanded along with higher education generally in the middle decades of the 20th century and played an especially important role as facilitators of Euro-ethnic Catholic regional elites. They still do, as the expansion of vigorous institutions like Loyola University in Los Angeles illustrates, but Mexican Americans are only a small part of the picture. Loyola L.A. boasts of its support for "minority" students, including Latinos who represent some 19 percent of their enrollment (Loyola Marymount University, n.d.), this in a region where over 80 percent of the Catholic population is Latino. Still, institutions like Loyola L.A. do enroll a significant proportion of the Latino middle class, reminding us how small that middle class actually is.

Of course, it is the nature of all churches and religious institutions of higher learning to judge themselves by essentially religious standards, which means spiritual rather than material dimensions. Tiny storefront churches, Korean megachurches, and the Holy Roman Catholic Church itself—all are presumably more in the business of saving souls than promoting upward mobility. As institutions, they must also attend to their own practical needs, and it is not a criticism to mention that institutional survival and growth have been at the center of Catholic official concerns since long before the current crisis. Whether or not the efforts of parish and other Catholic authorities to bind Latinos to the church are successful is beyond the scope of this chapter. But, returning a moment to the religious competition paradigm, it does seem that they are not doing a very good job on either side of the border. In Mexico, as throughout Latin America, the tradition of obedience to authority that the conservative church has so long relied on is breaking down, and the far more seductive and concrete charms of evangelical Protestantism have overwhelmed what remains of progressive Catholicism, in both its political and charismatic forms. All of these conflicting forces are also at play north of the border, particularly in those immigrant parishes and neighborhoods that continue to have a strong Latino identity and ties to Latin America.

Writings by such church leaders as Cardinal Mahoney of Los Angeles make it clear that they regard the infusion of Latino Catholics as the future of the church, but not only because of the numbers involved; they also see in them more willing sheep for their flocks: witness the belief that the new Los Angeles Cathedral will rally the faithful or the reliance on compliant Latina lay organizations as a counterfoil against the criticism of church protection for misbehaving priests (Watanabe, 2002). Time will tell if this calculation proves correct, but it is worth noting that in the history of American ethnic groups, acculturation has proved a very powerful force indeed. In its struggle for the loyalties of Mexicans and other Latino Catholics, let us hope that the church realizes that, ultimately, Latinos will no more be impressed than other American Catholics by cathedrals.

NOTES

I thank Richard Alba and Roger Waldinger for their valuable comments on an earlier draft of this chapter.

1.   This essay is based largely on secondary sources, including the websites of the Catholic Church and the National Catholic Education Association. Most general population data come from the U.S. Census Bureau website, and most information on Catholic membership and school enrollment comes from the official Catholic websites, which usually have more up-to-date information than printed sources. The sources of these quantitative data are not always made clear, and figures vary somewhat from website to website. The most recently available general surveys of the Latino population containing information about religious affiliation and comportment come from the early 1990s (de la Garza et al., 1992).

2.   Kumon is a Japanese-based tutoring company, with many centers in the United States that offer students after-school assistance with their English and math skills. Recently, Asian-American churches have begun offering copycat tutoring programs.

3.   The data on parochial education are drawn from the NCEA website; data on the population ages 5–18 by race is from the U.S. Census Bureau website.

4.   According to the NCEA website, the vast majority of Catholic students nationwide receive some financial aid, suggesting that the 5 percent rate receiving aid in Los Angeles may be oranges compared with the national apples. Like most "hard" data relating to Catholicism in the United States, these need to be taken on faith.

Part II

||||||||||||||||||||||||||||||||||||||||||||||||||||

Religious Conversion among Japanese and Korean Immigrants

The comparison of Japanese and Korean Americans was conceived as a way to examine how conversion to a mainstream American religion can happen as part of the assimilation of immigrant groups who bring nonwestern religious and cultural traditions to the United States. In these two cases, the religious traditions and experiences are similar, beginning with the primacy in their homelands of Buddhism combined with indigenous elements (Shintoism in Japan, shamanism in Korea). Moreover, Korean and Japanese American immigrant cultures are both heavily informed by a hierarchical sensibility of Confucianism and balanced by an equally strong sense of reciprocity and interdependence nurtured by Taoist and Buddhist institutions and thought. In addition, both immigrant communities have been influenced by a history of Christian missions and institutions in their societies of origin and a growing involvement with Christianity in America.

The comparison involves groups whose immigrations took place at opposite ends of the 20th century, but who both recognize generational differences in their experiences of adapting to American society. Consequently, the Japanese American group, whose history resounds with the first- through fourth-generational terms Issei, Nisei, Sansei, and Yonsei, is now concentrated in the last two of these generations, and a coherent literature testifies to the advanced state of its assimilation (Connor, 1977; Levine and Rhodes, 1981; Montero, 1981; Fugita and O'Brien, 1991; Sakamoto, Liu, and Tzeng, 1998). (There has also been a recent wave of Japanese arrivals, made up largely of management-level employees of Japanese firms sent to work in their American branches for fixed periods. Because they do not intend to settle permanently in the United States, these arrivals are not generally regarded as immigrants.)

Korean immigrants have come mainly since the 1965 watershed in U.S. immigration law, which finally dismantled the bars on Asian immigration, though a small number arrived in the early 20th century, before the bars were fully installed and others came as the brides of U.S. servicemen after the Korean War. They speak of the first generation and the second as having discrete experiences in the United States and distinguish the 1.5 generation, people born in Korea who came to the United States as young children and who experience elements of the generational perspectives of both immigrants and the American-born.

It therefore seemed plausible to take Japanese Americans as forerunners, whose experience would illuminate the options for religious incorporation available to Korean Americans. The questions that seemed initially to need addressing concerned what changes may take place to the beliefs, practices, and organization of the immigrants' religion as they settle into the American context, as well as how the immigrants and their children handle the tensions involved in adherence to an outsider religion in a society where Christianity in its various forms constitutes the paramount religious tradition. That acceptance of Christianity could represent an attempt to resolve this tension was apparent in the conversion of a significant fraction of Japanese Americans to Protestantism in the first half of the 20th century and in the evident strength of evangelical Christianity among Korean Americans today. But to what extent was the adoption of Christianity the major mode of accommodation to the American religious and social environment?

The chapters of our contributors have complicated the seemingly straightforward ideas that provided our starting point. To begin, the assumption that the religious backgrounds of the immigrants in the two groups are similar requires qualification. Buddhism and Christianity may represent the original religions of each ethnic group, but the ratio of Buddhists to Christians varies. Japanese American immigrants were mainly Buddhist, although some were Christian and more became so in America. Still more of their children joined the alien faith. Many Koreans who came to America were Christians before they made the journey; and even more joined Korean Christian churches in the United States. It is not clear whether a larger proportion of second-generation Korean Americans are Christians compared with their parents. This difference in religious composition has led to different intraethnic and interethnic dynamics as Buddhism has come to characterize Japanese Americanness, and Christianity, Korean Americanness—that is, what is perceived as authentic and standard within each group and by the mainstream society.

The chapters also underscore the primacy of race in any understanding of the experiences of these two Asian groups. The exclusions of Asian groups from the U.S. mainstream were extreme during the first half of the 20th century—a complete ban on immigration enacted by Congress during the 1920s; a bar on citizenship for the immigrants because of the racial provisions of the original 1790 law, which were affirmed by Supreme Court decisions in the early 20th century and remained in effect until 1952; and the infamous internment of Japanese Americans on the West Coast during World War II. These exclusions—even though they have been repealed and, in the case of the internment, have been officially regretted—have shaped the historical memories and thus the identities of Asian Americans in ways that make assimilation something other than a straightforward merging into the mainstream. The continuing stereotypes of Asians as "forever foreign," conveyed in backhanded compliments about English fluency and in insensitive questions about where U.S.-born Asian Americans are really from, engender a distance from the mainstream and a perception that whiteness is a requirement for inclusion in it (Kibria, 2002). Jane Iwamura's chapter (chapter 5) on the emergence of the internment experience as the foundation for a civil religion among later-generation Japanese Americans testifies to the continuing power of these experiences of racial exclusion.

The experience of racial difference on the part of otherwise assimilated Asian Americans raises questions about the role of religion as part of this process. By standard indicators, the assimilation of Japanese Americans has repeatedly been shown to be advanced: the later generations, with rare exceptions, do not speak Japanese; despite earlier barriers, their socioeconomic attainments have surpassed those of the average white American; and, most telling perhaps, their rates of intermarriage with white Americans are quite high (Qian, 1997). By the 1980s, some 63 percent of babies born to Japanese-ancestry parents were of mixed race, and in the great majority of cases the other race was white (Alba and Nee 2003). Korean Americans, though still concentrated in the first and second generations, are showing signs of following in this trajectory in, for example, their rapid conversion to English, high levels of education and professional attainment, and robust rates of intermarriage (Lee and Fernandez, 1998).

Yet the enduring experience of racial difference from the mainstream may keep Asians from reaching the stage where ethnicity is merely "symbolic," an option that may be exercised or not in some situations but otherwise has little import for everyday life (Gans, 1979; Waters, 1990; Kibria, 2002). The emergence of an Asian American pan-ethnic identity is one sign of distinctiveness, though it also may prove to be one respect in which the trajectories of Japanese and Korean Americans significantly diverge. When Japanese Americans were coming in sizable numbers early in the century, whites lumped them together with Chinese and other Asians as "Orientals" (Lee, 2001), but Japanese, Chinese, and other immigrant groups from Asia did not function in any meaningful way as a single group at that time. It was only in the 1960s and 1970s that various peoples whose ancestors derived from Asia began to band together and form an Asian American pan-ethnicity. A feature of Korean American life in the period of their highest immigration is that their ethnic connections and identities are able to function at two levels: Korean and Asian American. Pan-Asian civil rights and ethnic consciousness movements have created a political, social, and cultural space for Korean ethnic heritage to be valued and recognized. And the dominant racial group has been more disposed to accept Asians as legitimate members of American society. This general social trend, together with the fact that a majority of Korean Americans are Christians, has led to a higher level of acceptance of Korean Americans in the later period than was the case for Japanese Americans early on.

That race complicates the story of religious incorporation is indicated by how badly the classic work on religion, immigration, and American life, Will Herberg's *Protestant-Catholic-Jew* (1960 [1955]), a mid-20th-century book whose influence remains profound, stumbled on this core. Herberg, who saw religions as the primary groupings through which Americans could express their ethnic differences, did not attempt to make any sense of why Latinos who were Catholics and African Americans who were Protestant could not be fitted into his scheme. He dealt with these two significant exceptions in a footnote that states these "major groups stand measurably outside the division of American society into three [religious] 'melting pots.' . . . Their primary context of self-identification and social location remains their ethnic or 'racial' group" (1960: 42).

Herberg faced a similar difficulty when it came to Asian Americans, who constituted an additional exception: "Those of Oriental origin" (most notably women) are stigmatized as an "alien 'race'" and as a result, were relegated to "an inferior status in the social hierarchy" (1960: 36–37). The picture is doubly compounded by the fact that Asian immigrants had come to the United States as practitioners of non-Judeo-Christian religions—such as Buddhism, which Herberg pegs as an "exotic cult." The only recourse for the Asian American Buddhist was thought to conform to the "Anglo American ideal" and convert to Christianity (or Judaism). However, this sets up a further theoretical dilemma. If religion were to become the major legitimate means by which ethnicity is expressed—and this insight is the core of Herberg's famous thesis—what is left for Asian American converts to preserve and express (Yang, 1999: 132)?

Herberg's work prepared the way for what is now the dominant storyline about the religion-immigration nexus: namely, that religious adherence, regardless of the religion involved, is positive for successful incorporation into American society and generally helps make immigrants and their children into Americans (Foner and Alba, 2008; Hirschman, 2004). Assimilation is the salient theme, and it has found its way into the subsequent treatment of religion among Asian Americans, as, for example, in research on the "Protestantization" of the institutions and faith of the Japanese American community (Horinouchi, 1973) or in a much-cited article, "Becoming American by Becoming Hindu" (Kurien, 1998), which finds that Hinduism, albeit somewhat reconfigured for the new context, has helped Indian immigrants fit into American society and claim "a position for themselves at the American multicultural table."

The chapters here raise critical reservations about the validity of this storyline by underscoring how the ambivalences created by race are expressed in relation to religion. In particular, they demonstrate the way in which religious congregations, whether Buddhist or Christian, have been a site where different and at times conflicting stances of Asian Americans toward assimilation and their prospective membership in American society have been articulated. This point comes through sharply in the discussion by Lori Pierce, Paul Spickard, and David Yoo (chapter 4), which focuses on the Japanese and Korean American experiences before 1945. In this period, the Japanese overwhelmingly remained adherents of Buddhism, while the Koreans, reflecting in part the missionary work of American Protestants in Korea, were largely Christian—in fact, Methodist and Presbyterian. In each case, however, religion was accented by nationalism, for the Japanese tended to view themselves as emissaries of a modernizing nation and the Koreans to see their immigration and their Christianity as vehicles for their own anticolonialism at a time when Korea was under the domination of Japan.

Although conversion to the majority religion, Christianity, might have seemed especially protective for Japanese American Buddhists as a racial minority, they instead defended themselves against the prejudices that were widespread among white Americans (e.g., the charge of Mikado worship) by emphasizing the compatibility of their religious beliefs with democracy and the suitability for the American context of the Buddhist tenets of the equality of believers and the role of individual choice in the spiritual journey. Many Japanese American Christians emphasized assimilation as their predominant strategy, but their stance shifted once U.S. legislation of the mid-1920s had ended on racial grounds the possibility of further immigration from Asia. Cutting themselves off from their white-dominated parent denominations, they emphasized—perhaps, reemphasized, since their ties to Japan had never ceased—Japanese nationalism and, as the onset of war approached, some held that Japanese Christianity was superior to that practiced by U.S. whites, turning the notion of the adoption of Christianity as a form of assimilation on its head.

Jane Iwamura (chapter 5) updates this story to the ambivalent assimilation of fourth-generation Japanese Americans. Although the decline of separate ethno-religious organizations is obvious and the pattern of participation in mainstream religious institutions is probably similar to that of white Americans, Iwamura expands the categories of inquiry and detects a religious impulse that informs Japanese American identity in terms of a new civil religion. Historical trials, most notably internment, have forged a strong sense of racial-ethnic identity, cultural memory, and social justice among Japanese Americans that is uniquely expressed in modern-day ethnic institutions, such as the Japanese American National Museum and the annual pilgrimage to Manzanar. As Iwamura notes, "these organizations, projects, and modern-day rituals have become what is 'sacred' for the community—what binds it together and gives it a specific sense of meaning and mission." An examination of these seemingly secular practices reveals lingering patterns of religious belief and commitment that more conventional studies of religion and ethnicity miss and challenges straight-line assimilation models that have been used to characterize Japanese American religious life.

Sharon Suh (chapter 6) addresses the tensions over religious identity within the contemporary Korean American community, which to outsiders is dominated by evangelical Christians yet retains, quite visibly to insiders, a significant if small minority of Buddhist adherents. The visibility of the Korean Christian community occludes the continuing significance of Buddhism. Suh shows that Buddhists have responded to their minority religious status within their ethnic group by drawing sharp character and theological distinctions between the two traditions. In particular, she examines how Buddhists cite teachings within their own tradition in order to make claims for themselves as more open-minded, more self-reliant, more intelligent, more liberal, and, by extension, more "American" than their Christian counterparts. While the association of Buddhism with the highest values of American culture allows Buddhists confidently to respond to their minority status within the larger Korean American group, such claims do not necessarily serve to integrate them into mainstream America.

‖‖‖

4

Japanese and Korean Migrations

Buddhist and Christian Communities
in America, 1885–1945

Lori Pierce, Paul Spickard, and David Yoo

This essay has two tasks: to survey briefly the histories of Japanese and Korean American Christian and Buddhist communities between 1885 and 1945, and to discuss some of the analytical issues that arise as a result. Our concern is to draw attention to the broad historical context necessary to understand the effect that race had on the construction of religious and ethnic identities for these communities. Asian American religious identities have been complicated by American racial ideologies, which have conflated the categories of White, Christian, and American.

Japanese Migration

Japanese migrants began to come to the United States and Hawai'i in large numbers in the 1890s. They were preceded by a small number of students seeking western education that would serve the needs of their homeland, which was rapidly industrializing and beginning to make economic and political connections with the outside world. The main wave of Japanese immigrants—more than 200,000 of them between 1885 and 1920—originated in several southwestern rural provinces. They continued to come until 1924, when further immigration from Japan (as from Korea) was cut off by a U.S. immigration act. The Japanese never constituted more than 1.5 percent of the total flow of immigrants into the United States, although their political visibility vastly outstripped their small numbers.

The years from 1885 to about 1910 can be described as the frontier phase of Japanese American immigration. Almost all the migrants in that period were young men who worked in agriculture, mining, fish canning, lumbering, and railroad construction in the western United States and Canada, as well as in the newly acquired territory of Hawai'i. Japanese immigrants of this first generation—called Issei—were recruited by employers and labor-contracting middlemen. They moved frequently from region to region and from one sector of the economy to another. Nearly one-half began under indenture on Hawaiian sugar plantations, although before long most moved on to the continental United States or into urban occupations in Hawai'i.

This highly mobile population was, at first, without families in America and had few institutional roots. Gradually, some began to settle down, and the frontier phase gave way to the era of family and community building. Buddhist and Christian churches were among the first, fragile institutions to be built among Japanese Americans. This began in Hawai'i, where plantation life was geographically more stable than the migratory round on the mainland. Buddhist priests were initially sent as missionaries beginning in the 1890s. When Japanese men who immigrated to the continental United States began to settle down to run farms, work in city occupations, send for wives, and start families shortly after 1900, Protestant missionaries, who had worked among the earlier generations of Chinese migrants, turned their attention to the Japanese community, and tiny mission churches sprouted in several West Coast cities.

White Americans expressed early opposition to Japanese immigrants on racist grounds. They followed the lead of the anti-Chinese movement that had ended immigration from that country in 1882. The anti-Japanese movement began in the early 1900s, in both Hawai'i and the continental United States (Daniels, 1962; Okihiro, 1991). White Americans assaulted Japanese American individuals and businesses. Using racial language, they pushed for restrictions on Japanese American liberties and, ultimately, for their exclusion from the country. Whites decried Japanese and other Asian Americans as "unassimilable." Because they were Asians, they were ipso facto incapable of becoming fully American. Therefore, Japanese Americans were deemed unfit to remain in the United States.

The anti-Japanese race baiters fomented a crisis by trying to put San Francisco's Japanese children into segregated schools. This was followed by the Gentlemen's Agreement of 1907–1908, in which the United States coerced Japan into ending emigration by working-class men. When the men already here stayed and brought over wives, the anti-Japanese forces responded with alien land laws that forbade "aliens ineligible to citizenship" (i.e., Asians) to own or lease land. When those laws did not convince the Issei to leave, the United States passed an immigration act in 1924 that outlawed Asian immigration entirely.[1] Tens of thousands of Japanese Americans gave up on the United States and went back to Japan. The cutoff of immigration in 1924 gave the Japanese American community an unusual demographic profile. The immigrants and their children (Nisei) were separated not only by cultural experience but also by chronology. The bulk of the Issei were born before 1900, nearly all the Nisei after 1910.

Throughout the time period discussed in this chapter, about one-half the Japanese American population lived in Hawai'i; another one-quarter lived in California; the rest, about one-quarter, were in the Pacific Northwest, the Rocky Mountain states, and spread thinly across the continent. Japanese in Hawai'i had an intense community life, strong institutional ties to Japan, and an ethos that celebrated Japaneseness. In terms of concentration of population and close ties to Japan, California Japanese were somewhere between Hawai'i Japanese and the Japanese American populations in the Northwest and elsewhere, which were less segregated from White society.

Few Americans can be ignorant any longer of the travail of Japanese Americans during World War II (Daniels, 1995). In the spring of 1942, the long-simmering anti-Japanese movement bubbled over into the mass incarceration of 112,000 Japanese Americans on the West Coast. The concentration camp experience shattered Japanese American families and communities. Homes, farms, and businesses were lost. Morale was destroyed. The Issei generation never recovered. After the war, many Japanese Americans returned home to try to pick up the pieces of their lives. Others struck out for the Midwest and East. Continental Japanese Americans laid low for a generation, trying desperately to blend into the White American middle class (Nagata, 1993; Spickard, 1996: 133–60).

By contrast, the Japanese American population in Hawai'i emerged from the war with newfound confidence born of their experience with the outside world. Most of the soldiers in the celebrated 442nd Regimental Combat Team, the all-Japanese segregated unit that fought heroically in Europe, came from Hawai'i, not from West Coast concentration camps, although that distinction was blurred by the racial nature of the unit's identity. At war's end, Nisei soldiers came home to Hawai'i. In the next decade and a half, some among their number had taken over territorial politics and spearheaded the movement for statehood. Japanese Americans in Hawai'i remain a separate social and political group to this day.

So the Japanese experience in Hawai'i since World War II has been one of social and political prominence without blending into a wider community, whereas continental Japanese Americans have tended to seek absorption into the larger body of Americans. The 1960s saw the rise of a third generation (called Sansei) on the mainland. This group was, on the one hand, highly assimilated into White American society (note a nearly 50 percent outmarriage rate and the fact that almost no one spoke much Japanese). On the other hand, it was the Sansei who brought the West Coast Japanese communities back to life in the 1970s. They formed coalitions with Chinese, Filipinos, and others to make a new pan-ethnic identity they called "Asian American." They investigated the history of incarceration that their parents had tried to put behind them. This culminated, as Jane Iwamura shows (chapter 5), in the making of a new Japanese American civil religion around remembrance and redress in the 1980s and 1990s.

Japanese American Buddhism

Japanese emigrants transplanted Jodo Shinshu, Nichiren, Shingon, Tendai, and Soto Zen Buddhism to the United States. However, the single largest Buddhist institution in the United States before World War II was the Jodo Shinshu Buddhist Church, representing the Nishi (or Hongpa) Hongwanji (literally, the "West Temple of the Original Vow") sect. Some 63 percent of the Japanese immigrants to the United States and Hawai'i were from prefectures (Hiroshima, Fukuoka, Kumamoto, Wakayama, and Yamaguchi) that had the reputation of being dominated by this particular Buddhist sect (Kashima, 1977: 6; Spickard, 1996: 13–16). According to an early study, 75–90 percent of Japanese Buddhists in the United States are represented by Nishi Hongwanji (Kashima, 1977: 5).

Buddhism was first established in Hawai'i in 1889 when Soryu Kagahi conducted the first Buddhist service in Honolulu[2] and established the "Hawai'i Mission of Hongpa Hongwanji" (Dai Nippon Teikoku Hongwanji-ha Hawai'i). Kagahi was not an official representative of Jodo Shinshu headquarters in Kyoto, but he took it upon himself to investigate the necessity of establishing an official Buddhist mission in Hawai'i (Hunter, 1971: 32–36). Kagahi toured the islands during most of 1889, helping to raise funds to build a small temple on the Big Island. Between 1889 and 1897, fledgling groups on various islands continued to support the occasional itinerant priests, but there was not, as yet, any official support or recognition from Jodo Shinshu headquarters. It was not until 1897 that an official representative, Ejun Miyamoto, was sent from Japan to evaluate the needs of the Hawai'i Buddhist community. Shoi Yamada, who arrived in Hawai'i in 1897, became the first *kaikyoshi* (missionary priest) in Hawai'i. With official recognition and some funding from Kyoto, temple building in the islands escalated. By 1899, there were 6 official temples; by 1905, there were 14 (Hawai'i Hongpa Hongwanji Mission, 1989: 30).

Ejun Miyamoto repeated his efforts in 1898, arriving in San Francisco in July with Eryu Honda on a similar mission from Hongwanji headquarters. By the time they arrived, there was a sizeable community of Japanese immigrants, mostly men. Some were professionals—doctors, lawyers, and businessmen. Less than a week after Miyamoto and Honda arrived in San Francisco, many of these young men established the charter for the Young Men's Buddhist Association (Buddhist Churches of America, 1974: 45). Less than a year later, Shuye Sonoda and Kakuryo Nishijima were appointed as missionaries in order to establish the Buddhist Mission of North America (or the North American Buddhist Mission). In 1944, during internment, the mission officially changed its name to the Buddhist Churches of America.

Institution Building

Once the official missionary outreach was approved by sect headquarters and priests were dispatched, they were faced with the formidable task of reaching out to a population that was dispersed throughout rural countryside. In Hawai'i and on the continent, though the initial church was established in a large city—such as Honolulu and San Francisco—the bulk of the outreach to the Japanese community took place in outlying areas: on plantations and in the agricultural countryside of the Pacific Coast.

The North American and Hawai'i missions received nominal financial support from the sect headquarters in Japan, but they were entirely self-reliant when it came to fund-raising for projects such as temple building. One of the primary jobs for Buddhist priests was to help raise money and secure space by renting, leasing, or buying property. The importance of Buddhist churches in the life of the community can be demonstrated by the rapid rate of growth during the early 20th century. During the first 30 years of the 20th century, decades marked by a rapid growth of the Japanese American population, 29 temples were built on the Pacific Coast. By World War II, that number would reach 44 (Kashima, 1977; Buddhist Churches of America, 1974: 141). Temples were built in large population centers, but most were established in rural agricultural towns such as Watsonville, California, and Auburn, Washington. The community raised funds to buy or rent property, as well as to purchase sutras, ornamental decorations, and vestments for the church and priest and to purchase expensive statues of the Buddha or Shinran, the founding patron of the Jodo Shinshu sect.

Once established, the temple became the locus of Japanese American community activity. Aside from retail establishments, the church was often the only place where large numbers of Japanese could gather. In addition to holding weekly Sunday services and Sunday school for children, the temple was also the gathering place for organizations for young people (Young Men's and Women's Buddhist Associations, later known as "YBAs"), sports leagues, social clubs, boy scouts, *fujinkai*, the temple women's organization, and so on. Temples with large enough populations often hosted language schools—English or Japanese or both, depending on community needs. In Hawai'i, the popularity of Buddhist Japanese-language schools far outstripped those run by Japanese Christians (Hunter, 1971: 86–90). A Buddhist church, then, was often the focal point of the community and facilitated community organizing in addition to fostering religious faith. For example, the Waipahu Buddhist temple became a central gathering point for strikers in 1904 in Hawai'i (Okihiro, 1991: 43–45; Beechert, 1985: 197–99).

Community Life

Buddhist temples were often the focal point of Japanese American community life. This was especially true in rural, isolated communities or if the Buddhist church was the sole religious institution that welcomed Japanese membership. Buddhist missionary priests and their wives were called on to serve multiple roles in addition to their religious functions. While maintaining the temple as a place for worship and commemorative occasions, Buddhist priests and their wives were also expected to be social leaders in the community, participating in fund-raising for the temple and other local concerns, and educators, running Sunday religious schools and language academies. Since the temple was the center of the community, a gathering place for Buddhist and non-Buddhist holidays, Buddhist priests and their wives served as a direct connection to friends and family in Japan. They helped to retain Japanese customs such as the annual late-summer *obon* festival, even as they helped to ease the transition for Nisei from Japanese to Japanese American.

David Yoo (2000) has noted the importance of Buddhist youth organizations for establishing patterns of leadership, as well as helping Nisei meet potential marriage partners, business associates, and life-long companions. Buddhist churches hosted sports leagues, community service organizations, discussion groups, and social clubs. For Nisei in the continental United States, Young Buddhist Association meetings and conventions were often the only opportunity they had to socialize as a peer group. Going to school and living among White Americans, Nisei Buddhists took advantage of social occasions provided by the Buddhist church. By establishing youth organizations that were comparable with those enjoyed by other young people, Nisei Buddhists were able to establish and assert an identity that was a comfortable mix of Japanese, American, and Buddhist (Yoo, 2000).

Nisei often faced the pressure to convert to Christianity, especially if other family members converted or if the social life of their community made Christian conversion convenient or desirable. In Hawai'i, the Nisei generation was under far less pressure than on the continent to convert as a means to Americanize. The size of the Japanese community in Hawai'i mitigated some pressures, even though, because of their number, the Nisei were the focus of an intense Americanization campaign throughout the 1920s and 1930s (Tamura, 1994). Nisei Buddhists in Hawai'i had the advantage of a vast network of associates and strong community support. They also had the advantage of being able to express their unique cultural heritage in a multiethnic context that was also multiply religious. In that context, Nisei Buddhists expressed a greater degree of self-confidence in their religious identity than did their continental counterparts.

Japanese American Christianity and Nationalism

Christians were a distinct minority in the Japanese American community during the first four decades of the twentieth century. Some Issei came to the United States as Christians, having converted in Japan or coming from Christian backgrounds. Issei were also converted by Christian missionary outreach through churches and the YMCA, especially in urban areas such as Los Angeles, San Francisco, and Seattle. White Americans assumed that Japanese Christians would necessarily be better Americans, better able to assimilate into American culture. Because many White Americans assumed that Christianity was the natural companion to American nationalism, they believed that Christians would necessarily be or become better Americans. However, current research suggests that Christianity was not an adequate predictor of Americanization. In fact, quite the opposite was true.

Brian Masaru Hayashi (1995) examined exhaustively the records of three Japanese American churches of the evangelical Protestant sort from the 1890s to the 1940s: Japanese Union Church (which brought together formerly Congregational and Presbyterian congregations), Japanese Methodist Church, and Los Angeles Holiness Church. He found that the Christians in these churches adopted two different postures toward assimilating into American society in two successive periods. From the mid-1910s to the mid-1920s, Japanese American Protestants pursued a strategy of adopting American ways as much as they possibly could. This was the period of high tide for the Americanization movement that accompanied later Progressivism (Higham, 1975: 243–63). Issei Christians in this period were exhorted by their religious leaders, both White missionaries and Japanese American pastors (as, indeed, by Japanese consular officials), to accommodate themselves to American society. They were encouraged to speak English and dress in American clothes. Japanese American churches held classes where immigrants could improve their English and learn American table manners. They sponsored Boy Scout troops and held mother-daughter banquets.

Issei Christians sought Americanization with the goal of strengthening Japan. Sen Katayama said that he and his fellow students came to the United States "for the purpose of gaining true knowledge of higher civilization to educate and cultivate our minds . . . in the service of our native land" (quoted in Hayashi, 1995: 25). Hayashi interprets the Issei Protestants' Americanizationist impulse as a desire, not to give up their Japaneseness but to serve Japan—indeed, to prove the superior adaptability of the Japanese. He describes Methodist leader Kan'ichi Miyama as pursuing Americanization:

He and his band of student followers believed that Japanese Americans should adapt themselves to American culture and exhibit the best possible face before Americans. They encouraged moral reform work such as temperance, works of charity for indigent students, evening classes in the English language, employment introductions, and boardinghouse work in addition to evangelism. But at the same time, Miyama urged Japanese immigrants to remain true to their Japanese heritage. (36)

Yet Hayashi also quotes Miyama exhorting Japanese plantation workers to embrace American Progressive reforms in a manner that would remain true to Japan:

> Oh brothers! Let us consider it our honor that we are of the Japanese race. Let us undergo any tribulation in order that we may maintain our honor. Laziness and misdemeanors will not only bring distress on you but will also harm our unbroken structure which has existed from time immemorial. Such acts will also bring dishonor upon our 30 million countrymen in Japan. Let us lead reformed lives as of tomorrow! (36)

In the second period, from the mid-1920s to the onset of World War II, Japanese American Protestants were anything but assimilationist. In fact, they were among the leaders of the growing Japanese nationalist sentiment in Japanese American communities in those years. The decisive turning point was the Immigration Act of 1924, which barred further immigration from Japan. By that time, many Japanese Americans had worked their way into a tenuous middle-class position; this was especially true for members of Protestant congregations. The anti-Japanese movement and exclusion convinced many Issei Protestants that they could not count on America, not even on their co-religionists. Many went back to Japan. Those who stayed lost their enthusiasm for assimilating into American society and culture.

All the Japanese churches that Hayashi studied drew away from their White parent denominations in the latter 1920s and 1930s. They became self-supporting financially and no longer took direction from denominational headquarters. They gave up on the temperance and antigambling campaigns that they had pursued in the 1910s; they acknowledged that drinking and gambling were common Issei male pastimes, not objectionable activities. They lost any idealistic enthusiasm they might once have had for the American political system. Kan'ichi Niisato, a blind Holiness evangelist, railed against Franklin Roosevelt and the New Deal as "high-sounding and meaningless" (quoted in Hayashi, 1995: 84). Japanese

American Protestants revered the imperial family and celebrated the emperor's birthday. They sang the Japanese national anthem, "Kimigaiyo," in their sanctuaries.

Some even tried to blend Christian evangelism with the nationalist fervor that was growing in Japan. The Southern California Japanese Christian Church Federation proclaimed the superiority of Japanese Christianity over the American version: "We must introduce to Westerners in English the Christ who was revealed to Japan to correct the trend in America of straying away from the path of Jesus. . . . [We must show them the spirit of] bushido, loyalty, honesty, and gratitude." Holiness pastor Magojiro Furuya claimed that the God of the Bible was the same god as the Shinto sun goddess Amaterasu-omikami, who created the Japanese islands and their first emperor, from whom the present emperor was descended. He asserted: "God has given a special mission to the Japanese just as the Israelites were given a special mission. . . . Just as God consecrated the [Jewish] people and so prepared them to spread god's true way of salvation to the world from Israel, the Japanese are to liberate the world's colored races and are a specially chosen vessel" (both quoted in Hayashi 1995: 89–90).

One countertrend in Japanese American Protestant churches in this second period came as a result of the maturing of the Nisei, or second generation. Raised in American schools and streets, the Nisei generally spoke English better than first-generation Japanese and adopted the teenage styles of White Americans.[3] As the leading edge of their generation entered high school years in the 1930s, they began to demand worship services in English, basketball leagues, summer retreats, and other events that replicated the social activities and structures common for young people in White Christian and Japanese Buddhist churches. But Hayashi argues that the Nisei were not a force in their churches or communities in the prewar years, and that they followed their elders in that time of growing Japanese nationalism.[4]

Altogether, Hayashi concludes that "Japanese American Protestants were clearly *not* at the forefront of Japanese American cultural assimilation in the prewar period" (Hayashi, 1995: 6). Instead, he says, they represented an evangelical Protestant hybrid of Japanese nationalism and American cultural values. Evangelical Christianity introduced church members to new American holidays and to values such as temperance and social work, and it instilled in them loyalty to a transcendent god and an identity that indicated an adoption of a new existential outlook on the nature of life. But the faith did not inspire Japanese American believers to adopt many American normative values. Furthermore, it left the door open to secular political thought that undercut assimilation and provided an intellectual basis on which Japanese nationalism could develop. Its insistence on high ethical standards, its emphasis on missions and evangelism, and its teaching of submission to governing authorities fit with the Japanese belief in the superiority of their own culture and government and pulled Issei male church members along with their secular peers— and Issei women and their Nisei offspring—into the tide of Japanese nationalism in the 1930s (93–95).

So Hayashi challenges the idea that Christian involvement and commitment constitute an avenue of assimilation into the broader American society. On the contrary, he shows conclusively that Japanese American Protestants were among the most fervent supporters of Japan as World War II approached. As he says, "although the adoption of the evangelical Protestant faith certainly meant new values and a new identity, it did not necessarily mean a new American identity" (Hayashi, 1995: 7).

Religious Demography of Japanese America

If one had asked the Issei what their religion was when they boarded ship for America, the vast majority would have said Buddhist. Shinto, a religion that blended ancestor connection and nature worship, had become something of a cult expressing Japanese nationalism and emperor veneration by the 1890s. But most Japanese were as connected to Shinto as they were to Buddhism. Issei Christians numbered fewer than 10 percent of the immigrant generation.

Table 4-1 reports on several studies that asked Japanese Americans in various locations to identify their religion commitments. The trends are these: Between two-thirds and three-quarters of continental Japanese Americans identified themselves as Buddhists; most of the rest claimed Christian (usually Protestant) identities. The percentage of Buddhists was higher in the immigrant generation than among the Nisei; one-half or more of the second generation claimed a Christian religious identity. California had a higher percentage of Japanese Americans who were Buddhists than did the Northwest; Hawai'i probably had a higher percentage still.[5]

Many sociological studies presume that a person embraced only one religion: one was either Buddhist or Christian or Shinto. But quite a

TABLE 4.1
Japanese American Religious Affiliations

Place/Group	Year	Buddhist	Christian	Shinto[a]	Sample Total
Los Angeles	1924	3,140	972	780	4,892
California	1930	3,525	1,294		4,819
Issei		3,000	681		3,681
Nisei		525	613		1,138
Seattle	1936	800	1,200	120	2,120
Tule Lake[b]	1943	7,197	2,469		9,666
Former Northwest residents					
Total		2,360	1,096		3,456
Issei		1,364	335		1,699
Kibei		271	69		340
Nisei		725	692		1,417
Former California residents					
Total		4,837	1,373		6,210
Issei		2,360	452		2,812
Kibei		753	97		850
Nisei		1,724	824		2,548

NOTE: Issei, first-generation Japanese in the United States; Kibei, second-generation; Nisei, second-generation.
a. Only the Los Angeles and Seattle studies included a separate category for Shinto. Presumably, Shintoists are to be found among the Buddhists in the other studies.
b. The study made in the Tule Lake concentration camp also included a category for "secularists," which has been eliminated here.
SOURCES: Gretchen Tuthill, "A Study of the Japanese in the City of Los Angeles," M.A. thesis, University of Southern California, 1924, 66–67; Edward K. Strong, Japanese in California (Stanford, Calif.: Stanford University Press, 1968); S. Frank Miyamoto, Social Solidarity among the Japanese in Seattle, rev. ed. (Seattle: University of Washington Press, 1984), 45; Dorothy S. Thomas et al., The Salvage (Berkeley: University of California Press, 1952), 607.

number of Japanese Americans embraced elements of two or even three of these traditions. For example, Japanese American Methodists, Presbyterians, and Congregationalists in Los Angeles in the 1920s and 1930s held onto Shinto beliefs about the spirits of dead people. As Protestants, they were encouraged to believe that the spirit of a dead person immediately leaves the corpse and goes to Heaven or Hell. Yet these Japanese American Protestant churches regularly held *tsuitokai,* or wakes, with incense and food offerings, to placate spirits of dead people who lingered in the vicinity (Hayashi, 1995: 75–76). It is likely that most Japanese Americans, whatever their formal religious affiliation (or lack thereof) experienced elements of Shinto and Buddhist perspectives in their personal religious orientation.

Korean American History

In her pioneering 1937 master's thesis on Koreans in Hawai'i, Bernice Kim observed that, despite the internal diversity within this immigrant group, "one factor can unreservedly be said to have been common to nearly all Koreans, namely the Christian religion, a phenomenon in an Oriental group anywhere" (Kim, 1937: 137). From Kim's vantage point, any serious attempt to understand Korean Americans would have to take into account the centrality of religion in their process of migration and settlement. That insight has held true for Korean Americans from the very first arrivals in 1903 to the present day.

While no one would question the importance of religion for Korean Americans, very few studies have offered a sustained and nuanced treatment of religious experience. Historical and contemporary works have focused on institutional facts and membership figures. While important in providing some sense of the landscape, such treatments often neglect the complex ways in which religion, broadly construed, infused the worldviews and everyday lives of Korean Americans. Moreover, not enough attention has been paid to the ways in which religion has influenced the politics of community beyond the walls of the church, nor how matters seemingly unrelated to religion have been part and parcel of institutional churches and church-related organizations.[6] Such a study is beyond the scope of this comparative chapter, but an effort is made here to sketch out some of the questions and issues that can emerge when religion and migration and settlement are examined together.[7]

Religion, manifested in institutions, ideas, faith commitments, and ritual practices, has enabled Korean Americans to negotiate their identity and contextualize their experience. In the same vein, religion has provided its adherents with vital social services, racial-ethnic spaces, and a measure of faith and meaning. Recent studies point to the vitality of religion, evident in the nearly 3,000 Korean American Christian churches nationwide. While figures vary, survey data suggest that 65 to 70 percent of Korean Americans are Protestant, along with adherents of Roman Catholicism (10–15 percent) and Buddhism (10–15 percent) (Hurh, 1998: 105–15). Religion also informs the lives of men and women and families through personal and popular forms of religion and spirituality that intersects, spills across, and lies outside of formal institutions. It is clear that

Koreans in the United States—past and present—have been deeply influenced by the dominance, diversity, and, at times, divisiveness, of religious experience.

Korean Americans today number over 1 million persons, and religion, primarily Protestant Christianity, has been perhaps the most salient feature of their experience as a racial-ethnic community. Korean Americans have been in the United States for nearly a century, and their history has been marked by three waves of migration and settlement: the Early Years (1903–45), the Aftermath of War (1945–65), and Recent Arrivals (1965–present). After a brief overview of each wave of migration, we focus on the first period as a means of underscoring themes and issues that facilitate a comparative perspective on religion and migration with Japanese Americans during roughly the same era.

Early Years (1903–45)

The first wave of Koreans, numbering approximately 8,500 persons, entered the United States beginning in 1903, largely as a labor force for sugarcane plantations in Hawai'i. Religion played an important role from the very start, as recruiters for American companies in Korea called on Protestant missionaries in Korea to persuade those in their care to make the journey to the islands. As a result, Protestant Christians were among the first Korean Americans to venture to the United States, and as historian Wayne Patterson (2000: 7) has noted, immigrants overwhelmingly affiliated with Christian institutions after their arrival to Hawai'i.

Congregations on the plantations, in Honolulu and on the mainland, quickly became the gathering places for Korean Americans, serving as clearinghouses of information and social services. Churches also provided spaces, under the umbrella of religion, for Korean Americans to explore a wide range of issues, including their status as members of a racial-ethnic minority in the United States and their role in the independence movement to free Korea from Japanese colonial rule. Key immigrant and expatriate leaders such as Ahn Chang-ho, Pak Yong-man, and Syngman Rhee all were influenced by the reform-minded ideas based in the Christian institutions such as churches, schools, and hospitals that had helped shape their worldviews.

Moreover, Korean Americans looked to religion for a sense of meaning and comfort amid the harsh realities of life and labor that they encountered. At the same time, religion could also be a place of division, as churches and religious organizations could not but be enmeshed in the politics of community formation. For better and worse, religion, represented in the mix of the theological, cultural, political, and social, infused the lives of the majority of Korean Americans.

Aftermath of War (1945–65)

The fight for independence led by Korean Americans had entered a dormant period through much of the 1920s and 1930s, but it experienced new energy as events unfolded that culminated in a world at war. The jubilation felt by Koreans abroad at the end of the war, however, was soon met by the tragedy of the nation occupied by two global powers with competing agendas for the peninsula. Key immigrant leaders, entering the latter stages of their lives and representing immigrant organizations in Hawai'i and California, formed the Korean Delegation of America that headed back to Korea in 1945 to help in the reconstruction of the country. For so many Korean Americans who had waged a long battle for Korean independence, this period would be one of loss and heartbreak in which the bane of colonialism would be replaced by a people torn asunder (Kim 1971: 133–35, 146).

As Korean Americans witnessed and played a role in Korea's postwar future, approximately 14,000 persons—Korean wives of American servicemen and their children, war orphans, and professional workers and students—arrived in the United States during the second wave of migration, marked by the end of World War II and the Korean War (1950–53). Those in the Republic of Korea (South Korea) maintained strong ties to the United States via the military, educational institutions, and church-related organizations. Those ties provided some Koreans the means for starting new lives in America.

Sociologist Jung Ha Kim (2002: 193–95) has noted that the quality of experience for those who ventured forth during this period hinged on the themes of dislocation and home base. For the nearly 6,300 war orphan children who were adopted from 1955 to 1966, the choice to migrate was not their own, nor would they enter spaces in American society marked by an immigrant context. Close to two-thirds of the adoptees were Amerasians, the result of unions between Koreans and European and African Americans. In roughly the same period and in nearly equal numbers as the adoptees, Korean women came to the United States as "war brides."

These women lived largely segregated lives, near military bases and disconnected from other Korean Americans in part due to the lack of acceptance of outmarriage that existed within most immigrant communities. Many of these women would sponsor family members to immigrate to the United States in the post-1965 period. The final group were several thousand students and workers, many of whom had overstayed their visas and technically were illegal aliens. It is this third group that had the greatest level of contact with the existing Korean American institutions and communities.

The arrival of new immigrants during this period served as a precursor to the large wave of Koreans who entered the country in the post-1965 era from all three groups mentioned above. The aging and established prewar Korean American communities and institutions found themselves needing to adjust to immigrants who brought with them not only the effects of the war but also a different sensibility, given the changes that Korea had continued to undergo since most of the original immigrants had left their homeland at the turn of the century. To the extent that a merging of the older and newer populations took place, its results were mixed. Solidarity in terms of a common ancestry was strained by the fact that many of the children of the pioneer immigrants had come of age in the United States.

Recent Arrivals (1965–Present)

The passage of the 1965 Immigration Act by the United States removed long-standing restrictive and discriminatory measures that had been firmly in place since the passage of nativist legislation in 1924. Korean immigrants, along with many others from Asia, entered the United States in increasingly large numbers. At the peak in the mid-1980s, Korean immigrants topped 30,000 persons per year. This influx transformed smaller, historic Korean American communities in urban settings such as Los Angeles and New York; these newer immigrants make up the majority of the million or so Korean Americans in the country today. The boom in the population has been accompanied by an explosion in the numbers of immigrant churches, temples, and other religious organizations. This largely Protestant phenomenon in part reflects the growth and spread of Protestant Christianity in Korea, but it is also clear that many men and women have affiliated with churches only after their arrival in the United States.

Religion continues to be the heart of this racial-ethnic community, informing the daily lives of men and women in the midst of the pressures of economic survival and sociocultural adjustment set into motion by the migration and settlement process. Institutions range from small, house-based groups to megachurches that rival any religious organization in the country in terms of membership, programming, and resources. Religion has continued to play a critical social service function for Korean Americans, creating webs of relationships that attend to a host of needs immigrants face. That religious and racial-ethnic spaces have been intertwined has also been important for Korean Americans, as it has been for so many other immigrant groups throughout our collective history. Religious institutions have offered psychic and physical space within which individuals and communities can affirm traditions and customs from the home country, even while wrestling with the changes and conflict that can be engendered by new settings. As a source of faith and meaning and as a locus of ritual and spiritual practice, religion is a powerful and enduring influence in the lives of the diversity that is Korean America—from attending services in churches and temples to the less institutional, more popular forms of devotion and ritual activities.

Perhaps the defining moment of the post-1965 period is the 1992 Los Angeles uprising and riots. The ways that this event and its related issues have been refracted through the religious landscape of Korean America—from joint services with African American congregations and community assistance programs to apathy, denial, and neglect—suggest that while religion has been and continues to be at the core of this community, its nature is by no means uniform. The rise of second-generation, English-speaking Korean American; pan-Asian American; and multiracial ethnic institutions signals the dawning of a new era.

Reflections on Korean American Religious History (1903–45)

Peter Hyun's autobiographies chronicling his individual and family's experiences during this period reflect the complex and fascinating ways that Protestant Christianity infused the lives of many Korean Americans. The son of a prominent Methodist pastor, Hyun (1906–93) was one of the few, if perhaps not the only, Korean American eyewitnesses to the March 1, 1919, uprising that has served as an important marker for Korean resistance to colonial oppression by Japan. His journeys from Hawai'i to Korea to China and back to Hawai'i signal the kind of exilic and migrant status of many Korean Americans. Born on the island of Kaua'i, Peter's experiences are intimately connected to his father, the Reverend Soon Hyun, who played an important role in the March 1st uprising in Korea as well as independence movement efforts in China and the United States. The history of the Hyun family speaks to the pivotal role that churches and Christianity had in shaping the history of modern Korea and the Korean diaspora (Hyun, 1986, 1991).

As the primary site of migration and settlement, Hawai'i became home to immigrants who had come largely to fill the labor needs on sugarcane plantations. The Methodist mission sought to oversee the religious activities of Korean Americans within the first year of arrival, but immigrants had their own ideas about how they would congregate—a theme that would repeat itself throughout the period under study. The first organized worship service in July 1903 took place on Oah'u without the knowledge of the Methodist mission hierarchy. Indeed, religious life on the plantations reflected the agency of the immigrants as much if not more than it did the plans of denomination officials. For instance, Methodist superintendents lobbied sugar growers to help subsidize Christian work on the plantations with the rationale that Christian laborers would be more productive workers and less likely to leave the plantation for life in Honolulu. And yet, as Patterson has noted, Korean Americans were among the quickest to head to the cities (2000: 55–65).

Whether on the plantation or in the cities, immigrant Protestant churches served as the hub of the community—multipurpose spaces that served a range of needs for those who entered. In November of 1903, immigrant leaders in conjunction with the mission formed the Korean Evangelical Society, the forerunner of the Korean Methodist Church in Honolulu. The Methodist Church would serve as a pillar of the Korean American community in Hawai'i for decades (Choy, 1977: 254).

By 1916, there were 24 Methodist missions on the islands, and while the Methodists were the dominant Protestant group, an internal split soon created an independent church known as the Korean Christian Church (KCC). In a series of events that have become the stuff of legend, Syngman Rhee, future president of the Republic of Korea, but then an educator within the Korean Methodist mission in Hawai'i, broke with the denomination to form what would become the KCC in 1918 (Kim, 1971: 34–35). While this essay cannot detail the entanglements of religious and independence politics between the Korean Methodist Church and the

Korean Christian Church and their corollary organizations, it should be noted that these fissures created long-standing divisions among Korean Americans in Hawai'i and, to some extent, on the U.S. mainland as well.

As Koreans in Hawai'i braced themselves for World War II in the aftermath of Pearl Harbor, the Protestant Christian presence was firmly in place as the majority of immigrants attended Christian churches. Although numbers vary, one study states that there were about 1,000 Methodists, 200 Episcopalians, 2,000 Seventh-Day Adventists, 100–300 Catholics, and 1,000 Korean Christian Church members. In contrast, only about 30 Koreans claimed an affiliation with Buddhism (Patterson, 2000: 67).[8]

As Korean Americans in Hawai'i migrated further to the mainland, the Hawaiian patterns of community life also followed. Not surprisingly, immigrant Protestant churches in places like California became the primary vehicles for social services, political activity, and religious observance. In the fall of 1905, a small group of Korean immigrants in San Francisco formed a Methodist mission that met in a private home. Ryang Ju-sam, an evangelist from Korea en route to divinity school at Vanderbilt University, arrived in 1906, and in the wake of the city's earthquake, postponed his studies to help his compatriots who were in need of much assistance.

Ryang called on his church contacts and arranged for the rental of a three-story building that became headquarters for the Korean Evangelical Society. The use of the building was rich with symbolism. The first floor became the dining room and social center for residents who occupied the third floor, which had been converted into living quarters. In the middle, the second floor served two primary functions—worship space for religious services and a meeting hall for political groups. The ebb and flow that took place on each of the floors and the interchange between them suggest something of the organic nature of Korean American religious, political, and social life. After about three years, Ryang departed the city to take up his studies, but before then, he also started to publish the *Korean United Church News,* which disseminated information and opinion about Korea and Korean American communities to readers throughout the United States (Choy, 1977: 254–55).

Over the course of the next two decades on the mainland, Korean churches sprang up in nearly every settled community and rural waystation for migrant laborers. Korean Americans flocked to the churches for varied and multiple reasons. What they encountered was a flawed institution and leadership, but one that they claimed as their own. These immigrant churches occupied the heart of the community because people found in them a place that addressed their deeply felt needs. Whether through the social services provided, in the affirmation of one's racial-ethnic identity in the face of marginalization, or in the meaning derived from religious activities and worldview, churches could offer their congregants a sense of place amid the harsh realities of everyday life that most Korean Americans faced. That the politics of the community, including the drive for independence, ran through the Christian church makes these collective stories all the more interesting.

In the brief thumbnail sketch offered here, it is difficult to assess the richness and complexity of Korean American religious history in the period spanning roughly the first half of the 20th century. Much more needs to be done to unearth the stories that make up this history. The experiences of Koreans and Japanese in the United States hold important clues about the interconnected process of migration and religious life. It is to these issues that this essay now turns.

Japanese and Korean American Nationalism and Transnationalism

For both Korean and Japanese Americans, the fate of their respective home countries loomed large, even as they sought to negotiate their life circumstances in the United States. Perhaps all immigrants carry with them an abiding concern for their countries of origin, but the cases of Japanese and Korean Americans differed from European immigrants in that they were excluded from U.S. citizenship under the Naturalization Act of 1790, which extended it only to "free, white" persons. The inhospitable welcome these immigrants encountered only deepened the sense of pride in their ancestry.

Across the Pacific, the rise of modern Japan and its growing dreams of empire led to the annexation of Korea in 1910; that, in turn, launched the independence movement among Koreans at home and abroad. Several years earlier, full of imperial ambitions of its own, the United States, despite its treaty obligations to Korea, entered into a secret agreement with Japan, recognizing its control of Korea in exchange for noninterference in the Philippines (Choy, 1977: 64). The men and women who left their ancestral homes, while removed from the machinations of their governments, nevertheless would find their own lives entangled with fates of both the land of their birth and the country they adopted.

For Koreans, the independence movement against Japanese colonialism was at the core of their nationalism. An argument can be made that, although their numbers during the early years were small, the immigrant population in the United States was pivotal because of (1) the presence of key expatriate and immigrant leaders such as Ahn Chang-ho, Philip Jaisohn (So Chaepil), Pak Yong-man, and Syngman Rhee; (2) the funds that were generated by immigrants to support independence and relief efforts in Korea and in other locales; (3) ongoing ties to the United States, both to the federal government and to church organizations such as the Methodists, Presbyterians, and the YMCA; and (4) the efforts to publicize the plight of Koreans internationally (Choy, 1977: 141–89). The experiences of Korean Americans also raise interesting comparative possibilities with other immigrant groups during the same era who were fighting against colonialism in their home countries: the Sikhs in India and the Irish in Ireland. All three groups had organizations and movements based in the United States.

The linkages to the home country point to a related issue about how migration and religion inform the notion of the nation-state itself. For Koreans, the immigrant community in the United States viewed itself in part as a placeholder for Korea and Korean identity, especially as Japan systematically began to absorb their homeland into the Japanese empire. The Japanese ban against Korean language in the schools and public sites, a rewriting of history, and even a renaming of Korean cities and places—all sought to erase Korea as it was known before annexation by Japan. While Korean Americans were subject to immigration and the adjustments entailed in settling into life in the United States, they also saw themselves as an extension of Korea. This affected how they formed a sense of community, as well as how they negotiated the world around them in the United States.

Religion, specifically Protestant Christianity, played an important role in these thoughts about nation on several overlapping levels. First, American missionary Christianity was a formative and influential force on many immigrant leaders who attended Christian institutions like the Pai Chae School (Methodist) in Seoul. A mix of Christian teachings and American notions of democracy and individualism sparked the imaginations of young, reform-minded elites in Korea. These young elites represented a transitional link between the older, Confucian-based leadership tied to the royal court and the emergence of leaders who understood Korea's future to depend partly on embracing the ideas of the countries that were vying for influence in Korea at the end of the 19th century and the beginning of the 20th. This level may be thought of primarily in terms of the influence of religion on ideas and the shaping of worldviews.

In addition, Christian institutions, linked mainly to Americans, but also to Canadians and Australians, represented spaces in which Koreans could find a measure of insulation from the Japanese, before and especially after annexation. Church-related institutions were always a mix of missionary and native influence, but the realities of international relations came into play as the Japanese colonial government sought to deal with Christian churches. Of course, the Americans had their own conscious and unconscious agendas. An effort needs to be made to sketch out the ways that religion took on indigenous forms. Part of this would entail describing the internal diversity of Christianity within Korea and exploring how different strands coexisted in the face of mounting pressures brought on by the colonial presence of Japan.

For Japanese Americans, there was clearly an important linkage to Japan, because their departure, in part, had been set into motion by a nation engaged in rapid modernization. Historian Yuji Ichioka (1988) and others have commented on how the fate of Japanese Americans was deeply affected by U.S.–Japan relations, reflected in events such as the 1906 school incident in San Francisco and the 1937 Sino-Japanese War. Moreover, a direct connection existed between immigrants and their homeland through the practice of sending children to Japan to be raised by relatives. These second-generation Japanese Americans, known as "Kibei," spoke to the ambivalence that many immigrants felt about their place in the United States. The Japanese government, primarily through the consulates but also other means (e.g., newspaper editorials and surveillance) kept tabs on the immigrant communities, as they were concerned about how Japanese Americans affected Japan's image in the international community.

By highlighting nationalism and transnational realities for both groups, several insights into migration and religion emerge. The first is that migration itself must be viewed less in terms simply of what happened after arrival to the United States and more with regard to both ends of the journey. Only by sifting through the continuities and the contrasts will the adaptations become more evident. A second, related point is that there has been a tendency to view the "old world" traits of immigrants as transplanted to the new soil of the United States. While there is certainly a measure of truth to this perspective, the examples of Japanese Americans and Korean Americans challenge us to ask how it is that religion (and society) underwent change well before men and women boarded their ships for new destinations. Korean Protestant Christianity, for instance, entered the peninsula during a time of tremendous upheaval and instability. Not only was this religion a relatively new phenomenon, but also the worldview that immigrants took with them was undergoing much change. A third area specific to these two groups is the racialization of immigrants that spoke to their marginal status in the United States. Whether Buddhist or Christian, Japanese and Korean Americans had been legally and culturally relegated to the position of perpetual foreigners (Lowe, 1996).

Adjustment and Americanization

To ask whether religion facilitates or hinders adjustment to a new cultural context does not adequately describe the complexity of issues that surround the development of religion in these Asian American communities. A singular focus on assimilation obfuscates the more interesting and complex interrelationship between religious faith, race, and ethnic identity. For example, Hayashi's study challenges the prevailing notion that Protestant Japanese Americans would be more likely to demonstrate a stronger sense of Americanism than Buddhists. Neither did Korean American Protestants during the first half of the 20th century fit the stereotype of Christians being naturally better at demonstrating American values and virtues. The churches, by contrast, served to reinforce racial-ethnic ties and continued to do so because of two major factors: (1) the zeal for Korea's independence, which placed Korean Americans in an in-between place as immigrants in the United States, yet people whose ties to the home country were vital and on-going; and (2) the effects of racism that Korean Americans faced in the United States in terms of discrimination in occupation, housing, education, and so forth.

For Japanese Buddhists, the question of adjustment has traditionally been discussed in terms of the degree to which Jodo Shinshu Buddhism was assimilated by becoming "protestantized" in the United States. Sunday services and religious schools for children, hymn singing, pews, and youth social organizations have all been considered markers of the Americanization of Japanese Buddhism. These changes were interpreted as an attempt on the part of Buddhists to stave off an inevitable attraction that Nisei Buddhists would feel for Christianity. Buddhists, it was thought, imitated Protestant Christianity in order to keep the Nisei from asserting their American identity by converting to Christianity.

Buddhism in the United States did adapt to the American environment by making some of these superficial changes. But it is important to note that many of the adaptations that seem to mimic American Protestant Christianity had begun to take place in Japan during the turbulent Meiji era. Jodo Shinshu Buddhists were briefly persecuted as the result of their long history of cooperation with the government during the Tokugawa era. In addition, Christian missionaries began to challenge traditional Japanese religious culture by appealing to the spirit of modern reform that challenged conventional religious mores. Buddhists responded to the challenge of modernization posed by Christian missionaries by updating many of their forms and structures. The Young Buddhists Association, for example, was founded in Japan in 1894, to counter the popularity of the YMCA, which garnered attention and support through its progressive spirit of reform in urban Japan.

Japanese Buddhists in the United States who adopted strategies, forms, and ideas that were similar to those used by Protestant Christians were not just imitating their Christian neighbors because, as it was sometimes charged, they understood Christianity to be the superior religion. Buddhism was already undergoing profound changes *before* it was brought to the United States. Buddhists, like Christians, responded to the challenges posed by the modern era by becoming more politically progressive in their orientation and more focused on the needs of youth. In order to fully understand changes in Buddhism as it moved from East to West with migrant communities, we must be more conscious of the political and social dynamics that were already reshaping Buddhism in Japan during the Meiji period.

Once in the United States, Japanese American Buddhists frequently had to defend themselves against discrimination, both racially and religiously defined. Buddhism was often slandered (most often conflated with Shinto) and used as a justification for further restricting Japanese immigration. As non-Christians, Japanese immigrants were doubly suspect. American racial ideologies required that as members of a "yellow race," Japanese could never be considered fully American. This sense of radical otherness was often exacerbated by the fact that they were also non-Christian. Speakers for the community took great pains publicly to refute charges of "Mikado" worship and other canards that circulated in the press. There were a number of instances of Buddhist churches being denied permits to build or expand, and in Hawai'i the process of becoming registered as a nonprofit religious institution required a team of lawyers lobbying the governor on behalf of the temple (Kashima, 1977: 36; Hunter, 1971: 89).

Buddhists defended themselves, often in terms of American democracy and freedom. Yemyo Imamura, bishop of the Hawai'i Buddhist mission, argued that democracy was easily understood from a "Buddhist point of view." Writing during World War I, he contended that Buddhism in general and Jodo Shinshu Buddhism in particular were perfect expressions of the democratic ideals espoused by Americans. Since Buddhism emphasized the equality of all believers, as well as individual choice in the spiritual journey, a Buddhist faith was especially well suited for the American cultural context (Kashima, 1977: 32; Imamura, 1918).[9]

As minister to both the Issei and Nisei generations, Imamura and other Buddhist priests and community leaders were also careful to stress adaptation to the American environment, but never to the detriment of their Japanese Buddhist identity. Writing on the eve of World War II, Ralph Honda (1941), president of the Hawai'i Young Buddhists Association, expressed in no uncertain terms the attitude Nisei should take toward the coming confrontation. That he expressed his expectations in the form of the Eightfold Path, a central Buddhist ethical doctrine, illustrates the degree to which Buddhism for the Nisei generation had become identified with Americanism. If being a Buddhist meant having "right thought, right action, and right views," for example, being an American Buddhist meant adapting those Buddhist virtues for Americans in the coming conflict: right action, Honda argued, entailed "gain[ing] the confidence of our fellow Americans . . . [to] show loyalty and dependability. This also implies that we should refrain from thoughtless actions which might cause misunderstanding." Right livelihood required "remain[ing] law abiding citizens of our community and our country. We have before us an unparalleled opportunity to prove that we are good and loyal citizens by living rightfully during this crisis, even at the expense of self-sacrifice." Honda exhorted his fellow Nisei to redouble their efforts to be loyal Americans: "We are American citizens enjoying the rights and privileges that only a democracy can give. There remains but one view to take and that is to be loyal to our country, the United States of America."

Race and Racism

Because so little scholarly work has been done that explores the relationship between racial ideologies and religious identity, it is difficult to assess the impact of racism and racialization on Japanese and Korean American religious communities. We do know the practical implications of racial discrimination, in the form of exclusion, land laws, and day-to-day bigotry faced by the Japanese and Korean American Buddhist and Christian communities. For example, some researchers have suggested that the passage of the Immigration Act of 1924, which effectively cut off Asian immigration, had the effect of bolstering membership in Buddhist churches. In a 1932 study, Kosei Ogura argued that, in response to the blatant racism of the 1924 act, many who had previously been reluctant to actively identify as Buddhists in a Christian country now became defiantly and self-consciously Buddhist. Tetsuden Kashima concurred, noting that temple building had slowed after 1918 but picked up again after 1924 (Ogura, 1932; Kashima, 1977).[10]

Another logical result of racism against Japanese American Buddhists was evident in the days immediately after the bombing of Pearl Harbor. Although the North American Buddhist Mission immediately and unequivocally voiced its loyalty to the United States after the bombing, Buddhist priests were automatically targeted, arrested, and detained. Some were eventually sent to internment camps, but others remained in prison for the duration of the war.

For Korean Americans, a shared Protestant Christian faith did not serve as a bridge over the racial-ethnic divides that characterized their religious experiences. Ties to European American missionaries and their sponsoring denominations (primarily Methodist and Presbyterian) certainly influenced the shape of the Korean American and Japanese American Protestant religious landscape, but they did so primarily in terms of a paternalism that underscored issues of power and privilege rather than as a collective sojourn. Moreover, the core of the institutions, leadership, and lived experienced of religion was a racial-ethnic affair for both groups. While similar things could be said for many other immigrant groups such as Polish Catholics and Russian Jews who have settled in the United States, what set many Korean Americans (and other Protestants of color) apart is that race remained more or less a permanent dividing line that time did little to erase. It is telling that adherence to a shared Protestant faith has been effectively trumped by racial difference.

For example, in a report submitted for the 1924 Survey of Race Relations, William C. Smith documented the struggle of the Japanese community to build a Christian church in Hollywood. Members of the White (and ostensibly Christian) community organized to thwart their efforts to buy enough property to build a church and community center. To arouse community sentiment against the church, handbills were distributed, which read:

> Japs! You came to take care of lawns; we stood for it. You came to work truck gardens; we stood for it. You sent your children to our public schools; we stood for it. You moved a few families in our midst; we stood for it. You proposed to build a church in our neighborhood, but we didn't and we won't stand for it! You impose on us more each day until you have gone your limit! We don't want you with us, so get busy and JAPS MOVE OUT OF HOLLYWOOD. (1923: n.p.)

Korean Americans and Japanese Americans who called on their fellow believers discovered that religious allegiances rarely translated into a true sense of community. Arguably, most were not seeking such community, but in the limited contexts in which their worlds intersected, disappointment, frustration, and anger were commonplace. Japanese and Korean American Christians from the era under study (1885–1945) commented on the sense of exclusion and second-class status that did not just affect their overall lives in the United States but characterized their religious lives as well.

The religious histories of Japanese and Korean immigrant communities highlight the importance of race and racism in our understandings of migration and ethnic identity formation in the United States. If nearly all immigrant groups met with initial discrimination and prejudice, then the question remains why some groups soon left racialized disabilities behind while others endured such realities on more harsh and lasting terms. It is not by coincidence that, in the aftermath of Pearl Harbor, Buddhist priests and lay leaders were rounded up by the authorities because of their race and religion. Japanese American and Korean American Christians may have marginally benefited from their religious affiliation, but we know, of course, that such distinctions did not keep individuals and families from the camps or provide immunity from other hardships.

Moreover, the cases presented here raise the issue of how studies in immigration and religion have largely ignored the issue of race and racism.

Paying serious attention to this category of analysis and experience challenges the standard interpretations that dominate both scholarly and popular discourse about these subjects in ways that the chapters in Part II of this volume suggest. Although this comparison is directed toward Japanese and Korean Americans, both cases point to much longer standing matters of race and racism concerning Native and African Americans. While this essay cannot take up such themes, it is worth noting since, in part, we make a case that the dominant narratives of migration and religion in the United States begin to look quite different when race and racism operate as a central framework

NOTES

1. The lone exception was Filipinos. As natives of a U.S. colony, Filipinos were U.S. "nationals"—not U.S. citizens but free to come and go. That loophole was closed in 1934 by the Tydings-McDuffie Act.

2. Although Hawai'i did not become an official territory of the United States until 1898, by 1889, the processes that would facilitate its incorporation into the union were well under way. In addition, the close connection between the Hawai'i and continental Japanese migrant communities gives us some license in locating the first American Buddhist temple outside of the political boundaries of the United States.

3. Some adopted the teenage styles of Blacks and Chicanos; see Spickard (1999).

4. For the outside intervention that overturned Issei hegemony, see Spickard (1983).

5. For Hawai'i estimates, see Schmitt (1973) and Onishi (1937).

6. Several recent publications are beginning to address these kinds of issues, for example: Kim (1996); Kim (1997); Kwon (1997); Kwon, Kim, and Warner (2001).

7. This chapter focuses on the experiences of Korean American Protestants as the dominant group among immigrants and does not deal with other religious groups such as Buddhists and Catholics. Sharon Suh (chapter 6) takes up the theme of Korean American Buddhism in the post-1965 period.

8. Religious membership figures are difficult to verify in terms of accuracy.

9. Imamura wrote *Democracy according to the Buddhist Viewpoint* during World War I. It seems to be a rebuttal to American perceptions of Japan, and therefore Japanese immigrants, as autocratic and therefore un-American. Imamura gives an impassioned defense of Buddhism by demonstrating the fact that Shin theology was inherently democratic.

10. Of course, it could also be the case that temple building escalated in this era because of the number of children being born. Between 1910 and 1930, the number of Japanese on the Pacific Coast nearly doubled, mostly because of natural increase rather than immigration. The census of American internment camps indicates that the largest single group of Nisei was between 15 and 24 years of age in 1942, born between 1918 and 1927; see Spickard (1996), tables 2 and 6.

⁣⁣⁣⁣⁣⁣⁣||||||||||||||||||||||||||||||||||||||||||||||||||||||||

5

Critical Faith

Japanese Americans and the Birth of a New Civil Religion

Jane Naomi Iwamura

On a bright day in April, not far from Independence, California, several charter buses can be seen rambling down some old dirt roads in what appears to be the middle of nowhere. Although the scenery is spectacular—the dusty Owens Valley framed by snow-peaked mountains and a broad blue sky—one cannot locate the attraction. What are these people coming to see?

Photograph courtesy of Lauren Quock.

The dirt roads, as well as the abandoned concrete foundations that punctuate the acres of desert scrub, are part of the Manzanar National Historic Site. While many do come here as tourists, today's arrivals converge on the location with a different purpose in mind; they are on a pilgrimage.

In 2008, the Manzanar Annual Pilgrimage is in its 40th year. In the first, in 1969, some 150 young Japanese Americans journeyed to the site that once served as an internment camp in which their parents and grandparents were detained. One advised:

> The bitter cold and biting wind gave us our first lesson on how life must have been for the internees. Our humility was reinforced when we learned that what we had brashly called our "first" pilgrimage was for two Issei ministers, their 25th—Rev. Sentoku Maeda and Rev. Soichi Wakahiro are gone—but their spirits live on." (Manazar Committee, n.d.)

After this initial pilgrimage, hundreds more began to make the trip each year. Eventually, a dedicated committee of volunteers organized an annual event. The pilgrimage now takes place over several days and includes speakers, spoken word performances, contemporary bands, and Taiko drumming.

The crux of the program is the Saturday afternoon ceremony, which begins with the raising of the ten banners (representing each of the ten internment camps) and a roll call commemorating the former internees. At this moment, the crowd gathers in front of the cemetery monument— a "soul-consoling" tower or memorial to the dead erected by the evacuees during their internment—for a service of remembrance. Christian and Buddhist ministers, Catholic and Shinto priests preside and offer chants and prayers. The service is brought to a close as each participant places a flower on the monument—an offering in memory of those who died and suffered within the barbed wire that once enclosed the site. The offering also engenders a hope that such an injustice will never happen again and a commitment to make sure that it never will.

The pilgrimage is at once festival, political forum, and religious ceremony. In considering the relationship between Japanese Americans and religion, it would be easy to focus only on the interfaith service. However, the entire event has spiritual import. As Joanne Doi writes, such a pilgrimage for Japanese Americans represents a "sacred journey" that relives and recollects a "sacred story of suffering and spirit":

[It is] an attempt to regain our center as human persons and community by reconnecting to our history and each other on the periphery, on the margins. It is not escape but a return to the center of our history, the pivotal events that have marked us as Japanese Americans. In a paradoxical way, the center of our history located on the margins recreates and revitalizes as the truth of who we are shifts into place. (2002: 280)

The Manzanar pilgrimage and similar events and institutions committed to the preservation of memory reveal a dimension of Japanese American life that is rich and vital but seldom recognized by American studies and religious studies scholars alike. What has emerged from the collective experience of war and internment is a faith that is tied to no particular religious tradition but that takes racial-ethnic identity as its starting point. Post-immigrant Japanese Americans have developed no less than their own brand of *civil religion* that intimately links them to public life.

Historical trials, especially that of internment, have forged a strong sense of racial-ethnic identity, cultural memory, and social justice that is carried forward in contemporary institutions, such as the Civil Liberties Act of 1988, the Japanese American National Museum, and the pilgrimage to Manzanar. In significant ways, organizations, projects, and modern-day rituals such as these have become a "sacred" part of the community: they bind it together and give it a specific sense of meaning and mission that is distinctly religious in nature (on this sort of "popular religion," see Albanese [1996]). Along these lines, one needs to reconceptualize the spiritual legacy that has been passed on from one generation of Japanese Americans to another and to perhaps reconceive of the way in which we understand religion, immigration, and civic life and its relation to racial-ethnic identity.

Contours of Japanese American Religious Life

The majority of Japanese Americans who now reside in the United States are not foreign-born. Rather, they trace their descent from the largest influx of Japanese immigrants who arrived on America soil at the turn of the century. In search of economic opportunity, these immigrants were met by unfriendly labor conditions and anti-Asian prejudice. Despite these hardships, Japanese American communities thrived in America as the immigrant or Issei generation put down roots, reared their children (the second-generation Nisei), and established ethnic-specific networks and institutions, including Buddhist temples and Christian churches.

The history and travails of the Issei and their progeny have been well documented in numerous historical accounts, literary works, oral histories, and video documentaries. These works also include historical and sociological analyses of the role of religious institutions in Japanese American life. Many of these studies cite the significance of these institutions for the immigrant ethnic population, especially the Buddhist Churches of America (BCA), which has served a "key role in [Japanese American] survival and adaptation" (Kashima, 1977: xi; see also Yoo, 2000).

Nearly five generations since the arrival of the first immigrants, Japanese Americans are pegged as an American success story—not only in terms of economic achievement but also in terms of acculturation and the extent to which they are socially integrated into American society. Popular accounts feature Japanese Americans as a "model minority," increasingly assimilated into the American mainstream (beginning with William Petersen's oft-cited 1966 *New York Times Magazine* article). The scholarly literature seems to back up this view (e.g., Horinouchi, 1973; Levine and Rhodes, 1981; Montero, 1980; Morawska, 1994; Petersen, 1977). In these studies, religious affiliation and involvement in ethnic-specific religious institutions is often used as a measure of Japanese Americans' incorporation into American life and institutions (Montero, 1980; Woodrum, 1981).

Some would contend that the staggering decline in Buddhist temple membership is a sign of the continuing pattern toward complete assimilation. At its peak in 1960, BCA roll books listed approximately 50,000 families as official members of the church; in 1977, that number was cut in half (21,600); and in 1995, BCA membership was down to 17,755 families. Social scientific surveys confirm this trend, as Buddhist affiliation took a downward plunge (6–12 percent), with an accommodating increase in Christian, "no religion," and "other" categories. Because of this decline, one would hypothesize the eventual disappearance of BCA temples and ethnic-specific Christian churches. However, while there is definite "downsizing" taking place, these institutions continue to survive. A recent study highlights Japanese American Buddhism's resiliency along the West Coast, especially in areas that enjoy both a high concentration of Japanese Americans and an ethnically diverse population (Fugita and Fernandez, 2002). In the Christian case, several churches have redefined themselves as pan-Asian or multiracial institutions—a move that seems to challenge our understanding of a straight-line assimilation of Japanese American immigrants and their descendants (Jeung, 2004).

The above discussion provides a brief overview of how scholars have tackled the relationship between Japanese American religion and ethnicity. These analyses boast two salient features: (1) conventional definitions of religion and religious affiliation; and (2) a preoccupation with assimilation, specifically the way in which religious institutions factor into the assimilation process (but see Hayashi, 2003; Kurashige, 2002; Okihiro, 1984). As such, I would argue that the view we have of Nikkei religiosity and especially its relation to American public life is limited and potentially misleading.

First, conventional definitions do not help us conceive of how the early immigrants from Japan might have understood religion; rather, they rely on a western notion of religion as fairly contained systems of belief and practice (e.g., "Buddhism"). Furthermore, religion is seen as something discrete—a distinct part of human existence apart from the political, social, and cultural. For those migrating from prewar Japan, it is more accurate to think of these dimensions as incredibly fluid—a legacy that is interesting and necessary to think about in relation to their American-born children and grandchildren.

Second, assimilation models only look at the extent to which Japanese Americans adjust or "fit into" the current American milieu. Social scientists and others who use this model wish to analyze how much "they" (Japanese) have become like "us" (Americans), or at the very least discern the level to which the ethnic community has integrated into American society; the analysis of change is unidirectional. Such a framework downplays the community's own self-definition and blinds the researcher from acknowledging specific historical responses and unique contributions of the group. It does not allow one to consider the impact of Japanese Americans on American identity and experience (Alba and Nee, 2003).

Considering Japanese Americans within the larger history of American religions is tricky, and previous treatments offer only limited insight. Because of their status as ethnic and religious minorities, the study of Japanese American religious experience often finds itself between two bookends. On the one end, Japanese Americans are often compared with earlier European immigrants, who brought with them ethnically defined versions of their religious faith but who eventually adopted more "rational" forms of religiosity. On the other end, Nikkei religions, by merit of their Asian religious roots, are discussed in relation to recent Asian migrants, who arrived in the "post-65" era. In either case, Japanese American religions are still treated in scholarly writing as an *immigrant* phenomenon.

The term "immigrant" denotes an individual who was born outside of the United States but now makes the country his or her home. An "immigrant community" is an ethnic group mainly comprising such individuals who share the same ethnic background or come from the same country of national origin. Despite the usefulness of these concepts, they are technical definitions and do not necessarily capture Americans' everyday understanding of the term "immigrant." Indeed, the popular notion relies on this simple foundation but fuses onto it stereotypical meanings with which we are all familiar: the hopeful dreamer, hard-working migrant, out-of-place newcomer, ambitious foreigner, self-serving menace. These meanings have different accents and casts, depending on the racial-ethnic identity of the immigrant group, as well as their country of origin. As Lisa Lowe notes:

> Asian immigrants come as fundamentally "foreign" origins antipathetic to the modern American society that "discovers," "welcomes," and "domesticates" them. A national memory haunts the conception of the Asian American, persisting beyond the repeal of actual laws prohibiting Asians from citizenship and sustained by the wars in Asia, in which the Asian is always seen as an immigrant, as the "foreigner-within," even when born in the United States and the descendant of generations born here before. (1996: 5–6)

It is from this nexus of social meanings that I wish to discuss and consider Japanese Americans, religion, and public life. I would assert that no matter how long—that is, how many *generations*—one's family has resided in the United States, Asian Americans continue to be chained to their immigrant past (Tuan, 1999). Because of their racial uniform and religious background, they are often corralled with the newest wave of Asian immigrants. In everyday life, Japanese Americans (and Asian Americans of post-immigrant generations) rarely escape the question from a "kind" inquirer: "Do you speak English?" or "Where are you from?" or "Are you Buddhist?" Japanese Americans are saddled with the burden of acting as authentic translators for a Japanese religion and culture from which they are generationally and geographically removed.

This situation, however, does give rise to the interesting question: What happens to an immigrant group over time, especially when that group is perpetually linked to its immigrant roots, alien status, and foreign religious beliefs? In the case of Japanese Americans, such conditions have had traumatic consequences, which, in turn, have given birth to a new form of Japanese American civil religious consciousness.

Critical Faith

As historian Roger Daniels (2002: 303) notes: "The wartime exile and incarceration is the transcendent event of Japanese American history." The Nikkei community[1] suffered its most harrowing blow during World War II, as those of Japanese ancestry came under suspicion and West Coast Japanese Americans were rounded up and interned. More than any other, this event has become the defining moment in Japanese American history—the one that both informs and haunts Japanese American identity, collective and individual, to this day. Daniel's characterization highlights the overwhelming significance that wartime experience holds for Japanese Americans. But how, exactly, did this event shape Japanese American historical consciousness, and in what ways is the event "exceptional"—that is, beyond the realm of the everyday and formative of a larger sense of the group's mission and identity? How does it continue to inform Japanese American political and cultural pathways and take on an almost religious significance?

Scholarship that touches on the intersection of religion and civic engagement in Japanese American life often points out the ways in which ethnic-specific institutions fostered an ethical outlook in concert with American ideals or the cooperative merger of the temple and American civic institutions: for example, the Boy Scouts of America as a temple-sponsored organization (Kashima, 1977; Pierce, 2000). In a more critical vein, Gary Okihiro (1984) speaks about the way in which Buddhism and other folk religious practices functioned as a means of resistance during the internment period. And more recently, Duncan Williams (2006) critically assesses the government's treatment of Buddhist ministers during World War II in order to draw parallels between the plight of that period's Buddhists and post-9/11 Muslims—parallels that were immediately recognized by the Japanese American political and religious leaders after the fall of the World Trade Center. Here, the consideration of religious identity and its intersection with race offers insight as Americans struggle to deal with the non-Christian, non-White Other in their midst.

While these studies highlight the role that religion plays in Nikkei civic engagement, they reveal only part of the civil religious story. To offer a more illuminating picture of Japanese Americans, religion, and public life, one is compelled to background conventional definitions of religion and religious affiliation (Buddhist, Protestant Christian, Catholic, etc.), which characterize a great deal of the studies on Japanese American religions, in favor of a new lens. This lens should accommodate a sense of the religious that is more reflective of a Japanese American sensibility. David Hirano (1974: 2) states that "the difference between the American view of religion and the Japanese view is that the Japanese did not compartmentalize religion. Religion was a part of and inseparable from life." For immigrant Japanese Americans and, one may argue, their descendants, the boundaries between religion, politics, and culture are porous. In addition, one also needs to consider the elements of Japanese American religious experience that have been most defining for the community itself—for example, interdependence, reciprocity, care, and compassion (Clark, 2002). These values find their expression outside the bounds of religious institutions and affiliations, and they strongly link the individual's identity to a wider sense of the collective.

Such a sensibility is perhaps best illustrated through a concrete example. A third-generation Japanese American (Sansei) recounts how, during his time as a seminary student, he had the opportunity to meet Jitsuo Morikawa, a respected Baptist pastor and theologian in the Japanese American community.[2] He asked Morikawa what he should do after he completed his seminary degree. Instead of steering the young Sansei toward a career as a minister or pastoral care worker, Morikawa counseled that he should think about serving Asian American youth, *not* in a religious capacity but as an Asian American student services administrator who would help instill in these youth pride in their ethnic heritage and offer them a sense of belonging. The young seminary student did just that and now sees his work as a realization of his ministerial training and an extension of his religious background. Such stories as this are not uncommon and demonstrate an interwoven sense of religion (spiritual healing and development), politics (an awareness of discrimination and prejudice), and culture (kinship and acceptance) that is not confined to the walls of the church.

This understanding of religion is not one that is wholly unfamiliar to most in the United States. Perhaps the concept that best embodies this intermingling of the religious, cultural, and political is the one of American civil religion. This term achieved its greatest prominence, especially in academic circles, through the writings of sociologist Robert Bellah (1967). "Civil religion," according to Bellah (1975: 3) is "that religious dimension found . . . in the life of every people, through which it interprets its historical experience in the light of transcendent reality." For many in the United States, this "transcendent reality" is shaped by both the Christian tradition and Roman republicanism, which, in turn, lends meaning and justification to the principles of "democracy," "freedom," and "equality" before the law. Americans affirm their faith in these principles and to the nation through a shared set of "beliefs, symbols, and rituals" (e.g., the Bill of Rights, the Lincoln Memorial, the inauguration of the president). Civil religious institutions are historical creations, yet they need no justification. For instance, the Constitution "does not call upon any source of sacredness higher than itself and its makers." Ultimately, civil religion has an integrative function and binds the individual citizen psychically and spiritually to her fellow Americans and to the nation-state (Albanese, 1992; Wuthnow, 1998b).

It is both tempting and treacherous to think of American civil religion in relation to Japanese Americans—tempting, because the Japanese Americans are often upheld as a political "model minority." Despite the unwarranted suspicion and mistreatment Japanese Americans suffered at the hands of the government and their fellow compatriots during World War II, they have "proven" their loyalty and worth as U.S. citizens. They have fought meritoriously in battle and become dedicated public servants. As actor George Takei remarks: "We are part of the fabric of America, from U.S. senators to your schoolteacher to your local banker" (quoted in O'Neill, n.d.). In 1941 Japanese American Citizens League leader Mike Masaoka stood in front of the U.S. Senate and declared: "I am proud that I am an American of Japanese ancestry. I believe in this nation's institutions, ideals, and traditions; I glory in her heritage; I boast of her history; I trust in her future."[3] Masaoka penned this "Japanese American Creed" as a declaration of his community's allegiance to the country—an obvious proclamation of American civil religious faith.

It is treacherous to relate Japanese Americans to U.S. civil religion because not all Japanese Americans share Masaoka's fervent belief and unabashed patriotism (see, e.g., Hashima, 2007). There were those who questioned, if not actively resisted, the government's decision to intern 112,000 Japanese Americans, and this legacy of dissent has an active voice in the Japanese American community today (Abe, 2000; Muller, 2001). While

Bellah's American civil religion framework is able to accommodate this dissent, it does not necessarily draw our attention to the ways in which the Japanese American community has negotiated internal controversy, nor does it speak to the unique manner in which Japanese American civil religion is expressed. Japanese Americans did not adopt the larger American civil religious discourse part and parcel; to do so would be to retain a naive understanding and credulous embrace of the same institutions that were used to justify their internment. Rather, what emerges out of internment's legacy and an extended history of racial-ethnic oppression is something that one may call a "critical faith." This critical faith does not abandon civil religious principles (equality before the law, due process, and so on) but finds it necessary to reinterpret these ideals in relation to the Japanese American experience and to make known that experience (Alba and Nee, 2003; Kibria, 2002).

"Times of trial" radically redefine, if not create, civil religious expression. During these moments of crisis, the "deepest questions of national meaning" are raised that often require the formation of new myths, symbols, and rituals to support a transformed sense of a people's self-identity. The "time of trial" for Japanese Americans came in the form of internment—mass incarceration at the hands of the U.S. government. Japanese American historical consciousness is not something that was a spontaneous and sudden result of internment. Collectively, Japanese Americans did not seek reparations immediately after the war, nor did they readily acknowledge governmental injustice or even their own psychic trauma. Historical consciousness developed over time, as the community could articulate the abuses suffered and negotiate their own reflective response. One can see this development through a historical examination of the Nikkei debates over internment and the shift from a rhetoric of "loyalty" to one of "justice." From their efforts to properly memorialize the event to the hard-fought battle for redress, Japanese Americans began to realize their critical faith. And the arduous process of recollection and reclamation began to give shape to a new brand of civil religion—one in which it became the community's duty to recount the injustice and to make sure that it did not happen again.

Japanese American civil religion has taken on unique forms and is supported by its own set of sacred texts, sites, and rituals. Perhaps most foundational are two government documents that serve as historical bookends for the internment experience: Executive Order 9066 and the Civil Liberties Act of 1988. On February 19, 1942, Franklin D. Roosevelt formally approved E. O. 9066, which allowed for the forced removal and detention of Japanese Americans without trial or hearings. Nearly 50 years and eight presidents later, Ronald Reagan signed into law the Civil Liberties Act of 1988. Although Roosevelt's executive order was officially rescinded in 1976, the Civil Liberties Act carried full acknowledgment of the nation's wrongdoing by awarding a $20,000 reparations payment to each surviving internee, along with an official apology from the president made on behalf of the American people. Central to the apology was the acknowledgment that the government's actions "were rooted deeply in race prejudice, wartime hysteria, and a lack of political leadership" and that this moment in American history should not be forgotten or erased. The act, toward this end, also established a public education fund "to finance efforts to inform the public about the internment so as to prevent the recurrence of any similar event." In 2000, Reagan's words—"Here we admit a wrong . . ."—were prominently carved into the stone facade of the National Japanese American Memorial to Patriotism in Washington, D.C., as a permanent reminder of the nation's guilt.

Although the Civil Liberties Act brought a great deal of closure for Japanese American internees, former servicemen, and their descendants, it did not end the ordeal of the concentration camps and racial prejudice. The legacy of internment remains ever present for many Nikkei. Japanese American Nisei still deal with the psychological trauma and lingering feelings of guilt and shame over the event. (Japanese Americans define themselves generationally as Issei, the immigrant or "first" generation; Nisei, the first generation born in the United States, hence the "second" generation; Sansei, the "third" generation; Yonsei, the "fourth"; and Gosei, the "fifth.") Their progeny also suffer the effects of the violation, as Sansei, Yonsei, and Gosei "continue to search for a sense of cultural identity and historical integrity" (National Asian American Telecommunications Association, n.d.). Common to many descendants is an intense recognition of the suffering and sacrifice of the Issei and Nisei and the need to pay homage to their Japanese American ancestors. The collective memory of internment also compels Japanese Americans to forge sympathetic connections with other communities of color and new immigrant groups who are at risk of suffering the same racist mistreatment and propels an intense mission to safeguard against governmental injustice.

Executive Order 9066 and the Civil Liberties Act could certainly be read as significant historical markers in the development of a national or American civil religious sensibility: the former as a document that represents a shameful moment in America's past, and the latter as an acknowledgment of injustice, if not an act of contrition. However, incorporating these documents and events into the larger American civil religious frame easily erases the agency of Japanese Americans and the civil religious movement that developed to finally bring about the U.S. government's recognition of its misdeeds. It sweeps aside subcultural forms of opposition and resistance that can never be fully assimilated and stand as an "offense" to U.S. national life.

In the following sections, I discuss some of the texts, sites, and rituals that have come to form the basis of a Japanese American civil religion and then go on to analyze the patterns of religious practice and commitment that underwrite this civil religious engagement. My analysis here of the Commission on Wartime Relocation and Internment of Civilians (CWRIC) hearings, the Japanese American National Museum, and the pilgrimage to Manzanar describes the emergence of these events and institutions and highlights their status as significant expressions of a critical faith.[4] An in-depth understanding of Japanese American civil religion provides an example of political *and* religious resistance that has import for other marginalized groups who have formulated similar traditions and for those currently under siege who are engaged in developing their own critical response.

New Testament(s)

> For the forced incarceration during the war, which did so much to thwart my relationships with others, I am bitter. For the fear instilled in me at the hands of my own government, I am bitter. For the unnecessary feelings of shame inflicted on my father and my family for unfounded and never explained reasons, I am bitter.
> —former internee's testimony at the CWRIC hearings
> (quoted in Watanabe, 2003: 16)

The initial response to mass incarceration of many Japanese Americans could be encapsulated in the phrase "shikata ga nai," or "it cannot be helped now." The philosophy behind the term should not be mistaken as mere fatalism; rather, it implies the need to move on with life in the face of circumstances that one cannot adequately explain and does not have the power to change. As an ethnic group who had very little recourse at the time, Japanese Americans were served well by this principle. It allowed Nikkei internees to "concentrate on survival, rather than on the things they'd lost" (John Tateishi, quoted in Magagnini, 2001; see also Ishizuka, 2006: 125–26).

In hindsight, the phrase is associated with an attitude of passivity, and this passivity is then read as an essentialized part of the Japanese character. Such an interpretation, however, does not take into account the contextual use of the phrase. The intentional logic behind *shikata ga nai* is that one should not concentrate on the things one cannot change. As such, it bespeaks a spiritual philosophy that allows one to focus on the things one can do something about. The principle is also provisionally applied. As circumstances allow for greater action, *shikata ga nai* does not relieve one of responsibility. Its ultimate aim is not to debilitate but to revitalize in the face of adversities that seem beyond one's control.

As Japanese Americans regained themselves in the postwar years, a sense of what they believed could and should be changed grew. Nikkei, especially the Sansei generation, who participated in the civil rights and ethnic consciousness movements of the 1960s, actually served as a catalyst for this growing awareness (Takahashi, 1997). Through a framework of racial justice, Japanese Americans were able to fully recognize that internment was wrong; they were also able to situate the event in the broader context of the nation's racist history in which blacks, Latinos, and Native Americans were also victims. Ethnic pride, which these movements also encouraged, provided the impetus for cultural recovery and expression. Japanese Americans no longer needed to authenticate their identity vis à vis Japan or the United States but found it imperative to define themselves in relation to their own unique history.

For the Nisei, the process of regeneration and healing was complex. Silence was how this generation and their parents first responded to the event. However, plagued by the ghosts of the war and internment, they could not simply move on as if the past never happened; "I can never forget," as the Japanese American soldiers of the 100th Infantry Battalion and 442nd Regimental Combat Team proclaim (Chang, 1991). Bolstered by the Sansei example, many Nisei started to come to terms with the trauma that they and the Issei had suffered. They began to realize the import of their experiences and the need to make their stories heard so that their children would know of their suffering. These stories also were meant to serve as a reminder so that "never again shall any group be denied liberty and the rights of citizenship."⁵ "I can never forget" transformed into the injunction "Never forget," and an era of silence eventually evolved into an era of speech (Cheung, 1993; Yamamoto, 1999).

Hence, the interests of the various generations and groups of Japanese Americans did not coalesce naturally but entailed an extended process of negotiation and awareness. The Civil Liberties Act of 1988 was actually a result of the coalitional efforts of three distinct political groups within the Japanese American community: the Japanese American Citizens League (JACL), the National Coalition for Redress/Reparations (NCRR), and the National Council for Japanese American Redress (NCJAR), as well as Japanese American politicians and everyday citizens (on the redress movement, see Daniels, Taylor, and Kitano, 1992; Hatamiya, 1993; Hohri, 1988; Laremont, 2001; Maki, Kitani, and Berthold, 1999; Shimabukuro, 2001; Takezawa, 1995). While these organizations and their members were bitterly divided on certain issues (especially when it came to the issue of draft resisters and "no-no boys"—those who refused to take the government's loyalty oath during wartime), they did agree that the U.S. government had committed a grave injustice against the Nikkei community and that this betrayal needed to be fully acknowledged to the satisfaction of the community. They also agreed that the story of Japanese Americans was one that needed to be recorded and told for the sake of all in the United States.

The institutionalization of memory therefore becomes significant in the larger mission of education and healing for Japanese Americans. The ways in which memory is reenacted and repurposed lend Japanese American civil religion its distinctive character. One of these ways was made most evident in 1981 at the congressional hearings held by the CWRIC. The commission was established to determine whether the incarceration of Japanese Americans during World War II constituted a military necessity. It also sought to assess the impact of internment on the Japanese American community. More than 750 Japanese Americans in six cities offered emotional, often heart-wrenching testimony to the committee. For these individuals, their families, and the community at large, the hearings proved a cathartic experience: "Nisei testified and spoke of the humiliating and degrading treatment experienced by these American citizens simply because of their race" (James Okutsu, quoted in Spickard, 1996: 155).

These testimonies not only chronicled severe financial, cultural, and personal loss but also gave expression to years of anger, frustration, and rage.

The CWRIC issued its formal report in 1983, finding that "military necessity" was not at the heart of the government's decision to incarcerate West Coast Japanese Americans; rather, "race prejudice, war hysteria, and a failure in [U.S.] political leadership" were the decisive factors (U.S. Commission on Wartime Relocation and Internment of Civilians, 1997). In its report, the commission recommended redress for Japanese Americans, including a reparations payment to each evacuee. While the Civil Liberties Act of 1988 and the presidential apology that accompanied it stand as landmark documents, it is the individual testimonies of the 750-plus internees that are equally if not more significant. In the fullest sense of the word, these accounts form a "testament": tangible proof, a statement of belief, a legacy and covenant. They bear witness to the injustice suffered and introduce into congressional record the good faith and sacrifice of a marginalized people. Furthermore, these testimonies serve as cautionary tales of the type of oppression that racial and religious minorities can experience, not only at the hands of fellow citizens but also the U.S. government. As humble, yet passionate reminders, they also reveal that such abuse does not end with the traumatic event or with its disclosure but reverberates through the group for generations.

By all accounts, the CWRIC hearings were a turning point in the struggle for redress. They galvanized the Japanese American community and lent the cause a broadbased support. As Nisei publicly shared their testimonies and heard those of others, they realized that they each had an important story to tell. Common in theme, but individually distinct in detail, these stories spiritually bind Japanese Americans together and are referenced again and again in historical documents, in lesson plans, and by the internees and their families themselves.

Re-Siting Memory

In the heart of the Little Tokyo district in downtown Los Angeles, one can cross over to the north end of First Street onto a large plaza. Looking to the left, one sees a beautifully ornate yet understated doorway that was once the entrance to the Nishi Hongwanji Buddhist temple. Looking to the right, one is struck by a more imposing structure—a contemporary pavilion of glass, steel, and brick. In feel and design, there is a stark contrast between the two buildings. However, both structures are meant to

The Japanese American National Museum

form an integrated unit as part of the Japanese American National Museum (JANM).

Viewed together, the two Los Angeles buildings provide a historical metaphor for Nikkei identity. The temple, which initially housed the museum's exhibition space, was built by Japanese immigrants in 1925. Designed by Edgar Cline, it is an eclectic mix of Japanese temple architecture and the Egyptian revival style that was popular in the United States in the 1920s. As is the case with many immigrant churches, the building served a number of functions: worship space, social hall, movie theater, and rental office space. Japanese Americans during the war used the temple to store their belongings as they were led off to internment.

In 1969, the Nishi Hongwanji congregation constructed a new temple just down the street—grand in proportion and Japanese in design. As JANM curator Karin Higa remarks: "[The new temple] seems to reflect the sixties and seventies longing for authenticity and ethnic identity" (quoted in Moffat, 1993: 1). After the old temple was abandoned, it fell into disrepair and was eventually taken over by the city. It sat, ready for demolition, until it received a new lease on life in 1986 as the proposed site of the new museum and was carefully restored and retrofitted.

In relation to its ancestral relative, the pavilion reflects a postmodern sensibility. The building's materials and design were chosen to "express the Japanese reverence for materials and craftsmanship, [while] at the same time creating forms that are bold and contemporary and reflect in an abstract way the rich urban context" (Japanese American National Museum, "Architectural Fact Sheet," n.d.). Both in the reflection of the curved glass wall and in its complementary building materials, the pavilion intentionally mirrors and enters into a dialogue with the older temple. By considering the architecture of both buildings, one can sense an increasing comfort and conscious embrace of the Japanese American past. However, this new ethos does not romanticize that past and attempt to re-create it in every detail; instead, it pursues a conversation with what has gone before.

The JANM began in 1982 as a joint effort between Little Tokyo businessman and former internee Bruce Kaji and Japanese American war veterans Young Oak Kim and Y. B. Mamiya. The museum received nonprofit status in 1985, and over the course of the next seven years, Kaji, Kim, and Mamiya, as well as a dedicated corps of volunteers, raised the more than $10 million needed to renovate the old Buddhist temple. Although the museum was without a building throughout the 1980s, it hired a full-time curator/researcher, who embarked on developing its collections, including an extensive photo and moving image archive. It also designed and sponsored its first installations and exhibited these "beyond its metaphorical walls" in Honolulu, New York, and Los Angeles.

The JANM opened its real doors in 1992. The museum then set its sights on the construction of a new pavilion to house its growing collections and staff; six years and $45 million later, JANM realized that goal as well. The 85,000-square-foot pavilion features a national resource center, life history studio, education centers, and stone and water garden, as well as exhibition and museum staff space. The expansive central hall allows for large-scale special events and lectures. While corporations and government agencies provided the bulk of the funding for both building projects, the museum also received amazing widespread assistance from Japanese Americans. In addition to financial support, Japanese Americans across the country generously donated many of the artifacts and photos that now make up the museum's collection (Kikumura-Yano, Hirabayashi, and Hirabayashi, 2005).

JANM is set apart from other ethnic museums around the country (Berger, 2003), not only in terms of its size and resources but also in terms of its aim: "The mission of the Japanese American National Museum is to promote understanding and appreciation of America's ethnic and cultural diversity by preserving, interpreting, and sharing the experiences of Japanese Americans" (Japanese American National Museum, "Mission," n.d.; see also Nishime, 2004/5). While the institution's raison d'être derives from the quest to document the Japanese American experience and preserve historical memory, this memory is harnessed for a larger goal: "to promote understanding and appreciation of America's ethnic and cultural diversity."

This mission is at once general and specific. It is general in the sense that it reaches for universal significance: it pushes Japanese American identity beyond itself. At the same time, it sees Japanese American experience as offering relevant lessons and insights for others in the United States. This universalization is not abstract, however. The museum's definition of "Americanness" clearly highlights the ideal of cultural diversity, tackling issues of difference as its primary concern. Here, cultural memory is consciously deployed as a safeguard "against the prejudice that threatens liberty and equality in a democratic society" (Japanese American National Museum, "Mission").

JANM's mission is reflected in its exhibits and programming. While much of the gallery space is dedicated to chronicling the Japanese American experience through historical exhibits, the museum also has sponsored shows dedicated to Flo Oy Wong's work on Angel Island and Asian American immigration, contemporary art by Los Angeles artists, and the community history of the multiethnic Boyle Heights area. The museum also sponsors discussion forums, craft classes, artist talks, walking tours, and a wide variety of performances.

Finally, the museum's Life History Program seeks to document the histories of individual Japanese Americans through oral and videotaped interviews, as well as written texts. This is arguably JANM's most significant program, since it perfectly engenders the goals of the museum:

> Oral history is particularly important for the Japanese American community. As a community of color, our history is often marginalized from the mainstream record. Oral history provides a way for marginalized communities to record and interpret the meaning of historical events from their own perspective. No longer is history told about them, but rather history is told by them. (Japanese American National Museum, "Museums Life History Program," n.d.)

As the program description suggests, oral history constitutes a privileged method and important community practice. Similar oral history projects by other Nikkei organizations and educational institutions across the country abound (Hansen, 1995). Like the personal testimonies offered by former internees at the CWRIC hearings, these accounts uphold the uniqueness of individual lives and offer a multidimensional, multiperspective view of social forces and events that have shaped the Japanese American collective psyche. History becomes something that is not authoritatively dictated and officially sanctioned but is mutually informed and more wholly realized; every person has an important story to tell.

In essence, JANM has come to embody the spiritual ethos of the community. The museum becomes a sacred storehouse of cultural memory and spiritually links current generations of Japanese Americans with their immigrant ancestors. By visiting the museum, second, third, fourth, and subsequent generations of Japanese Americans in a sense pay homage to their forebears. In relation to American public life, JANM also concretizes a sense of mission as it compels museum visitors to confront issues of racial oppression, historical injustice, ethnic identity, and cultural survival (for alternative views of the museum, see Fujitana, 1997; Ishizuka, 2006; Kikumura-Yano et al., 2005; Kurashige, 2002; Yoo, 1996). Through its various exhibits, programs, and, indeed, the very physical presence of the museum itself, JANM enacts a critical faith—a faith in its ability to "transform lives and strengthen community," as well as to "create a more just America and, ultimately, a better world" (Japanese American National Museum, "Mission").

Rituals of Remembrance

Words, images, and sounds all serve as important avenues of memory. However, as S. Brent Plate (2002: 196) comments: "Memory is not an activity of the mind only, but of the body and of the minds and bodies of others. . . . Remembering is a dynamic, interactive process." Rituals play an important role in the preservation of memory as they involve the active bodily participation of all those who are present. Japanese American civil religion similarly involves rituals that bring a community together to remember the past for the sake of the present. These modern-day rituals, such as the annual pilgrimage to Manazar that opens this article (and the Tule Lake Pilgrimage, which began in 1974), initially brought together Japanese Americans, mainly Sansei, who often lived in the shadow of their parents' and grandparents' silence, and helped them begin to recover a shattered past. As Joanne Doi (2002: 277; see also Doi, 2007) explains: "These [events] were attempts to search out the truth of the history bound up in the silence of the Nisei and the classroom. The magnitude of the silence of the Nisei helped form the voice of the Sansei; the Nisei's absence of outward emotional response mobilized the Sansei to begin to speak out." In a significant sense, the annual pilgrimages and Days of Remembrance[6] prepared the way for more intense struggles (the fight for redress) and extended projects (the Japanese American National Museum).

Manzanar Pilgrimage 2003. Photograph by author.

Even though many of the ambitious goals of the Japanese American community have been realized, the pilgrimages continue to fulfill an important function. Nisei join their children and grandchildren on these journeys, and the rituals have become intergenerational affairs. As such, they provide the opportunity to share long-suppressed stories and feelings with one another. The pilgrimages also draw non-Japanese Americans from a variety of racial-ethnic backgrounds. At the Manzanar pilgrimage ceremony, Latino schoolchildren can be seen lining the rows in front of the cemetery monument. They, along with Arab Americans, African Americans, Jewish and Anglo Americans, as well as other Asian Americans, listen to the prayers and chanting of the various priests and place flowers on the monument.

As many note, the flower offering is one of the most powerful parts of the service. Through the act of the offering, individuals forge their own relations to the past and contemplate the larger forces that led them to this place and time. They enter into a sacred economy in which the ancestors are enlivened and past, present, and future meld into one. At the very least, they are caught up in the communal nature of the moment. At the end of the ceremony, participants are invited to dance the *Tanko Bushi* (coal miner's dance). This traditional dance, associated with Obon odori festivals observed at Buddhist temples throughout the United States, is performed to honor the dead—most notably to recognize their true unselfish nature and celebrate their release. Those who join in the dance may not fully understand the religious dimensions of the ritual, but they realize their movements in bittersweet and now hopeful remembrance. Through sound, motion, and rhythm, participants become bonded with their Japanese American ancestors and to one other. For the people who share in the annual pilgrimages, psychic connections are highly specific, as each participant is drawn into the history of internment and is led to consider the consequences of injustice and betrayal, as well as to recognize perseverance and reaffirm hope. On multiple levels and in multiple ways, the pilgrimage ritual encourages a spiritual reconciliation and healing that other ethnic institutions—secular and religious—do not usually provide.

Equally significant, the pilgrimages nurture a strong political awareness among its participants. In 2003, for instance, the Manzanar Committee chose "A Call to Action: End Racial Profiling, Speak Out for Peace" as the pilgrimage's official theme. In the 9/11 aftermath, Japanese Americans readily see the government's detention of Arab, Muslim, and Sikh citizens as eerily similar to their own experience. Japanese American organizations were some of the first to protest the unfair treatment of these marginalized groups. As such, there have been new alliances forged among various communities, and many Japanese Americans are discovering that their historical experience is more relevant than ever before.

Unlike the government's response in 1942, President George W. Bush in 2001 made a forthright appeal to the American people to treat Americans of Arab, Muslim, and Sikh descent with "respect and dignity" soon after the fall of the Twin Towers. While Bush's plea drew from the rhetoric of liberal multiculturalism, statements issued by Japanese American organizations politicized the situation by drawing attention not only to the government's racist history but also to "the link between domestic and foreign policies, or U.S. state racism at home and U.S.-led wars abroad" (Naber, 2002: 226–27). The stance of these organizations remained critically watchful; the necessity to act propelled by their own unique historical calling: "We should step up and speak out. . . . Maybe [Muslim

Americans] can't make any statements against the war because they are feeling so targeted just like we did" (Lisa Nakamura, quoted in Naber, 2002: 227).

Religious Patterns of Commitment

The year 2004 marked an important event for the Manzanar Committee, the Japanese American community, and those who joined the pilgrimage annually: the U.S. Park Services officially opened the Manzanar Interpretive Center at the Manzanar National Historic Site (Creef, 2004; Hayashi, 2003). The Interpretive Center, much like the Japanese American National Museum, features interactive exhibits chronicling the wartime internment of Japanese Americans, as well as the rich history of the area, educational programs, and its own oral history project. In addition, the on-site "museum" includes a reconstructed guard shack and mess hall. In the back of the center is a screen that lists the names of the 10,000 people interned at the camp. The (re)construction of the camp and its educational arm, the Interpretive Center, appears to bring Japanese American history back into the American civil religious fold. As Sue Embrey, the longtime Manzanar Committee chair seems to concede: "The Interpretive Center is important because it needs to show to the world that America is strong as it makes amends for the wrongs it has committed, and that we will always remember Manzanar because of that" (Embrey, 2004). A year later, however, the committee reaffirmed the critical function of the Manzanar Pilgrimage. Embrey proclaimed, "We need to make sure history doesn't repeat itself. Muslim and Arab Americans are being held at Guantanamo Bay without charge or trial. It reminds us of the Issei who were also held without charge for many years during WWII" (Embrey, 2005).

In 2005, history came full circle as the Japanese American National Museum's sister institution, the National Center for the Preservation of Democracy, made its home in the old Nishi Hongwanji Buddhist temple. With its aim to "promote the principles of democracy, diversity, and civic involvement" (National Center for the Preservation of Democracy, "Vision and Mission," n.d.), the National Center appears in lockstep with an American civil religious agenda. But a closer look reveals the center's particular standpoint—one that is informed by its Japanese American historical roots. Its premier exhibition, "Fighting for Democracy"—available both in virtual and physical form—takes the visitor through a series of

Memorial service for Japanese American Servicemen killed in action. Gila River Relocation Center, Arizona. Photographer unknown. War Relocation Authority.

exercises or scenes that juxtapose and connect the lives of Mexican Americans, African Americans, Filipino Americans, Chinese Americans, and other ethnic minorities in the United States during World War II (National Center for the Preservation of Democracy, "Fighting for Democracy," n.d.). While great care is given to highlighting the diversity of wartime perspectives, it is the Japanese American experience that anchors the exhibition and demonstrates the center's emphasis on the "fragility" of individual rights and freedoms.

In an important sense, Japanese American civil religion remains in constant dialogue with its American counterpart—sharing much of its language and principles. But the texts, sites, and rituals that inform its stance remain historically unique. They are also influenced by religious and cultural traditions and ways of engaging the world that differ from the religious patterns of Christianity and Roman republicanism that undergird American civil religion (Bellah, 1975). Attention to these traditions and spiritual sensibilities is the key to fully understanding the distinctiveness of Japanese American civil religious formation and the spirit that sustains its vision.

Models for understanding the contours of a racial-ethnic group's civil religious engagement do exist. For instance, Jonathan Woocher (1986) delineates the process for American Jews. He outlines a number of Jewish American secular organizations in which ethnicity and religion merge to create a sphere of moral commitment and concern. Japanese Americans, likewise, draw from a traumatic history to create their own civic sphere. The Nikkei example also presents a unique and interesting perspective. Because of the religious diversity of the community, Japanese American civil religious expressions is usually not tied to one particular religious tradition; Japanese Americans had to negotiate, if not transcend, their particular religious affiliations. For the Issei and Nisei generations, such affiliations created cleavages within the community and even contentious rifts within families to the point that some Buddhists and Christians did not speak to each other. The mere fact that Japanese American Buddhists, Protestant Christians, Shintoists, Catholics, and others were interned both gave rise to a common experience to which these different groups would eventually refer and compelled them to find language and rituals that bridged their respective worldviews and sectarian concerns. This is not to say that particular religious traditions were abandoned for a more secular mode of engagement; rather, Japanese Americans found concepts that were faithful to those traditions and drew from a broadly conceived Japanese American spiritual culture. The language Japanese Americans use to express their commitments therefore may not stand out as religious. At the same time, it is subtly underwritten by a transcendent sense of identity and mission forged in the historical trials of internment and war, as well as informed by their particular spiritual culture.

Gary Okihiro (1984), in "Religion and Resistance in America's Concentration Camps," begins to investigate the sources that would foster a Japanese American civil religious outlook. In his investigation of "ethnic religion" in the camps (a term he uses interchangeably with "ethnic culture"), he isolates two "fundamental features of Japanese religious belief": (1) filial piety and ancestor worship; and (2) closeness of man, gods, and nature (225). The first dimension is especially relevant to an understanding of Japanese American civil religion:

> Filial piety, ancestor worship, and family and ethnic collectivity were cultural values which were emphasized in the home and stressed in the Buddhist churches and Japanese language schools. Those internal values were reinforced by external forces such as anti-Japanese agitation, barriers to Nisei assimilation and restrictive employment opportunities, and the concentration camps themselves which were pointed reminders to the Nisei that they were not considered to be "true Americans." (227)

Furthermore, this view of everyday relations and the collective was buttressed by a sense of heritage and peoplehood that was not necessarily tied to either the Japanese or the U.S. nation-state. The invocation of *Yamato damashii* ("Japanese spirit"), while seen by Wartime Relocation Authority officials as an expression of pro-Japan sentiment, was often rather invoked by Nikkei to summon the "customary virtues of perseverance, loyalty, forbearance, and sacrifice for the common good" (Okihiro, 1984: 228).

Viewing Japanese American spiritual culture in this integrated fashion allows one to identify the distinctive framework on which a Nikkei critical faith is built. The language of "paying respect" is often invoked during pilgrimages to internment sites, as are notions of "remembrance." These spiritually infused concepts and practices are linked to the ways Japanese Americans honor the dead across religious and sectarian lines. Homage to ancestors is most formally ritualized in Japanese American Buddhist traditions, in which loved ones who have passed away are memorialized through ritual activities that take place in the home, the temple, and the cemetery. (These traditions are also informally practiced by Nikkei Christians.) A person's death is marked not only by a funeral but also via a series of memorial services, both privately held by the family and publicly recognized by the *Sangha,* or congregation. While the details and sentiment surrounding these services vary according to Buddhist denomination, such rituals have genealogical links to *senzo kuyô,* or Japanese ancestral memorial rites, that are observed on a regular basis and which reinforce a sense of the ongoing interconnectedness between the living and the dead. Within this spiritual economy, the dead do occupy a distinct realm—but one that is in constant engagement with the living and is experienced more as part of the "seamless social continuum" (Pye, 1984: 61) than as a radical departure. Memory, therefore, is something that must be continually cared for and ritually maintained.

The Manzanar Pilgrimage and Days of Remembrance can be viewed as a *kuyô,* in which participants remember their Japanese Americans forebears and the event that so disrupted their lives. But perhaps more to the point, these events memorialize the *social death* of Japanese Americans— their racial exclusion in the United States—and ritually reaffirm this historical moment and social fact. Participation in these annual gatherings, therefore, is an obligation that redeploys memory in service of the living (including future generations) and can be distinguished from similar American civil religious rituals of memorialization, such as the Gettysburg

Address. In this "Lincolnian 'New Testament' among the civil scriptures," the Civil War is reinterpreted within the rubric of Christian sacrifice and viewed as an event that demands "a new birth of freedom" (Bellah, 1967). In contrast, Japanese American civil religion views death—both individual and social—not simply as a sacrifice in this Christian sense of unimaginable act and necessary rebirth but more as an extension of life that tempers the living. The dead—which here includes a sense of what used to be (Japanese American life before internment) and what they had hoped to become (fully accepted American subjects)—are ever present, but they only remain present through continual acts of attention and care.

Senzo kuyô also sheds light on the centrality of oral testimony and oral history for Japanese Americans. Within the religious cosmos of Japanese and, arguably, Japanese Americans, individuals do not exist as autonomous beings but as part of a network or web of human relations. As Dorinne Kondo (1990: 9) notes, within the Japanese worldview, there is a "fundamental connectedness of human beings to each other."

One of the wellsprings of such an understanding can be traced to the Buddhist tradition, including metaphors of "Indra's net" or, still closer to home, "The Golden Chain"—a verse that many Japanese American children learn as part of their Pure Land Buddhist upbringing:[7]

> I am a link in Lord Buddha's golden chain of love that stretches around the world. I must keep my link bright and strong. I will try to be kind and gentle to every living thing, and protect all who are weaker than myself. I will try to think pure and beautiful thoughts, to say pure and beautiful words, and to do pure and beautiful deeds, knowing that on what I do now depends my happiness and misery.
>
> May every link in Lord Buddha's golden chain of love become bright and strong and may we all attain perfect peace.

In Amida Buddha's "golden chain," each link is important, and one realizes not only that one's existence depends on others but also that one's life and actions are integral parts of the chain. In this everyday religious saying and its broader religious context, the significance of each person is recognized, and each one makes an important contribution to the whole. This sense of interdependence permeates relations among the living, as well as relations between the living and the dead. Such a framework lends each person's life, his individual perspective, an integrity and importance all its own.

While the "group orientation" of Japanese and Japanese American subjects is often emphasized in scholarly and popular accounts, a sense of the group—whether family, workplace, or nation—is inextricably tied to the value and worth of each individual. Again, through participation in memorial services, Japanese American religious subjects perform and embody this worldview as they both remember those loved ones who have passed away *and* reaffirm their ancestors (and ultimately themselves) as part of a larger network. The centrality of oral history—the need to capture individual voices and stories—emerges from this spiritual ethos. As previously mentioned, no one person's story takes precedence, but each provides a unique reflection of the collective experience (as each jewel in Indra's Net reflects the whole of Buddha nature). And without these individual pieces, the collective no longer exists or does so in an impoverished manner. As each person's life contributes to the chain of being, each person's testimony about internment and its legacy becomes a necessary component in the Japanese American civil religious framework.

The testimonies that make up the CWRIC hearings and other oral historical accounts therefore provide the epistemological foundation for Japanese American historical consciousness and its vision of justice ("coming to know") and the ontological foundation of its meaning and mission ("coming to be"). In a similar vein, the Japanese American National Museum as a repository of memory emerges as a key site and expression of this particular ethic that simultaneously recognizes the integrity of individual experience and the way in which this experience is interwoven into the larger fabric of communal meaning.[8] The museum on many levels can be likened to a Japanese home altar in its structure and function—formal and resolute in its overall focus, yet improvisationally defined by its Japanese American historical actors, supporting members, and multicultural viewing public. Indeed, the interactive experience JANM encourages through its exhibitions, programs, and collection processes serve to weave Japanese American individual lives into the larger frame (in the same way that the Buddhist practitioner brings his or her own history to a home altar through *ihai* (mortuary tablets), photographs, and personal reflection). History becomes enshrined in the museum—in a way that does not simply commemorate but also enlivens.[9]

The spiritual economy that I have described is not meant to essentialize the Japanese American character. The religious and political diversity of Japanese Americans must be recognized, and one should note that a good degree of conflict and difference has always characterized Japanese

American life throughout its 150-year history. As David Chidester and Edward Linenthal (1995: 15) emphasize: "Sacred space is inevitably contested space, a site of negotiated contests over the legitimate ownership of sacred symbols" and meanings. Younger generations of Nikkei will undoubtedly bring their particular outlook and experiences to the continuing endeavors and concerns of the "community" and forge their own connections to the past (Nakamura, 2006). Still, when consensus does emerge, as, for example, with the Nikkei movement for the passage of the Civil Liberties Act or Japanese American participation on annual pilgrimages, it is important to articulate the patterns of civil religious engagement and the spiritual worldviews—not so readily apparent—that lend ongoing meaning to Japanese American struggles for justice and expand the dominant civil religious perspective.

TO REMEMBER IS TO ACT

Without being imprisoned in Gila Relocation Camp, How would I have become aware of the Buddha's compassion?   —Kakichi (quoted in Kimura, 1976: 151)

In his seminal essay, "Religion and Ethnicity in America," Timothy Smith (1978) speaks of immigration as a "theologizing experience" (see also Orsi, 1985). The uprootedness and displacement that migrants inevitably experience is written into new forms of religious belief and practice. While immigration certainly prompted religious innovation among turn-of-the-century Japanese Americans, it did not serve as the group's touchstone. Far more inexplicable and traumatic was the legalized and wholesale discrimination that ensued. Spiritual crisis came through internment.

Times of trial are often specific to a group and subculturally defined. "A shared experience, no matter how unjust the circumstances, creates an intimate and kindred universe for those who share it," in Karen Ishizuka's (2006: 124) apt words. For racial minorities and other marginalized groups, these times of trial are often instigated by U.S. institutions and quickened when the promise of American civil religion is not fulfilled. In response to such crisis, marginalized groups are compelled to develop their own civil religious faith—related to but distinct from U.S. national expressions. Japanese Americans offer an especially paradigmatic case, but one is able to discern similar civil religious movements among Mexican Americans (the Chicano/a vision of Aztlán or the embrace of César Chávez as a civil religious figure), African Americans (forms of black nationalism and pan-Africanism), and Native Americans and indigenous peoples (struggles for land rights and nationhood). Arab Muslims and South Asian Sikhs in the shadow of 9/11 have also drawn from the example of their historical predecessors. As appeals to the American civil religious principles of tolerance and toleration become increasingly ineffectual, immigrant groups currently under siege are beginning to develop their own distinctive civil religious consciousness that is true to their voice and their vision (Pew Forum, n.d.).

At crucial moments, American civil religion and minority civil religions can converge (as is the case with Martin Luther King Jr. and the civil rights movement, frequently referenced in national address, or the designation of Manzanar as a national historic site); because of the persistent inequities, however, they can never wholly unite. Minority civil religious expression, such as the critical faith of Japanese Americans, therefore becomes crucial in the sustenance of a particular group *and* for the nation as a whole. It is not simply a transcendent sense of its own origins and calling that keeps American civil religion accountable (as Bellah contends), but competing civil religious institutions and forms wrought through the suffering of the nation's oppressed that calls out and ultimately humbles.

Robert Orsi, in his exploration of contemporary Catholic faith, speaks about the way in which the history of Catholics can be seen as a *braided* one—one in which the lives of Italian Catholics remain woven with one another and with others despite dispersal into the suburbs and city. Braiding also means that "linear narratives so beloved of modernity—from immigration to assimilation, from premodern to modern, from a simple faith to a more sophisticated faith and so on—are not simply wrong but . . . mask the sources of history's dynamics, cultures' pain, and the possibilities of innovation and change" (Orsi, 2004: 9). In the case of Japanese Americans and other immigrant groups, a critical faith—forged on American soil—offers unique expression of their historical experience and religious roots. It also has come to braid or weave together across time and space the lives of Japanese Americans with one another and with those that suffer similar oppression.

Racial prejudice has had a harrowing effect on Japanese Americans. The documents, sites, and rituals of Japanese American civil religion help the people emerge from their painful history and make good of that past. As the above sketch reveals, the institutionalization of memory becomes the occasion for education, political action, and healing. While one hopes that intolerance and discrimination are a thing of the past, Japanese Americans are well aware that there is no guarantee that this is or ever will be the case. This vigilant attitude is indeed at the heart of Japanese Americans' critical faith. *Shikata ga nai.* There is nothing I can do to change the past. *Shikata ga nai.* But there is something I can and must do now.

NOTES

This chapter first appeared as Jane Naomi Iwamura, "Critical Faith: Japanese Americans and the Birth of a New Civil Religion," *American Quarterly* 59/3 (2007): 937–68. It has been revised for this volume.

1. The term "Nikkei" is generally used to refer to Japanese emigrants and their descendants, especially to those Japanese who migrated to North America and Latin America during the Meiji period. In this essay, I use the term interchangeably with "Japanese American," since Japanese Americans often refer to themselves as such. The designation also recognizes a growing awareness among Japanese Americans of their connections with Japanese in Latin America and Cuba.

2. This conversation took place in the 1980s. To read more about Morikawa's legacy, see Morikawa (1990) and Nagano and Malcomson (2000).

3. This amended version of Masaoka's statement is inscribed on the National Japanese American Memorial to Patriotism in Washington, D.C.

4. Other monuments dedicated to the Japanese American wartime experience that can be considered civil religious expressions include the National Japanese American Monument to Patriotism in Washington D.C. and the Go for Broke Monument in Los Angeles. They do not seem to garner as much multigenerational Nikkei participation and support, however, and their foundations have been primarily maintained by older volunteers. The National Japanese American Monument has especially aroused conflict within the Nikkei community.

5. These words are attributed to Ben Tamashiro, who served as part of the 100th Infantry Battalion ("Ben Hiroshi Tamashiro," 2004).

6. The Day of Remembrance takes place every February 19—the day that President Franklin D. Roosevelt signed Executive Order 9066. In 2007, the U.S. House of Representatives passed H.R. 112 and officially designated February 19 as the National Day of Remembrance for the Japanese American Internment.

7. The Pure Land tradition traces its roots to India and China. This sect departs from other strands of Buddhism in that salvation no longer depends on one's merit or individual efforts but is achieved through the invocation of the Buddha's name ("Namu Amida Butsu"). Amida Buddha, the Buddha of Unhindered Light, provides the focus of the practitioner's faith and devotion.

8. It is interesting to note the ways in which the museum's fund-raising campaigns are informed by a Japanese religious sensibility. As Audrey Lee-Sung (2005: 67) writes: "In considering support for the institution, many individuals made gifts in memory or in honor of their first-generation parents or grandparents." This practice of remembering family members through financial donation (*orei*) is common among Japanese American Buddhist practitioners.

9. For a discussion of the religious economy of the Buddhist home altar in Japanese American contexts, see Iwamura (2003).

6

Buddhism, Rhetoric, and the Korean American Community

The Adjustment of Korean Buddhist Immigrants to the United States

Sharon A. Suh

In examining the Korean American community in the United States, one cannot overlook the fact that religion constitutes a primary characteristic of this immigrant group's process of adjustment and acculturation. However, while most studies of Korean American religions bring sustained attention to the role of Korean Christian churches in the maintenance of ethnic identity and aiding the process of transition to life in the United States, scant attention has been paid to the existent Buddhist communities in Korean America (Hurh and Kim, 1990). Perhaps this oversight can be attributed to the widely held assumption that most Koreans living in America are Christian. Yet despite the phenomenal numbers of Korean American Christian churches in the United States, there remains a substantial number of Korean Americans who affiliate themselves with the Buddhist tradition (Hurh, 1998: 106).

Although it is known that 70 percent of the Korean American population identifies as Christian, of which 40 percent converted to Christianity after immigration, it is difficult to accurately assess the number of actual Buddhists in the Korean American community since many Buddhists purposely avoid drawing attention to their religious identity within the ethnic community out of concern over social and business relationships with Christians. Sociologist Won Moo Hurh maintains that, currently, Korean Americans who affiliate themselves with the Buddhist religion comprise only 1.5 percent of the entire population of Korean Americans living in America (Hurh, 1998). According to the abbot of one of the largest Korean American Buddhist temples in the United States, however, Buddhists comprise approximately 10 to 15 percent of the Korean American population.[1] Most Korean American Buddhists are quite cognizant of their numerical minority within their ethnic group, knowledge of which is often gained through experiences of marginalization by the larger Korean American Christian community, which often views Buddhism as a relic of the past or as "devil worship," since Buddhism denies the ultimate existence of God.[2]

Based on in-depth qualitative interviews conducted with 50 male and female members of the Los Angeles–based Sa Chal temple, one of the largest Korean American Buddhist temples in the United States, in this chapter I examine the contemporary context of Korean American Buddhism.[3] In so doing, I look at the role of Buddhism in the Korean American community and the Buddhists' responses to their new religious minority statuses. One of the primary findings of this study indicates that, for this particular immigrant group, being Buddhist in a largely Christian Korean American community often results in an ideological and rhetorical struggle over authentic identity. That is, paradoxically, a Buddhist identity can be constructed by Korean Americans to resist the notion of "Americanization" and acculturation and, at the same time, be invoked to valorize the Korean American Buddhist community's ability to embrace popular values of democracy and self-reliance associated with attaining the "American dream."

In particular, I have found that many respondents react to their minority status in the Korean American community by engaging in a struggle to prove that (1) they are more authentic Koreans than their Christian co-ethnics, and (2) they are more successful Americans than their Christian co-ethnics. Due to fear of jeopardizing potential social and economic relationships with fellow Korean immigrants of the Christian tradition, this struggle tends to occur on a private internalized level. While the struggle may not be explicit, it nonetheless draws important attention to the complex relationship between their religious and ethnic identities.

Buddhists largely associate Buddhism with a nationalistic sense of Korea and therefore see it as an authentic marker of Korean identity. In this instance, the Buddhist religion is constructed as a barrier to an undesired "Americanization" compared with the Christian religion as practiced by Korean Americans, which is characterized as overly "westernized." In other words, Buddhists often make the claim that since Buddhism existed in Korean before Christianity was introduced in the 18th century and also, perhaps, because it is different from the dominant American religion, Buddhism is the more *authentic* religion associated with Korean identity.

At the same, Buddhists are aware that Christianity has long been associated with modernity and contributed to earlier Korean immigration, particularly during the first wave arriving in the United States, and that Buddhism has often been associated with backwardness and inferiority. In response, many Buddhists assert that they are also *simultaneously* better Americans because their own Buddhist doctrines of self-enlightenment are more commensurate with notions of American democracy than are Christian doctrines, which they associate with a lack of free will.

Here I examine the complex and, at times, paradoxical relationship between maintaining a Buddhist identity as a marker of *Korean* identity and, at the same time, a marker of a successful *American* identity. It is by looking at the Korean American Buddhist community that one can gain a new perspective on the relationship between religion and immigration for a specific ethnic group. In this particular case, religious identity can be said to both resist and enhance the experience of immigration to the United States and the construction of identity as Korean Americans.

Being Buddhist in a Christian World

The Christians think that Buddhists are devils and that you only have to believe in God to be saved! In Korea, Buddhism was the original teaching but now they [Christians] think of it as the devil. I used to follow my younger sisters to church when I first got here because I wanted to learn something about Christian beliefs. But now, even though I don't go to church anymore, my sisters still think I believe in Christianity. They don't know that I go to temple because I don't tell them. If they knew they would keep asking me why I didn't believe in God and they would keep on bothering me. But belief is my own choice, so I don't want to hear any protests. I don't say a word; I just go alone to temple diligently and think of the Buddha inside my heart.

—Mrs. Oh, a 51-year-old Buddhist woman living on her own in Los Angeles

That a woman should find it necessary to hide her Buddhist identity from her own sisters (themselves previous Buddhists) illustrates the reality that many Korean Buddhists encounter on a daily basis: the ubiquity of church affiliation among Koreans living in America. For most Korean Buddhists, it is common for fellow Koreans to assume a priori that their religious identities are Christian, for most people assume that "all Koreans are Christian," and many Buddhists like Mrs. Oh above choose not to divulge their Buddhist identities. Below, I examine Buddhist responses to the increasing Christianization of the Korean American community to reveal (1) how a Buddhist identity shapes an individual's response to religious marginalization within his or her own ethnic community, (2) how a Buddhist identity can lead to the development of high self-esteem despite this religious minority status, and (3) how the Buddhist injunction of "knowing/finding one's mind" has been interpreted as a strategy of self-elevation in relation to their Korean American Christian counterparts.

Because Buddhist teachings are believed to foster open-mindedness, self-knowledge, and independence, many members of Sa Chal believe that, despite the apparent success of Korean American Christianity in providing for the needs of its worshippers, it is actually Buddhists like themselves who are better capable of adjusting to life in America. For Buddhists in this study, the psychological virtues cultivated through Buddhist practices and the ability to "find and know one's mind" are equated with what are esteemed as the highest virtues of American culture—self-reliance, the ability to make it on one's own, open-mindedness, and democratic values. The capacity to acculturate and become " American" serves as the terrain for competition with Korean American Christians whose teachings are held to foster dependence, narrow-mindedness, and weak-mindedness—the very opposite of what "Americanness" connotes. In this way, Buddhists maintain that rather than the higher numbers of worshippers, better economic resources, and facility in the English language that the churches possess, it is the psychological strengths found in Buddhism that lead to actual success in the United States.

Yet what it means to be American and to successfully adjust to life in this country is not uniform but, rather, highly contradictory. On the one hand, being American signifies an erosion of traditional Korean values that hold families together; this negative connotation leads to the equation of Buddhism with an authentic Korean identity in contrast to Korean Christians, who are criticized for being duped by western culture. In this instance, we find that many Buddhists disparagingly characterize the postimmigration conversions of Koreans to Christianity as a cheap form of Americanization. Yet, ironically, this situation produces the unexpected result of Buddhists then competing with Christians over what it means psychologically to be an American. Thus, on the other hand, the positive attributes of American culture that motivated many Koreans to immigrate in the first place—better opportunities, more freedom, and self-reliance— are then equated with what it means to be a Buddhist.

The oppositional rhetoric of identity espoused by men and women at Sa Chal signifies here that what it means to be Buddhist is used in different contexts to develop self-esteem in response to a perceived double psychological burden—being an ethnic minority in the larger United States and being a religious minority in the smaller Korean American community.

Growth of the Church in the Korean American Community

The rapid multiplication of Korean American Christian churches comes as no surprise to Buddhists at Sa Chal. In fact, many Buddhists complain that they are often urged to convert to Christianity while they shop at Korean markets, do business with fellow Koreans, and meet with friends. Even their children are pressured to convert at their high schools and colleges where Korean Christian church groups are becoming an increasingly powerful presence. One Sunday afternoon at Sa Chal, Michael, a 14-year-old member of the temple's youth group, complained to his friends about how "an old woman kept following [him] in a car and tried to give [him] flyers to come to her church!" Kristine, a college student, sympathized and added: "Once I was in the Korean market and some grandmother tried to get me to go to her church but I told her I was Buddhist. She then got really upset and told me that it was wrong for young people to believe in Buddhism!" Both students rolled their eyes in exasperation and sighed, "Christians just don't understand about free-choice!" Despite these two examples, fewer and fewer Korean American students have been attending Sa Chal services over the years.[4]

Aware of the decreasing numbers of Buddhist youth attending temples, the abbot of Sa Chal has been working feverishly to attract more members to Sa Chal through an increased recruitment campaign in Korean-language newspapers, radio, and local television spots. As recently as January 1999, Abbot Lee opened an art gallery on the first floor of the temple in an effort to attract more Korean Americans who may be interested in shows dedicated to contemporary and traditional Korean art from Korea and the United States. That Christianity looms large in this plan was noted even in the abbot's sermon after the gallery's opening reception, in which he informed worshippers how excited he was that even Korean Christians attended the event and "were so surprised that we Buddhists could do something as big as this!" The abbot also converted one of the first floor spaces of the temple into a Buddhist bookstore in the hopes of attracting more Korean Buddhists from the local Koreatown district.

While these programs have the specific goal of *pogyo,* or the dissemination of Buddhism to the Korean and, recently, non-Korean community, they also reflect the struggles Buddhists encounter as they move from a historical position of relative religious strength in the homeland (28 percent of the entire population in Korea) to a marginal position in Los Angeles. The everyday reality of Korean Buddhists living in the Korean American communities of Los Angeles can be characterized as increasingly Christianized. This situation becomes readily apparent through a cursory drive down the busy Wilshire Center district of Koreatown, where churches dot the commercial and residential streets that make up this urban sector catering to Korean immigrants. Some of these churches are established within mainline American Protestant churches and have their services after English services of the churches that they rent. Others are located in small residential homes that, on Sunday mornings, are lined with cars crammed onto the driveways and in the streets. Some are even located in commercial buildings with signs out front welcoming visitors and members with Korean-language signage.

Many factors help explain the rise of Christianity among Korean Americans, factors that make them one of the largest Christian groups among all Asian Americans, second only to the Filipinos (Hurh, 1998: 107). Briefly, these reasons can be attributed to the predominantly Christian immigrant population comprised of urban, middle-class individuals who first came to the United States in 1903–5, when newly converted Christians comprised 40 percent of the nearly 8,000 Korean immigrants to first land in Hawaii. For these immigrants, "to become a Christian in Korea meant to become Westernized or Americanized" (Hurh, 1998: 109). In addition, a number of factors have led to the phenomenal growth of Korean American churches, including the provision of social services, psychological comfort, and opportunities to worship and socialize with fellow ethnics and the religiously pluralistic nature of American society in which religious distinctiveness has played an important role in the preservation of cultural and ethnic identities (Shin and Park, 1988).

Anthropologist Kyeyoung Park further attributes the growth of Korean Christianity to the dual role of promoting economic success and attainment of the American dream and the preservation of ethnic identity. According to Park, "Korean devotion to small business success is ideologically intensified at the church," where rotating credit clubs (*kye*) are established among church members to finance businesses and where labor pools and business networks abound (1997: 186–87). Yet, despite the increasingly large percentage of Korean Americans who self-identify as Christian (70 percent for those living in Los Angeles and 77 percent for Chicago), most adult Buddhists I encountered at Sa Chal express no interest in converting to Christianity.

The Buddhist Response

In response to their smaller population in the United States, temple members claim that the only way to effectively reach out to the younger generation of Buddhists is through the education of the parents, who would then bring their children to temple with them. Some parents maintain that the temple should be held responsible for passing the tradition onto students and providing English-speaking Dharma instructors who could then teach the children about Buddhism. Others at Sa Chal advocate that the only way to spread Buddhism throughout the Korean American community is to offer programs that appeal to men, for if more men were interested in Buddhist temples, then membership would double. Yet a significant portion of the remaining members have come to terms with their newfound minority status within the Korean community by invoking Buddhist discourses on karma and Buddha Nature, where individuals are held to be their own agents in determining their religious identities. Many parents thus argue that their children must make up their own minds about which religion to follow, for Buddhism "is about karma" and "awakening the Buddha Nature." Therefore, children must not be "forced to become Buddhists."

Implicit in these statements is a strong distinction drawn between Christians, who are viewed as "too aggressive" and coercive in their efforts at proselytization, and Buddhists, who are praised for being more liberal and independent. Ironically, however, this emphasis on Buddhist karma and self-agency has had the unintended consequence of an increasing Christianization of many second-generation Buddhist children who simply choose to socialize with their Korean American peers, most of whom are heavily involved in the church. Accordingly, many Buddhists envy the style of proselytization of the churches and the ministers' efforts to attend to the social, economic, and psychological needs of their congregants. In many ways, Buddhists at Sa Chal long for a monastic clergy that could provide the type of personal connection they perceive to exist between minister and churchgoer. Furthermore, most Buddhists lament the fact that the majority of Korean Buddhist monks in Los Angeles cannot speak English—a major deterrent to reaching out to the younger generation offspring of current worshippers at the temple.

Yet, given the slight percentage of Buddhists in the Korean immigrant community and the large percentage of former Buddhists who convert and seem to enjoy a more economically successful life (according to my participants), what is it that makes Buddhists maintain their religious identities? In other words, why have Buddhists at Sa Chal sought to remain Buddhists, even when their own children and siblings are turning to the Christian church? Furthermore, what does being a Buddhist in a Christian world mean for the person who consciously chooses not to convert? Does he or she equate being Buddhist with a stronger sense of self, open-mindedness, independence, and, by extension, "Americanness," despite or in reaction to his or her minority status? It is to these questions that I have sought answers and interpretations among members of Sa Chal, for these are some of the primary concerns and the "stakes" involved in the religious practices of contemporary lay Korean Buddhists in the United States. Not one of my participants at the temple remains unconcerned about these issues since all of them have had family members convert and have themselves felt the pressure to convert. In fact, most Buddhists at Sa Chal have had the experience of attending church, either by going to a missionary school in Korea or by going to church in the United States with a friend or family member.

Of the 50 Buddhists interviewed for this study, most participants appear rather flexible about passing down their religious traditions to their children. Although most parents prefer to see their children attend temple as devout Buddhists, members' responses center on two main reasons for their flexible views:

1. Since karma (*innyon*) plays a large role in Buddhism, most participants believe that their children will become Buddhist if and only if they have a certain past relationship based on karma. In other words, since Buddhism is about self-awakening, a Buddhist identity cannot be forced on a person.

2. Since Christian churches have become a hot spot for young adult socialization, most Buddhist mothers and fathers would rather see their children mingling with fellow Koreans who have similar values outside of religion than spending time with non-Koreans.

Parents ease the anxiety they feel about their children's informal conversions by maintaining that they themselves have a more profound understanding of Buddhist doctrines, which necessitates their acting in a more liberal fashion. For these Buddhist parents, children must be allowed to act according to their own karma. Thus, when comparing themselves with Christians, Buddhists at Sa Chal pride themselves on their more democratic natures.

Women's Responses

Mrs. Jin, a 50-year-old mother of two sons in their early 20s, vehemently believes that her children should choose their own religion. Even though she herself lived as a Buddhist nun for ten years in Korea before getting married at the age of 28, she still believes that it is more important for her sons to choose for themselves what religion they want to practice. For Mrs. Jin, above all, this choice is the measure of what being a Buddhist is about; in fact, she even encouraged her two sons to go to church so that when they decided for themselves what religion to practice, they would make an informed decision. She explains:

> Even I sent my kids to church, why did I send them to church? I told them that they should try going to church and try to compare the merits of each faith. Since I have taken them to temple with me since they were young, they were not influenced by [Christianity]. Rather than telling them not to go to church, I told them that they should try to understand the Christian faith in God so that later on, if they chose to believe in Buddhism, their beliefs would be deep and strong because they have chosen for themselves. For us [parents] since we have had such a strong and deep faith in

Buddhism, we can't just convert to Christianity so easily, but my kids didn't have that experience. So I told them to go to church.

Here we find Mrs. Jin's negative value judgment about conversion to Christianity, which she views as a lack of true faith and an easier pathway to follow.

Mrs. Jin's comments also indirectly draw a contrast between Buddhism and Christianity, where the latter is interpreted as a religion demanding strict adherence to a specific set of beliefs. Buddhism, however, "is about having to control oneself so that nobody is going to tell you to come and go [to temple], for Buddhism is not about evangelization [like the Christian churches are], it's not like that" at all. Citing Buddhism's more liberal attitude, Mrs. Jin says that she goes to temple "because the desire rises out of my own heart." In other words, religion for her is something that is self-motivated, and it is the individual who controls one's own fate.

Although she wants her own kids to attend the temple, she is also well aware that the church offers many services that are appealing to immigrants, including youth, like social or business services and personal connections with fellow members. This outreach to immigrants and their children is something that she believes that the Korean monks at Sa Chal have failed to achieve. She disapproves of the monks' failure to take an active role in helping immigrants adjust to life in the United States. Because of it, Mrs. Jin claims that many Korean immigrants convert to Christianity because it provides an "easier" path to adjustment. Yet Mrs. Jin herself still chooses to struggle on her own and, in so doing, believes that she maintains her integrity as a Korean Buddhist. Her own experiences of dislocation in a new world where she still cannot speak the language have led to an isolation that she had hoped the Buddhist temple would help combat. This, however, has not been the case for this woman who now spends most of her days either assisting her husband in his acupuncture and Oriental medicine clinic on the first floor of their home in Koreatown or socializing with her neighbor, a fellow Buddhist member of Sa Chal.

While Mrs. Jin leaves the responsibility for the religious identity of her sons to karma, when karma does not work in her favor she then holds the monks responsible for making her sons Buddhist. That she is bothered by the fact that her sons are not Buddhist comes through in her disappointment over the scarcity of young Buddhist women in the Korean

American community with whom she can match her sons for future marriage. When asked if she preferred her sons to eventually marry a Buddhist or a Christian, she responds:

> If they have chosen to believe in Buddhism then a Buddhist will be good. If they chose Christianity then a Christian would be good. Whatever they want to be is fine. But Buddhist girls that go to temple don't exist! So there are no people for Buddhist kids to marry. Right now, at Sa Chal too, there are only older bachelors and old maids! Young people who go to temple don't exist! So, even if you want to find them, you can't! Our family has gone to a matchmaker and asked them to find a Buddhist spouse for our sons, but they said that we had to go to church to find a daughter-in-law! But if our sons marry a Christian . . . well people who go to church don't do *chaesa* (ancestor memorial rites). So, then people without ancestors won't even have descendants come to look after them . . . [and still] the Christians will not do *chaesa*. The Buddhists hate that! They agonize over that! But there are no Buddhists available! If we don't do anything about that then Buddhism will not survive! The temples will survive for those monks who are here now but after them, they will disappear. If you have a monk, you have to have worshippers! If you only have a monk and no worshippers, how is Buddhism going to survive?

Mrs. Jin's comments illustrate the anxiety she feels over her sons' disinterest in Buddhism, for here she views Christianity as a direct repudiation of an authentic Korean past. Although she is extremely concerned about the future of her family, Mrs. Jin's attitudes toward Buddhism and monks at the temple are highly contradictory: on the one hand, she wants to tout self-reliance and coming to one's own decisions without relying on outside help; on the other hand, at the same time, she is highly critical of monks who do not offer any kind of help in practical matters such as caring for new immigrants like the churches do. Her comments also illustrate an awareness that Christianity is succeeding in gathering the support of younger generations of Korean Americans, a situation that is both threatening and, at times, enviable.

Throughout my interviews at Sa Chal, comparisons were constantly drawn between Buddhist and Christian doctrines, with Buddhism usually being described by women as a more independent practice that relies on the self as the arbiter of experience. Included in these descriptions of Buddhism is the characterization of the religion as free and without intrusion in one's personal life. For Dr. Lim, a 46-year-old woman who recently converted to Buddhism after her second marriage, Buddhism seems to provide less stress in her life, for it has far fewer rules and regulations. Dr. Lim was raised as a Buddhist through the influence of her grandmother when she was a young girl growing up in Korea. Yet like many Korean women, she converted to Christianity after her first marriage, for her "first husband's family was a Christian family and they told [her that she] had to go to church together."

Based on her experiences at both a Korean Christian church and a Buddhist temple, Dr. Lim indicates that she prefers Buddhism to Christianity because the former offers her much more flexibility to do as she wishes. She explains:

> At church, all you have to do is believe in Jesus and you'll receive help, but here at the temple they don't have that [philosophy] of just believing in someone else. So it seems like the dharma is a little more liberal, it's not exclusive and Buddhists don't believe that "only my way is the right way." There really are some easier things about [the temple]. At church, first of all, you always have to attend services, there are so many meetings and they always tell you to go to them. If you don't go, then a phone call comes . . . and also they say that you *have to* proselytize. If you don't do it very well then they sort of publicly recognize it. But if you go to the temple and say that you couldn't proselytize other people, it's just not a big deal; but in church it's sort of a sin.

In her comments we clearly see that the independence of Buddhism is believed to foster the democratic value of freedom of religion.

She nonetheless acknowledges that for some people the Korean Christian church offers opportunities for socializing and making business connections that might, in fact, be more beneficial for her own clinic:

> There are too many churches aren't there? Korean people believe too much in blessings [from God]. The reason why there are so many churches here . . . is that people are lonely and think that they should go to church so they can meet with other Koreans. Another reason is because of business. We have heard . . . if you do a business like I do, when you know a lot of people through church you get closer to them and can find more potential clients so that's why a lot of people go as well. . . . Some traditional people will preserve their [Buddhist identities], but if a person doesn't believe in

Christianity [in America] then there will be very few people around like
that person and so that person can't really do much.

Dr. Lim attributes the main difference between Buddhism and Christianity to a question of agency. She believes that Christianity teaches that all
one has to do is believe in God and that all will be taken care of if one
is faithful. Buddhism, in contrast, teaches one about self-reliance, an aspect of the teaching that all my participants have cited as one of the most
important aspects of Buddhism. This characteristic self-reliance leads to
agency and, by extension, the instantiation of the American values of independence, which a Christian dependence on God and the church is believed to prohibit. Because Buddhism does not interfere with her personal
life, Dr. Lim maintains that she will continue practicing Buddhism with
her husband. Although she does have a 16-year-old son, she continues to
allow him to attend her old church and believes that it is up to him to
"choose for himself what religion he will follow."

Aware of the discrimination that many Buddhists feel in the Korean
American community, Chin Mi Young, a divorced 52-year-old mother of
one, responds by drawing a strong distinction between the self-knowledge
and reliance derived from Buddhist practice and the dependence on an
outside agent found in Christianity. Mrs. Chin arrived in the United States
in the spring of 1992 and has since then been divorced from her husband,
a Christian. A member of the Buddhist choir, she attends Sa Chal weekly
and devotes much of her time socializing with her fellow Buddhist friends
when she is not working as a babysitter for two Korean children. As a
child, Mrs. Chin attended church a number of times and also had a friend
who was a minister in the United States. Yet after attending this friend's
church a number of times, she found that

> in Christianity, you ask for your well-being. In Buddhism, though, you
> are the subject and therefore you have to come to a realization of yourself
> and discover your well-being through the teachings. I find this to be more
> practical in daily living. In Christianity, you are not the subject, you leave
> everything up to the spirit [of God to decide]. This does not make sense to
> me because if you need to go somewhere, you have to know the directions
> for getting to that destination.

In her comments, Buddhism is held to be the more practical and modern religion that creates a strong will. Mrs. Chin further equates the

conversion from Buddhism to Christianity with loneliness and weak-mindedness and believes that because Christians help people find jobs and visit their homes, the weak-minded are more likely to switch religions. As she puts it, "I think that most people convert because they are lonely but the ones that stay Buddhist are strong-minded and will always stick with Buddhism."

Mrs. Chin also finds Christianity to be rather coercive for, as she puts it, Christians "believe one should believe in one god, only their God, and if you don't believe then you can't go to heaven. Christianity tells people that if you don't follow the ways of God, then you will not go the right path." She then contrasts this with Buddhism where "there is a philosophy which shows a way of living that people can experience and choose for themselves." For Mrs. Chin, "people should experience and decide for themselves" which religion they choose to follow, again a very American value.

Many women at Sa Chal believe that Christianity fosters an overly dependent relationship on a force outside oneself: that is, on God. For these women, Buddhism is viewed as a more sophisticated teaching that encourages individuals to develop strength and courage through self-knowledge and self-reliance. Thus, even though Christianity might attract a greater number of Korean immigrants, it is the Buddhists who are said to be more successful at withstanding life's ups and downs, particularly the psychological struggles of immigrant life. Kwak Soo Young, a nursery school teacher in her early 50s who attends Sa Chal every few weeks, was raised as a Buddhist in Korea and eventually married a fellow Buddhist. She has lived in the United States since 1982 and has three children ages 27, 29, and 30. Although she used to bring her kids to temple with her, now she no longer attempts to bring her adult children to worship services because temples do not seem to offer much personal support. She explains:

When you go to temple, the monks don't say things to you like "Welcome!" to make you feel comfortable. The monks just look at people and say, "Oh you're here." That's a problem for Korean Buddhism but for the monks, they have these rules regarding their existence and so it is sort of hard to get close to them. But once people immigrate, if you go to the airport there will be a lot of ministers there for the sake of preaching. Ministers that you don't even know will come up to you and ask people, "Oh did you just immigrate here? What church do you belong to?" They ask them all these things and if they don't have a car, they [recent immigrants] are given a ride somewhere. But really, what monk exists who would do that sort of thing?

Although she originally raised her children as Buddhists, she also claims that "it is not so much that you really teach your kids about religion but that you show them what you are doing and they eventually will follow on their own" if they choose. This flexible attitude toward her family's religion is also reflected in her early experiences of allowing her children to attend church so that they could spend time with their fellow Korean friends, a point of great concern for Mrs. Kwak.

Yet, although she claims that Buddhism is about free choice, she limits this association to religious practices alone. When it comes time for choosing an appropriate spouse, she practically shouts, "Marry an American? No, never!" Despite this seemingly contradictory interpretation of Buddhist doctrines of karma and self-reliance, she explains, "Ever since my children were young, I told them that getting married isn't just about two people, it's about the whole families as well." Fearing a language and culture gap between the families, she explains, "to the mother and father, it would be so hard because there will no longer be that tie with parents and you will be further apart." So, to her children she often warned that "you have to think of how many other people are going to be uncomfortable about the decision that you make and not just think about yourself!" Buddhist doctrines of karma and free choice, then, have their proper application in choosing religious affiliation but not in choosing the proper mate. Here we find a distinct irony where Korean cultural values run counter to the individualism and independence she values in being American, which indicates that there are some aspects of American culture that she chooses to ignore.

While many women respond to the rise of Christianity with both admiration and disdain, others have had direct experiences of proselytization from friends and family, leading them to often subvert or hide their Buddhist identities among Christians. Such is the case with In Soon Song, a woman born to Korean parents. During college, In Soon moved to Japan and married a Japanese Buddhist. Mrs. Song arrived in Los Angeles in September of 1999 to live with her two sons, who are currently attending high school in the United States. Although she grew up in a Buddhist household in Korea, she is the only one of her siblings who has remained Buddhist. Her older brothers have converted to Christianity, and her children in the United States do not attend temple at all. While living in Japan, In Soon felt very at home practicing Buddhism since "there are so many temples and small shrines wherever you go walking along that you can stop and bow at." In the United States, however, churches seem to dominate, especially within the Korean community.

In fact, since coming to the United States, Mrs. Song's religious choices have received much scrutiny within her circle of Korean female friends, all of whom are heavily involved in the church. She expresses her frustration with her Christian friends who, as evangelizers, insist on converting her and not respecting her own decision to remain a Buddhist:

> A month ago, I met a classmate who is now a very close friend. But this friend goes to church and in my English class, all my friends want to take me to church and they are after me about it all the time. But this is what I have to say to them: "As I live, I look for religion but religion should not be most important thing between us because you are my close friend. Since you are a deep Christian you go to church diligently and I go to temple diligently because I am a Buddhist. Our religions are different. But since we met outside the church, don't talk to me about going to church." I have another friend who is a *chondo sa* (evangelizing woman). She prays everyday at the church and always wants me to come to church. Since this *chondo sa* kept asking me to just come to church with her, I finally said that I would think about it. Then she says, "Well first go to temple and then plan to go to church afterwards." So, I came to Sa Chal early one morning and finished my prayers in the *bopdang*, I didn't even get to eat because there were two church people waiting right outside for me Sa Chal in their car! So, I did my bowing to the Buddha and since I made a promise, I went to church.

Because of the constant pressure she received from her friend, Mrs. Song eventually began to tell her that she could not get together on Sundays anymore because she was too busy and she realized that many of her friendships were dependent on sharing the same religious affiliation. In many ways, Mrs. Song has been extremely disappointed since she is living alone with her two sons away from her friends in Japan. Meeting friends through her English classes seemed to be an ideal situation, but these friendships began to change once it became apparent to her friends that she did not wish to attend church.

Nowadays, she explains that in her English classes, when her classmates and instructors discuss weekend plans, Mrs. Song keeps silent about her temple attendance and admits, "I just say that I am going to do some sports or go to the health club. Since I play golf, I just say that I am going golfing." In this way she is able to avoid the gaze of Korean women who might criticize or proselytize her into going to church, even though she has no interest at all in doing so. In many ways, In Soon keeps her Buddhist identity hidden among Christians, for she fears being singled out for being too different. She told me a story of one of her Buddhist girlfriends whose livelihood in America depends on the suppression of her religious identity:

> If you want to do business anywhere around here, Korean Christians will always ask you what your religion is. So the owner of the business will say things like if your household is not Christian, then you can't do business here. Since they said that to my friend, she said that she couldn't say a thing about being Buddhist and so she replied, "I am non-religious," when they asked her what religion she was. She couldn't say that she believed in Buddhism! She wanted to come here to America and look for a job but each time she went looking, [employers] would ask what religion she was and if she was a Christian. Since there are so many difficulties for my fellow Koreans who live in America, I think that half of them change their religions for the sake of making a living and finding jobs. So, when I heard that from my friend, my heart hurt so much! When you come here [to the United States] you come for the sake of business and making a living. If you go to the Christian religion, it seems that your life is easier, it is good for finding jobs and so there are some people who will go to church, I have seen a lot of people doing that, for the sake of living standards. And when I see that my heart really hurts. Even now, when I go to school, on Fridays our American teacher always asks us students, what are you going to do this weekend? As soon as he asks that, then if there are ten people they will all say "church."

For Mrs. Song, Christianity symbolizes an easier lifestyle but also a marked betrayal of Korean tradition. As a Buddhist who understands self-reliance, she is not afraid to be alone in American and, in fact, takes pride in being independent.

Men's Responses

The topic of Christianity and business success emerged as one of the most common distinctions drawn between Christians and Buddhists by men at

Sa Chal. Most men insisted that Koreans frequented churches over temples because at church, one could bring along business cards and expect to find both jobs and potential customers, and a system of business was facilitated by the ministers. These comments often reflected a sense of envy among Korean American Buddhist men at the perceived ease through which Christian men could pursue economic success with the support of the religious community. Nonetheless, not one male respondent indicated that he wished that the Buddhist temple and the monks would perform similar functions or that the temple ought to provide business opportunities between members. Rather, most men indicated that the monks should spend less of their time involved in worldly affairs and more time involved in studying the sutras and Buddhist philosophy.

In fact, unlike the women, most male respondents believed that the monks should be responsible for offering Buddhist sermons that provided less daily advice on how to survive as an immigrant in the United States and more time on disseminating Buddhist teachings. Implicit to this critique of current monks at Sa Chal is a belief that lay men should have more responsibilities in the general and administrative affairs of the temple; such responsibilities were thought to encourage male participation and, at the same time, detract from the monks' respectability. Some participants even went as far as to say that such activities on the part of the monks were done out of a desire to spread their own names throughout the Korean public. In other words, many male members of the temple want the monks to remain "traditional" and withdrawn from American culture.

This critique of monks illustrates a male desire for self-elevation through high-status positions with an ethnic group that are unavailable to them outside the Korean American community. This yearning for status within the temple leads many of them to compare the temple with the many Christian churches that offer both ritual and administrative positions. Furthermore, since Buddhist men are highly conscious and, at times, envious of the economic and social benefits of belonging to the church, many have responded to this situation by highlighting what Buddhism has to offer that Christianity cannot—independence, self-reliance, and freedom. These three benefits are held to be more important than business success and social prestige, for they are not contingent on what Buddhists deem a submission to an outside agent other than oneself—compliance to authority figures like God, Jesus, or ministers. Furthermore, they are held to be compatible with American democracy and values of independence.

Jae Woo Shin, a 28-year-old student of Eastern medicine, maintains that Buddhist meditation and worship focus on self-awakening as opposed to reliance on an outside force like God as the means for religious salvation. It is this difference of agency that appeals to him, for Buddhism teaches him to depend on and awaken himself. After visiting a number of Protestant churches in Korea during his sojourn in the U.S. Army and while living as a college student in Iowa, he explains: "I believe in Buddhism because I don't believe in any God or other person. If I go to heaven when I awaken, then I go by my own self-effort. But the church believes in many things like that God will actually pick you up and save you." Jae Woo prefers to rely on himself, a desire consistent with his motivations for remaining in the United States—to develop independence and live free from social constraints he still finds in Korea's Confucian culture. Based on his early experiences as a foreign student living in Iowa during his undergraduate years, he sympathizes heavily with new immigrants to the United States and even admits that he originally started attending a Christian church because he wanted to learn English. In the early 1990s, there were no Buddhist temples for Jae Woo to attend in Iowa, so he began to attend a church where he could take free English classes and meet up with other Koreans.

As this Buddhist sees it, the church is "the easier way," but for those "who *really* believe in Buddhism, they will come to the temple." That there are fewer Korean Buddhist temples for people to attend indicates to Jae Woo that those who do manage to worship as Buddhists in America are more faithful and more independent. Furthermore, since he posits that independence and self-reliance are the hallmarks of American culture, he believes that in the future, Buddhists will have an easier time adjusting to American culture since they share the same values. Mr. Shin enjoys the fact that as a religion of independence and self-reliance, the Buddhist attitude of free will enables him to attend different temples if he so chooses. For the moment, however, he usually just attends Sa Chal services because, as he puts it, "I don't want to talk to a lot of people at temple and . . . if I go to Sa Chal, there are so many people and I don't have to meet them all, so I just feel more comfortable on my own."

For Mr. Hong, a 70-year-old gentleman who reads the Diamond Sutra, Heart Sutra, and Thousand Hand sutra every morning from 5 to 7 AM, religion is a matter of personal choice. The father of four children who don't attend temple, he explains that Buddhists believe that "it is up to yourself [to choose] your own religion, so I would tell them that if they were going to be Christian, they would have to decide that for themselves." Like Mr. Kim, Mr. Hong says that he comes to temple to cleanse his mind, although he has attended church from time to time to be with his children. Citing the differences between the two religions, he states:

> Buddhism does not believe in any kind of god like the Christians do. We Buddhists think that you have to awaken your own mind by yourself. [Christians] completely cling to God for everything, but Buddhism is about awakening one's own mind and then enabling your morality to rise. If you increase your morality, then you are practicing Buddhism.

According to Mr. Hong, although many people convert to Christianity from Buddhism upon arrival in the United States, they "don't convert because they really want to believe but because they are isolated . . . and so if they go to church, they meet other immigrants and people they know." For him, Buddhism symbolizes wisdom and a natural ability to "make it" in the new world, whereas Christianity symbolizes a blind faith in ministers and God to make life more fruitful. Despite the large presence of Christians in the Korean American communities, he has no fear or concern for the future of Korean Buddhism and firmly believes that to be Buddhist is the better and more intelligent option:

> If you look at it, Christians are coming back to the temple. A lot of old people are doing the same because there's a lot of lies in their beliefs [in the church] and so they come back to Buddhism because they are of a true nature. Ministers say to live and believe in them and believe in God but the monks say that you have to awaken your own mind. Ignorant people think that if I believe in God then I will live well and be well off. So ignorant people tend to follow that way. But a smaller number [of people], if they have knowledge and know how, then they decide to come back over this way [to Buddhism].

The strength of character he associates with Buddhism leaves him confident of both his own future and that of his fellow Buddhists in the larger Buddhist community.

A 53-year-old man born in Seoul who has lived and studied in Korea and China, Dr. Jin arrived in Los Angeles in 1997 to open up his oriental medicine clinic in Koreatown. He contends that missionization of the second generation will be a very difficult task since Buddhism in Korea has historically concerned itself less with the day-to-day task of bringing in more adherents and more with "lofty philosophical concerns." Dressed in a blue and maroon traditional Korean style suit that he wears every day, Dr. Jin sits behind his desk looking very much like a Confucian scholar. The only time I have seen Dr. Jin at Sa Chal is at the 25th-year anniversary, even though he has spent much time in Seoul as a Buddhist youth leader working to teach Buddhism. In fact, he has known Abbot Lee since this time in Korea, and the two of them have a long established friendship. Yet, while in America, Dr. Jin feels very little need or inclination to attend temple on a regular basis. When asked about the current state of religion within the Korean American community, Dr. Jin agreed that Christianity has been more successful in attaining converts for reasons he attributes to the different roles of the minister and the monk.

Throughout our conversation, he posits that, traditionally, monks have not fulfilled the task of offering services to the laity, yet upon their arrival in America, it is precisely these services that immigrants seek out. Because monks are considered religious virtuosos by temple members, they historically have not provided for the economic and social needs of worshippers. The minister of a church, however, has traditionally played more of a role in offering advice and counsel to church members; because of this relationship, Dr. Jin maintains that immigrants feel more comfortable seeking out the support of a church.

Dr. Jin also believes that it was the rise of Confucianism in Korea that brought about the distinction between gender roles that discouraged men from attending temples in Korea. Hence even today, women occupy the majority of temples in both the United States and Korea. This gender distinction also serves as one of the main reasons behind the rise of Christianity and the departure of men from Buddhist temples. Dr. Jin also maintains that women usually went to temples to pray for the well-being of their families but that, lately, "men are probably still too embarrassed to publicly worship at temples since Buddhism had been so denigrated as low class during the Yi dynasty." Dr. Jin's comments illustrate why some Buddhists choose to hide their religious identities or seek out the social comforts and benefits offered through the churches. But these Buddhists, according to Dr. Jin, are "not real Buddhists, for real Buddhists who have a knowledge of the philosophical tenets of Buddhism, an understanding of the sutras, and a desire to attain enlightenment could never convert!"

Dr. Jin is quite proud that he has remained a Buddhist, for being a Buddhist is much more difficult a task to accomplish:

Christianity has the Ten Commandments which are really easy—don't steal, don't kill, etc. But Buddhism does not have any commandments, instead it talks about purifying the mind. When I look at the church's Bible and the Buddhist sutras, I think that the Buddhist sutras are better, but if someone doesn't understand them, they might decide not to go to temple anymore. The church, however, talks about things very simply and the most important thing is just that you shouldn't consider anyone higher than [God, Jesus] or the minister. . . . Buddhism is a religion based on awakening for the sake of enlightenment, so one devotes oneself to worshipping and reading the sutras. The aim . . . is enlightenment, it's all about enlightenment. So it is harder to understand Buddhism and read the sutras.

Although Christians may think that Buddhism is a more traditional and, therefore, less modern and less sophisticated religion, Dr. Jin maintains that being a Buddhist is intellectually more challenging. Relying on oneself to purify the mind and understanding the sutras is not something everyone can do. Those who lack the mental apparatus to do so tend to go the church where one only needs to follow the Ten Commandments, which are already laid out for the individual.

Perhaps the individuals most affected by the rise of Christianity within the Korean American community are those students who encounter Christianity on a daily basis. For many Buddhist youths at Sa Chal, Christianity plays an important role in their everyday interactions with their co-ethnic friends. Encouraged by their parents and comforted by the familiarity afforded in such friendships, Korean Buddhist kids are often challenged by their own Christian friends to attend churches. For many of these students, such invitations to come to church serve as a source of pressure because if they do attend church, they will participate in a religious practice counter to their parents. Yet, if they do not attend churches and Christian activities, they may risk losing the friendships they have with fellow Koreans. It is a very difficult social position that the students find themselves in: not only are they a perceived minority in the larger context of American culture, but also they have to defend their religious identities. Based on my interactions with Buddhist students, it appears that religion and choice are very much at the forefront of students' relations with other Korean Christian kids. The questions of the validity of Buddhism and the issues of conversion seem to emerge quite a bit in everyday life. Yet, there are also those students who deeply pride themselves on being Buddhist, despite their acknowledgement that

Korean Christian churches often provide services and company that temples do not.

James Jang, a 21-year-old college student, maintains that being Buddhist is synonymous with being independent, a characteristic far more important than being a dependent, albeit comfortable, Christian. James maintains that he was "practically born in a Buddhist temple since [his] grandmother was the head of her own temple." "Since she was a nun," James fondly recalls, "me and my mom used to go there almost everyday. So, I literally grew up in temple." For James, being a Buddhist has never been a source of stress or embarrassment, for despite having numerous Korean Christian friends, his religious practice is something that he is drawn to for personal and not social reasons.

Nonetheless, James does envy the Korean Christian churches for providing what the temple does not: a strong sense of community. Based on the few times he attended churches with his Korean friends, he comments:

> I don't know why but the Christians have a really good sense of community building. I think it sort of goes back to the question of whether or not a religion can provide some sort of social activities. As Buddhists, we are used to sitting in a room, meditating and praying. But Christians are used to praying, singing, and going out to reach for other people. They go to a particular house weekly and practice a service there and that provides an opportunity for other people to meet one another. For those people who [immigrated] to the United States who are really unfamiliar with the culture, tradition, and language, they kind of long to [keep] being Korean even before they even decide to make themselves United States citizens. So they go out looking for people who can understand them and who speak the same language, know the same culture and traditions. I think that's what created a whole different community of Christians. But as far as the Buddhists are concerned, I see a lot of individualism among Buddhists in Los Angeles.

The churches better fulfill an immigrant's need for comfort among fellow ethnics and opportunities to socialize as a group to escape the challenges of adjusting to life in a new country. Yet James remains extremely proud of his parents and himself for not hiding their religious identities, no matter what the social and economic consequences may be. Here we find that Buddhism is held to be the tougher yet ultimately more rewarding path. James's belief that the Korean Christian church has a stronger sense of community building has been echoed throughout my interviews with members of Sa Chal. As noted earlier in this chapter, many men and women express envy at the church's commitment to meeting and greeting new immigrants at the airport and offering more opportunities for becoming involved in social activities and receiving support. Yet, despite the obvious benefits to such activities perceived by the Buddhists, they also perceive such activities as unnecessary to being a Buddhist, for, as many members put it, "being a Buddhist is about doing things on your own." This belief, according to Sa Chal members, rests in the philosophical belief in self-reliance and self-awakening.

Conclusion

In this chapter, I show how religious affiliation represents more than different spiritual orientations and practice. For example, "to be Buddhist is to be Korean" implies that religion and ethnicity are intricately bound. This association of Buddhism with an "authentic" Korean identity enables some Buddhists to distinguish themselves from Korean Christians whose faith is then interpreted as an adoption of western ideals. In many ways, the large-scale conversions of Koreans, both in Korea and in the United States, to Christianity are a central concern and perceived threat to Buddhists at Sa Chal, who disparagingly attribute those conversions to an easy form of "Americanization" and "weak-mindedness." The perception of Christian churches dominating Korean immigrants through their powerful resources can also be found in the rhetoric of Buddhist remissionization and reeducation of Korean Americans espoused by many temple members.

Throughout this chapter, I also show how views of the other (Christians) play a crucial role in understandings of the self in the negotiation of identities and the development of self-esteem for temple members, and I draw specific attention to the tension and irony in the association of Buddhism's injunctions of self-reliance and independence with the cardinal virtues of American culture itself—independence, self-rule, and democratic values. By contrasting their own beliefs and practices from Christians who are defined as "weak willed," "overly dependent," and "coercive," Buddhists indirectly claim that, despite the better economic success enjoyed by Christians in churches, such Christians are not as "American" as the Buddhists because their practices are too dependent on others for support.

A Buddhist identity and the rhetoric of self-reliance are thus heavily tied to improving one's self esteem, both as an immigrant and as a Korean American living in a Christian world. Buddhists are seen as better Americans while, paradoxically, Korean Christians are seen as too westernized for having adopted Christianity. This paradox reflects tensions between the pros and cons of American values. Yet, "to be Buddhist" is to be independent from the majority, which, for many participants in this study, enhances self-esteem. Buddhists thus construct themselves simultaneously as more authentic Koreans *and* better Americans.

NOTES

1. Based on interview with the abbot of Sa Chal Temple, in Los Angeles, CA.

2. Both Kyeyoung Park (1997) and Won Moo Hurh (1998) equate Buddhism with antiquated practices. Many participants in this study informed me of the common equation of Buddhism with "devil worship" that they experienced among their Korean American Christian counterparts.

3. The actual name of the temple where I conducted my research has been changed in order to protect its identity. Similarly, all names of interview participants in this study have been changed.

4. From my own observations, I noted that from the period between June 1997 and June 1999, the Buddhist youth group attendance dropped over 50 percent: from 25 students to just under 14 students. According to the remaining students, those who left went to church, which offered better opportunities to meet up with friends and because English was the primary language of communication.

Part III

Incorporation of New Religions into American Society by European Jews and Arab Muslims

The main reason for this volume's comparison of the social incorporation of Jewish and Arab Muslim immigrants is that they have each introduced to America a minority monotheistic religion that competes with the existing Christian hegemony. But, like Catholicism, which spread across the American social landscape with the settlement and integration of German, Irish, and Italian immigrants, Judaism became accepted as an American charter religion and part of a religious triumvirate celebrated by the mid-20th century as the nation's Judeo-Christian heritage. At question today is whether Islam will be able to attain a similar charter status in an expanded definition of that heritage. One reason to anticipate such acceptance will occur is that Islam shares historical and theological roots with Christianity and Judaism, notably in their recognition of Abraham as a founding prophet and, as Muslims say, in being religions "of the book." But, despite these similarities, the differences over which the adherents of each of these religions have ostracized, punished, and battled one another for centuries suggest that accommodation will be difficult to attain. Nonetheless, because of the American constitutional separation between church and state and protection for individuals' freedom of worship, Protestants, Catholics, and Jews have been able over a century of contention to work out something close to a pluralistic modus vivendi that would seem in the long term capable of including Muslims as well.

Despite the seeming entrenchment of ethnic and religious pluralism in America, there are still reasons to wonder if or how Arab Muslims and Islam will become accepted by other Americans. An important difficulty is that relations of Arab Muslims with other American ethnic and religious groups are greatly influenced by events outside of the country, particularly in the Middle East. Conflicts between Arabs and Israelis over land

and governance have recently been subsumed within a wider strategy of the United States to transform the region through a "war against terrorism" declared by President George W. Bush after the September 11, 2001, attacks against the World Trade Center and Pentagon and the resulting military occupations and wars in Afghanistan and Iraq. The simplistic, but yet persistent, self-fulfilling prophecy that these issues reflect a broader "conflict of civilizations" between the Christian West and Islamic East inflames relations between Muslims, Christians, and Jews, not only in their efforts to shape U.S. government foreign and security policies but also in everyday domestic life.

Yes, in the face of these intergroup rivalries and friction, the 20th-century experience of Jews from their arrival as immigrants to their acceptance as a fully American ethnic and religious group—including how they fought and largely overcame anti-Semitism—stands as a model for Arab Muslims who today find themselves in a similar situation as they seek a place in American society. The contemporary version of this story stresses that acceptance came in tandem with social mobility, very evident for the second generation of eastern European Jews by the mid-20th century, and involved even a racial redefinition of Jews to place them incontestably in the white population (e.g., Brodkin, 1998; Foner, 2000). In both respects, the story of the acceptance of Jews offers hope to Muslims, whose educational attainment and professional standing locate them, on average, in the middle class or higher, and whose ancestors come in general from outside of Europe.

That the following chapters about Jewish and Arab Muslim immigration and the role of Judaism and Islam in their incorporation address similar issues, through from different perspectives, enabling instructive comparisons of similarities and differences in both group's responses to the difficulties that they have faced. Calvin Goldscheider (chapter 7) and Arnold Eisen (chapter 8) bring a historical perspective to understanding the transformation of Jewish immigrants into an American ethnic and religious community. Beginning with differences between immigrant parents and their children over their understanding of themselves as God's "Chosen People," Eisen emphasizes the distinctive experiences, attitudes, and formulations of subsequent generations as they reinterpret and balance the religious and cultural meanings and significance of being both Jewish and American. Goldscheider traces the coherence of the Jewish community over the same stretch of time, examining the familial and institutional means by which Jews have sustained an ethnic identity and a communal coherence on the basis of changing but shared underlying values. Looking back at the past from the vantage point of a group whose identity and continuity are no longer shaped by the "force and meaning" of anti-Semitism, the authors are oriented less by the earlier concerns of Jews as they sought acceptance in American society than by contemporary worries about whether the Jewish community will lose its religious, cultural, and group distinctiveness through cultural and social assimilation. While both chapters conclude that assimilation leads to Americanized reidentifications and reinterpretations that might perplex earlier generations, they affirm the viability of a continuing Jewish religious and social community within the context of American pluralism.

In contrast, Yvonne Haddad (chapter 9) and Ann Chih Lin (chapter 10) present the situation of Arab Muslims as being more like that faced by Jews in the past when hostility and discrimination raised barriers and doubts regarding the possibilities for acceptance and the mode of their incorporation. Haddad distinguishes between the histories and experiences of Arab and Muslim immigrants and subsequent generations before examining how those who share these overlapping identities today are treated by the American government and society and remain uncertain as to the viability of their collective coherence and the extent that America can ever really become their homeland.

In contrast to Jews, as Haddad describes, Arab Muslims share cultural and religious identities with broader and more diverse populations. To a great extent, American Arabs have an original common language and a common regional history, but the majority practice various forms of Christianity and other religions, including Judaism. American Muslims include not only those of Arab descent but also larger numbers of African Americans and recently arrived immigrants from diverse cultural and national backgrounds in South Asia and, to a lesser extent, Africa. These groups also differ in their adherence to distinctive Islamic traditions, including Sunni, Shi'a, Druze, and other sects. Within the context of this diversity, Haddad emphasizes the efforts that Arab Muslims have made to create national organizations, employing one or both identities at different times and in changing national and international contexts to defend and promote their interests and establishment within the larger society. These organizations seem parallel to, and at times were modeled after, similar antidiscrimination, civil rights, and religious organizations created by Jewish immigrants to confront anti-Semitism, gain rights, and promote domestic and foreign policy goals.

Lin focuses more closely at the contemporary experiences of first-generation, Arab-Muslim immigrants who are concentrated in the metropolitan Detroit area of Michigan. This group includes Iraqis, many displaced by the Gulf War, and new members of more established Yemeni, Palestinian, Syrian, and Lebanese communities. This chapter pays less attention to the role of national politics and institutions than to the familial networks and communal organizations through which Arab Muslims seek to adjust to everyday and local American life.

We believe that a comparison of the experiences of Jews and Arab Muslims in America offers an original and instructive lens through which to view the challenges that each group has faced—and is facing—as it adapts to, and changes, American society. In particular, the struggle of each to maintain distinctiveness and identity while making a case for inclusion and respect within the American polity, and the extent to which this struggle is shaped by diversity and conflict internal to each group, show striking parallels. At the same time, contrasts between their experiences also reveal important differences about the social and political contexts within which each group lives today.

Neither Judaism nor Islam has a centralized religious hierarchy with the authority to define what "true" religious practice entails. For neither does a place of worship automatically define a community. These facts of religious organization grant these communities a great richness of belief and practice; at the same time, they pose a central problem for their survival. How does a noncentralized religion create the kinds of institutions, networks, and shared beliefs that give identity and practice any communal meaning? Equally important, how can these communal meanings be defended against hijacking by any particular sect or scholar?

Goldscheider and Lin propose that the answer lies less in specifically religious organization than in the internal structures—family, neighborhood, profession, and social network—that connect individual Jews or Arab Muslims. These patterns of interaction can be dictated by extended families who live close to and socialize with each other, by attendance at the same universities and in pursuit of the same occupations, and by concentration in a few metropolitan areas and within particular neighborhoods in those areas. They can also be influenced by the creation of community centers around places of worship or by such alternatives to places of worship as advocacy groups and charities. Without these types of interaction—which are often tangential to religious doctrine or belief—the persistence of Jewish or Muslim identity, not to mention Jewish or Muslim impact on American life, would be impossible.

But if religious identity depends in some part on social organization, it cannot be reduced to it. Eisen and Haddad depict the vibrant debates over orthodoxy and theology that characterize modern Judaism and Islam. Though class and gender matter, these debates do not follow either neatly; though they are linked to practices and customs, it is impossible to infer belief simply by looking at customs. Indeed, one of the distinguishing characteristics of both American Judaism and American Islam seems to be the willingness to reinterpret traditional symbols and accepted verities, all the while claiming that these are not reinterpretations but, rather, the "true" understanding. Another is the great range of religious leaders and spokespeople, each with a contending perspective but none with the authority to end debate. The failure—or perhaps unwillingness—to understand these important points has played into anti-Semitic and anti-Muslim actions and bias in the United States, when the religion and its adherents are vilified by association with some particular Jewish or Muslim "representative," even if that person speaks and acts for no one but himself.

These parallels should not blind us to important differences in the development of American Judaism and Islam. Eisen explains how "Americanness" became a central theme in the efforts of American Jews to define their faith. "Americanness" is a theme in Haddad's chapter, too, but so is the global context: Muslims exist in a world community of Islam where the most influential teachers and scholars are almost entirely located outside of North America. While American Jews in the 20th century could claim, with some justification, that Jewish scholarship and practice was centered in the United States, the many variants of Islam all over the world both enrich the faith in the United States and add exponentially to the difficulties of defining it and including it unproblematically under the umbrella of an American identity.

These debates must also be put in the context of how they affect—or do not affect—the practice and beliefs of the majority of these faiths' adherents. Here the history of Judaism in the United States illustrates the challenges that Islam will face. Religious practice and belief are perhaps always determined as much by individual and familial choices as by commonly acknowledged doctrines. At the same time, a central tenet of Islam is that all believers are part of the *Umma,* or universal community. Thus, variation in practice and belief can be problematic for Muslims in ways that they are not for Jews. In addition, unlike Judaism, which has become both ethnicity and faith for American Jews, Muslims in the United States still have distinctive ethnic backgrounds and social customs in addition to their faith. This again puts pressure on Muslims to work toward a unity that may create more division than community.

Both the Jewish and the Arab Muslim communities have had to construct a life in the United States, as well as a religious mission befitting their new environment. For the American Jewish community, shaped by their role as the "Chosen People," lured by the possibility of security and assimilation, and refocused in the 1970s on Israel's survival, the fear of "decline" and disappearance has been a constant consideration. That fear finds expression in issues as different as the formation of new denominations and the changes wrought by intermarriage. It also has taken form in the unifying support for Israel, a "homeland" that most have never lived in.

Conversely, among American Muslims, conflicts between the United States and Arab countries create other kinds of considerations: Islam as threatened by U.S. power versus Islam as a salvific force in American life. The casual stereotyping that Arabs and Muslims see in the news media or in entertainment, the willingness of the United States to use military force in the Middle East, and the hostility of a culture that Muslims often see as individualistic, immoral, and materialistic all lead Arab Muslims to fear that they will not be assimilated but destroyed by America. At the same time, many Arab Muslims also see in the United States a land of great promise and opportunity: a land where worship is not restricted by secularist governments fearful of popular Islamic movements, a land in which a vibrant economy and education system allow families to prosper, and a land in need of the moral compass and lessons in compassion that Islam could provide. Nor is it uncommon to hear Arab Muslims say that in the United States there is the chance to nurture universal Islam, with so many Muslims of different races and ethnicities in the same place.

In this environment, the topic of Israel is particularly charged for both groups, affecting their relationship to each other, their relationship to the American polity, and, ultimately, their sense of what kind of Jews or Muslims, and what kind of Americans they will be allowed to be. For American Jews, Israel is a symbol of survival, and American support for Israel is necessary to guarantee it. For American Arabs, Muslim or Christian, American support for Israel is seen as a threat to the survival of Palestine and to the holy sites in Jerusalem. These foreign-policy questions spill over easily into the ways that Jews and Arab Muslims interact with American civil society. For Jews, who over the years have built an effective and sympathetic group of lobbying organizations, the protection of Israel's special relationship with the United States is also a way of holding together a community that many activists feel might otherwise disappear. For Arab Muslims, who both admire and resent the ability of Jewish groups to get wider support for their goals, the success of Jewish groups often seems to underscore their own lack of integration into American civil society and their lack of effectiveness as either a self-protective or salvific community.

Thus, Israel is not only a concern that American Jews and Arab American Muslims battle over; it is a guidepost in each community's understanding of self. It encapsulates, as each of the chapters in this section does, how Jewish and Arab Muslim immigrants to the United States have sought to maintain their own identity while changing it to meet a new environment. It shows how religion has been intimately intertwined with participation in civic life. Perhaps most intriguingly, it suggests how the Jewish experience over a century and a half may contain clues to the ways that the Arab Muslim experience will develop as they seek to become fully American and yet also authentically distinctive.

7

Immigration and the Transformation of American Jews

Assimilation, Distinctiveness, and Community

Calvin Goldscheider

Large, cohesive, and powerful Jewish communities have emerged in the United States, where Jews define themselves and are comfortable both as Jews and as Americans. Most have long-term roots in America and have developed lifestyles and cultural forms, along with complex local, national, and international institutions, that enrich their ethnic and religious expressions. These multigenerational communities do not appear to be ephemeral. Their Judaism and their Jewishness are expressed in diverse and changing ways that challenge simple assumptions about the total assimilation of ethnic white minorities and the demise of religion in modern society. For while Jews have assimilated and become secular in some ways, their communities have become more cohesive and viable in other ways, developing new expressions of Judaism in a secular context and of Jewishness in an open pluralist and ethnically diverse society. They are well integrated into and share much of the broader national culture and society in which they live; yet they remain distinctive communities.

Instead of asking whether the grandchildren and great-grandchildren of eastern European Jewish immigrants to America are assimilating or whether they are surviving as a community (they are doing both), social scientists have reformulated the central analytic questions about Jews and other ethnic and religious minorities in the United States:

> What factors sustain ethnic and religious continuity of American Jews in the absence of overt discrimination and disadvantage?

What structural and cultural forces sustain continuity in the face of pressures toward the disintegration of the uniqueness and distinctiveness of their communities?

The short answer to these questions is that communal institutions and social and family networks, the structural underpinnings of communities, using Jewish values as their themes, are the core elements sustaining communal continuity. Institutions construct new forms of Jewish cultural uniqueness that redefine their collective identity.

Three features of social life form the basis for my assessment of the transformation of American Jews: (1) I focus on the structural, not only the cultural, features of Jewish communities; (2) I emphasize the contexts (networks and institutions), not only the values that distinguish Jews from others; and (3) I target communities and families rather than individuals as the units of theory and analysis. To assess the formation and developments of the community over time, I argue that we need to examine the quality of Jewish communal life in its broadest meaning. With the emergence of the fourth and later generations, distance from immigrant origins has faded as the major axis of change in the community. Although individuals exit and enter the community, the institutions and the collectively shaped culture sustain continuity and commitments.

There are many entry points to the analysis of American Jewish communities. I begin with a review of the formation of the American Jewish community and the role of immigration at the turn of the 20th century in that process. The historical context shapes the basis for understanding the roots of the community, the routes immigrants have taken out of the community, and the transformations they have experienced. In the process, I note some of the distortions that have characterized our understanding of the immigration process of American Jews. Building on a more systematic understanding of immigration, I then turn to the major changes in the quality of life that have characterized the community, including the changing stratification and family patterns of American Jews, and conclude with some notes about networks and institutions.

Social class and family patterns of American Jewish communities are the core of their generational continuity, and institutions are the sources of their distinctiveness. Jews have been transformed from an immigrant group defined by a combination of religious and ethnic distinctiveness to an American ethnic community defined by a distinctive cultural construction of Judaism and Jewishness with central features that are particularly

American. This transformation makes historical comparisons by generation particularly problematic and cross-national comparisons using similar indicators of continuity distorting. I argue for the importance of context and structure for comparisons over time and the life course, exploring distinctiveness in a wide variety of spheres.

Several analytic themes shape my orientation. First, changes over time in the characteristics of Jews and their communities do not necessarily imply the decline of community or the total assimilation of Jews. There is no simple inference that can be extrapolated from change to communal continuity. Hence, the identification of changes over time may imply the transforming of community but not its disintegration. Second, my focus is on the cohesion of communities, based on the extent and contexts of intragroup and intergroup interaction along with a shared constructed (and changing) culture. These contexts of sharing and interaction may occur in specific institutional or religious contexts but are likely to occur in the daily round of activity associated with the multiple spheres of social activities—work, school, neighborhoods, leisure, and family. Nevertheless, an examination of interaction in any one sphere may not have implications for interaction in other spheres. Third, time can be viewed both in terms of generations, historical context, and in terms of the life course. I expect that ethnic and religious identity, at both the individual and communal levels, varies over time as context changes. The life course is one perspective at the microlevel for studying a variety of unfolding and emerging changes in the context of ethnic communities.

A wide variety of structural and institutional features link Jews to one another in complex networks and mark Jews off as a community from those who are not Jewish. These features include family and social connections; organizational, political, and residential patterns; and religious and ethnic activities that can reinforce the values and shape the attitudes of American Jews. I review below some of these core features to identify their role in the integration of Jewish immigrants into American society. At the outset I reiterate that institutions play a powerful role in ethnic communities as they continually construct the cultural basis of community. Family and social networks reinforce shared cultural constructions of Judaism and Jewishness.

Immigration and Origins

Immigration from the countries of eastern Europe in the 1870s through the 1920s became the demographic foundations of the contemporary American Jewish community. Drawing on significant proportions of Jewish communities of origin, the immigration involved 2.5 million, mostly urban, Jews. It was a collective and voluntary migration, reflecting the push of economic and political constraints in places of origin and the pulls of opportunities in places of destination. In turn, immigration was facilitated by powerful kinship networks. Social and ideological changes had already characterized immigrants and their communities before they left, resulting in the greater receptivity of immigrants to the opportunities in America. The combination of selectivity, American economic context, volume and characteristics of immigration, the role of networks, and the presence of other ethnic and religious groups as part of the immigration stream shaped the nature of the first generation of American Jews from eastern Europe.

The volume of immigration and the distribution of immigrants converted the scattered local American Jewish communities into a national ethnic group, from a population of 200,000 in 1870 to over 4 million in the mid-1920s. The guiding ideology of this immigration, transferred from eastern Europe, was secular-socialist, not religious. It was ethnic Jewishness in the broadest sense, not narrowly defined Judaism, that characterized the immigrant community. The economic motive underlying the immigration was dominant (an escape from economic discrimination and oppression, not just the fear of pogroms); the capitalist goal of the immigrants was to take advantage of the economic opportunities (grounded in political opportunities) that were available in America.

The heaviest volume of Jewish immigration from eastern Europe occurred between 1904 and 1908, when 650,000 Jews arrived, and in 1913 and 1914, when an additional 0.25 million arrived. In no year was Jewish immigration more than 14 percent of general immigration, and more often than not it was less than 10 percent. Aided by local and national Jewish American organizations, informed and supported by extended family members and persons from their towns of origin, the overwhelming majority of Jews remained in America, coming with family members or bringing them in subsequent years. The permanent family and community-based immigration of Jews made it reasonable for them to invest in learning English, to form families, and to finance the education of their children. With little or no incentive to return to places of origin, with economic opportunities available in America, and with help from earlier Jewish immigrants from Germany, Jews from eastern Europe became citizens in their new homeland. They competed well with the millions of other immigrants who were more rural and less permanent (for an overview, see Gorin, 1992; Goldscheider and Zuckerman, 1984).

To assess the impact of the receiving society on Jewish immigrants, we need to identify immigrant selectivity. All Jews did not come to America, even when there were no restrictions on immigration from Eastern Europe. Indeed, most Jews remained in eastern Europe, and Jewish population size there increased precisely during the period of mass immigration. As in other migrations, younger adults were more likely to move and were selective on socioeconomic grounds. Property owners and those with good jobs were least likely to migrate. The poorest and the least educated were also less likely to have the resources to move. There was a much higher proportion of skilled laborers and a much lower proportion of unskilled workers among the immigrants than among the Jewish labor force in eastern Europe. Pressures to move were greatest in urban areas where Jews were squeezed during the early period of industrialization. Emigration occurred among those whose skills were most transportable. As in other immigrations, those most receptive to change were already somewhat freed from the constraints of family and tradition and already experienced some social and economic mobility. Family migration was more characteristic of Jewish immigrants than of other immigrants.

Most of the religious leaders and their closest followers remained in Eastern Europe. They correctly viewed America as threatening to their authority and their religious traditions. As they defined America the *trayfa medina*, the "impure country," the socialists and secularists, who were disproportionately among the immigrants, saw America as the "golden land" and the "promised land." They brought with them the cultural societies, unions, and political parties of eastern European Jewry, leaving behind the religious institutions, including the religious educational institutions.

Most Jewish immigrants did not sever their ties to their places of origin, even as they became American. Kinship and friendship ties were the bases of further immigration of relatives and friends from communities of origin. Chain migration, not return migration, was a dominant feature of eastern European Jewish immigration to America. Forms of international ties developed among Jewish immigrants, shaping networks of support and interaction among immigrants and their children. Settlement and organizational patterns in America reinforced ties to communities of origin. Building religious and welfare institutions, coming from the same region, living close together in neighborhoods, immigrants conveyed to their children the sense of community and culture of places of origins, including the depths of their Jewish identification. By the first and second decades of the 20th century, thousands of independent *landsmanschaften* and local immigrant organizations existed in American cities where Jews were concentrated.

The immigrant generation was residentially concentrated in particular neighborhoods, in a few large cities, dominated by New York (by 1920, almost half the Jews in the United States lived in New York and almost two-thirds lived in three states; almost 85 percent were concentrated in cities of 100,000 or more population, compared with less than 30 percent of the total population; only 3 percent of the Jews lived in rural areas, compared with 46 percent of the total population). The economic activities of Jewish immigrants distinguished them from those they left behind in places of origin and other immigrants. The overwhelming concentration of immigrant Jews in skilled labor provided Jews with enormous structural advantage over other immigrants in the pursuit of occupational integration and social mobility. There emerged a distinct overlap among Jewish immigrants of ethnicity and occupation with very powerful economic networks, occupational niches, and occupational concentration (Kuznets, 1960; Lieberson, 1980; Goldscheider and Zuckerman, 1986).

Their social and economic background, residential and occupational concentration, and family characteristics allowed immigrant Jews to take advantage of the expanding educational opportunities in America. Working in more skilled and stable occupations, Jews earned more money than did other immigrant groups. This facilitated their investment in the education of their children. Over time, the direction of the links between occupations and educational levels reversed, allowing those with better educations to obtain better jobs. But the mobility away from neighborhoods of initial settlement and to new jobs and higher levels of education were carried out as a group process. Attending college, for example, usually occurred among commuters (who lived at home); new communities of Jews were created even as they moved away from family. By 1920, at least 80–90 percent of the students enrolled in City College and Hunter College in New York were Jewish. Before Columbia University instituted restrictive quotas after World War I, some 40 percent of its student enrollment was Jewish (Steinberg, 1974; Perlmann, 1988).

The immigrant generation could not shed their Jewishness even as they would change it. Their foreignness and their structural and cultural features prevented or constrained their full assimilation, as did the discrimination they encountered. Residential, educational, and occupational networks joined family and organizational networks to reinforce a cohesive ethnic community. These bases of cohesion would inevitably change as the children of immigrants moved to new residences, attended new schools, obtained new jobs, and faced the economic depression of the 1930s and the war in the 1940s. Yet the children of immigrants were raised in families where an ethnic language was distinctive, where cultural closeness to origins was undeniable, where families were cohesive and supportive, and where networks and institutions were ethnically based. Combined, these powerful elements made the second generation Jewish by both religion and ethnicity. But their ethnicity (in the sense of national origin) was fading, and their Jewishness was becoming Americanized, defined by religious differentiation. Although sharply different from the Jewishness of their parents' generation, their children's Jewishness was clear and distinctive by American standards. The critical issue of change and continuity among Jewish Americans focuses initially on generations in the sense of closeness to foreign origins and to length of time in American society. The continuation of integration into the third and fourth generations, distant from cultural origins, raises directly the question of the changing culture (i.e., quality) of American Jewish life.

At work, in neighborhoods, in schools, as well as in religious, political, and social activities, immigrant Jews and their children were interacting with other Jews. Yiddish and socialist schools and newspapers competed with public and religious schools. Credit associations, *landmanschaften*, local fraternal and communal institutions appeared and expanded. While learning English, Yiddish remained the language of business and social life among Jewish immigrants. Even when their children rejected Yiddish as their language, it was still the cultural environment of their upbringing. In the pre–World War II period, most Jews in America interacted with other Jews in their community. The number of bases of cohesion among Jews was large indeed. The overlap of occupation, residence, and ethnicity was as high in America as anywhere in urban Europe. Jews left the Old World behind, not all of it to be sure, to become American. Their Jewishness was conspicuous by their background, culture, and social structure.

Stratification

What happened to the community and ethnic and religious identity among the descendants of immigrants? Clearly, the third and later generations faced a very different social and economic context. Shaping generational social and residential mobility was the role of the educational and occupational opportunity structure and, in turn, the basis of new forms of communal cohesion. I, therefore, begin the review of the transformation of American Jews with stratification since it is a key structural condition that affects cohesion within Jewish communities in the United States. I review the occupation and education of Jews using evidence from 1910, 1970, and 1990 national data sources (U.S. censuses and sample surveys) on Jewish men and women and in comparison with other white non-Hispanics. First the long-term changes in Jewish American stratification and its continuing distinctive communal patterns are described. These changes are then linked to selected measures of the intensity (or quality) of American Jewish life, examining the impact of educational attainment, occupational type, and occupational concentration on religious and ethnic Jewish expressions. The evidence provides a basis for assessing the consequences of the changing stratification profile for the continuing developments of the American Jewish community.

Education

The story of the changing educational profile of the American Jewish community from the turn of the 20th century to its end is for the most part clear and well known. Jews in the United States have become the most educated group of all American ethnic and religious groups, of all Jewish communities around the world, and of all Jewish communities ever in recorded Jewish history. This is quite a feat, given the low level of education of the American Jewish community three to four generations ago, and this accomplishment reflects both the value that Jews place on education and the educational opportunities available in the United States. Over 90 percent of contemporary American Jewish young men and young women go on to college, and they are the children of mothers and fathers who also have studied in college—two generations of men and women who are college educated. Many have grandparents who have exposure to some college education. Increases in the educational level of the American

Jewish population have been documented in every study carried out over the last several decades, and the level attained is a distinguishing feature of American Jewish communities. It may be a core value of contemporary American Jewish culture.

National data sources allow us to analyze this dramatic change in detail. Using both the 1970 and 1990 National Jewish Population Surveys, along with comparable data on the non-Hispanic white population from U.S. census and Current Population Survey data, I constructed the educational attainment levels of American Jews born in the pre-1905 period to 1950–60. These cohorts show how school enrollment ranged from the first decade of the 20th century through 1990s. These reconstructed data highlight several important features of the educational transformation of American Jews (see the statistical details in Goldscheider, 1997b).

First, cohorts of Jewish men and women born before 1905 had relatively low levels of education that first increased for men and then for women. Viewing these cohorts as the experience of a generation, Jewish men and women born in the first decade of the 20th century aggregated at low levels of education. Even those who completed high school were exceptional within the Jewish community, as well as among their non-Jewish age-peers. Those growing up at the end of the 20th century are college graduates; those not completing college have become clear exceptions among Jews. In contrast, those born in the 1920s and 1930s attained a much greater range of educational levels than the cohorts born before or after them. These middle cohorts lived through a period of transition in the schooling of American Jews, where the rate of educational change and the choices about whether to continue schooling at various stages were at a maximum. The transformation from a generation characterized by low levels of education to a generation where two generations of Jews are characterized by college levels of education is clearly reflected in these contrasts. The generation of educational transition and heterogeneity was also the generation of greatest tension between foreignness and Americanization. Hence, generational conflict was greatest during this period.

These educational data refer to individuals, retrospectively constructed, with generation and compositional changes inferred. Cross-sectional views that are contemporary with the periods examined are powerful additional reminders of how the community appeared educationally at various points. The 1910 U.S. census provides us with a brief glimpse of educational patterns for Jews and others. Data on literacy point to lower levels among Jewish men than others in 1910 and significantly lower levels among Jewish women than either men or other women. So the educational starting point for Jews, most of whom were recent immigrants in 1910, was lower than others. Estimates of school enrollment by age in 1910 suggest that Jewish children aged 14–18 were less likely than native whites to be in school and even less than some other immigrant groups. But Jewish men who were born in the United States had much higher enrollment levels and the highest estimated years of schooling completed. Moreover, comparing national data on two cross sections of Jews and others in 1970 and 1990, encompassing the variety of cohorts that characterized the American Jewish community at those two points confirm three central points about the educational transformation of Jews: (1) Jews have become a community with distinctively high levels of education and higher than others in the United States; (2) there has been a systematic increase in the levels of education over the last 30 years, reducing only marginally the gap between Jews and others; and (3) the Jewish community as a whole has become more concentrated at the upper end of the educational distribution, reducing the educational heterogeneity among Jews and thereby increasing the structural basis of community and the commonality between generations.

Occupation

How have these educational patterns been translated into occupational changes? What have been the changing patterns of occupational concentration among both men and women? Consistent with the literature (e.g., Chiswick, 1991; Kessner, 1977; Lieberson, 1980; Goldscheider, 1986) and with the educational patterns, 1910 census data show that a majority of American Jews (i.e., those who were living in households where Yiddish was the mother tongue) were either skilled or semiskilled workers. Few were professionals or managers. When Jews worked in white-collar jobs, they tended toward "sales" and not "clerical" work. Jewish women in 1910 were heavily concentrated in these same categories of blue-collar work, and few were in professional and managerial jobs or in sales. At the turn of the 20th century, Jewish men were distinctive in their greater concentration in sales and, along with Jewish women, in their lower concentration in jobs classified as "service." Jewish women were exceptional in their very high concentration in skilled and unskilled work. Thus, Jewish occupational distinctiveness at the turn of the 20th century in the United States was not the result of their position in jobs at higher levels but in their involvement in sales or in factory work.

In the two generations to 1970, the Jewish occupational pyramid was up-ended: it shifted from having 55 percent of the males in worker or service positions in 1910 to having 69 percent in professional and manager positions in 1970; from 73 percent of the Jewish women with jobs classified as worker or service categories in 1910 to 46 percent in professional and managerial jobs in 1970 and 37 percent in clerical jobs. Between 1970 and 1990, there was an increase in professional occupations among Jewish men and women, along with a rather sharp decline (over 50 percent) in managerial positions among Jewish men.

Despite these radical shifts over time, the Jewish occupational structure remains distinctive in the United States when compared with white non-Hispanics in metropolitan areas. Particularly conspicuous is the greater concentration of Jews in professional jobs, paralleling their educational attainments. We compare the occupational concentration of Jews and non-Jews from three additional perspectives: (1) the extent of self-employment, (2) the specific jobs Jews have within broad occupational categories and their concentration within them, and (3) the proportion of the total occupational distribution that is captured by a small number of jobs.

SELF-EMPLOYMENT

The data from the 1910 census subdivide employment status into three categories: employer, own account, and working for wages. Not surprisingly, almost everyone worked for wages in 1910—Jews and others, men and women. Nevertheless, Jewish men were much more likely to be self-employed or to be an employer than were others. One-third of the Jewish males who were working were self-employed, compared with 16 percent of the total population. Estimates from the 1970 and 1990 National Jewish Population Surveys suggest that the proportion of self-employed Jewish men declined between 1970 and 1990, from 38 percent to 32 percent. The level of self-employment remains high for Jewish men, and its pattern contrasts with the total population, which experienced an increase from 10 percent to 15 percent. Thus, despite some convergence in the level of self-employment between Jewish and other males, the Jewish level continues to be distinctive. Even as the level of self-employment remained higher among Jews, the meaning of self-employment has also radically changed. Self-employed professionals and self-employed tailors not only require different levels of education but also are likely to have different implications for generational occupational transfers and for ethnic networks.

The data also show that Jewish women were not very different from other women in their employment status, suggesting that gender differences in employment (not only in jobs) were more distinctive between men and women than between Jews and others. As with men, the level of self-employment among Jewish women remains distinctively higher than others.

OCCUPATIONAL CONCENTRATION

A key theme in the analysis of educational and occupational changes over time has been how the intergenerational social mobility of American Jews has allowed them to become integrated into the mainstream of American life. However, social mobility has been a group phenomenon occurring to significant segments of entire cohorts and, hence, has resulted in educational and occupational reconcentration rather than simple assimilation. I have already noted the changes in the educational concentration of Jews—Jews moved from high levels of educational concentration at low levels of educational attainment to a greater diversity of educational levels during the transition, and then to a new intensity of concentration at high educational levels. The same pattern emerges for occupational shifts that have led to reconcentration from 1910 to 1990.

This reconcentration can be observed when specific jobs are examined, not only for the standard occupational categories that the census has categorized. I organized the specific jobs that accounted for 50 percent of the total occupational distribution of Jews and calculated as well the percentage of the total population in these specific jobs. The data show that 50 percent of all working Jewish men were located in only six specific occupations in 1910, which encompassed only 11 percent of the total population. The concentration in skilled and semiskilled work and also in specific jobs was even greater for Jewish women than for both Jewish men and the total population. Over 50 percent of the Jewish working women in 1910 were located in only five occupations; only 12 percent of the total female population were in these occupations.

In 1970, almost 30 percent of Jewish men were in managerial and administrator positions, compared with 7 percent of the total white population. Lawyers, accountants, and physicians accounted for a disproportionate number of Jewish male occupations, as did retail and wholesale sales jobs. In each case, these areas of job concentration were significantly greater for Jews than for the total white population. But the range of jobs diversified as the location of jobs within the occupational hierarchy increased. Jewish women were also concentrated in a limited number of jobs in 1970. Like most women, they were disproportionately secretaries, with only small differences between Jewish and other women. Compared with other women, a significant number of Jewish women were managers and administrators, schoolteachers at all grade levels, sales workers, and sales clerks. The much broader number of occupations characterizing Jewish men and women in the 1970s than in 1910 reflected the educational changes and widening of the occupational opportunities as the American economy developed, as a general character of the country as a whole and among Jews in particular. Both occupational diversity and new types of occupational concentration emerged among Jews by the 1970s.

These patterns continued through the 1990 period. Again, examining particular jobs and the number that accounts for about one-half of the job distribution of Jews reveals both a significantly longer list in 1990 than in 1970 and a continuing occupational distinctiveness of Jews, when compared with the total population. In 1990, as before, occupational distinctiveness continued, along with the dispersal of Jews within the American occupational structure. Comparing 1970 and 1990 shows the shift away from managerial positions toward both more specialized and new professional jobs. Where comparisons with the non-Jewish occupational distribution is possible, the continued distinctiveness of the distribution of jobs among Jews becomes evident, even as the number of jobs that make up one-half of the occupational structure increased. There was a shift in jobs among Jewish women in the two decades to 1990, parallel to the changes for Jewish men. Jewish women in the labor force moved out of secretarial work toward greater job diversity and professional jobs, although the impression remains of continued gender segregation in the workplace among Jews as among others.

Implications of Stratification for Jewishness

What do these stratification changes imply for the continuity of the American Jewish community? There are two views. On the one hand, increases in educational attainment and the diversification of occupational types result in greater interaction with "others" who are not Jewish. These new contexts of interaction between Jews and non-Jews challenge the isolation and segregation of Jews and, in turn, the cohesion of the Jewish community. The institutional contexts of schooling and the workplace may also expose Jewish Americans to new networks and alternative values that are not ethnically or religiously Jewish. The combination of interaction and exposure may result in a diminishing of the distinctiveness of the community over time through family changes and generational discontinuity.

There is another side of this picture: the commonality of social class among Jews and the distinctiveness of Jews relative to others are important sources of cohesion of the Jewish community. Jews are both marked off from others and linked with other Jews by their resources, networks, and lifestyles, which are the obvious implications of their occupational-educational distinctiveness and high levels of attainment. To the extent that community is based on shared interaction among members and a common set of values and lifestyles, these occupational and educational transformations among American Jews are significant bases of communal cohesion. The mobility of Jews away from the occupations characteristic of the immigrant generation has been a dominant theme in research. Missing has been an emphasis on the new forms of concentration that have emerged.

The alternative outcomes of the educational and occupational transformations that Jews have experienced in 20th-century America are often presented in oversimplified and extreme forms. Clearly, American Jews cannot be characterized as either a totally assimilated community (in the sense of the loss of communal cohesion) or as an isolated, totally cohesive community. There is no consensus about how or even what to measure to assess the quality of Jewish life in America at the end of the 20th century. Nor is there sufficient evidence about the nature and implications of the networks that Jews have developed over the life course and generationally. So the emerging balance of Jewish communal life and its linkage to the educational and occupational changes experienced by Jews cannot be assessed fully.

Specific national data on selected aspects of Jewish expression can be linked to the educational and occupational patterns that we have outlined. A review of some analytic explorations along these lines is suggestive. Measures of Jewishness that tapped the multidimensional ethnic and religious expressions of Jews in 1990—including seasonal ritual observances (Passover and Hanukah), traditional rituals (Kashrut and Shabbat observances), organizational participation (Jewish educational and organizational activities), associational ties (Jewish friends and neighbors), philanthropy (contributions to Jewish charities), and intermarriage attitudes—were related to the occupational and educational characteristics of households. Not surprisingly, the results are complex. Several core results are revealing. First, many of the education and occupation measures are not related directly to contemporary indicators of Jewishness but operate in the context of the family life course (e.g., age, family structure, presence and ages of children). Occupation was only weakly related to most of the factors that were examined. It appears that the commonality of jobs and self-employment are not directly linked with religious and most ethnic ties.

The data are consistent with the argument that the meaning of self-employment and occupational concentration has altered over the generations and, hence, the implications of these factors for Jewish continuity may also have changed. In the past, educational attainment and occupational mobility were linked to disaffection from the ethnic community. That is no longer the case. The absence of a relationship between occupation and measures of Jewishness may also imply that having these occupational ties is a sufficient basis for Jewish interaction and Jewish networks. If occupational concentration substitutes for Jewish communal and religious networks, then we should expect that the relationship between social class concentration and measures of Jewishness would be weak. There are no measures of ethnic economic resources, ethnic networks, and ethnic business connections to test out these arguments directly.

The data also show that several indicators of education reinforce and strengthen Jewish expressions, particularly those that are tied to participation in Jewish communal activities and ties. College education seems to promote Jewish-related activities for the age group below age 45, although this is less the case among older cohorts. In this sense, the relationship between attending college and Jewishness that was negatively related to Jewishness in the past had changed significantly by the 1990s. Again, this is consistent with the view that the Jewish alienation presumed to be associated with higher levels of educational attainment occurs when higher education is an exceptional group feature characteristic of the few. When exposure to college and university education is an almost universal experience for American Jews, its impact on Jewishness becomes minimal (e.g., Wilder, 1996).

Finally, there is no systematic evidence from these results that the changed stratification profile results in the abandonment of the American Jewish community in terms of the wide range of Jewish expressions. There is no systematic relationship between becoming a professional, working for others, being in a job where there are few Jews, on the one hand, and most, if not all, of the measures of Judaic expression as individual measures or as part of a general index, on the other.

Contexts of Assimilation

Neither high levels of educational attainment nor being in managerial and professional jobs weakens the intensity of Jewishness in all of its multifaceted expressions. It is likely that the commonality of social class among American Jews and their very high levels of educational and occupational reconcentration are not sufficient to generate the intensive in-group interaction that characterized the segregated Jewish communities in some areas of eastern Europe and the United States a century ago. The benefits of these stratification transformations in terms of networks and resources have not re-created the cultural and social communities of Jews of a different era. Nevertheless, the evidence indicates that the emerging social class patterns are not a threat to Jewish continuity in the transformed pluralism of American society.

The educational and occupational transformations of 20th-century America mark Jews off from others and connect Jews to one another. The connections among persons who share history and experience and their separation from others are what social scientists refer to as "community." The distinctiveness of the American Jewish community in these stratification patterns is clear. When these stratification profiles are added to the residential concentration of American Jews, the community features become even sharper. Many have noted the move away from areas of immigrant residential concentration, the residential dispersal of American Jews, and the reshaping of new forms of residential concentration for the second and later generations of American Jews. The national data on educational and occupational concentration only begin to tell the story of new forms of community interaction. The residential and occupational concentration of Jews, attendance at selective schools and colleges away from home, and work in selected metropolitan areas have resulted in a geographic concentration of American Jews that is astonishing for a voluntary ethnic group several generations removed from foreignness and not facing the discrimination of other American minorities.

The value placed by Jews on educational attainment as a mechanism for becoming American (and obtaining good jobs and making higher incomes) clearly is manifest in the context of the opportunities open to Jews in the United States. Their higher level of education and their concentration in professional and managerial jobs has not led to the "erosion" or total assimilation of the Jewish community. While these stratification changes may result in the disaffection of some individual Jews from the community, it may also result in the greater incorporation within the Jewish community of some who were not born Jewish, as well as the general attractiveness of the community to Jews and others.

Educational, residential, and occupational concentration implies not only cohesion and lifestyle similarity but also exposure to options for integration and assimilation. Education implies exposure to conditions and cultures that are more universalistic and away from ethnic-based education, even when most Jews are sharing this experience and are heavily concentrated in a select number of colleges and universities. If high levels of educational attainment and occupational achievement enhance the choices that Jews make about their Jewishness, then Jewish identification and the intensity of Jewish expression are becoming increasingly voluntary in 21st-century America. In that sense, the new forms of American Jewish stratification have beneficial implications for the quality of Jewish life. There is a balance between the forces that pull Jews toward each other, often referred to as "assimilation," so that they share what we call "community"—families, experiences, history, concerns, values, communal institutions, rituals, religion, and lifestyles—and those that pull Jews away from each other. The evidence available suggests that the pulls and pushes of the changing stratification profile toward and away from the Jewish community are profound. They are positive in strengthening the Jewish community and represent a challenge for institutions to find ways to reinforce their communal and cultural benefits.

One of the core values of contemporary American Jewish culture is education. There is a paradox in this context: The secular educational attainment so distinctive among Jews and derived from Jewish values is not only un-Jewish in content but is viewed by some as the source of assimilation. Better-educated Jews, so it is often argued, are exposed in colleges to either secular or Christian values (or both) and are influenced by Americanism, meet non-Jewish persons whom they marry, and as a result become less Jewish, more assimilated, and over time are lost to the Jewish community. So, the circle is complete: distinctive Jewish values result in high educational attainment of Jews, which, in turn, seems to be responsible for the assimilation of Jews!

Clearly, secular education is not the source of assimilation since many well-educated Jews remain attached to the Jewish community; the evidence available points unmistakably to the absence of any systematic relationship between years of education and types of Jewish expression—religious or ethnic. In the past, however, education was associated with a decline of Jewishness. And the data also show that particularistic Jewish education is not deteriorating, since so many young and older Jewish adults are obtaining a superior Jewish education in a wide variety of Jewish institutions and in diverse packaging.

There are two important points to stress about education in the past. Educational attainment in the past was one powerful path toward social mobility. Education led to better jobs, higher incomes, escape from poverty of the unskilled and skilled labor characteristic of parents, and, in turn, an escape from the neighborhoods and networks that consisted of the foreign-born. Education was a means or escape from the association of foreignness with a foreign language, a foreign culture, and foreign parents. For many, education was the escape from Jewishness and Judaism. In short, education was the path to becoming American but required leaving the community.

Education has almost always been celebrated among Jews, with pride in the group's accomplishments. When children and grandchildren became doctors and lawyers, skilled business people and teachers, it was thought that this was the "Jewish" thing to do. But in those early years there was a cost. The cost was for Judaism and Jewishness and, more important, for relationships between the generations. Although parents encouraged their children to obtain a high level of education, the lifestyle associated with higher education often meant conflict between parents and children who had different educational levels and between siblings and peers who had different access to educational opportunities.

But looking beyond the costs, we now appreciate the value of education over the last two generations. Here the value of education has not lessened, but the opportunities have increased and spread. Education has not disrupted Jewishness but increased generational similarities and removed one source of the generation gap. So the meaning of two generations of college-educated Jews becomes not simply a note of group congratulations and pride, not only a changed relationship to Jewishness as a basis of intergenerational commonality. Educational attainment has become a feature of families that is not disruptive and points to sharing and common experiences.

So an analysis of educational attainment points to the increased power of families, the generational increase in resources, and the common lifestyles that far from dividing families again bind parents and children together to a network of relationships. These emphases on education and achievement, as well as family cohesion and values, have become group traits that make the Jewish group attractive to others. Unlike in the past, when interaction and marriage between Jews and non-Jews was also a mechanism of escape from Jewishness and foreignness, the Jewish group has now become attractive to others because of their family and communal traits, particularly education. And, like education, intermarriage cannot have the same meaning in the new context of generations as it did in the older context of rejection and escape. By binding the generations, education has become a family value.

Intermarriage and Families

If family is important and its meaning has changed, we need to directly confront the increasing rates of intermarriage among third and later generations of eastern European Jewish immigrants. Intermarriage has become an obsession of Jewish communal leaders, some social scientists, many journalists, and Jewish parents.

For a community to survive or to flourish, some attention needs to focus at the most elementary level on generational renewal. An ethnic or religious group requires particular attention to generational replacement. Institutions without people become heirlooms to be preserved in museums, as relics of the past and interesting artifacts for archeologists and historians. For continued survival, institutions must focus on demographic continuity. To do so requires attention to renewal; in the American context, generational renewal is anchored in the family.

The family has changed so much in the last several decades that the immigrant great-grandparents might not recognize it; we hardly do. And in the context of family and continuity, we confront what some consider the most "threatening" group process to emerge: intermarriage between Jews and non-Jews. In general, I think that the Jewish community's concern with intermarriage is misleading and misdirected.

In the past 100 years, although intermarriage rates were low, the phenomenon had been devastating. Those who intermarried repudiated their religion, their families, and their communities. And their religion, families, and communities abandoned them. The loss was to their generation and an irrevocable loss to the generations that would have come. So the obsession of the American Jewish community with intermarriage as threatening to the community is understandable. However, the context of American Jewish communities and the circumstances of the lives of American Jews from 1970 to 2000 have changed. The changing integration of American Jews is associated with the increasing social contact between Jews and others. Universalistic criteria have opened choices in residence, jobs, and marriage. The move toward non-Jewish circles is particularly conspicuous in choices of spouses and neighbors.

We focus on intermarriage between Jews and non-Jews precisely because it symbolizes the nature of Jewish/non-Jewish interaction and, by inference, the potential weakening of the Jewish community. It directly addresses the question of Jewish values. The issue in a voluntary community is who is a member and affiliated with the community. Being Jewish in America and being part of the community is a question of who is in the Jewish group—not only who you marry but also the Jewishness of the next generation and, hence, the continuity of the community. In America, by and large, Jewish group membership is voluntary, based on a social and not a biological or a religious legal definition. It is informal, group membership, but it is no less powerful.

The evidence shows that most American Jews continue to be Jewish by the standards of being born into a Jewish family. But there is an increasing reality of new Jews in the United States. Being Jewish and the process of conversion to Judaism or making commitments to the Jewish community varies through the lifecourse. Jewish identification increases as families are formed and children need to be educated. And the major source of Jewish identification for American Jews is ethnic-communal, not narrowly religious. Therefore, the issue is not intermarriage but Jewishness in the family and household: that is, how people conduct their lives and raise their children and are linked to their extended family and the broader Jewish community.

What is some of the evidence? There is no question that there have been increases in rates of intermarriage between Jews and non-Jews in the United States. In the past, Jewish men married out more than Jewish women, but that appears to no longer be the case. Since women tend to take a more active role in the home, this change was a basis for concern in the past, but now Jewish women who marry out may want to reinforce the Jewishness of the home. There is also no simple association between intermarriage and alienation from the Jewish community. The relative rates of generational continuity of the intermarried within the Jewish community (i.e., how many children raised in households where one or more persons was not born Jewish remain Jewish in a variety of ways as they form their own families) have changed over the last decade as the levels of intermarriage and conversions have increased, and as the levels of acceptance of the intermarried within the Jewish community have increased as well. So now what happens to the spouses and the children of those who marry out? Are they always lost to the American Jewish community?

The attached diagram (Table 7-1) is an exercise. I have made up the numbers based on some evidence to illustrate some of the popular misconceptions in understanding intermarriage rates. In the first generation, let us suppose that there are ten couples. Half of the couples are Jewish by birth; 70 percent of the couples are Jewish either by birth or by religious conversion. Looking at individuals not couples shows that of the 15 Jews in this generation (or cohort), 10 are married to born Jews (or 66 percent). In this generation, there are 15 born Jews and 2 conversions to Judaism—hence, a gain of two Jews to the Jewish community. A demographic gain for the Jewish community with an individual rate of intermarriage of 33 percent (when 5 out of 15 born Jews marry persons not born Jewish) and a couple intermarriage rate of 50 percent. So when one-third of the Jews marry non-Jews and one-half of the couples consist of Jews marrying born non-Jews, the Jewish community gains two additional Jews. This gain occurs when conversions to Judaism or identification with Jewish families take place among only 40 percent of the non-Jews who marry Jews (two out of five). In short, there can be group gains with high individual or couple intermarriage rates.

The key question, some may argue, is the second generation, the children of the intermarried. I agree, but in ways that the data show may be surprising. This time we look at the second generation. For this exercise, I postulate an estimated 15 Jewish children, assuming each couple in the first generation has two children. This is exactly the same number of Jews as in the first generation. How does this come about? We are assuming that each of the Jewish couples has two Jewish children and that the converted or identified Jewish families each have two Jewish children. We are also assuming that only one out of six children of families where Jews are married to nonconverted and non-self-identified Jews will be Jewish. What would be the case if one-half of the intermarried had children who were raised as Jews rather than one out of six? I should note that the actual figures seem to be that about 40 percent of the children of Jewish intermarriages are identified as Jewish and 60 percent are identified by their parents as Jewish or as noncommitted.

The lessons to be learned from this simulation are twofold:

TABLE 7.1
Intermarriage Diagram

	First Generation	Second Generation
1.	Jew**Jew	Two Jews
2.	Jew**Jew	Two Jews
3.	Jew**Jew	Two Jews
4.	Jew**Jew	Two Jews
5.	Jew**Jew	Two Jews
6.	Jew**Non-Jew Converted	Two Jews
7.	Jew**Non-Jew Converted	Two Jews
8.	Jew**Non-Jew (Not Converted)	One Jew and One Non-Jew
9.	Jew**Non-Jew (Not Converted)	Two Non-Jews
10.	Jew**Non-Jew (Not Converted)	Two Non-Jews

Note: In the first generation 50 percent of the couples are both Jewish by birth; 50 percent of the couples involve one partner who is not born Jewish.

Of the 15 Jews in this generation, ten, or 67 percent, are married to born Jews.

There are 15 born Jews and two conversions to Judaism, hence a gain of two Jews in this generation.

There are an estimated 15 Jewish children in the second generation, assuming each couple in the first generation has two children and only one out of six children of families where the non-Jewish partner did not convert was raised Jewish . This number of Jews is the same number as the number born Jewish in the first generation.

High intermarriage rates of individuals and couples may result in group stability when conversions or Jewish identification occur. More important, numerical stability with intermarriage occurs when children are raised as Jews. Intermarriage is not the question, but generational continuity is—that is, the Jewishness of homes and families.

A generation perspective is needed to identify who are raised as Jews and, more important, who grow up to be Jewish and have a Jewish family. The question becomes, how many of the children are raised as Jewish and encouraged to want to be Jewish as adults?

What do these patterns add up to? It is clear that formal conversions to Judaism or identifying with the Jewish group are paths to raising Jewish children, adding religion to the ethnic dimension. There are large numbers of non-Jewish-born persons who identify themselves as Jews and who are identified as Jews by their family, friends, and the Jewish community, without formal conversions, and who are engaged in family, communal, and organizational activities that are Jewish. There is also increasing evidence that nonconversion at the time of marriage does not foreclose the possibility of conversion to Judaism at a later point in time. Jewish identification and practices at the time of marriage do not remain constant over the life course. Therefore, it is *not* marriage per se or a particular religious ceremony but the context of the household and family, doing things Jewishly that creates the potential for demographic continuity.

It is particularly important to reiterate that the Jewishness of the home is not limited to religious practices or ritual observances. This is the case as well for the Jewishness of couples where both spouses were born Jewish. Rather, family, communal, and associational *networks* are the key indicators of Jewish continuity. Institutions are community ways to organize these networks. Institutions create the content of Jewish identity and the changing cultural values of the group. Even using religious affiliation, the majority of intermarried Jewish couples, including those without conversion, identify with a religious institution, occasionally attend religious services, and perform religious seasonal rituals at only slightly lower levels than are observed by born Jews married to born Jews (see also Cohen, 2001).

Thus, intermarriage and disengagement from the Jewish community are no longer synonymous. Since those who intermarry are often not less attached to the Jewish community and no less Jewish in their behavior and commitments, increasing rates of intermarriage by themselves are poor indicators of the weakening quality of Jewish life. Intermarriage is not necessarily the final step toward total assimilation. In most intermarriages, the *Jewish* partner remains attached to the Jewish community, and unlike in the past, in many cases, the non-Jewish-born partner becomes attached to the Jewish community, as do many of the children of the intermarried, through family, friends, neighborhood, and Jewish organizational ties. Many of their friends are Jewish, many support Israel, and many identify themselves as Jews. And some proportion of spouses and their children formally convert to Judaism, many becoming Jewish under the direction of religious leaders and their institutions.

In conjunction with the increasing rate of intermarriage, and associated with its high level, has been the increasing acceptance of the intermarried by Jewish families and by the secular and religious institutions of the community. Unlike in the past, the intermarried are more likely to be accepted and even welcomed in the Jewish community. Hence, when taken together, the research evidence shows that intermarriage should not be viewed as the quintessential indicator of assimilation among American Jews. The increasing rate of intermarriage therefore does not necessarily mean declines of the Jewish community. Intermarriage may even imply strength when significant proportions of the intermarried are actively involved in being Jewish and practicing Judaism. High intermarriage rates unambiguously mean that the networks of Jews are touched, affected, and linked to the intermarriage issue and that the proportion is larger than the percentage who are currently intermarrying. There is hardly a Jewish household in America that has not experienced the taste of intermarriage of a family member, a neighbor, or a friend.

Therefore, whether intermarriage should be treated as a sign of erosion of the American Jewish community depends on the Jewish commitments of the intermarried to the Jewish community and the eventual commitments of their children. Much depends as well on how the Jewish community, the formal religious and secular institutional structure, accepts and nourishes linkages between those born Jewish and those Jewish by their identification, commitment, and conversions. It is important to see the issue of intermarriage from the perspective of the next generation, young adults who have been raised with an open positive value of family and community and who struggle with the question of what the community and the family will do in enhancing the acceptance of new family members. So while marriage may be based on individual decision-making, marriage links families and families are the basis of community. Marriage and the formation of new families are critical for the quality of American Jewish life in the 21st century.

Concluding Thoughts

Jews in America are surviving; indeed, some Jewish communities are thriving. Contemporary American Jewish communities have resources, money, education, health and talent, and organizations and institutions on a scale that is unprecedented in historical memory. The survival of American Jews is less threatened by external forces than ever before. Indeed, the external forces bring together the diverse communities that are American Jews and create the new basis of culture and commitment. Most Jews in most Jewish communities in the United States have found unparalleled freedom and choice. And the amazing fact of our day is that when confronted with freedom and choice, most Jews choose to be Jewish rather than something else. Shared lifestyles, common background, similar educational levels, common culture, agreed-upon goals about Israel and communal survival, and extensive and diverse institutions and organizations cement the religious and ethnic distinctiveness of American Jews. All this occurs in the context of the powerful forces of integration and assimilation. Indeed, it may be because of the openness and pluralism of American society that American Jewish communities remain distinctive.

The Jewish community has constructed for itself three compelling arguments about the Jewish past and present. Somewhat oversimplified, these arguments are as follows. The first argument is that Jewish communities have moved over the last century from communities based on religion and religious activities to secular communities. In modern, open, voluntary societies, Jews, like others, have become more secular and less attached to religious activities, religious institutions, and a religious way of life. Whatever religious orientations their grandparents and great-grandparents had, today's Jews have fewer of them. Religion is simply less central to their lives today, so it is argued. Judaism, has itself become secular. This is the so-called secularization theme.

A second argument focuses on the ethnic or the peoplehood dimension of Jewish identity. Jews in the past, so the argument goes, had a distinctive sense of being a people apart from the Christian and Muslim societies where they lived. Being a minority meant lack of access to opportunities and exposure to discrimination in everyday life. Those features were the minimum consequences of minority status of Jews everywhere. However, with increasing openness of society, the expansion of political rights and economic opportunities and the acceptance of Jews into society, the ethnic component has diminished. As other white immigrant groups, Jews have assimilated into western societies. Jews have accepted their new situation and have been accepted by others. As generational distance from ethnic origins has increased—most contemporary American Jews do not have grandparents who have experienced living outside of the United States—the ethnic distinctiveness of American Jews has faded. Jews have become thoroughly American. So the second argument suggests that ethnic identity recedes and ethnic assimilation occurs over time.

A third argument follows directly from the secularization and assimilation arguments and combines the first two. It argues that as religious identity weakens and ethnic identity fades, the Jewish community weakens. What remains, therefore, is the need for external stimuli to ignite the dying embers of Jewishness. At times, these sparks come from some ethnic cultural attachment and pride in a new nation-state (Israel) or some recognition of Jewish vulnerability to external forces that threaten survival. Thus, as secularization diminishes the Judaism component and assimilation decreases the Jewish ethnic component, there remain few internally generated Jewish values or features of Jewish culture to sustain a community. As Judaism and Jewishness fade, so the argument goes, nothing beyond externals can form the basis for the future growth of Jewish communities outside of the state of Israel. These three arguments about secularization, assimilation, and cultural distinctiveness have in one form or another informed discussions of contemporary American Jewish communities.

A systematic body of evidence, I submit, challenges these arguments. The paths Jewish communities have taken in modern, open pluralistic societies are certainly not fully described by these themes. The dichotomy between religious and ethnic identity is not as useful among Jews as among other groups. Jews are not simply a group other than Protestants or Catholics, Mormons or Muslims. American Jews are also not simply like Italian Americans or Hispanic Americans. The institutions that Jews have developed, the networks they have established, the families they have valued, and the concerns over external events in the globalized world of the 21st century are powerful bases for American Jewish cohesion. The commonalities of educational and occupational experiences over two generations, along with the power of institutions that search for new ways to construct the core of Jewish culture, reinforce continuity as they generate and reflect change. These bases are not the same as they were in the past. And the bases of community are unlikely to be the same in the future for the fifth and sixth generations of American Jews of eastern European ancestry. Whatever form it takes, the commonalities of lifestyle, stratification, and family will be the basis of the institutionalized construction of American Jewish culture.

‖‖

8

Choosing Chosenness in America
The Changing Faces of Judaism

Arnold Eisen

Some 70 years ago, as the children of the massive eastern European Jewish immigration to America moved to take full advantage of the unprecedented opportunities available to them, the major question debated in countless Jewish sermons, newspaper articles, plays, novels, and theological writings was whether and how Jews could continue to remain apart *from* American society and culture at the same time as they moved to become a full part *of* it. Hyphenated identity, a Jewish desideratum since the start of the modern period, finally seemed attainable. "America is different," Jews proclaimed, because it seemed, for the first time really, that they were not. This achievement, or the prospect of it, ironically brought the Jewish community face to face with a new sort of "Jewish problem," long anticipated but never before actually encountered—a question that still looms large in Jewish debates today. What can it mean to be Jewish in the absence of palpable Jewish difference? Identity, for two millennia a given, has become a persistent question in the United States over the past century, made such by the fact of American openness and diversity.

In part, it must be recognized, the source of the question does not lie in sociological transformation but in theological perplexity. For centuries, Jews had seen themselves, and had been seen by Christian or Muslim neighbors, as a people blessed and cursed with a unique divine covenant and mission. By the early decades of the 20th century, however, many Jews no longer believed that God had chosen their ancestor Abraham to perform a special task in the world, delivered the Israelites from Egypt, or issued a special revelation to them at Mount Sinai; they no longer expected that God would one day send the Messiah to redeem Jews from the lands to which they had been exiled as part of a divine plan for the world's education and salvation. Enlightenment had had its impact on many future immigrants even before they left the "old country" for the new, and in America the ancestral beliefs seemed still less compelling. A survey done in the 1930s indicates that the doubters had come to include a majority of the community's rabbis (Zeitlin, 1945). More than 70 years later, while belief in God as personal being or force remains high among Jews, traditional tenets of faith are held outside the Orthodox world by only a small minority (cf. Eisen, 1983; Cohen and Eisen, 2000).

These *theological* issues surrounding chosenness, however, have from the outset been framed, shaped, and exacerbated by the *sociological* transformation to which I have already alluded—one that continues to exert a major influence on Jewish belief and practice alike. For centuries, the claim to divine election has been given force and meaning by ghetto walls and everyday discrimination, and, in turn, has made sense of that isolation. Jewish self-definition became quite another matter when Jews sought and then achieved full participation, as one among a number of ethnic and religious immigrant minorities, in a society to which they, like all the others, belonged and called home. Hence the vexing and impassioned communal debate over Jewish distinctiveness and purpose that consumed Jews of the "second generation" and has not abated since. As one leading communal figure posed the matter in 1943, "Nation, people, religion— what are we?" (Morgenstern, 1943). It was already clear that hyphenated identity could not mean simply joining a given and stable Jewish selfhood to new American conditions and surroundings. Indeed, the very presence (or possibility) of the hyphen necessitated the interrogation of Judaism and Jewishness, as well as the effort to construct new meanings for Americanness. Recent decades, carrying on that discussion, have witnessed a new concern: the meaning of selfhood as such at a time of unparalleled individualism on the one hand and remarkable cultural diversity on the other. Both developments have immensely complicated the conception and formation of identity among Jews, as among all other groups.

My purpose in this essay is to reflect further on this theme, drawing on recent research into American Jewish identity, as well as recent writing on American religion and ethnicity more broadly. The study of 20th-century American Jews and Judaism has for some decades focused on the ways in which Jewish thinkers and the Jewish "laity"—whether of the "second," "third," or "fourth generation" from the point of immigration— have fashioned through ideas and institutions alike a set of new Jewish self-definitions designed to suit the new realities of diversity and actual or hoped-for pluralism. For all that "Jews *are* different" to some degree from other American religious and ethnic minorities—in large part because they have generally claimed that their identity partakes to some degree of *both* sorts of identity rather than only one—the study of Jewish debates on the matter should prove helpful in understanding other groups as well: "It could be argued that all immigrant ethnic identities in America have been tied at first, at least to some extent, to particularist religious affirmations. It is certainly true that they exhibited differences more substantive than those who defined the conditions for their acceptance would allow" (Eisen, 1983: 178). Jews have not been the only American immigrants and descendants of immigrants to face the choice between continued distinctiveness and incomplete assimilation on the one hand, with consequent testing of the limits of pluralism, or, on the other hand, the reduction of ethnic and religious distinctiveness to the "symbolic" dimensions described by sociologist Herbert Gans (1979). "To be other in America," I wrote 20 years ago, "has in practice proven a combination of the two: pretending a greater sameness than exists while at the same time claiming for otherness a greater substance than in fact remains to it" (Eisen 1983: 178). I hope to help explain why this continues to be the case in our day.

Judaism in the Second Generation (ca. 1925–50)

Calvin Goldscheider's essay in this volume (chapter 7) has well summarized the demographic, occupational, political, and social dimensions of Jewish adaptation and adjustment to America in the 1920s and 1930s. In the words of a leading rabbi of the "second generation," Milton Steinberg (1955 [1934]: 23–35), American Jews of that period stood between two worlds: one in which they could no longer live, the other of which would not admit them. Judaism as believed in and practiced by immigrant parents was unappealing. America, at a time of economic depression and rising anti-Semitism, was barring or closing doors it had promised to open wide, and "only a people of acrobats could preserve a semblance of poise on a footing so unstable" (247). The rabbis, for their part, strove to make Judaism relevant to, and so viable in, these changed and difficult circumstances. Several of the strategies that they pursued to that end are particularly noteworthy.

American Jewish thinkers of all denominations (but none so much as Reform) traded on the resonances of the Bible, and of chosenness in particular, to join Judaism with American ideology (cf. Eisen, 1983: 37–41). Leo Jung, the prominent Orthodox rabbi of the Jewish Center in New York City, declared in a 1939 sermon titled "Sinai and Washington" that Jews and Americans shared a divine mission to humanity: "And the Father of man bethought himself, and sent men to look for the country of their dreams where the song of the Lord might be sung." The leader of Conservative Judaism, Louis Finkelstein, devoted a major scholarly work on *The Pharisees* (1938) to showing the identity between rabbinic teachings and the Puritan ideals that were the basis of American democracy. Simon Greenberg, another leading Conservative thinker, wrote in 1945 that since the Bible's influence on American democracy was so well known, he would instead discuss "democracy in Post-Biblical Judaism." Reform rhetoric was in general the most extravagant: "Here in the New Jerusalem of America, planned as a spiritual Zion by its founding fathers and brought into being by revolutionary patriots imbued with the God-inspired liberalism of the prophets of Israel, the concept of this country as a citadel of social justice and warm-hearted humanitarianism was a natural one" ("Democracy in Post-Bibilical Judaism," 1945: 1–9).[1] Note that Jewish apologetic in this 1951 address also serves the purpose of intra-Jewish debate, pitting Reform Judaism against "other less progressive Jewish movements." But thinkers of all movements laid claim to the ideological alliance between democracy and Judaism, in one way or another invoking God as its source. The hyphen linking the two halves of American Jewish selves, they hoped to show, linked all Americans to all Jews, because the highest ideals of the two were in fact one.

Chosenness could only play the dual role assigned to it by American Jewish leaders—at once connecting Jews to America and rooting them in their own past—if the doctrine could be interpreted in ways that did not conflict with current Jewish theological assumptions and sociological necessities (or desires). The doctrine seemed essential to the maintenance of Jewish distinctiveness, but its traditional meanings (or what these seemed to be) were impossible to affirm; the result was a concerted and persistent effort at reinterpretation. Reform thinkers generally understood chosenness as a Jewish mission to humanity. The purpose of Israel's covenant was universal service. Julian Morgenstern, head of the Hebrew Union College (Reform's rabbinical seminary), proclaimed in 1945 that "we of the Reform wing conceive of Israel as a people, a chosen people, endowed from the very birth with a genius for seeing God in every aspect of existence and of interpreting all of life, nature and history from the standpoint of the one, eternal God" (14). The traditional belief that God had chosen Israel meant, to modern minds, that "Israel chose God as his ideal of service, the province of religion and ethics and morality—all values emanating from God—as its domain of self-expression and self-realization."

Mordecai Kaplan, a Conservative rabbi who argued over the course of a long career that Jewish beliefs and institutions needed "reconstruction" in order to suit the radically new conditions of Jewish life, rejected the notion of chosenness entirely because it rested in his view on an unscientific belief in a "supernatural God," immorally connoted superiority over other groups, and ill-befitted the Jews' status as citizens of a pluralistic democracy (1934: 15–24). He urged replacement of election with a notion of "divine vocation or calling," which would not involve "any of the invidious distinctions implied in the doctrine of election, and yet [would] fulfill the legitimate spiritual wants which that doctrine sought to satisfy." Many are called, we might say, but few are chosen (Kaplan, 1948: 229).

Kaplan's Conservative colleagues chose for the most part to reinterpret the doctrine of election rather than abandon it. They denied that it carried connotations of superiority or demands for isolation, and they reinterpreted the claim to divine revelation of the Torah—in their view the principal element of Israel's uniqueness. Rabbi Ben Zion Bokser, for example, argued that all groups were equally chosen by God, for each was a unique vehicle of His revelation and an instrument of His purposes in history. In this sense, the Jews as a distinct community had been "divinely chosen both as to the causes that have fashioned it and as to the mission of universal service which it is obligated to perform in the world." Jews say that [God] chose Israel, wrote Finkelstein, "in the sense that Israel was more keenly aware of his being than other peoples" (quoted in Eisen, 1983: 107–11). Orthodox thinkers, of course, did not need to engage in such equivocal affirmations, both because their theologies permitted and demanded a more robust view of election and because their constituency remained, until after World War II, far more of an immigrant rather than a second-generation community.

My point in this brief survey of how American thinkers reinterpreted one central doctrine of their tradition is twofold. On the one hand, inherited religious beliefs and practices can only be seen by its adherents through the lenses of their own experience. Biography and culture always mediate tradition. The transformed conditions of Jewish life in America both elicited new selections from the repertoire of tradition and precluded older readings. Some Biblical verses and themes assumed new importance or took on new meanings, just as the Hanukkah celebration assumed greater urgency in the context of America's Christmas, and Passover became a "festival of freedom," the observance of which in many homes came to include the singing of Negro spirituals. On the other hand, religion continued to serve its role as "model for" life outside its precincts. Chosenness helped Jews to understand who they "really" or "essentially" or "eternally" were as individuals and as a group, and so what they should and should not be doing, as Jews or Americans or both. The lesson could be more distinctiveness, or less; more concern with social justice, or reinforcement of conventional morality; support for one version or another of Zionism (in the years before Israel's creation) or opposition to all forms of Zionism on the grounds that Jews had a mission to perform among the nations, not as a state among states.

Kaplan perhaps drew the most far-reaching conclusion from the encounter with election: Jews had to abandon not only the claim that God had chosen them but the definition of themselves as a religion:

> Now that the aura of divine election has departed from his people, and his Jewish origin brings with it nothing but economic handicaps and social inferiority, the Jew rebels against his fate. . . . He has to evolve some new purpose in life as a Jew, a purpose that will direct his energies into such lines of creativity as will bring him spiritual redemption. (1934: 15).

None of the existing religious options were satisfactory, Kaplan argued, neither Orthodoxy (because it clung to "supernatural" claims that simply were not credible in the face of modern science and rationality), Reform (because it had abandoned the notion of Jewish peoplehood with its key component of allegiance to a homeland in Zion), nor Conservative Judaism (because it had never followed through on its own guiding convictions but had waffled and equivocated so much that Kaplan divided his treatment of the movement into two chapters, which he called "Right Wing of Reformism" and "Left Wing of Neo-Orthodoxy"). Kaplan urged that, instead of debating the proper course of Judaism as religion, Jews stop conceiving of Judaism as a religion at all but regard it instead "in its totality," as a civilization.

His "social scientific" argument for the switch went as follows: "To be different may mean to be both other and unlike, or, to be other only. Otherness is different in entity, unlikeness is difference in quality" (1934: 177–78). It was a mistake to see Jews as Americans in every respect but one: religion. That definition via "quality" could not work when "what is at stake in our day is the very maintenance of Jewish life as a distinct societal entity. Its very otherness is in jeopardy." Kaplan reasoned that if otherness could be taken for granted, "the element of unlikeness will take care of itself." Judaism had always been, and should once again be, far more comprehensive than Jewish religion. "It includes the nexus of a history, literature, language, social organization, folk sanctions, standards of conduct, social and spiritual ideals, esthetic values, which in their totality form a civilization." Judaism, we might say, should not be a set of beliefs or purposes—an "ism." Rather, it should be the culture of the group to which Jews knew themselves to belong.

He called this an "intuitional approach" and asserted, in an extravagant passage, that "attachment to Judaism has always been derived from just such an intuitional attitude toward it. The various interpretations of Jewish doctrine and practice, the abstract values and concepts, are but the formal afterthoughts of that intuitional attitude" (182). Jews had uttered and found meaning in the credo of Jewish faith, the Shema Yisrael prayer, "not because of the abstract idea of absolute monotheism which it is supposed to express, but simply because it provided the thrill of being a Jew." Kaplan hoped to reconstruct Judaism as civilization—its land, its language and literature, its folk-customs, its communal institutions—in the belief that renewed excitement in Judaism—that is, at being a Jew—would follow.

I shall leave aside the many vexing issues associated with Kaplan's functionalist reinterpretation of Jewish practices and beliefs, including his idea of God as a set of forces at work in history and the cosmos, in order to focus on a matter far more relevant here: the possibilities and limitations of what Kaplan called "living in two civilizations." Kaplan's many ruminations on the subject remain of interest, some 70 years after he published them, because he was not only exceedingly perceptive but extraordinarily conflicted. He repeatedly called, on the one hand, for a "maximalist Judaism," noting that a civilization, any civilization, "demands that the foundations of personality in the child be laid with the materials which the civilization itself supplies" (1934: 196). Jewish attachment to a homeland in Palestine, study of Hebrew, immersion in Jewish history, obligations to Jewish philanthropies, and observance of mitzvot (understood by him not as commandments but as "folkways") would make for an identity far more comprehensive than religion alone could provide, even if that religion were Orthodox.

The problem, of course, is that all this activity would be over and above Jews' full participation in American cultural life, which came more naturally and was ready to hand. Kaplan himself urged Jews to live in two civilizations, not one. At moments of clarity he was forced to acknowledge that Jews in America could never "live Judaism" as their "primary civilization" or even as a "co-ordinate civilization" as they might in a situation of real cultural autonomy (1934: 215–16). Judaism in America could "survive only as a subordinate civilization. Since the civilization that can satisfy the primary interests of the Jew must necessarily be the civilization of the country he lives in, the Jew in America will be first and foremost an American, and only secondarily a Jew." The two sides of the hyphen, we might say, were not and could not be equal. Indeed, Kaplan's call for a "maximalist Judaism" meant, in fact, "a maximum program of Jewishness compatible with one's abilities and circumstances" (1934: 220; 1948: 445). These would likely be severely limited.

Still—and this is how Kaplan got around the problem of cultural primacy—America was simply not constituted at the moment to provide Jews or Gentiles with the self-fulfillment (he called it "salvation") that they required. The citizen of the modern state turns to its culture only for "his literary and esthetic values" and of course owed the state duties of civic allegiance. Gentile Americans, possessed no less than Jews of hyphenated identities, turned to "Christian civilization" for "moral and spiritual" values. Kaplan repeatedly cited American Catholics as a model of what he had in mind for his readers (e.g., 1934: 217, 250). Jews did not have the option of seeking salvation as their Christian neighbors did, all the more so, Kaplan wrote because Gentiles were not yet prepared to accept Jews on their own terms, and begrudged Jews' corporate life as equals (280). All the Jew wanted, he wrote poignantly, was that Gentiles "not monopolize his life [so] as to leave no room in it for the Jewish civilization" (234).

Then, 14 years later, after urging Jews to identify spiritually and culturally with the nations among which they live (1948: 102), Kaplan argued in a remarkable passage that Jews in the United States should turn to America for "economic and social security" (437). For "moral and spiritual security"—for all that really mattered, we might say—there would be Judaism. If their culture were suitably reconstructed, if it were shorn of outmoded beliefs and useless institutions, if its synagogue were revitalized by new liturgies, its traditions outfitted with new meanings, and its institutions equipped to meet all of a Jew's needs, material and spiritual (synagogues subsumed, for example, into all-purpose "community centers")—why would Jews *not* turn to it for their fulfillment? Where else *could* they turn?

The inequity of value that we noticed earlier, in Kaplan's talk about the "zones" of Jewish life, has now been decisively reversed. Judaism's side of the identity hyphen occupies a lot less space than America's, as it were, but claims a lot more quality time. I think we would not stretch the point too much were we to say that in Kaplan's view (as in that of many other American Jewish religious thinkers of all denominations, then and since) America is depicted as means, while Judaism is end. America is body, and Judaism is soul. America is external, and Judaism is internal. America is now, and Judaism is forever. American values, for all they are identified with Judaism, are sometimes good and sometimes not so good (Kaplan was remarkable for his critique of the damage caused to body and soul by capitalism), while Jewish values—once they have been "revalued" to suit the present day—are always prized. In a word: America rescues, but only Judaism saves.

And still, Kaplan knew, Jews resisted their own salvation through Judaism. The societal and cultural reality around them was simply too powerful. In passage after passage in *Judaism as a Civilization*, Kaplan calls for renewed involuntarism in an attachment he knows full well is now utterly voluntary. The man who interpreted heretofore-obligatory *commandments* as freely chosen *folkways* writes that every people's collective will "takes the form of law." The group tells its members what they must do—and punishes those who disagree: "If, then, Jewish nationhood is to function in the diaspora, its principal manifestations must be this very element of involuntarism characteristic of national life" (1934: 292–93). Kaplan's diaries from the period, only recently published, reveal the extent to which he despaired of ever getting American Jews (including his own family) to see the light (Scult, 2001). The reason, in part, was that they, like him, had internalized universalist Enlightenment notions, and so could not lend credence to the particularist beliefs on which their tradition seemed to rest. In part, too, they, like him, had embraced Emancipation, and so opposed with all their hearts any bar to their successful integration into American society. But there was another reason, to which Kaplan recurred at several points in the book: anti-Semitism. Jews made their decisions under considerable pressure.

One example of external suasion will have to suffice here. *The Christian Century* magazine, principal organ of liberal Protestantism, featured regular criticism of Hitler and of anti-Semitism in America throughout the mid-1930s. But in 1936–37 the magazine aroused Jewish ire when it ran a series of editorials arguing that Jews could find a legitimate place in America only if they defined themselves as a religion and not as "a particular race" or "hereditary group" ("The Jewish Problem," 1936; "Jewry and Democracy," 1937; "Why Is Anti-Semitism?" 1937). Hostility to Jews arose because of Jewish exclusiveness, the magazine asserted. The real question at the bottom of Jewish-Gentile relations in America was this: "Can democracy suffer a hereditary minority to perpetuate itself as a permanent minority, with its own distinctive culture sanctioned by its own distinctive cult form?" Jews persisted in keeping themselves apart because of the "illusion that [their] race, [their] people, are the object of the special favor of God" ("Jewry and Democracy, 1937: 735–36). They had to realize that "the only religion compatible with democracy is one which conceives itself as universal, and offers itself to all men of all races and cultures. The Jewish religion, or any other religion, is an alien element in American democracy unless it proclaims itself as a universal faith, and proceeds upon such a conviction to persuade us all to be Jews" ("Why Is Anti-Semitism?" 1937: 862–64).[2] The message was clear. Particularist beliefs and practices carried a price, and Jews had to decide if they wanted to pay it. The more distinctive they remained, and the more that distinctiveness was a matter of group identity rather than individual choice, the less acceptance they could expect from other Americans. Jews responded to this challenge, and others like it, by pointing to American principles of religious freedom, or ethnic and cultural pluralism, or both. Jews were one of the three great American religious groups. Will Herberg's *Protestant-Catholic-Jew* (1960 [1955]) is the key title in this connection—a book written by a Jew that accords Jews, despite their relatively small numbers, the same status and importance as Protestants and Catholics. Rabbis and other communal leaders were likewise the principal proponents of the idea of the "Judeo-Christian ethic." Others, such as the philosopher Horace Kallen (1970 [1924]) and anthropologist Melville J. Herskovits (1990 [1941]), argued for a notion of cultural pluralism that would include Jews by rendering them analogous to Irish or Italian or African Americans. Kaplan, as we have seen, reminded everyone that all Americans—Jews and Gentiles alike—possessed hyphenated identities. Jews were not unique in their uniqueness, not distinctive by virtue of their distinctiveness, but precisely the opposite.

These defenses of cultural and religious diversity continue in our day. Before turning to them, however, I briefly examine debates over chosenness in the "third generation:" the postwar period when American identity became more secure, and Jewish identity—haunted by the Holocaust, bolstered by the creation of Israel—seemed once again an option to be asserted.

Judaism in the Third Generation (ca. 1950–75)

Jewish religious thought from the late 1940s through the 1970s has a different tone and purport than comparable writing from the preceding decades, in part because a "Jewish state" was now a fact rather than an aspiration or source of communal contention and the Holocaust had lent added urgency and pain—as well as inescapable reality—to the notion of Jewish uniqueness. The change had other sources as well. For one thing, America was different. Virtually all remaining barriers to Jews' full acceptance in American society—occupational, residential, political—fell one after the other in the wake of the war. What is more, a widely noted if short-lived "religious revival" in the 1950s spurred renewed popularity for theology and theologians and sent Americans back to church, especially in the suburbs to which they now moved in large numbers. Jews, as they moved outward from the cities, constructed new and imposing synagogues at major intersections.

The vast majority of the community was now removed by two generations, at least from the point of immigration. It was highly educated and increasingly successful. Jews were less averse to public expressions of their Judaism, as long as these seemed to be sanctioned or encouraged by Christian neighbors. They also became more open to or even eager for religious observances such as Passover, as long as these met a set of conditions first enunciated by sociologists Marshall Sklare and Joseph Greenblum (1967). Jewish practices had to carry universalist messages, to take place in private space and time, and to be child-centered. Most important of all, perhaps, no activity proposed to Jews, public or private, could seem to threaten the delicate and newly won peace that America now seemed to afford them. Philip Roth's story from the "third generation," "Eli the Fanatic" (1994), captured these calculations beautifully. Looking back on the period, Nathan Glazer suggested that a historian of ideas should one day try "to determine just how the United States evolved in the popular mind from a 'Christian' nation into a nation made up of Protestants, Catholics and Jews" and "how the Jewish group, which through most of the history of the United States has formed an insignificant percentage of the American people, has come to be granted the status of a most favored religion" (1972: 1).

My concern here is the change in Jewish theology that resulted from and further shaped that process. Two developments relating to chosenness are especially germane. First, a number of secular Jewish intellectuals came to see their work, and their status as artists, as expressions of an alienation, which, in turn, stemmed from—and, indeed, constituted— their Judaism. Jewish authors in America, wrote Irving Howe, could not but feel " a profound, even a mysterious sense of distinctiveness. . . . What [they] make of it in the context of their experience, how they transform, play with, and try sometimes to suppress it—this forms the major burden of their art" (1977: 3–4). Or, as Roth put it, "There were reminders constantly [in childhood] that one was a Jew and that there were goyyim out there. . . . [One had to] create a moral character for oneself. That is, one had to invent a Jew" (1963: 21, 39).

Second, rabbis and theologians restored election to a central place in Jewish belief and urged their readers to accept and enhance Jewish uniqueness rather than seek to blur or obliterate it. Arthur Hertzberg wrote that Judaism could survive in America only by "emphasizing what is unique to itself and by convincing its children that that uniqueness is worth having" (1964: 7–9). America was exile, he asserted, in clear contradiction with the widespread conviction that America was *home* for Jews, meaning that Zionism meant not the ingathering of all Jews but support for a home needed by *other* Jews, who were not lucky enough to have one in America: "The essence of Judaism is the affirmation that the Jews are the chosen people: all else is commentary" (Hertzberg, 1966: 90).

Emil Fackenheim (1970), like several other thinkers who began publishing in the late 1940s and early 1950s in new journals established then for that purpose, asserted that Jewish commitment entailed "mystery" and "scandal" which would not yield to rational inquiry. Abraham Heschel (1968) sought to arouse wonder, awe, and the sense of the ineffable to provoke the ultimate questions, which he believed only the personal God of the Bible could answer. "Israel has always been a mystery to Israel. But it is a mystery on its own terms," wrote Arthur Cohen (1971: 84). Eugene Borowitz (1973) reasserted the primacy of covenant, precisely as a Reform Jew committed to autonomy and heavily influenced by Kant.

It would be wrong to attribute such beliefs to the majority of American Jews, though lack of data precludes any certainty as to what most

Jews did or did not think about God and Judaism. I have characterized the variegated pattern of Jewish decision-making about distinctiveness in this period, conscious and unconscious, as a "halfway-covenant" with Jewish tradition (Eisen, 1983: 148). Jews were at home in America—but not entirely so. Intermarriage rates through the mid-1960s remained low. Most Jews numbered only other Jews among their closest friends. They identified with one or another of the Jewish religious denominations—but synagogue membership and attendance, like home ritual observance, were not high. Yet there were persistent and widespread signs of new interest, even before the renewed communal attachment that came with the 1967 war and the sudden outpouring of attention to the Holocaust several years later.

Herberg's famous notion, borrowed from Arthur Hansen, of the third generation returning to the religion of the grandparents, partly out of rebellion against the rebellion of the parents and partly because they no longer had to struggle free of a heritage their parents had rejected for them, captures some truth where American Jews are concerned. But it misses the abiding ambivalence, rejection, and regret. The truth in Herberg's generalization relates to the difference it made for Judaism that the vast majority of American Jews in the third generation were no longer immigrants or children of immigrants—and so had very different concerns. They were no longer oppressed by an identity they had inherited but in search of an identity that they could choose—a selfhood that could then carry the force of having chosen them. Borowitz claimed, in fact, that Jews clung to a greater particularism than they were willing to avow, masking significant commitments behind trivial choices: "God lurks behind the chopped liver" (1973: 125–28).

Theology for all that remained an elite pursuit among third-generation American Jews. Systematic articulations of belief were few and far between, while American Jews responded to powerful images such as election and rituals such as Passover. Belief remained idiosyncratic, and observance eclectic.

The reason, in part, is that most people are by definition not intellectuals and so remain uninterested in highbrow pursuits such as theology. But disinterest in Jewish theology on the part of American Jews of the third generation had at least two other causes, I believe. One is that theology is inherently particularistic. It concerns a *single*-faith community and its relation to God. Theology thrives on challenges from the outside but is designed by insiders for insiders. It articulates the truth that they come to know by being who they are—and not others. Jews in America, as we have seen, resisted this degree of distinctiveness and were uncomfortable with traditional notions—revelation at Sinai, special protection by God, chosenness—which seemed to imply or demand it.

The other, borrowing a phrase from Jacob Neusner (1979), is that theology is "life reflected upon," and so requires "life lived" on which to reflect. American Jews lacked a coherent communal way of life on which their theologians could meditate and to which it could lend meaning. The community had disintegrated to a significant extent. Jewish law had been repudiated by all but a small minority, primarily Orthodox. The idea of a Jewish mission provided an invaluable sermonic theme for Reform rabbis, in part because it rhetorically conjured up the illusion of action, of Jews doing something for God or the good—something distinctive and unique—among Jews whose Jewish activity was minimal. American Jews, we might say, were willing or eager to embrace a modicum of distinctiveness, a degree of chosenness—a "halfway covenant" with their tradition— but they were not prepared not to accept a *theology* of chosenness that came complete with beliefs in particular revelation and redemption, let alone a unique way of life to go with these. Hyphenated identities require hyphenated theologies—or, as I have suggested, they subvert the effort at theology altogether.

Judaism in the Fourth Generation (ca. 1975 to the Present)

All this began to change in the 1970s. Israel and the Holocaust for the first time took center stage in a communal agenda. which one analyst (Woocher, 1986) has aptly named "sacred survival." It was not clear what Judaism entailed, or why Jewish distinctiveness was important, but it was urgent that both continue. Fackenheim gave eloquent (and problematic) articulation to this sentiment in his famous invocation of a new "614th commandment," uttered by the "Commanding Voice of Auschwitz," which supplemented and even took precedence over the traditional 613: "Thou shalt not give Hitler posthumous victories" by abandoning Jewishness, Judaism, or trust in humanity (1970: 84–98).

Jewish "federations," the community's umbrella for charitable organizations, used this appeal to bolster support for overseas causes including Israel, as well as social service agencies in the United States—this as concern steadily mounted over rising rates of intermarriage and assimilation.

(Starting in the 1980s, the latter concern far eclipsed the former; Israel declined in importance as a locus of identification or a motivation of fund-raising.) Rabbis, joined by some younger Jews who had participated in a countercultural movement of lay-led, egalitarian communities called "havurot," protested that survival without content was pointless and would not work. In the 1980s a series of new developments took place, all of which placed renewed emphasis on the religious or transcendent meaning of Jewishness.

Reform prayer books, for example, were revised to include more Hebrew and more of the traditional liturgy. At the same time, the movement urged more observance by its laity (voluntarily chosen by individuals, of course), and its rabbis and theologians expressed new sympathy for the language of mitzvah, reinterpreted to bear more (but not all) of the traditional force of binding commandment. "Tradition" became still more prominent as the "god-term" or authority in all movements, but especially in Conservative Judaism, which continued to claim (as against Reform) that it had never abandoned the authentic tradition, embodied in Jewish law, while (as against Orthodoxy) adopting law and tradition to new realities. Reconstuctionism, since the 1960s a separate movement complete with its own seminary, journal, lay and rabbinic organizations, and ideology, sought more aggressively than either Reform or Conservative Judaism to appropriate elements of "new age" religiosity and and respond to widespread interest in "spirituality."

All three movements had decided by the mid-1980s to ordain women as rabbis, as well as to afford women equality in other aspects of ritual observance. Reform and Reconstructionism broke with Jewish law by recognizing the children of Jewish fathers and non-Jewish mothers as Jews (called "patrilineal descent"). Conservative rabbis, like their Orthodox colleagues, did not. Modern Orthodox Jews found themselves pulled "to the right" by ultra-Orthodoxy, the continuing success of which has borne witness not only to the surprising appeal of separatist communities and premodern theological claims but also to the increasing willingness of Gentile Americans to tolerate substantive difference, at least in the religious sphere. One would be hard-pressed to find more salient markers of Jewish transformation in the period than the impact of feminism on the one hand and the success of Orthodoxy on the other.

Both these phenomena, though they stand in some respects at opposite ends of the spectrum, can usefully be seen as responses to a set of developments characteristic of Judaism throughout the modern period (Eisen,

1998: 242–63). They involve, first, a *calculation of distinctiveness:* just how different the Jews involved wish to be from their surroundings, how much difference each particular observance entails, and how much the relevant surroundings will bear. Second, they demand or resist *the explanation of particularist practices in universal terms* deemed compatible with the Jews' status as citizens of a diverse and pluralistic society. Modern Orthodoxy has by no means been immune to this dilemma, and in the wake of the September 11 terrorist attack, an ultra-Orthodox organization took out an ad in the *New York Times,* expressing sympathy and solidarity for fellow Americans of different faiths in a fashion more typical of religious colleagues to their left. (A Greek Orthodox church ran a similar ad on an adjacent page, with similar wording, to similar purpose.) Third, American Jews of all denominations responded to the powerful *appeal of ancestors:* the desire to walk in the ancestors' ways, to feel their presence by engaging in ritual activities that they too had observed, sometimes with the help of inherited ritual objects, and so to feel their presence and enjoy their blessing. Fourth, many Jews and their rabbis continue to *search for authority,* without ever finding it or wanting to find it; they prefer to see themselves as seekers after truth rather than as people who possess it. Like Christian contemporaries studied by Robert Wuthnow (1998a, 1999) and Wade Clark Roof (1993, 1999), they believe it right that each person on his or her own spiritual journey arrives at his or her own ultimate convictions (and is free to depart from those convictions for others, at a later point in the journey), and they hold it wrong to accept the teachings of religious authorities. The point is to *struggle with* God rather than (merely) to *believe in* God. Contemporary rabbis are fond of pointing out that "Israel" is the name given to Jacob after he has "wrestled with God," the apparent meaning of the words of which the name is composed.

Sociologist Steven Cohen and I (2000), interviewing moderately affiliated Jews of the baby boom generation from all across America (not the 20–25 percent who are most active Jewishly, or the comparable group which is least involved), and supplementing those interviews with a 1,000-person survey of a representative sample of American Jewish adults, found that all these trends are very much in evidence at the start of the 21st century. Our study of the "habits of the American Jewish heart" reveals the same tension between individualism and communal commitment first articulated by Robert Bellah et al. (1985). Among Jews, too, the first language spoken is "individualism," autonomy, freedom, the "sovereign self," its claims voiced at every point of every interview. Community, as Bellah put it, remains a "second language," spoken not as often and not as well. The Jews we interviewed resent it when anyone tells them what they "must do" because they are Jews or in order to be a "good Jew." They reserve the right to decide what they will observe and how they will observe it. What is more, if they cannot find personal meaning in observance, they will let that observance lapse—and feel that they are right in doing so. "Sacred survival" no longer compels them. The "public Judaism" of federations, support for Israel, and remembrance of the Holocaust has lost much of its appeal.

Yet the people we interviewed are Jewishly active enough to earn the title of "moderately affiliated." They are not ashamed of being Jews and are proud of the tradition from which they are free to select. Their declarations of autonomy go hand in hand with the belief that a person born of at least one Jewish parent (or converted to Judaism) is a Jew for life, and—even if he or she never performs a single distinctively Jewish act—no less a Jew than any other. Holding fast to this conviction, our respondents can rest assured that their children and grandchildren will be Jewish to the end of time, barring conversion to another faith. They respect the right—and not just the obvious ability—of their children to choose an identity other than the one that they themselves had been given and had confirmed. They hope for them, above anything else, that they be happy. But they also allow the hope that the next generation will find meaning, as they did, in Jewish tradition: choosing a manner of chosenness, individually tailored to suit their needs, which will be a source of blessing.

The major source of meaning that our interviewees found in Judaism was ritual activity performed in the home with children. Those whose children had grown up and left home looked back wistfully to Sabbath dinner tables and Passover seders with their children, or they looked forward to sharing those activities with grandchildren. At a time of extreme mobility and individualism, when many Americans live far from close friends and family, and when ascribed communal loyalties cannot define the self one chooses to be, meaning in life centers more on members of one's intimate family, especially children. American Jews seek to link that source of meaning to the rituals and tradition that they share with their own ancestors, thereby rooting themselves and that which they pass on to ancestors as well as to descendants. Intermarriage seems less and less a bar to such observance; even when both spouses are Jewish, we found, Jewish ritual activity is a subject of negotiation like any other and takes place when one spouse—usually the female—feels strongly about it; ritual finds a mode and meaning of observance with which the other can be satisfied. Initiative where private observance is concerned now seems overwhelmingly to rest with women—home and children, even in two-career families, remaining primarily the responsibility of wives and mothers—even as the role of women in public leadership roles such as the rabbinate continues to grow dramatically.

The synagogue is widely valued as an extension of family, as a site where community and tradition can be experienced, and as a place for quiet introspection apart from the harried workweek—though fewer than half of American Jewish adults are members of synagogues, and the vast majority of members attend only infrequently. God is believed in far more widely as a personal deity or force(s) in the universe than one might have imagined (56 percent in the survey "definitely" believe "there is a God," and another 27 percent that this is "probably" the case [Cohen and Eisen, 2000: 219])—but not the Jewish God of synagogue liturgy. American Jews believe, when they believe, in a universal and personal God. They find this God in nature, in their children, in the kindness of strangers, in history, and sometimes even in synagogue.

Among men as well as women, we discovered, ethnic as well as religious Jewish involvements and activities are often fraught with ambivalence. Jewish commitments are transmitted, after all, by parents (or had been rejected by parents whom our interviewees had rejected in turn by turning back to observance). They also involve demonstrations of distinctiveness with which many Jews are still uncomfortable, even in the privacy of their own homes.

Other essays in this volume, and particularly those by Yvonne Haddad (chapter 9) and Ann Chih Lin (chapter 10) in this "quartet," chart similar calculations of perceived and desired distinctiveness, a similar concern with family combined with significant differences of ethnic/religious activity according to gender, and similar concern for the demands of authenticity of belief on the one hand and accommodation to the new realities of America on the other. One suspects that as Arab and Islamic communities become more removed from the "old countries" and more exposed to the cultural pressures of contemporary America, they will exhibit more of the individualism we found to be prominent among American Jews.

Cohen and I titled our study *The Jew Within* to capture the degree to which Jewishness at the turn of the new century, a full three generations since the massive immigration of Jews to America, seems less and less a matter of public declarations and commitments and more and more an identity performed in the intimate spaces of home and family or even *inside* the individual self. Jews can pretty much select freely from the repertoire available to them. For one thing, American tolerance of religious and cultural distinctiveness has greatly increased, particularly when that difference is expressed in the private sphere and when the people expressing it are linked by class, race, and ethos to the still-regnant majority culture. Nor is there much Jewish communal pressure, outside Orthodoxy, to bend Jews in the direction of behavioral or ideological conformity. Choosing a degree of chosenness, therefore, does not appear to threaten autonomy, all the more so if the Jews involved come from nonobservant or intermarried homes. Christian neighbors, too, are seen to choose, and switch, their own communal allegiances. At the same time, adult education courses and the huge outpouring of Jewish books in recent decades, readily available in national chain stores and via the internet, have combined to make Jews far more knowledgeable than ever before about what their choices are.

Kaplan would likely have been happily amazed at the sheer number of activities available to Jews who wish to "live two civilizations"; he would have felt vindicated, too, by the eagerness of many American Jews (including a candidate for the vice-presidency) to identify with both civilizations and even, to varying degrees, to regard that identity not merely as an ethnic attachment parallel to that of Italian Americans or African Americans but to find religious meaning in it. While "ethnicity" and "religiosity" are for many Jews largely "symbolic" in Gans's sense; and while, as Richard Alba (1990) has pointed out, these differences are no longer "structural"—that is, they do not have constraints imposed by birth, occupation, or place of residence (but see Goldscheider's essay in this volume, chapter 7, on the continuing distinctiveness of Jewish patterns).

Nonetheless the hyphenated identity of American Jews seems in a great many cases to go deep beneath the surface. It reaches as it were to the heart of selfhood. The survey data confirm that American Jews overwhelmingly *want* their differences to run deep, and they value America precisely for permitting a degree of distinctiveness at the same time as it binds Jews up in a wider world, enabling them at once to be *part of,* and *apart.*

Conclusion

As one looks forward from the turn of a new century toward the likely developments that will shape American Judaism in coming decades, one question stands out: What does it mean to be a self in a multicultural society—or, in a more recent formulation of the question that Jews and other minorities have been wrestling with for over a century—what does it mean to be a *multicultural self* in a society that may or may not prove open to the public expression of substantial difference, religious or cultural? Does it make sense to speak of "the self" at all, at a time when the self can choose so often and so richly from so many different options— when, indeed, the very notion of "the self" is held up to postmodern questioning?

Kaplan recognized in 1934 that "to admit the Jew on a basis of complete equality, the nations would have to be tolerant of the cultural differences among their own groups instead of trying to cast them into a uniform mold" (280–81). The additional issue now seems to be whether it still makes sense to speak of "the Jew" or "the Christian," the Italian American or the Mexican American. Definite articles seem inadequate to the task of identifying fragmented selves who may no longer even be in search of wholeness. The effect on their religions and cultures is likely to be profound.

The philosopher Jeremy Waldron, for example, regards the various sources that make up his identity as so many pieces which need not add up to make one whole; he equates allegiance to a Catholic or a Methodist church with the taste for campfires as opposed to operas (1995: 93–100). If churches die out because cosmopolitan selves have no need of them, Waldron writes, "it is like the death of a fashion or a hobby, not the demise of anything that people really need" (100).

This is exactly the sort of selfhood that Michael Walzer has in mind when critiquing the "postmodern project" of " a life without clear boundaries and without secure or singular identity": "The associations that these self-made and self-making individual form are likely to be little more than temporary alliances that can be easily broken off when something more promising comes along" (1997: 88–90). Walzer favors what he considers the best of the emerging American reality: "namely that we are both this and that; that there are still boundaries, but they are blurred by all the crossings" (90). The hyphen, he writes, should work as a plus sign rather than a divider and should enable Americans to live on either side, or both (1992: 17, 45). Others find even this formulation too constrictive, too essentialist. The self is what it is, and will be whatever it becomes.

It may matter differently, in this context, that American Jews still enjoy the luxury of appropriateness from received (or newly created) ethnic and cultural traditions. Jewish individuals, like Jewish organizations, can be "ethnic" when it suits them and "religious" when that seems preferable; they can be equal partners in the Judeo-Christian ethic, or they can be "private celebra[nts] of cultural difference," as one historian nicely puts it, in the context of "public assimilation to putatively American behavioral norms" (Greenberg, 1998: 57). American Jews are also overwhelmingly white, of course, as well as highly educated and affluent. Their difference is any number of ways especially safe—and, to that degree, untypical.

Jewish numbers, however, remain relatively small—about 2 percent of the American population—and shrinking every year. This may close off options available to larger groups, or it may spur individual activity born of anxiety about collective disappearance. It seems likely that Jewish patterns of distinctiveness and integration—of boundary maintenance, boundary crossing, and boundary definition—will depend more than ever for their success on the willingness of other Americans to follow similar patterns, and on the willingness of American elites and institutions to countenance the public expression of serious difference. Horace Kallen wondered aloud in the final paragraph of his classic essay, "Democracy versus the Melting Pot," whether "the dominant classes in America want such a [pluralistic or multicultural] society" (1970 [1924]: 120–21). This of course remains an open question, in 2008. Its answer for Jews and Judaism will depend as well on the ability of Jewish religious thinkers to interpret their tradition in ways that not only legitimate other religions and cultures—this task is revolutionary enough—but value those cultures precisely in and for their difference.

Judaism (like Islam and Christianity) has yet to find actual *value,* as opposed to mere inevitability, in the possession of hyphenated identity. Religions have never been known for their pluralism; American ethnic groups, on the other hand, have yet to resist the pressure to move from substantial to symbolic difference—or to engage other groups in a way that goes beyond mere toleration or coexistence. Both sorts of difference, religious and ethnic, are being tested and stretched by the presence in large numbers of individuals and groups who are visibly distinct in new and different ways—and who do not positively value the liberal traditions to which all American minorities, religious and ethnic, have submitted heretofore.

The outcome is uncertain, to say the least. It seems fairly certain, however, that the choices surrounding chosenness by Jews and others will likely be a very different enterprise in the 21st century than it was in the 20th, for immigrants as well as descendants of immigrants, for all that the need to calculate perceived and desired distinctiveness, to enact participation and apartness, is a constant.

These choices will draw on different meanings of self and other, will involve different notions of personal and collective boundaries, and will invoke different notions of ethnicity and perhaps of religion. Most important of all, perhaps, the processes of constructing self and community will proceed in the full awareness that parallel processes are transpiring among *other* ethnic and religious groups, the members of which—the boundaries of self and group now being so permeable—may not be "other" at all but part of "we" or "I." Kaplan would likely have been neither pleased nor displeased at this prospect but rather perplexed and uncomprehending, and he is not the only one.

NOTES

1. See also Greenberg's later statement, "Judaism and the Democratic Ideal" (1966) in Foundations of a Faith (New York: Burning Bush Press, 1967), 13–34, and his recent reiteration in *The Ethical in the Jewish and American Heritage* (New York: Jewish Theological Seminary of America, 1977).

2. A similar complaint about "Pluralism: National Menace" appeared on June 13, 1951 (701–2). Yet elsewhere the magazine considered Christianity itself to be a culture, not a religion, expressing the fear that the culture of America would be other than Christian ("God-Centered Education," 1937: 542–44).

|||||||||||||||||||||||||||||||||||||||||||||||||||||||||||||||

9

The Shaping of Arab and Muslim Identity in the United States

Yvonne Yazbeck Haddad

The al-Qaeda attacks of September 11, 2001, on the World Trade Center and the Pentagon are repeatedly depicted as having "changed America forever." Whether or not such hyperbole is justified, there can be little doubt the event reverberates in all spheres of American life, particularly for Muslims and Arabs living in the United States. As it is still too soon to know for sure, future scholars will have to investigate such questions as the following: Have the attacks had a lasting effect on Arabs and Muslims and their integration and assimilation in the United States? What permanent impact, if any, will reactions to the attacks have on the unfolding of the articulation of Islam in the American public square? Certainly the U.S. government is currently attempting to play an important role in such a reformulation of Islam through its attempts to identify, one might even say create, a "moderate Islam," one that is definitively different from the Islam espoused by the attacks' perpetrators.

How Arab Muslims in the future will adapt to and become incorporated into American society will be influenced by a number of factors, including not only by their history as immigrants and their ongoing ties and identification with the Middle East and Islam but also by their reception by American society and U.S. foreign policy toward the Arab region and its Islamic peoples. These interrelationships are examined in the following pages topically and chronologically.

Since Arab Muslims began to emigrate to the United States in notable numbers at the end of the 19th century, they have been received with uncertainty, suspicion, and, at times, hostility. Their situation and history seem similar to that of immigrant Jews who, when they arrived from eastern Europe in considerably larger numbers at the end of the 19th and beginning of the 20th centuries, also introduced a religion that was not yet accepted as part of American national identity. Jewish immigrants experienced prejudice and discrimination. Yet, as described by Calvin Goldscheider (chapter 7) and Arnold Eisen (chapter 8) in this volume, over time and as a result of considerable struggle, American Jews overcame much of the institutional, social, and political exclusion that they at first confronted. Judaism along with Protestantism and Catholicism became widely accepted as America's Judeo-Christian heritage.

Whether and how Arab Muslims will similarly be able to establish themselves remains uncertain. Although some Arab Muslims see in the experiences of Jews and other religious minorities possibilities for their own incorporation into an increasingly pluralistic American society, they have at times also experienced considerable hostility to their inclusion from other Americans, including some Jewish leaders and organizations. Those responses, particularly in the context of the post-9/11 American "war against terrorism," have become especially problematic for Arab Muslims as they seek to come to terms with both their history and their future prospects in America.

This chapter first presents a brief description of the identities and numbers of Arab Muslims who have come to reside in the United States. This introduction is followed by historical accounts of their experiences and adaptations as Americans, with attention to their different identifications, first as Arabs and then as Muslims, and how they have been received by other Americans in relation to both identities. The chapter concludes with a review of the challenges that Arab Muslims have faced since 9/11 and their efforts to establish their place and voice within the context of American ethnic and religious pluralism.

Arab Muslim Identities and Numbers

Because of their dual religious and cultural identities, Arab Muslims in America can identify and affiliate with two larger, somewhat overlapping, international populations. As speakers of Arabic, they can find ethnic and geographic commonality with others of Middle Eastern and North African origins, Christians and Jews as well as Muslims. As Muslims, they can identify with a wider Islamic religious community, or *umma*, whose members derive from various cultural, geographic, and national origins, including not only Arabs but also Pakistanis, Indians, Africans, and American-born Muslims, the largest percentage of whom are African Americans. In their adaptations to American society, Arab Muslims have variously deployed these two identities and the potential memberships and alliances they allow in their relations, both with one another—overseas and inside the United States—and with others within American society.

There are no accurate figures for the number of Muslims in the United States. Neither the census data nor the records of the Immigration and Naturalization Service provide any information on religious affiliation of citizens or immigrants. Consequently, there exists a great disparity in the estimates of their number in the United States. The estimates range between 2 million as reported by the American Jewish Committee (Cho, 2002) and as many as 11 million as claimed by Warith Deen Muhammed, leader of the Muslim American Society (MAS), the largest African American Muslim organization. The Council on American-Islamic Relations (CAIR) reports in all of its communiqués that there are 7 million Muslims in the United States. While the numbers are contested, it is generally agreed that they are significant. The larger the community, Muslims believe, the greater its potential impact in the political arena and its influence on policy. The figures appear to be of similar importance to some Christians and Jews who started over a decade ago warning about the "imminent threat" of Muslim presence in America (Kramer, 1993; Pipes, 1990).

An estimated 3 million Arabic-speaking people (and their descendents, a few of whom are in their sixth generation) now live in the United States, constituting about 1 percent of the population, the majority having arrived during the last third of the 20th century. The community is still in the process of being formed and re-formed as policies by the American government regulate the flow of emigration from their countries of origin. Legislation limiting immigration, as well as American foreign policy and the prevailing American prejudice against Arabs, Muslims, and Islam, has at times accelerated and at others impeded the integration and assimilation of the community into American society.

The Arab community in the United States is noted for its diversity, which is evident in its ethnic, racial, linguistic, religious, sectarian, tribal, and national identities. Today, Arab Americans are dispersed throughout the United States; two-thirds of them living in ten states, and one-third living in California, New York, and Michigan. They appear to favor urban areas, as about one-half of them (48 percent) live in 20 large metropolitan areas, with the highest concentrations in Los Angeles, Detroit, New York, Chicago, and Washington, D.C. About one-quarter of them (23 percent) are Muslims (Sunni, Shi'a, and Druze) and constitute a minority within the Arab American community, the majority of whom are Christian[1] with a small Jewish minority (Dahbany-Miraglia, 1988; Sephardic Archives, 1986; Zenner, 2002). They are also a minority (25 percent) within the Muslim American community, which includes an estimated 33 percent South Asians and 30 percent African Americans.[2]

Immigration of Arab Muslims

Arab Muslims arrived in the United States as part of three waves that included various Arab and Muslim populations. Early-19th-century immigration from the Middle East ended with the interruption of World War I and the imposition of immigration by the National Origin Act of 1924. After World War II, a second wave of immigration began with the recruitment of students from Arab countries, some of whom settled here and attracted others. Finally, the relaxation of restrictions that began with the 1965 reform of immigration laws has provided opportunities for the entry of larger numbers of Arab speakers and of Muslims from more widely diverse national and religious backgrounds.

A few Muslim males from the Syrian Province of the Ottoman Empire (today's Syria, Lebanon, Jordan, and Palestine/Israel) began arriving in the United States in the 1870s. They were rural migrant laborers hoping to make money and return to live in their homelands (Aswad, 1984; Hagopian and Paden, 1969; Hoogland, 1987; Neff, 1985). Their success, the deteriorating economy in the Middle East, and the subsequent famine precipitated by World War I brought about 4,300 additional Muslims to the United States between 1899 and 1914 (Moore, 1995). The flow of immigration was interrupted during the war. Subsequently, it was curtailed by the National Origin Act of 1924 that restricted the number of immigrants from the Middle East to 100 persons per year.

The early immigrants were classified by the officials of the Immigration and Naturalization Service (INS) as coming from "Turkey in Asia." They resented the Turkish designation since many were running away from Ottoman conscription and oppression, as well as the Asian designation since it excluded them from becoming citizens. By 1899, the INS began to add the subcategory of "Syrians" to their registration (Mokarzel, 1928). That became the identity of choice, as argued by Philip Hitti (1924) in his *The Syrians in America,* who insisted that Syrians were distinct from the Turks and have made great contributions to human civilization. Among themselves, they talked about being "wlad 'Arab," children of Arabs, a reference to the language they spoke.

The early Muslim immigrants from Greater Syria to the United States were few in number. They came to the United States when racism and nativism were paramount, when "Anglo conformity" was promoted as the norm for citizenship and the Protestant establishment determined what "American" was. Like the millions of immigrants who passed through Ellis Island, they followed the patterns of integration and assimilation that refashioned them into American citizens. Their names were anglicized: Muhammad became Mo, Rashid became Dick, Mojahid became Mark, and Ali was recognized as Al. They dug ditches, laid down railroad tracks, peddled, and later opened grocery stores and other businesses that catered to ethnic needs. Their children went to public schools and worked in factories. They enlisted in the American military during World War I and II and served with distinction.

The second wave of immigrants came after the end of World War II, when the United States assumed responsibility for the security of the oil fields in the Middle East and recruited students from the newly independent Arab states to study at American universities with the expectation that once they returned to their home countries they would constitute an important asset to U.S. interests. They were predominantly of middle-class and upper-class urban backgrounds, with intimate experience of living in pluralistic settings. A large number were graduates of foreign educational institutions run by secular and missionary groups in the Arab world. Their instruction had been primarily in foreign languages and in western curricula: American, British, French, German, and Russian. Two-thirds of the students married American wives. A large number of them decided to settle in the United States. Abdo Elkholy's (1966) study of Arab Muslims in Detroit, Michigan, and Toledo, Ohio, estimated that the total number of Muslims of Arab origin in the United States was 78,000, the majority of whom were from Lebanon. The other estimated 30,000 were from eastern Europe (Albania and Yugoslavia), Pakistan, and Turkey, with a few Tatars from the Soviet Union.

The revocation of Asian exclusion by the 1965 immigration act dramatically altered the constituency of the Muslim population of the United States. It brought immigrants from all areas of the Arab and Muslim world, and these new immigrants were more representative of the existing ethnic, national, and religious diversity. They included a large number of highly educated, socially mobile, professional Muslims, part of the Arab and South Asian "brain drain," and more women. Meanwhile, the opening of the doors of emigration, the changes in immigration laws, and the lottery system that gave visas to winners from all over the world brought a different "kind" of immigrant. All social and economic classes from villages, towns, and cities stretching from Morocco to Yemen are represented. The majority of new Muslim immigrants came from the subcontinent of Asia: India, Pakistan, and Bangladesh. The latest arrivals included a substantial number of refugees from countries wrenched by civil wars and often suffering the results of western exploitation. Some have called them the "collateral damage" of American foreign policies in such countries as Algeria, Iraq, Lebanon, Somalia, Palestine, and elsewhere. Among them are some of the poorest of the dispossessed, with little or no formal education. They are more concerned about survival than with issues of identity and assimilation. Along with the refugees are those seeking political asylum from Algeria, Libya, and Tunisia and other autocratic regimes.

The Arab Muslims of the United States reflect the religious and sectarian divisions of the population of the Arab world. The largest group is Sunni. The percentage of the Shi'ite population in the United States is presumed to be larger than what obtains in the Arab world, due to the fact that their areas of residence were devastated by war (especially in southern Iraq and Lebanon). The Shi'ites include Ithna 'Asharis (or Ja'faris) from Iraq, Lebanon, and Syria; Isma'ilis from Syria; Zaidis from Yemen; 'Alawis from Lebanon and Syria; and Druze from Israel, Lebanon, Palestine, and Syria. All of these groups have established their distinctive community organizations in the United States. They generally affirm that there are no differences between Shi'is and Sunnis. Since the American intervention in Iraq, incidents of increased tension between the two groups in the United States has been reported. While both may worship in the same mosque, there have been disagreements over whether members of the two communities can intermarry or whether one group can perform the burial prayer over a deceased person from the other.

Immigrants from the Arab world also reflect the variety of minority and ethnic communities that constitute the populations of these nations, including Armenians, Assyrians, Chechens, Circassians, Kurds, and Turcomans, who have been subjected to the Arabization programs of Arab governments since independence. Many in these groups tend to dissociate themselves from Arab identity once they emigrate. Some do identify as Arabs or as Arab Americans, and others have set up lobbies in Washington collaborating with pro-Israeli groups and are engaged in defaming Arab nations. The Arabic language may seem to be the strongest common bond among Arabs and an initial indicator of ethnic identity; however, the variety of dialects makes it difficult, for example, for Maghrebis (North Africans) and Mashreqis (from the Levant and the Arabian Peninsula) to communicate. For most, the common language is English.

Those who emigrated in the second half of the twentieth century brought with them diverse national identities, developed by their nation-states to inspire loyalty among their citizens so they would defend national security against outside enemies. For immigrants, their attachments to these national identities are continually tested by events in their home countries and by American foreign policy toward their countries. Such home ties became strained during the Gulf War in 1990–91 when Gulf Arabs questioned the authenticity of "Arabness" among citizens of the northern states (Egypt, Jordan, Morocco, Palestine, Syria, and Tunisia) who opposed Saudi Arabian and American retribution against Saddam Hussein. Gulf Arabs dismissed them as "Arabized" peoples who did not understand the threat that Saddam's military posed to the Gulf states. At the same time, some Arabs of the northern tier criticized Gulf Arabs as greedy and gullible and accused them of contributing to the disempowerment of the Arab people in their willingness to spend tens of billions of dollars to support American destruction of Iraq and empower Israel in the process.

Not all Arabs living in the United States are immigrants. Those who are in the United States on a temporary basis include migrant laborers who come from different countries, with the largest number from Yemen (Abraham, 1977, 1978).[3] They, along with émigrés and political and religious refugees, influence the assimilation of Arab immigrants as they focus on events overseas. They live in limbo awaiting a change in the political circumstances in their home countries. A third group are the thousands of students attending various colleges and universities throughout the United States. Other temporary residents include tourists, business people, and relatives. They also include a large contingent of diplomats to the United States and the United Nations from 56 Islamic nations who continue to be active in Arab and Islamic affairs.

Two international Islamic organizations, the Muslim World League (MWL) and the Organization of Islamic Conference (OIC), are recognized by the United Nations as nongovernmental organizations and have diplomats in New York City. The Muslim World League had extensive involvement with Muslim organizations in the United States in the 1980s. It organized the Council of Masajid (places of worship) in North America, provided imams from overseas for the leadership of 26 mosques, and funded Islamic activity in the United States. Several other Arab nations, including Egypt, Iraq, Libya, Kuwait, Qatar, and the United Arab Emirates have funded publications and mosque construction, among other projects.

Becoming American

There are very few studies that document the Americanization of Arab Muslims in the United States. Two pioneering studies, those by Abdo Elkholy in the late 1950s and by this essay's author, Yvonne Haddad, with Adair T. Lummis in the early 1980s, explored different ways in which Arab Muslims were adapting to American culture.

In the late 1950s, Elkholy attempted to assess the acculturation and assimilation of two Muslim communities after an incubation period of at least a quarter century when immigrants from the Middle East lived in isolation. Elkholy concluded that their practice of Islam was facilitating their assimilation. The immigration quota system of the 1920s, the depression of the 1930s, and World War II limited communications and further immigration from the region. Elkholy focused his investigation on whether "adherence to the old religion which differs from the religion prevailing in the adopted culture," and particularly to Islam, are an impediment to the assimilation of immigrants of Arab ancestry into the United States. He concluded that they are not. Focusing on two Arab American Muslim communities (some of whom were fourth generation) living in Toledo, Ohio, and Detroit, Michigan, Elkholy found that, although the two communities were formed by immigrants arriving at the same time from the same area of Lebanon and were identical ethnically and religiously, the Toledo community was both more assimilated and more religious (Elkholy, 1966: 15–16).

Elkholy determined that the factor that appeared to have the most impact on Arab Muslims' assimilation was their occupation. The Detroit community was predominantly working class, lived in a ghetto-like environment, maintained traditional perceptions of the family, perpetuated sectarian conflicts, and had virtually no interaction with non-Muslims

(Elkholy, 1966: 18). In contrast, Elkholy described the Toledo Muslims as liberal, "Americanized by liquor." The members of the Toledo community had higher incomes, largely as a result of their engagement in the liquor industry and ownership of 30 percent of the city's bars. Aware that Islam forbids alcohol, they did not consume alcohol themselves but rationalized selling it (58). Although they had lived in disparate parts of the United States before settling in Toledo, they were generally related to one another, displayed a greater harmony between the generations, and appeared to share a common goal of preserving their middle-class social status. Although they attended mosque services, they appeared to ignore important Islamic prescriptions. For example, they prayed on Sunday in the mosques without performing the required ablutions. They also maintained social relations with Christians, attended social events in churches, and displayed an American flag in the mosque (34, 37). Generally ignorant of Islamic prescriptions and ritual, the young members of the Toledo mosque used the building primarily as a social center.

In Detroit, young Muslims were living through an economic recession. Elkholy disapproved of their leisure activities—their preferred music for dancing was the Lebanese dabkeh (1966: 33)—and described them as "scores of idle, jobless young men" who spent their time gambling and fighting between cliques. They were, he went on, engaged in "night life activities of the Moslem 'beat' generation" and were "religiously weak." He attributed their behaviors to their authoritarian parents, and he saw the mosque as a place for "men" who were "aged and backward" (90).

Elkholy noted that factors leading other immigrants to assimilate in the United States, such as language acquisition and preference for middle-class areas of residence, were also melding Arab Muslims into American citizens. He argued that Islam was functioning as an assimilating religion by bringing the communities together as they began to shed their ethnic identities. In fact, he observed that the third generation in Toledo was more religious, while that of Detroit was more nationalistic, and that strong religious affiliation in the Toledo community accelerated, rather than hindered, its assimilation (1966: 69, 95, 98).

A quarter century after Elkholy's study, Yvonne Haddad and Adair Lummis (1987) interviewed members of five Muslim communities. They found that acculturation and assimilation were progressing among Muslims, despite the influx of a large number of new immigrants from different areas with distinctive identities. The study focused on five groups of early Arab Muslim settlers in the United States, four of which had established mosques by the 1930s (in Dearborn, Michigan; Toledo, Ohio; Cedar Rapids, Iowa; and Quincy, Massachusetts) and another, comprised primarily of Pakistani immigrants, that had established a new mosque in Rochester, New York. The 1985 survey noted that the traditional role of the imam had been transformed, even though a few of the imams, who were supported by the Muslim World League, had attempted to replicate the tradition of authority that obtained overseas. In several instances, the imams were overruled by their congregations, who had invested the decision-making role in the mosques' elected executive committee. From being a leader of prayer, the imam in the United States had taken on the role of a pastor, providing counseling and instruction in the faith, representing the community to the general public, participating in interfaith activities, and defending the faith.

The Haddad and Lummis survey found that over two-thirds of the Muslims sampled had a graduate degree, making this the best-educated Muslim population in the world. Their educational achievement was also well above the national average of the United States. While it is possible that only the highly educated chose to participate in the study, further research revealed that these immigrants emphasized college education as a means to social and economic mobility. As American higher education expanded in the 1960s, a large number became professors at universities.

While a significant number of this group became professionals and business people in the United States, it was mostly the immigrants who were admitted on preference visas after 1965 who became doctors and engineers. They brought with them a special enthusiasm for these two professions, as they are highly prized in the Arab world as a means to social and economic mobility. Many parents pressured their sons to follow in their footsteps. In the middle of the 1990s, the children of this group began to specialize in law, journalism, and the social sciences.

The Haddad and Lummis study confirmed Elkholy's findings that the Americanization of Arabs includes adopting values that are contrary to Arab customs, particularly in choosing a marriage partner. Whereas arranged marriages are still in effect in large parts of the Arab world, the Arab Muslim communities of Detroit and Toledo in Elkholy's study considered marriage to be a matter of personal choice, with courtship emulating American patterns. But the majority (71 percent) had married Muslims. Although about one-half of each community (45 percent in Toledo, 45 percent in Detroit) opposed the marriage of females to non-Muslims, Elkholy also found that two-thirds of the people interviewed would not oppose interfaith marriages, if the spouses were allowed to practice their faiths (1966: 31–32, 70). More recently, while arranged marriages have continued to be the norm among the majority of the children of recently arrived immigrants, especially those from small towns and rural areas, new means of matchmaking have been devised, including advertising in ethnic and religious magazines and through an internet service. On college campuses, many young Arab Americans have become indistinguishable from their colleagues in that they go to bars, date, drink, and smoke pot.

Elkholy had concluded that Muslim women increased their participation in public life as part of their Americanization. The later research survey of Haddad and Lummis revealed an important fact in Dearborn: women had been the primary instigators in establishing the mosque. They not only took the initiative in securing a place for the religious and social activities of the community, but also they raised the funds necessary, through bake sales and door-to-door soliciting. They managed the activities in the mosque facilities, arranging for weddings, receptions, and *haflehs* that included dancing. The influx of new immigrants into Dearborn, primarily Yemeni male migrant laborers with a different cultural understanding of the role of women in society, created a crisis in the community. The Yemenis, who wrested control of the mosque through the courts by arguing that its extrareligious activities were un-Islamic, dispatched the women to the basement and restricted their access to the mosque through a separate door. Thus the new immigrants attempted to re-create their notion of Muslim society in the American context. Other actors, primarily the recently imported foreign imams, who were hired to run the mosques, attempted to enforce traditional gender segregation. Scandalized by the dancing and social events taking place in the mosque, they insisted the mosque be used exclusively for prayer and religious instruction.

The majority of the Muslim women in the United State during the 1960s did not veil. Veiling was generally perceived as part of the maintenance of old customs, which were already dying out in Middle Eastern urban areas (Elkholy, 1966: 70). Haddad and Lummis corroborated Elkholy's findings of Americanization, confirming that the degree of strictness in adhering to "Islamic dress" varied from one mosque to another (1987: 126–27). Some mosques permitted women to attend prayer in knee-length skirts and no head coverings, whereas others insisted that women cover all their bodies and in some cases provide them with wraps (132). The more recent arrival of new immigrants who believe that the covering of woman's hair is a divine commandment has led to an increase in the number of women voluntarily donning the *hijab,* even though in many cases their mothers had never worn one and their grandmothers had cast it away in the 1920s and 1930s. Also recently affecting the role of women is the immigration of Muslims from South Asia who advocate traditional customs, including even the banning of handshaking between the sexes (134–36).

Women's religious activity has been mostly restricted to "sisters" groups. Although women for some time have led study circles that focus on Islamic knowledge and the teachings of the Qur'an, these generally have been conducted in private homes. By the 1990s, some Muslim women had begun to make their contributions to public life as academics, teachers, and researchers. Some were working through the Islamic historical and juridical sciences to reinterpret and provide new insights into Islamic knowledge and have published many studies on the role and status of women in Islam. In an effort to influence the cultural and social restrictions on women, some have offered new and progressive insights and interpretations grounded in the text of the Qur'an and the example of the Prophet Muhammad.

Unlike in Muslim countries, in the United States mosque attendance is a family affair rather than a strictly male activity. Muslim women do attend *jum'a,* Friday communal prayers, albeit in smaller numbers than the Sunday family prayers. In some mosques, women's allotted space for prayer is located at the back of the prayer hall behind the men. At other mosques, they are at the side, often separated by a barrier or a curtain. Occasionally, women pray in a separate space such as a basement, a loft, or an auxiliary room where they can watch the service on closed-circuit television. Most women interviewed found the separation helped them to concentrate on prayer rather than on members of the other sex.

While researchers have found that Arab Muslims have been cautiously open to religious and sociocultural change within the context of their local communities, their adaptation to living in America has also been shaped by broader national and international political forces. In this regard, U.S. government policies toward Arab and Israeli conflicts in the Middle East have had a particular influence on Arab Muslim's identification as Americans, as it has had on American Jews.

Arab Experience of America

Who is an Arab? What is an Arab? How does one become an Arab? These are questions that were hotly debated in the formative period of the modern Arab nation states during the first half of the 20th century and continue to generate a great deal of discussion both in the Middle East and among Arab Americans. An Arab nationalist identity was proposed as the foundation for a modern state that would consider as Arab all who speak the Arabic language and identify with Arab history and culture, regardless of whether they were Muslims, Christians, or Jews.

This multireligious view was promoted primarily by Jews and Christians in an effort to carve out a national identity where religious minorities would be recognized as full citizens. This view was also propagated by some Arabic-speaking Muslims who in the 1920s opposed the Young Turks who were seeking to "Turkify" all ethnic and tribal groups resident in the Ottoman Empire. Today several other meanings may be given to the word "Arab." One, for example, restricts the term to those who are native to the Arabian Peninsula as opposed to those who live in the "Arabized" northern tier (Iraq, Lebanon, Syria, Jordan, Palestine, Egypt, and North Africa). Another, much broader, definition is based on citizenship in any of the 22 Arab states that are members of the Arab League.

In a manner of speaking, immigrants from the Arab world are veterans of the struggle to modernize and westernize in the context of the colonial and postcolonial eras. In the United States, they perceive a nation that has some very strong institutions, that sees itself a model democracy, and that welcomes all who choose to share in the American dream. It seems to be a nation that advocates openness and pluralism as foundational principles of its polity. But somewhere behind these principles, Arab immigrants suspect the possibility of an anti-Saracen heritage as much or more anti-Arab and Muslim as anti-Semitic (Daniel, 1993; Kiernan, 1972; Tolan, 2002; Young, 1990). Such suspicions have been raised by the popular media; surveys of the news, cinema, school texts, and other sources of public information have documented how widely Arabs, Muslims, and Islam have been represented stereotypically as "outsiders" or "others" whose inferior, barbaric, sexist, or irrational beliefs and customs should be condemned if not eliminated (al-Qazzaz, 1975; Griswald, 1975; Jarrar, 1976; Karim, 2000; Malek, 1996; Perry, 1975; Said, 1997).

Arab Americans have attempted to synthesize their experiences of America with the Arab and Muslim experience of a dominant "West" during the history of European colonial expansion and subjugation of the Muslim world beginning in the 16th century and lasting through the first half of the 20th century. Attempts to perpetuate western domination of Arab nations have been perceived as continuing through American intervention in the area since the 1950s and support of Israel's expansion and settlement in Palestine and surrounding Arab states. The American government's support for autocratic regimes that appear to be client states and its war on terrorism, implemented through regime change in Afghanistan and Iraq, are widely perceived by the Arab and Muslim world as a war on Islam, consistent with this historical pattern.

Encounter with Zionism

The early immigrants from the Middle East were concerned about the fate of their relatives back home in the aftermath of World War I. A few lobbied the U.S. government to help create the Arab state promised in the Faisal-McMahon correspondence, and some Maronites worked for the creation of Greater Lebanon (Smith, 2004: 61–64). However, the majority of immigrants did not appear to be interested in political activity. Indeed, most of their early organizations were social, ethnic, or religious in nature.

The Syrian and Lebanese American Federation of the Eastern States was formed in Boston. Its membership included a variety of organizations that were social clubs, cultural groups, and charitable organizations. In 1932, the National Association of Syrian and Lebanese-American Organizations was formed and later the National Association of Federations. In the early 1950s, the federation sponsored a convention in Lebanon to foster good will between the United States and Syria and Lebanon. There is little evidence that the majority of the membership, a substantial number of whom belonged to the second and third generations, had any awareness of events overseas or the geography of the Middle East. Some of them had even contributed to the United Jewish Appeal (Hagopian, 1975–76). By the late 1950s and early 1960s, the National Association of Federations ceased to exist.

In the 1940s, the Arabic-speaking immigrants in the United States began to feel uncomfortable as the Zionist campaign for the recognition

and support for the state of Israel became intense. Among the slogans adopted by the Zionists were "A land without a people for a people without
a land."[4] The immigrants knew better. Not only was Palestine populated
with Palestinians, both Christian and Muslim, but some of the immigrants still had relatives and friends in Haifa, Jaffa, Ramallah, Beit Jala,
Jerusalem, the Galilee, and elsewhere.

The most galling Zionist slogan openly solicited funds for the eradica-
tion of Arabs: "Pay a dollar, kill an Arab." It had a great impact on Sayyid
Qutb, an Egyptian author on a scholarship in the United States between
1949 and 1951. An agnostic, he returned home totally disillusioned with
the United States, which he characterized as racist, anti-Arab, and anti-
Muslim. Back in Egypt, he became active in the Muslim Brotherhood
movement and became the greatest advocate of Islamism as an alternative to capitalism and communism, as a system that guaranteed justice
and equality and where there is no distinction based on color or national
identity.

By the 1950s, the impact of the conflict in the Middle East on the Arab
Muslim community in Detroit was palpable. Elkholy (1966: 18) noted that
they emphasized that they are Arab, regardless of whether they emigrated
from Lebanon, Iraq, Syria, or Yemen. One interviewee told Elkholy:
"Wherever a party is opened in the name of the Prophet, no one is particularly moved. If it is opened in the name of God, no one cares either. But
the name of Gamal Abdel-Nasser electrifies the hall" (48–49). He attributed the phenomenon to the "continuing threat posed by the existence of
Israel and Nasser's resistance to Israel and the Western political pressure."

A substantial number of the new Muslim immigrants brought a different identity, one fashioned by devastating experiences of war and conflict
in the Middle East, including the Israeli attack and catastrophic Arab defeat
(al-Nakba) in 1967, the failed Arab counterattack in 1973, the Israeli invasion of Lebanon in 1982, and the massacres of Sabra and Shatila in 1983. The
Lebanese civil war, in which Maronite Christians sided with Israel against
the Palestinians, led to Muslim distrust of Arab Christians. The new immigrants represented a generation that had wearied of an Arab nationalism
perceived to have failed to deliver on the hopes of the Arab people for justice for the Palestinian people, for parity with the West, and for input into
the world order. Their identity was shaped by the ideology that was beginning to sweep across the Arab world, one that affirmed religious identity as
a means of resistance to fundamentalist secularism, promoted by a variety
of regimes in the Middle East, as well as to hegemonic "Judeo-Christianity,"

experienced as the dominance of expansionist Israel as supported and empowered by Western nations. They had come to subscribe to some form of Islamic identity and included a small minority who favored "Islamism" as the only way to foster unity and strength to combat what was perceived as the incessant efforts to undermine Islam and Muslims.

Among the Arab Muslim immigrants who came to America in the 1980s were some who had witnessed the 1979 Iranian revolution and concluded that it demonstrated the power of Islamic identity in mobilizing the population to dethrone the shah, whom many saw as the mightiest of tyrants, yet a lackey of the United States and Israel. For some, these experiences generated the view that Arab nationalist identity was a colonial construct devised to divide and dominate Muslims as separate ethnic, racial, and language groups. The new understanding was that only an Islamic identity, creating solidarity between Muslim nations, can provide the necessary resources to fight for Muslim causes. The Arab states, went this line of thinking, would be empowered by the broader Muslim support from Indonesia, Pakistan, and elsewhere.

But an Islamist identity did not prevail among Arab Muslim immigrants in America. American hostility toward Arab nations at the time of the 1967 Israeli preemptive strike against Egypt, Syria, and Jordan led some community leaders to believe that the American public was uninformed about the facts of the conflict in the Middle East. This perception led them to form the first organization to assume a hyphenated identity and coin the term "Arab-American." The Association of Arab-American University Graduates (AAUG) was formed in 1967 by graduate students, professionals, university professors, lawyers, doctors, and veterans of the Organization of Arab Students (OAS). It reflected an Arab nationalist ideology that made no distinction among its members based on religious affiliation or national origin. It placed special emphasis on producing knowledge and educating both its membership and the American public about the Arab world.

The Arab American organization immediately became a target of the Zionist lobby, which began to portray Arab activists as spies and propagandists for foreign interests (Hagopian, 1975–76: 101; Hussaini, 1974). The *Near East Report* devoted several issues in 1969 alleging the presence of Arabs to be a threat to the United States.[5] The expressed concern was over Arab "propaganda" on American campuses. According to one analyst, the report's editors found "the Arab viewpoint reaching American ears was of equal concern as alleged security threats" (Fischbach, 1985: 89). The report warned Americans that Arab students may harbor *fedayeen* among them and that Arabs were trying to infiltrate leftist organizations. To silence critical voices on university campuses, other groups lobbied to cut federal Title VI funding, which was in part intended to support the training of area-studies experts for government service. The lobby also funded opponents of politicians who questioned American support of Israel, including Senator Percy of Illinois and Senator Fulbright of Arkansas, both of whom may have lost reelection as a result (Findley, 1989).

Other American Arab organizations were established by the second and third generations, veterans of the earlier federations. They were formed to defend the civil and political rights of the community and to respond to U.S. government policies that targeted Arab Americans, such as Operation Boulder, which was launched in 1972 by Richard Nixon's administration after the massacre of Israeli athletes at Munich. The U.S. government sought the help of the Israeli government and pro-Israel organizations in the United States to spy on the community.[6] It shared intelligence with the Israeli government and, many Arab-Americans believed, adopted the Israeli suspicion of Arabs being terrorists (Fischbach, 1985). The FBI began to compile dossiers on organizations and on members of the community by tapping their telephones and gathering information about their political ideas, the journals to which they subscribed, and their circle of friends (Bassiouni, 1974; Hagopian, 1975–76). Under Operation Boulder, the Arab community was intimidated by FBI investigations, restriction of movement by Arabs in the United States, and deportation of hundreds on technical irregularities. At the same time, new immigration from the Arab world was restricted. Although Operation Boulder officially came to an end in 1975, harassment of politically active Arab Americans continued, with the apparent purpose of discouraging their political activity. The massive scrutiny did not result in identifying any anti-American activities (Jabara, n.d.).

Other government actions and policies increased the marginalization of Arab Americans and heightened their anxiety. Using the Freedom of Information Act, the Arab community learned that the U.S. government was considering the use of two military compounds in the South for the possible internment of Arabs and Iranians, as had been done to the Japanese during World War II. They were shocked by the way that anti-Arab perceptions were encouraged by the ABSCAM investigation, when FBI agents masqueraded as Arabs in order to bribe members of Congress (Berman, 1982; Shaheen, 1980).

Many Arab-Americans saw these events as comprising a discriminatory campaign against persons of Arab origin to offend the dignity of many Arab Americans, particularly those American-born of Syrian and Lebanese origin who viewed themselves as loyal and law-abiding Americans (al-Qazzaz, 1997) and who had fought to defend the United States and its interests and values in both World War I and II. In response, in 1972, second- and third-generation Lebanese Americans organized the National Association of Arab Americans (NAAA), which was modeled after the pro-Israel lobby, the American Israel Public Affairs Committee,[7] in order to educate Arab Americans about the political process, as well as arrange for them to meet with members of Congress to discuss issues of great concern to the community. In addition, the American-Arab Anti-Discrimination Committee (ADC) was founded by former American-born Senator James Aburezk and James Zogby, both of Christian Lebanese origin (Orfalea, 1989). It was modeled after the ADL (Anti-Defamation League) to fight racism, prejudice, and discrimination against Arabs. It is currently the largest grass-roots Arab organization, with chapters throughout the United States.

The Arab American Institute (AAI) was established by James Zogby in 1984 when he split from ADC in order to encourage Arab Americans to participate in the American political system by voting and running for office. It has sought to establish Democratic and Republican clubs, such as those active in the presidential campaigns of Jesse Jackson (1988), Al Gore (2000), and George W. Bush (2000). Arab immigrants generally lack experience in political participation, fear the consequences of political involvement, and have no experience in coalition building. Major political candidates, including George McGovern, Walter Mondale, Joseph Kennedy, and Mayor Wilson Goode of Philadelphia, have shunned their support and returned their financial contributions because they are perceived as a liability, often out of fear of antagonizing the pro-Israel lobby. For example, in the 2000 New York senatorial contest, Republican candidate Rick Lazio depicted Arab and Muslim contributions to Hillary Clinton's campaign as "blood money," which led her to return the donations. As a result, many in the community feel disenfranchised, given the importance of donations in providing access to elected officials and determining U.S. policies.

All of these Arab American organizations were formed by coalitions of Christians and Muslims who had immigrated or descended from immigrants from Arab homelands. The founders shared experiences and interpretations of events in the Middle East and concerns about U.S. policies toward the region. Together they confronted what they saw to be unfair Zionist and U.S. government stereotyping and intimidation. By engaging in the political process they sought to get America to live up to its democratic values vested in the judicial system and guaranteed by the Constitution and Bill of Rights.

Muslim Experience of America

Once the pioneer Muslim migrants from the Arab world decided to settle in the United States at the end of the 19th and beginning of the 20th century, they were eager to belong, and in the process they tried to interpret American culture as compatible with Arab concepts of virtue and honor. They emphasized the similarities between Islam and Christianity and the respect Islam has for Jesus and his mother Mary. Early records show that they were dispersed throughout the United States and initially tended to socialize with Christian and Jewish immigrants from the Arab world. They sent their children to Christian parochial schools in order to imbue their education with ethical values. It was not until the 1930s that they began to have structures dedicated for Islamic services. In communicating with the American public, they tended to talk about the Qur'an as "our bible," the mosque as "our church," and the imam as "our minister." Their great-grandchildren are now indistinguishable from other Americans. Their dispersion and isolation, as well as the hardships they went though, led to little organized activity. Some belonged to the Syrian and Lebanese Federations.

Abdullah Igram of Cedar Rapids, Iowa, a veteran of World War II having experienced marginalization in the American military, worked to bring Islam and its adherents into the mainstream by seeking recognition from President Dwight D. Eisenhower. He requested that the religious affiliation of Muslims be recognized by the U.S. military, which previously left it blank on their "dog tags." In 1953, he called for a general meeting of Muslims, and members from 22 different mosques and centers in the United States and Canada participated. The next year they formed the Federation of Islamic Associations (FIA) in the United States and Canada. It eventually had a membership of 54 mosques and Islamic centers. Reflecting the constituency of the Muslim population in the United States in the 1950s, the majority of the congregations of these mosques were Lebanese.

Muslim immigrants of the 1970s often found the cultural accommodations exacted of earlier immigrants to America too high a price to pay, especially after America had begun to define itself as Protestant, Catholic, and Jewish. They rejected aspects of the American social and spiritual life that they found to be abhorrent, even as they enjoyed America's economic opportunities and freedom of religion, association, and speech. They accused the earlier immigrants of diluting important Islamic traditions, rituals, and distinguishing characteristics. They believed that difference and distinctiveness are a necessary means of affirming a place for Islam. Their conscious religious observances and their publications emphasized the great importance of the manner of prayer and how women were to dress, walk, and talk. Rather than stressing the commonalities with American culture and religion, they put the emphasis on the differences. Some leaders were confident that Islam is the perfect way and the cure for all that ails America.

Other factors contributed to the development of Islamic institutions in the United States in the 1990s. For one thing, there was a dramatic growth in the number of Muslim immigrants to the United States between 1970 and 1990, creating a larger group of practicing Muslims. Many came from the middle and lower-middle classes in rural areas and elected to maintain their traditional dress, while finding in mosque institutions a support system that helped them establish networks to find jobs and companionship.

The last decade of the 20th century ushered in a new phase of Muslim integration and assimilation into the United States. Several factors coalesced to bring about a major transformation in the Muslim community. The Gulf War of 1990 marked the end of financial support from Saudi Arabia and other Gulf nations. Initially, the withdrawal of support had a devastating effect on Islamic projects in the United States. Both FIA and ISNA (the Islamic Society of North America, which was formed in the early 1980s by Muslim students who had decided to settle in the United States) shut down their operations for lack of funds to pay their staff. But communal paralysis did not set in. Several leaders welcomed the freedom from dependency and began to work to establish permanent Islamic institutions. In the process, the power shifted from umbrella organizations to decentralized leadership, the independent mosque executive committees. While ISNA reopened with a skeleton staff, its ability to guide the progress of Islam nationwide had been greatly diminished. Its journal, *Islamic Horizon,* continues to be distributed nationally, and its annual conventions draw about 30,000 Muslims. It has recently started hosting academic conferences on "Islam in America," "Islam in Prisons," and "Islam among Latinos," which provide important insights on the daily life of Muslims in North America.

While the 1980s saw the development of Arab American organizations interested in public policy, the 1990s introduced several politically oriented Islamic organizations. The American Muslim Alliance (AMA) was formed in California in 1989 by Agha Saeed to empower Muslim participation in voting and running for office. Others include the American Muslim Council (AMC, founded in 1990), the Council on American-Islamic Relations (CAIR, 1994), and the Muslim Public Affairs Council (MPAC). Their goals generally paralleled those of the Arab organizations of the 1980s. Several of the leaders were alumni of the Arab American groups who saw a need to create Islamic institutions that would engage non-Arab Muslims in supporting political and civil rights issues relevant to the growing Muslim community.

With the election of Bill Clinton as president of the United States, Muslims perceived a major transformation to occur in the political allegiances of government policy makers. In their eyes, Clinton was beholden to the Jewish community because of its extensive support during his campaign. At the urging of Senator Joe Lieberman, Democrat of Connecticut, the new administration brought 27 activists from the pro-Israel lobby into government and placed them in charge of Middle East policy. During his two terms in office, they were able to weave the U.S.-Israel relationship into a seamless entity. It appeared to Muslims and Arabs that U.S. interests in the Middle East were being subsumed under the primary interests of Israel.

At the same time that the foreign policy initiatives of the government were deemed anti-Palestinian and anti-Muslim, the Clinton administration initiated a policy of symbolic inclusion of American Muslims. Periodically, leaders of the various Muslim organizations were invited to public events and occasionally had an audience with policy makers and talked about their issues. Hillary Rodham Clinton hosted the first *iftar* dinner, the break of the fast of Ramadan, at the Department of State. Although some in the Muslim leadership were enamored by what they perceived as an elevation of their status, they were fully aware that, though they could voice their concerns during these brief encounters, they felt they had no influence on policy.

Confident in an American Muslim future, Muslims in various suburbs and cities stepped out of the shadows and became more visible. They turned to their own resources and began building mosques and Islamic centers, whose number grew from 598 in 1986 to over 1,250 by 2000. Some of the mosques built in the middle of the century were architecturally nondescript and were remodeled or replaced by new structures with minarets, copulas, and domes, symbols of Islamic architecture. A few of the mosques started social and welfare organizations (such as soup kitchens and free medical clinics) to serve the needy in America, breaking with the practices of earlier generations who sent their *zakat* (tithe that is one of the requirements of Islam) funds to support the poor relatives and the dispossessed of the lands they left behind. Over 200 Islamic schools were established. Islam was entering the mainstream, and the Muslim community decided that it is in America to stay. It consciously began to put its imprint on the American landscape, a permanent settlement set in brick, concrete, tile, and stone.

Meanwhile, Arab American identity had become associated with Christians and secular Muslims from the Arab world. The growing consensus among Islamists was that Arab identity had been divisive and had led to the disempowerment of the Arabs. From their perspective, anyone who identifies as Arab places national over religious identity. Increasingly, Muslim immigrants from Arab nation-states identify themselves either as Muslim or by the citizenship they held prior to emigration: Egyptian, Palestinian, Syrian, and the like. Very rarely do immigrants assert, "I am an Arab Muslim," unless they are from the Gulf area or are trying to make a linguistic or geographical distinction. For many in the third wave of immigrants, "Arab" became a secondary modifier of identity, depending on context. Their primary identities may be Shi'i, Muslim, Lebanese, Arab, or American, depending on the circumstances.

Whereas early mosque activities centered on fostering a social community that shared a common faith, in the 1990s the mosque became a center for creating an Islamic ethnicity based not only on a shared faith but also on a shared worldview that envisioned a Muslim community engaged with American society, taking its place in the American religious mosaic.

Aftermath of 9/11

While scholars have been studying the immigration and integration of Arabs and Muslims in the United States and comparing their adjustment to that of other initially ostracized religious groups such as Catholics and

Jews, in the aftermath of 9/11 it may also be helpful to compare the status and treatment of Arabs and Muslims with that of Germans during World War I, Japanese during World War II, and Jews during the cold war. The policies adopted by the Bush administration are reminiscent of measures adopted during these critical moments in American history that suspended American legal protection of all citizens and identified some as a threat to the nation.

The last wave of Muslim immigrants consciously and deliberately stepped out of the isolation that the immigrants of the 1960s and 1970s had maintained because they feared for the survival of Islam as an American faith. Muslims embarked in the 1990s on a policy of engagement with American society that culminated in their joining Arab and Muslim political organizations and, for many, publicly supporting the George Bush–Dick Cheney ticket in the 2000 presidential election. The impetus for this support was the fact that Bush had met with the leadership of Arab and Muslim organizations and listened to their concerns, while the Democratic candidate, Al Gore, had ignored them. Furthermore, during the presidential debates, Bush had questioned the fairness of the profiling of Arabs and Muslims. After Bush took office, however, his administration shied away from engaging with the Muslim community. This policy changed after 9/11 when Bush visited the Islamic Center in Washington, D.C., and, in an effort to calm public anger—but to the consternation of many of his supporters—he declared Islam a "religion of peace."

The attacks of 9/11 appear to have settled ongoing debates among policy makers in the United States about American security and foreign policies. After the collapse of the Soviet Union, a growing number of political officials had begun to identify "fundamentalist Islam" as the major imminent threat to U.S. interests, just as some Israeli leaders had done for several decades. The attacks of 9/11 revealed the view of a growing number of Beltway pundits and journalists that Israel and America were becoming targets of anti-Jewish and anti-Christian hatred.

Also subscribing to this view were elements of the fundamentalist Christian community who, following the Israeli victory of 1967, shifted their interpretation of contemporary signs that the end of time was near to predict that a major battle between Jews, now restored to Israel, and Muslims would herald the return of the Messiah. Such Christian fundamentalists welcomed the intensification of conflict between the two faiths as a signal of the final redemption of the Jews. Leading ministers denounced Islam and its prophet in a manner that reminded some Muslims of the discourse that launched the Crusades and justified European colonization of Muslim nations.

Because most of the men who carried out the attacks of 9/11 were Arab Muslims, the initial impact of the event on the Muslim community was one of deep shock and fear of a potential backlash. Many Muslims were subsequently surprised and pleased by those Christian and Jewish communities who supported them. They were grateful to the rabbis and ministers who volunteered to stand guard at mosques, schools, bookstores, and other Islamic institutions to keep avengers away. They were amazed at the number of American women who donned scarves for a day in solidarity with Muslim women who veil. They were also touched by the little gestures of kindness from neighbors who offered to act as escorts or purchase groceries. They were pleased that Americans were finally interested in Islam and were reading about the religion and getting acquainted with the tenets of their faith.

For Muslims, the most distressing measure adopted by the government in response to 9/11 has been H.R. 3162, commonly known as the USA PATRIOT (Providing Appropriate Tools Required to Intercept and Obstruct Terrorism) Act of October 24, 2001, which has in essence lifted many civil liberty protections for Muslims and Arabs in the United States. An estimated 5,000 young Arab and Muslim men have been put into detention under the act. Further, the act sanctions the monitoring of individuals, organizations, and institutions without notification. Its provisions have been protested by the American Bar Association, the American Librarians Association, and the American Civil Liberties Union. Several Arab and Muslim organizations have recently sued the American government, insisting that this act is un-American. Former Congresswoman Mary Rose Oakar, president of the American-Arab Anti-Discrimination Committee, declared that the act was "completely incompatible with basic civil liberties, most notably freedom from unreasonable search and seizure by the government as guaranteed by the Fourth Amendment to the Constitution."[8]

Meanwhile, the identification of a terrorist in the United States has slowly mutated from "Arab" to "Muslim." The critical transfer became embedded in U.S. law when Congress passed H.R. 1710, the Comprehensive Antiterrorism Act of 1995, after the Oklahoma City bombing. Among other security measures, the bill sanctioned airport profiling of potential terrorists. The profile was not of a Timothy McVeigh but of an Arab or a Muslim. Arabs and Muslims are concerned that, while the Antiterrorism Act has sanctioned the incarceration of Arabs and Muslims with secret evidence, the Patriot Act has sanctioned their incarceration with no evidence.

Many of the security measures adopted by the Bush administration were perceived as being anti-Muslim rather than antiterrorism. When the American government set up an office in the Department of State to engage in liberating Muslim women, many Muslims interpreted it as a virtual declaration of war against a Muslim definition of the role of women in society. They questioned whether this really meant liberation from Islam and its values. U.S. embassies began to monitor textbooks in Muslim countries for antiwestern, anti-American, or anti-Israeli content, giving the appearance to some that the only "Islam" that could be taught is one approved by the CIA. Fearful of the transfer of funds to terrorist organizations, the American government began monitoring nongovernmental civic, charitable, and religious organizations and, in effect, assumed a veto power over *zakat,* through which American Muslims support orphans and widows overseas.

Equally troubling were raids on the homes and offices of national Muslim leaders in northern Virginia, which were perceived by Muslims as a sign that the U.S. government was looking for a new leadership. The arrests were particularly surprising to Muslims who had criticized these leaders for cooperating too closely with the American government. The raids raised questions about what kind of Islam America will tolerate. Several of the individuals who have stepped up and volunteered to lead the Muslims into "moderation" have been supported and funded by various agencies of the U.S. government. Their mission is to provide new reflections on and interpretations of Islam. They have opened offices and are in the process of leading others into "right thinking." To date, these leaders appear to have few followers as they are widely perceived by Muslims as agents of the effort to undermine Islam.

Other profound changes appear under way, their ramifications still unfolding. For the majority of Muslims who emigrated with the idea that, if things did not work out, they could always return home, the attacks appear to have settled the "myth of return": Muslims are here to stay. Unconsciously, they have slowly become American and relish the freedoms that American society provides. The question for this group is how to adjust to the intensified scrutiny by anti-immigration organizations and government security agencies that demand repeated public demonstrations of patriotism and allegiance to America and its government's policies. Many Muslims had a hard time convincing their fellow Americans that, because

America had been attacked, they too felt attacked. Their repeated denunciations of terrorism as un-Islamic did not seem to be sufficient. Some offered to act as a bridge linking the U.S. government with Muslim organizations overseas and governments in heavily Muslim countries. Others volunteered to serve in the armed services. Thousands volunteered to act as translators, though few were hired due to heightened suspicion of their ethnicity or religious affiliation.

That the whole Muslim and Arab community was placed under scrutiny brought about other changes. Muslims feel that now there is little room for public conflict. A new relationship has opened between mosqued and un-mosqued Moslems, who previously tended to disagree on issues pertaining to integration and assimilation. But in the post-9/11 policies adopted by the government and in the tone assumed by some of the press and evangelical clergy, both groups became targets of hate, discrimination, and profiling, regardless of their religious or political adherence. Sermons in mosques became restricted to devotional topics. Islamic literature that used to be available for free distribution disappeared from most public places. Self-censorship extended to websites and their recommended links.

Another noticeable change has been the increased prominence of Muslim women in the public square. Feeling threatened by insecurity and vulnerability, after 9/11 a few women took off the veil to avoid attacks, but many others put it on. As men began to keep a low profile, women took charge. Many Muslim women assumed important positions in the administration of Islamic institutions and as spokespersons and defenders of the community. In this period of tribulation, rather than remaining relegated to the "sisters" committees, which had typically been designated as "parallel but equal," men and women became "together and equal." They raised funds for the victims of 9/11 and coordinated blood drives for the wounded. They also marched to protest discrimination against Muslims. At the same time, concern over the government's policy of incarcerating or deporting males for infractions of the law placed some women under duress. They became reluctant to report domestic problems in order to safeguard their husbands' and their children's future.

Also noticeable is the fact that the community embarked on coalition building with human rights, religious rights, and civil rights groups. Relating to non-Muslims became a priority. They promoted interfaith occasions, inviting churches and synagogues to come and visit the mosques and engage in dialogue. They joined national organizations that were seeking justice against corporations and sweatshops, working for the protection of the environment and peaceful resolution of conflicts. They began to seek to build coalitions with civil liberties organizations. Sill, many felt that because of their ethnicity or religious affiliations they no longer had the luxury of disagreeing with government policy. While freedom of thought is a right for all Americans, there seemed to be an exception if they were Arab or Muslim. The Bush stance in his fight against terrorism that "You are either with us or against us" appeared to leave no room for an independent interpretation of the meaning of being a Muslim.

America, a Home for Arabs and Muslims

For over a century, immigrants from the Arab world have prospered in the United States. They have "made it" by working hard, carefully shedding their particular cultural distinctions, compromising and blending in. Yet they have not as yet been welcomed as a group into the American mainstream. The Christians among them who have achieved leadership positions, some even as high as elected governors and senators, have mostly abandoned eastern Christianity, whether Orthodox, Melkite, or Maronite, and joined mainline American churches. Many Muslims question whether the price of belonging in America is contingent on the renunciation of Islam. They are still waiting to be accepted on their own terms into the American definition of its constituent faith communities.

From the outset, officials in the U.S. government have raised questions about the fitness of Arabs to qualify for citizenship in America based on issues of race and color.[9] Spooked by the influx of large groups of immigrants (predominantly from southern and eastern Europe) during the first two decades of the 20th century, the American public appeared little inclined to welcome Middle Easterners. For example, a judge in South Carolina ruled that, "even though they may look white," Lebanese immigrants "are not that particular free white person" designated by the 1790 Act of Congress and hence not entitled to citizenship (Samhan, 1987: 14). After a decade of legal debates, the American courts ruled that they qualified as white and were therefore able to become citizens.

In the post–World War II period, when the United States was reinventing itself as a pluralistic society, immigrants from the Arab world found themselves publicly and deliberately excluded from the American mainstream. Many felt that what amounts to anti-Arab racism is rooted in the

Arab-Israeli conflict: "It has been not so much Arab origin as Arab political activity in America that has engendered a new form of 'political' racism that takes prejudice and exclusion out of the arena of personal relations into the arena of public information and public policy" (Samhan, 1987: 16). They see that this political exclusion has been propagated by their political rivals, such as the American Jewish organization that tagged Arab American activists an "artificial constituency," a sort of illegitimate group of foreign agents undermining Israel (Groot and Rosen, 1983). This eventually brought a variety of government agencies, including the CIA, INS, FBI, and IRS, the Department of State, and the Customs Service, to coordinate their monitoring of the Arab-American community in an effort to ferret out terrorists and intimidate the community, weakening its effectiveness and scaring off its allies and sympathizers (Fischbach, 1985).

The 1990s witnessed an increase in hostility toward Arabs and Muslims in the United States. The hostile atmosphere appears to have been encouraged by several interests. They include the conservative wing of the Republican Party, the religious right, the pro-Israel lobby, and leaders of autocratic Arab states. Events overseas precipitated measures that led to racial profiling and targeting of Arabs and Muslims, along with a growing atmosphere of hostility toward Islam. An act of Congress, a decision of the Supreme Court, and a presidential executive order legitimated the incarceration of Arabs and Muslims using secret evidence. In a sense, they were treated as different from other citizens of the United States since they were denied the basic presumption of innocence until proven guilty. Thus at the beginning of the 21st century, the United States, once again, seemed to question whether the members of one group have the same rights as other citizens. This time, the discrimination is based not on color or political affiliation but on the perennial fear of the Arab "Saracen" and the commitment to an Islamic ideology.

A number of events in the late 20th century appear to have had a profound effect on the formulation of Arab American and Muslim identity in the United States. Events that heightened Americans' negative perceptions of Arabs, Islam, and Muslims include the Israeli preemptive strike on Egypt, Syria, and Jordan in 1967; the oil boycott of 1973; the Islamic Revolution in Iran in 1979; the Rushdie Affair of 1989; and the Gulf wars. The 1967 war provided the impetus for the formation of the American Arab organizations that sought to ameliorate the negative image of Arabs in America, to provide a venue for airing their frustration, and to give accurate information. They attempted to redress what they perceived to be the one-sided reports about the Arab and Muslim world and sought to exercise their political rights to have an input into the shaping of policy. The Islamic Revolution in Iran and the anti-Muslim sentiments generated in the American media with headlines about "America Held Hostage" focused Muslim attention on the unforgiving and sustained rejection of political Islam. It raised questions about American support for Israel, which defines itself as a Jewish state, and the American rejection of Muslim attempts to create Islamic states.

The Gulf wars brought to the fore a new generation of Arab and Muslim activists seeking to change American policies by operating within the system. The majority does not approve of either of the American wars on Iraq, not because they are fond of Saddam Hussein or his policies but because they are not convinced by the justification of the government for launching the attacks. They believe, rather, that the U.S. government did not give diplomacy a chance but was bent on destroying Iraq's army in order to maintain Israeli domination of the Arab world.

Unlike the activists of the 1970s, the newest generation of Arab Americans is not spending time on establishing umbrella organizations, writing constitutions for these organizations, or running elections for officials or spokespersons. Rather, they have adopted modern means of communication, including the internet, to create networks committed to justice and peace. They collaborate with existing organizations for human rights, minority rights, and religious rights. These Arab American activists are mostly in their 20s and 30s, and they take American values very seriously. They believe that they are working to create a better America, one that is not blinded by special interests but is truly guided by the values it preaches. In the process, they believe that they are truly Arab—truly American.

The new immigrants who came as adults in the 1960s with preformed identities and a distinctive worldview are in the process of negotiating their identity in a hostile American environment. Increasingly, their children are reshaping them into Americans. For the children, America is the only homeland they know. They often repeat, "I want my parents' religion but not their culture." The parents, in contrast, have been teaching their Arab culture as Islam, and they want to keep their children within the tradition. It is too early to guess where this process will lead, especially in light of American hostility to nonprivatized Islam. Increasingly, they are being asked to define themselves vis-à-vis America. What does it mean to them to be an American? Do they want to be an American or a hyphenated American? Do they think of themselves as Muslims living in America? Do they think of themselves as American Muslims, or do they think of themselves as Americans who happen to be Muslim?

While the answers to such questions may vary, there is no doubt that the American public, the American security apparatus, and the American government are increasingly demanding a clear and unequivocal answer. In the process, many young people who grew up identifying themselves as American and Muslim are experiencing relentless prejudice and discrimination. As one woman put it, "I feel American, I bleed American, but my country denies me that identity because I am a Muslim." Tempered by prevalent hatred and "othering," many are reidentifying themselves as Arab American or Muslim American.

NOTES

This essay is based on the Charles Edmondson Historical Lectures delivered at Baylor University in 2001. It is reproduced with the permission of Baylor University Press. Yvonne Haddad (2004), *Not Quite American? The Shaping of Arab and Muslim Identity in the United States* (Waco, Tex.: Baylor University Press).

1. The Christian communities are remnants of early Christian churches. Among those who identify their churches as "Orthodox," for example, are the Byzantine, Assyrian, Jacobite, Coptic, and Gregorian rites. Each of these churches has its Catholic Uniate counterpart, those who have established fealty to the Vatican. More recently, Arab countries have seen the establishment of new churches representing Protestant denominations (predominantly Anglican and Presbyterian) with smaller Lutheran, Baptist, Jehovah's Witnesses, Pentecostals, and other evangelical and sectarian Christian churches. It is estimated that Catholics (Roman Catholic, Maronite, and Melkite) constitute 35 percent, Orthodox (Antiochian, Syrian, Greek, and Coptic) 18 percent, and Protestants (Episcopalians, Baptist and Presbyterian) 10 percent. See Arab-American Institute, "Demographics," n.d.

2. It is estimated that 3.4 percent are from Sub-Saharan Africa, 2.1 percent are European, 1.6 percent are white American converts, 1.3 percent are Southeast Asians, 1.2 percent are Caribbean, 1.1 percent are Turkish, 0.7 percent are Iranian, and 0.6 percent are Hispanic. See U.S. Department of State, 2002.

3. In addition, an estimated 13,000 Muslims of Arab and Pakistani background are currently living in fear of imminent deportation because of irregularities in their immigration status.

4. Michael Palumbo, "Land without a People," at http://www.geocities.com/CapitolHill/Senate/7891Palumbo_chtr1.html, 4.

5. For example, those of May 14 and October 29, 1969.

6. *New York Times,* May 24, 1973; *Washington Post,* October 15, 1972.

7. Jerome Bakst, "Arabvertising: The New Brand of Arab Propaganda," *Times of Israel,* April 1975, 15–23, cited in Hagopian (1975–76: 111).

8. Other Arab American and Islamic organizations that joined ADC in the brief include Muslim Community Association of Ann Arbor, Arab Community Center for Economic and Social Services, Bridge Refugee and Sponsorship Services, Council on American-Islamic Relations, Islamic Center of Portland, and Masjid as-Sabir of Portland.

9. 213 Fed. 812 (District Court, E.D. South Carolina, 1914), at 357, cited in Moore, (1995: 53); Khalil Bishara, *Origin of the Modern Syrian,* cited in Suleiman (1987: 44).

Muslim, Arab, and American
The Adaptation of Muslim Arab Immigrants to American Society

Ann Chih Lin

The religious beliefs of immigrants have always been an important factor in their adaptation to American society. Religion instills an important sense of identity and purpose. It is often the source of rituals and practices that bind communities together and preserve cultures. It can provide social networks and organizational resources to help immigrants gain power and influence and combat prejudice and discrimination in their new society.

Among today's Arab migration to the United States, Islam can play this important role. But as has been the case with other non-Christian religions, Islam also faces barriers from American society. Particularly after September 11, 2001, social prejudice toward and the lack of understanding about Muslims and the comparative scarcity of Muslim institutions in American society mean that Muslim-Arab immigrants face particular problems as they work to create a flourishing community in the United States.

The conjunction of religious belief and social prejudice is, of course, not new in American history. As Calvin Goldscheider describes (chapter 7), the experience of prejudice is an integral part of the Jewish experience, shaping Jewish institutions as well as beliefs about how to be American and how desirable Americanness is. Based on interviews with first-generation Arab immigrants, this chapter explores the same dynamic among Muslim Arabs today. Their sense of separateness created by the knowledge of prejudice and difference creates two primary pathways to incorporation: either through personal networks and effort or through organizational channels. In the first, religious faith and cultural practices are undergirded not by institutions but by family and friends in one's private life. Such immigrants understand that their commitments are marginal in American society, and they accept this marginality without resentment or surprise. At the same time, they also claim a set of American interests and opportunities, a set that they believe all residents, of any creed or color, share. Thus their private and closely guarded faith and sense of culture neither conflicts with nor influences their American identity. In the second, by contrast, other Arab Muslim organizations sustain—indeed, help to create—the sense of community among immigrants who are touched by and belong to them. These immigrants, usually wealthier and more educated than the first group, seek to create an American identity that embraces and incorporates their faith, their political and social ideals, and their right to stand at the center of their new country.

The immigrants whose experiences are described in this essay are first-generation Arab immigrants in the metropolitan Detroit area of Michigan. The Arab immigration to Michigan is over 100 years old and continues to this day: Iraqi immigrants, many displaced by the Gulf War, have joined older communities of Yemenis, Palestinians, Syrians, and Lebanese. The Arab-origin population here is second only to the metropolitan Los Angeles area in size and is still the most concentrated community of Arabs in the United States (Arab American Institute, 2002; Schopmeyer, 2000). The area includes a city, Dearborn, which has a multitude of businesses, religious institutions, and community groups catering to Arab immigrants and their descendants, as well as both public and private schools where Arab children are concentrated. But Arab-origin residents are also well represented in the suburbs and smaller cities of the area and within the Detroit city limits.

The age, size, diversity, and institutionalization of the Detroit Arab community has consequences for the institutions and patterns of identification that we describe. First, it is a community of both old and new immigrants and institutions. Immigrants can choose among multiple hometown and home country associations, both new and established mosques, ethnic and religious social and advocacy groups, and parochial, charter, nonsectarian private, or public schools. This means that the histories of different periods of immigration are all represented in local groups; in Detroit, different eras of immigration coexist.

Second, living in a Muslim Arab community—as opposed to either an Arab or a Muslim community—is possible in Detroit because of the large Arab population. Some mosques in the Detroit area are multiethnic, with membership that includes South Asians and American Muslims, but many others are not.[1] In other parts of the country, where Arabs are a minority of Muslims, this is less possible.

Third, in many ways, the diversity of identity choice described here is made possible by the size and scope of the community. This is not a community that has no choice but to unite and overcome differences to compensate for its small numbers. Certainly the Arabs in this area still face discrimination and prejudice, and they may often have common interests. But the size of the community is such that there are a variety of ways to combat common enemies or pursue common goals, as well as ways to find community without engaging in battle.

The diversity of the community from which these immigrants come has several implications for research and scholarship on Islam and its contributions to the incorporation of immigrants from the Middle East. First is the importance of evaluating not what role Islam has in the adaptation of Arab immigrants but what role one's Muslim *community* has. An immigrant may be religious, even observant, but the institutional and communal forms of her observance—not the religion itself—are what play the primary role in her adaptation. Second, and closely related, is the importance of class. When the institutional and communal forms of religion are so significant in incorporation, incorporation will, in turn, be mediated by socioeconomic class, both in the kinds of organizations with which people identify and in the kinds of networks that develop as a result. Third, gender is at the center of questions of identity. In part this is because immigrants use changes in family and gender roles as one way to mark their adaptation—or resistance—to American society. But it is also because women's activity, or lack thereof, shapes many of the organizations to which immigrants belong. Fourth, what happens in the second generation, as well as in generations beyond, depends on yet a further element: the ability of communal interaction and institutions to claim the attention and allegiance of these immigrants' children and grandchildren.

As both Calvin Goldscheider (chapter 7) and Arnold Eisen (chapter 8) make clear, the institutions that characterize an immigrant population upon arrival, or even long settlement, evolve, in Eisen's words, to both "connect [immigrants] to America and root them in their own past." As the Muslim and Arab institutions described by Yvonne Haddad (chapter 9) evolve, both in response to life in America and in response to global

Islam, they will attract different segments of the second and third generation and change the future of Muslims, Arabs, and America.

Sample and Study Design

This chapter is based on in-depth qualitative interviews conducted between 1998 and 2000 with 92 Arab immigrants, half male, half female, from the Detroit metropolitan area, an area that has the highest concentration of Arabs in the United States.[2] All emigrated to the United States as teenagers or adults and have been in the United States for at least five years and as many as 50. They occupy a variety of economic circumstances, from women on welfare to storekeepers to small businessmen to wealthy suburban families, and live in a variety of neighborhoods, from majority-Arab streets in Dearborn to upscale suburbs. At least 25 percent are Christians, both Orthodox and Catholic; the other 75 percent are Muslim: Sunni, Shi'a, and Druze. They claim seven nationalities of origin—Palestinian, Syrian, Lebanese, Iraqi, Jordanian, Algerian, and Egyptian—and 10 sending areas, including all of the above as well as Morocco, Saudi Arabia, and Canada. Some 67 percent are citizens; all but 2 percent of the rest have permanent residence.

Amaney Jamal, my colleague on this project, and I recruited respondents through personal networks in mosques and churches, by approaching staff and clients in the waiting room of a social service agency catering primarily to Arab Americans, through a radio advertisement, by introducing ourselves to customers in restaurants and Arab-owned stores, and through referrals from various acquaintances. The resulting sample is not statistically representative of the Arab community in Detroit or in the United States. However, we deliberately attempted to maximize the diversity of our respondents, with the intention of learning about the immigrant experience both within and outside of ethnic enclaves and ethnic-primary social circles.

Maintaining Community through Family

Omar, an autoworker, settled his family in the United States after several years of commuting between Detroit and his hometown in Lebanon. He owned a store for a while, then sold it; his son now has a small business.

His small but comfortable house is filled with solemn-eyed grandchildren; he sent his son back to Lebanon to marry a cousin and bring her here. As the interview progresses, Omar's sister, a woman of 60, and his nephew come by to sit on the porch and drink tea. In the midst of this family network, he is clearly a respected and important person.

Asked about community events, he frowns: "I don't get involved with these things. I don't like to show or emerge in those things." The mosque? He goes occasionally, primarily on holidays, but is not part of any active community center. But he does have an active social life: "Every week almost I go to a wedding. If I get an invitation, it's because people respect me. So any invitation I get, I reciprocate because it's out of respect. That means I was not forgotten."

Many immigrants are like Omar. They respect their cultural traditions and the commandments of their faith: "We came from the Middle East. Our culture and traditions are different. The freedom here is for the people of this country. I came from outside. Either I adjust to the freedom of the people here, or I can reserve my own traditions. I am not forced to adjust to the freedom here if it clashes with my own norms." He maintains these norms in his family: his wife covers her head; his son married in the family and continues to live with his parents. He also maintains them because he is embedded in a social network of family and friends, which reinforces his own beliefs.

Immigrants like Omar are strongly attached to their Islamic beliefs and behavior. But their beliefs and behavior are private: their religion does not enter the public square. When Omar talks about his faith, the emphasis is on "his" faith: "Everybody has their own religion. And religion goes back to Allah. A person can preserve their religion if they are Muslim or Christian. And the system here allows this." He simultaneously believes that he is an outsider, accepting the limitations of that role, and sees the benefits, for him, of being included in the protections that all Americans have: "The people here are convinced with the type of freedom, type of lifestyle they have. We come from outside and we cannot force them to adjust when they are convinced with their own standards. We can observe our own traditions because the American system and the law here allows us to. And we need to respect this as well."

The distinction that Omar draws between "the people here" and "us," where he is at once part of "the people here" and yet different from them, carries over into his political life. Omar has strong beliefs about the unfairness of American policy in the Middle East: "U.S. foreign policy is biased in favor of Israeli interests. And the U.S. government itself knows this. And I wish the U.S. government treats everyone for their own rights. It should treat everybody fairly, not in a biased manner." He knows of two famous Arab American politicians—James Zogby, who is the leader of the Arab American Institute, a lobbying group in Washington, D.C., and Spencer Abraham, at that time a U.S. senator from Michigan. Of the two, he prefers Zogby: "He has more courage. And he is more straightforward. And I have no doubt that Spencer Abraham tries to defend Arab rights, but probably because of the situation Zogby is in, he is better able to speak on Arab issues." In other words, he has not only a critique of American foreign policy but some knowledge of Arab American leaders who make that critique. But Omar, who says that he votes, also says that he does not base his vote on foreign policy issues. Instead, when he talks about voting, it is "as an American," which to him means on issues like social policy, health care, and the economy: "Of course, as an American I care about the domestic issues, because what happens in the U.S. affects all people in the U.S. Its economy and social life are important. . . . I am part of America, and any prosperity affects me, and any recession will impact me." He usually votes for Democrats, who "work for domestic issues: poverty, health care, retired and Social Security."

Immigrants like Omar have not abandoned either their cultural or their religious practices to become American. But these cultural and religious beliefs do not influence their public behavior. This is not because they think such beliefs unimportant. Rather, they have a particular notion of what it means to be American—a small core of shared interests, surrounded by a larger, but private, set of personal beliefs. This approach to American public life is less a choice than a response to a particular set of structural conditions and cultural expectations. The lack of organizational connection in these immigrants' lives and the types of employment they engage in coincide to make their stance toward American life reasonable.

The first thing to notice about Omar's religious practice is that it is not dependent on mosque attendance or other kinds of organized communal activity. Islam is a noninstitutional faith: like Judaism, the rituals of faith are lived through daily life and personal practice. While there is a rich tradition of Islamic scholarship and study, in practice, faith is transmitted as much by family and community as by doctrine and teaching. Mosques do not correspond to a particular geographical area in the way that Catholic churches correspond to a parish. Men go to mosques to pray in the Middle East, but not necessarily for other activities. Women pray in mosques as well, but many women do not have the habit of going to a mosque.

For many Muslims, therefore, mosques do not play the organizing role that churches played for Catholic neighborhoods and American Catholicism (Gamm, 1999; McGreevy, 1996). Nor do other organizations substitute. Immigrants like Omar are embedded in an extended network of family and fictive kin, often from the same village or region, produced by chain or colocated migration (Suleiman, 1999; Shryock, 2000). But the very presence of these strong ties can inhibit the need to build community through formal organizations. Those who did are primarily active in hometown societies. More often, however, visits to one's friends and kin, or informal gatherings at a restaurant or someone's store, serve to satisfy the need for social ties.

The privatized community that this kind of social interaction supports is also undergirded by particular forms of employment. Many in this group run small businesses, sometimes in conjunction with paid employment; women tend not to be employed or to be employed in family businesses. When women do not work, their interactions tend to be with other women in their social network, around children or family affairs.

These types of work lead to distinctive kinds of social and political networks. Those working in auto plants or in service jobs, for instance, will have non-Arab coworkers and will often belong to a union. To the extent that political discussion happens on the job and political organizing occurs through worker institutions (such as unions), these immigrants can participate. But their participation is likely to follow the interests of the majority: that is, the non-Arabs and nonimmigrants who share those networks with them. The United Auto Workers (UAW) takes stands on domestic issues such as Social Security; it is less likely to take a stand on foreign policy issues such as the Israeli-Palestinian conflict. Thus the politicization of Muslim immigrants through these work networks is unlikely to lead to opportunities to put their distinctive political concerns on the table.

Even when issues regarding the rights of Muslims arise, the context of a diverse workplace suggests that these will be judged not with reference to Muslims' particular needs but by the same rules that govern any other religious accommodations. As a result, such networks are likely to foster the belief that "American" political issues are domestic issues, not foreign policy ones, and that religious issues are political only insofar as they involve parity of religious treatment.

A different set of factors affects those who own small businesses (David 2000). Entrepreneurs often have the opportunity to interact with city government and other business owners. But such businesses often involve long hours and substantial family labor. Thus, until they are successful, small business owners tend not to have the time or inclination to participate in ethnic or religious organizing. As one storeowner told us, "I have this shop. I never visit. I take no vacation. I devoted all my life to my family. I work hard to raise my family, I open this store seven days a week." Unless they work within the Arab American enclave, they are also unlikely to be drawn into organizations such as the Arab American Chamber of Commerce.[3]

The role that women play in the formation of community is particularly important here. As discussed in the next section, many of the pan-ethnic Arab and Muslim organizations that the immigrants mentioned are staffed either by paid professionals or by the volunteer work of mothers who are part-time or full-time housewives. Women whose networks revolve around family and fictive kin (unrelated individuals whose close, significant relationships take on characteristics of family relations), however, seldom participate in such activities. This may be partly due to lack of education, but it also reflects differences in types of socializing. Lana, a housewife, is a case in point: her husband works in a deli, she receives some public assistance for her children, and they live in a neighborhood one street away from her husband's mother and two houses away from her husband's uncles. Apart from visits to them and to one friend with children about her age, she says:

> I don't go nowhere, just stay home. Like yesterday—I have a car, where I'm going to go?—they [the kids] bored, everybody here, the Arabs I know, they left. I stay outside by myself. They [the kids] told me, please take us all. So I drive the car around and around, for half an hour, then come back home." Instead, "I help my neighbors when they cooking, or something like that! I do a lot of things like that. [*Are they Arabs?*] Arabs. I help my mother in law too. . . . I speak to American neighbors most of the time, but they don't came visit and I don't go—just outside.

Women, who are considered and consider themselves as safeguarding culture in their own practice and in their children's upbringing, also tend to be more worried about negative American social influences. As Lana explains:

I come here. I have to be more responsible for myself. I have to talk nicely, I have to sit nicely, more than in my country. Because—this is America. . . . [*Do you have to be more responsible for yourself in the U.S. because Americans are different?*] Yes. [*So you want to show that you're Muslim.*] I'm Muslim. I have to be more worried about myself.

This, as well, leads to a focus on monitoring and guiding children: "It's the way you raised, like how I'm gonna raise my kids, they gonna grow. If I raise them good, and trust them, take care of them, they gonna be, *inshallah*, good guys. But if I raise them like hit them, get sick of them, then they show it, they gonna raise the way they grow from the house."

It is important to point out, however, that even for people like Lana, who are quite isolated from much of American society, isolation is not the same as rejection. Indeed, Lana is quite adamant not that she is American but that America guarantees her the right to mingle when she wishes. American, she says,

don't make no difference, so they give us citizenship, they treat us same thing. We can go buy anything we want, we can go anywhere we want, same thing like American people. [*So you said Americans treat Palestinians just like any other people?*] Even we go, we wear scarf, everybody knows we are Muslims, we go shopping, we go malls, we go anywhere we want to. Nobody bother us, nobody say you have to go this lane, or you can't buy this. No. I never heard about that.

In general, then, this group has created a private practice of ethnicity and religion (Gans, 1982 [1962]; Alba, 1990; Waters, 1990). In this way, the group's practice is similar to mainstream conceptions of ethnicity as choice. Because it is not attached to social institutions, it is very vulnerable to change. Its maintenance depends on close ties between kin—ties that can change when families become more prosperous and move away, when new immigrants from the home country stop arriving, or when the children develop new friendships or marry outside the group. To the extent that chances of economic progress are not blocked, the children and grandchildren of these immigrants can also easily end up identifying simply as Americans of Arab descent, without an ethnic or religious component to their identification as American.

People in this group do have the potential to adopt a pan-ethnic Arab or Muslim identity. Current events, such as the conflict in the Middle

East, can lead to more contact between these people and pan-ethnic institutions via participation in protests or other community activities. Omar, for instance, has participated in one demonstration: a trip to Washington, D.C., to protest the massacres in Qana. That demonstration was organized by the local Lebanese Club. But this participation is sporadic and usually does not lead to sustained activity. Omar did not consider the protest a political action: "It's not about the war and political factions, which is something we don't have anything [to do] with. This is about innocent children." The demonstration was a well-planned one; Omar recalls "meeting with five or six members of Congress at the hotel, and they tried to pressure Israel about this." Yet this event, though clearly one that Omar is proud of, did not encourage him to join the Lebanese Club or other ethnic organizations in town.

The need for religious institutions—for instance, the incorporation of a mosque, the formation of an Arabic or Islamic school, the provision of social services—can also lead to more interaction with both American and pan-ethnic groups. For Mahmoud, a restaurant owner with six children, "the only thing I do is probably the kids' school, that's the only thing I work with after work hours, working with the school and the community to keep the school going." Yet his efforts on behalf of the local Islamic school have also put him in touch with a group of local citizens protesting the war against Iraq, and, in fact, he contributed money and signed on to an ad condemning the bombing. Mahmoud is suspicious of politicians:

> I'm not a Republican, I'm not a Democrat. And that's why I don't vote for the president, because it don't matter whether he's a Democrat or a Republican. Both the same to me. [*What makes them the same?*] Well, let me tell you something, I'm sure you know this, but they stand out there to be elected, they can tell you whatever you want to hear, and when they get into the office, someone put a gun to their neck and say, don't do anything, just follow the rules.

And yet his continuing involvement with the school has the potential to draw him back into expressing his political beliefs on an issue-by-issue basis, because the institution itself draws new people, some of whom may have a different understanding of politics and convince him to join in.

Maintaining Community through Organization

Najwa is a friendly woman of 45 with seven children from 8 to 25 years old. She meets us in a local bookstore at the end of a day in which, we discover, she has taught school, ferried her children around to activities, prepared dinner, and picked up a friend to meet us. Wearing the hijab, a long-sleeved blouse and blazer, and a long skirt, she is full of energy and chatter, despite the summer heat and her long day.

Najwa married in Syria right after high school and came to the United States as a young wife. Her older children went to public schools, in which she was an active volunteer and member of the school's parent-teacher organization (PTO); later, as more South Asian and Arab Muslims moved into her area, she helped to organize a private Islamic school. While doing this, she also earned a B.A. in education, which gave her the certification necessary to teach elementary school. Now she teaches part-time in the Islamic academy and runs a local social service organization for disadvantaged children, while raising her two youngest children and keeping track of the older ones.

For Najwa and her family, the mosque is not only, as it is for Omar, a place to celebrate holidays. Instead, it is a community center. She meets weekly with other women in a study group. Local politicians go there during election campaigns to give speeches. It is a place where her Syrian family mixes with an international group of people, including Arab Muslims, Africans, Asians, Europeans, and American converts: "You know, when we go to the Detroit mosque my children feel awkward. They say how come everybody is Syrian? In our mosque [we have people] from all over the world. . . . I tell them that's the past and our mosque is the future—humanity coming all together."

Nor is the mosque the only place where Najwa meets others. She participates in a half-dozen different groups and activities, including a group of Arab Christian and Muslim women working on voter registration and social services assistance for Arab women in the metropolitan area. She gives talks introducing Islam at the local university and at area churches, and she is an avid member of the audience at public events on international issues. In her old neighborhood, she worked with her non-Arab neighbors in groups such as Neighborhood Watch, but since they moved, she says regretfully, she's been too busy to get started again.

Most immigrants in this category do not have the energy or the executive abilities of Najwa; she would be a standout in any community. But while Najwa's talent is an individual characteristic, her many activities illustrate the role of religious and ethnic organizations, like the ones Haddad describes in her chapter, in building a Muslim American community. Unlike Omar, Najwa's practice of religion and ethnicity within organizations integrates them with her Americanness rather than remaining separate from it. Unlike Lana, she transforms her nurturing of family into nurturance of a larger community. The critical difference is her translation of "community" from the strong ties of friends and family to "the strength of weak ties"—connections to people who are not one's family or close friends (Granovetter, 1973).

Rather than interacting primarily with a smaller version of her community in the Middle East, as Omar and Lana do, Najwa functions in a much more diverse set of networks that includes Muslims from other Arab countries and non-Arab countries; Arab Christians; and non-Arabs who are interested in international affairs, enrolled in college courses, or residents of her old neighborhood. This allows for coalition building, in ways that strengthen the ethnic or religious community, and that, over time, may increase others' knowledge and acceptance of it.

Najwa's experiences provide two examples. When the Islamic school was first proposed, some people in the township opposed it. But at the time, the mosque community had already formed ties to local politicians: "Being close to the people in power in our township helped us—helped our cause in court, because [of] our numbers. They care about the vote now because we are clustered. We support by voting for them. . . . We have people . . . who [are] willing to give donation and do what it takes to be involved." Another example of deliberate coalition building comes in Najwa's discussion of Mercy International, a Muslim charity:

I think Mercy now they are try to be helpful to communities, to society like Red Cross. When they had Oklahoma bomb like you know they were there. The Mercy International were there and they tried to give blankets and give food and give shelter to the people who got affected. So they were helping out. And when they had the flood in the Midwest a few years back they were giving support and help. So I think they are trying prove their humanitarian cause and showing that they could be effective. [*So you think there is perhaps a perception that they are not humanitarian that kind of prevents them from becoming more effective?*] I think people when they see things made by other than the mainstream people here they think that maybe you have your own agenda. So they don't trust you that much in the beginning. So you have to prove yourself first. I think most of them are proving themselves.

Najwa recognizes here that others treat her community with distrust or distaste. But instead of drawing back into the community, as Omar or Lana might, she describes a process of mobilizing allies and persuading opponents that their fears are misplaced. The implicit assumption here is that these issues and groups are part of the American political system; unlike Omar, Najwa does not distinguish here between "American" interests and her own. Put another way, Najwa takes it for granted that tasks like the establishment of an Islamic academy and improving the reputation of Mercy International are not foreign issues but American ones.

This is a classic form of participation in a pluralist system, and it requires resources—votes, campaign donations—and some knowledge of which non-Arabs or non-Muslims might be interested in alliances. Both resources and knowledge are more available to relatively prosperous immigrants with education and social status. As Najwa says, "The generation before us were not that educated in the system and they didn't know much. They were mostly workers and people who were just trying to make it in life, so they weren't thinking of essential issues in their life besides their breadwinning and their day-to day."

But the attraction to groups organized around common ethnic or religious interests is not simply that of the luxury of resources and the longer view. Middle Eastern immigrants of higher socioeconomic status are attracted to groups like the Council on American-Islamic Relations (CAIR), the American-Arab Anti-Discrimination Committee (ADC), the Arab American Institute (AAI), the Association of Arab-American University Graduates (AAUG), and the American Muslim Council (AMC) because discrimination is perceived in class-specific ways. Those who perceive discrimination are often not the poor, who suffer structural injustices that they cannot trace to their ethnicity or religion, but the successful, who see that despite their success they are not treated as well as others with the same credentials or resources (Lin, Hackshaw, and Jamal, 2001). Discrimination is an issue for them precisely because they expect to be treated as other Americans.[4]

Women of higher socioeconomic status, whose families have the financial ability to allow them to volunteer and who themselves have extensive education, in both secular subjects and on Islam, play a particular role in maintaining those organizations Women like Najwa actively helped to create, and now sustain, all of the organizations mentioned above (Hatem, 2001). Many of these women work part-time—partly to keep themselves available for family responsibilities, partly in deference to a traditionally gendered division of labor. Their extra energy, and their talents, go into pan-ethnic groups. But even women with full-time careers feel that they have a responsibility to build and nurture the culture and the community. This nurturance is expressed in terms of morality. Najwa says:

> I think we should voice our concern and our opinion because I listened to [a lecture that] said one congressman was making his vote based on one person [one person's opinion]. . . . So hearing that, you know, your voice has weight—you shouldn't belittle what you can do. Everybody you have effort [you can make an effort] and you should at least clear your conscience. You [should do] your duty concerning what you believe in.

There is an interesting contrast here with the moral concerns of Lana, who understood her obligations to the Muslim community primarily in terms of how she behaved and how others might perceive her. The notion of a moral duty to express one's opinions and to influence the public sphere for good lifts the notion of morality from one of private behavior to one of communal responsibility.

This reading of morality among the women in this group, in particular, is evident even when they do not participate in organized religious activity and do not consider themselves observant. Leila is an elegantly chic real estate broker from an upscale suburban neighborhood. She is Muslim but is not active in a mosque community: "I'm Muslim, but I was raised going to a French Catholic school, so I believe that all humans are the same. There is one God, the same for all of us, and he is worshipped by all people. I believe that religion tells us we should treat all people fairly and sincerely." She serves on the board of a local social service organization that specializes in services to new Arab immigrants, and she is the treasurer of a cultural association, "mostly people established here, who want their children to learn about their background and their culture." She also participates in the local chapter of the ADC, which, though it is a secular organization, she supports in part because of her religious beliefs: "I feel it's degrading to be racially discriminated against, because human beings are the same all over. . . . In our Muslim religion, they say humans are equal, there's no difference between Arabic, non Arabic, white, black, Oriental; the only difference is being honest and have good morals."

This is not to say that men are not active in creating a pan-ethnic identity or in maintaining its organizations. But more than women, men who are active in pan-ethnic groups often have professional and personal reasons for their participation. They may work with Arab clients or find that Arab professional or business organizations provide leadership opportunities. They may also take salaried positions, especially in advocacy organizations that allow them to use their professional training and provide a springboard for them to "speak for" the community. Others, more often volunteers, may also be people who were active in Middle East politics and see pan-ethnic groups as a way to continue their political activities in exile. By contrast, men who do not derive any professional benefit from their participation in such groups tend to participate less, or less actively. They may lend their financial support, but it is their wives who attend meetings and organize events.

What kind of community, of either ethnicity or faith, do these immigrants create? While the process that creates them is similar, the substance and characteristics of these communities themselves are quite different. For some, like Najwa, residence in the United States allows the opportunity to build a truly universal Muslim community. At the core of Islamic teaching, no ethnic criterion differentiates Muslims from one another. All Muslims who uphold the *shehada* and follow the five pillars of Islam are part of the Islamic Umma. As the Prophet Muhammad says (peace be upon him): "There is no differentiation between an Arab and a non-Arab except in piety." The universality of Islam, especially in the wake of discrimination after 9/11, can even be understood as a way of dividing the community.

There are, of course, other interpretations of the Qur'an. Some argue that the *ayah*, "O mankind, we created you from a male and a female and made you into nations and tribes so that you may know one another," suggests that Allah acknowledges that there are ethnic differences among us. We should recognize our differences (first) and then know one another (second). In general, however, many Muslim immigrants make the point that the faithful practice of Islam precludes identification as "Arab" or "South Asian," white or black. For them, even when they support the goals of Arab pan-ethnic groups, that identity cannot be paramount.

The implications of this for communal identity are fascinating. Just as today there is little differentiation between third-generation German and eastern European Jews, one could imagine, over time, the creation of a Muslim community without specific ethnic referents. In such a community, South Asians, Arabs, African Americans, and others might not only worship together but also share common political and social agendas. Even if ethnicity were not cast away entirely—and the different histories of Jews and Muslims in their home countries suggest that the parallel is not perfect—one could yet anticipate strong and stable coalitions between Muslims of different ethnicities.

Najwa's statement—"In our mosque [we have people] from all over the world. . . . I tell them [my children] that's the past and our mosque is the future—humanity coming all together"—suggests the possibility of such an outcome. Within many of these multiethnic mosques, immigrants have told us of campaigns on behalf of Bosnians as well as Palestinians, of concern for Pakistan as well as Iraq. Certainly the major American Muslim organizations—CAIR and AMC—have made a point of cultivating multiethnic leadership (Leonard, 2003). Yet there are also reasons to expect that this transformation may be difficult. Most of the major mosques in the Detroit area are dominated by one nationality group—whether Lebanese, Syrian, Palestinian, or Yemeni. Moreover, mosques, which are independent and which call their own clergy, differ not only by sect but also by practice. Doctrinal stands, which include rules about women, social interaction, and observance, often differentiate one mosque community from another. Clergy and funding add another layer of complexity: Who is qualified to serve as a leader? What differences might there be in leadership in the U.S. context? Should one seek or accept money from the Middle East?

Another factor in the creation of identities is the prominence and activity of a different definition of community: pan-ethnic, nonreligious Arab organizations, such as the ADC. Individuals who identify as "Arab" and who support these organizations may be religiously observant themselves. But the discussion within these organizations, even when it concerns antireligious bias, takes place without reference to religious values. It would be wrong to think of such organizations as hostile to religious involvement, or vice versa. It is not an overstatement, however, to say that in these groups and as part of this identity, religion is a private right rather than a communal characteristic. Thus discrimination against Muslims or anti-Muslim stereotypes are considered wrong, not because Islam needs to be defended but because all religions should be. Understanding religion as "private" allows for a membership that is both Christian and Muslim and that varies in its degrees of observance.

Many immigrants support both Muslim and Arab advocacy groups with no sense of conflict. One woman active in her local mosque told us, in reference to the ADC, "I think they are doing a good job, but they are not a religious organization—it's an Arab group. So their agenda is mixed, but that's not an issue for us." For others, though, the conflict is less easily bridged. Some in pan-ethnic groups fear identification with Muslim extremism or are afraid that religious divisions between Muslims and Christians might come to characterize agendas and leadership. Others in Muslim groups, led by influential clerics such as Taha Jaber al-Alwani, scorn association with groups that downplay religion.

But perhaps the most important obstacle to the development of vibrant pan-ethnic Arab or Muslim coalitions comes not from the membership of such groups but from the extent to which such groups can expand beyond their relatively elite, well-educated base. As discussed here, many immigrants who have no intention of relinquishing their culture and religion also will not entrust that culture and religion to organizations. Within a pluralist society, however, it is organized interests that wield social and political influence. Put another way, for faith to shape the integration of Arab immigrants in the United States in ways that will have a long-term impact on American society, that faith will have to be carried by institutions.

Conclusion

The two categories described here—a privatized form of community shared with friends and family and a more public form shaped through and by organizations—are not the only ways that Muslim Arab immigrants create community in the United States. Immigrants who emigrate with their village or spiritual leader will often create tight-knit associational lives after they settle in the United States. Because these associations tend to be closed (or at least invisible), not only to non-Arabs but to other Arabs as well, membership and participation can exacerbate isolation instead of combating it. Other immigrants, especially after intermarriage, establish social networks with non-Arabs and non-Muslims. While they may consider themselves Arab and Muslim and may attend the occasional festival or religious service, they are not and would not consider themselves part of an Arab or Muslim community.

There are also other providers for the many social goods—language, news and gossip from home, guidance about religious matters or U.S. oddities, help with business ventures, even camaraderie and social support—that ethnic or religious organizations have always provided. The internet, for example, can allow people to maintain virtual communities with friends and relations in their country of origin; satellite TV can provide both news and entertainment, in Arabic, originating throughout the Middle East and also in the United States. The effects of these communication options are not yet clear. It is possible that organizations might find it hard to compete with their virtual counterparts. But it is also possible that those who make the most extensive use of new communication technology use it to add to, not replace, other sources of information and friendship.

What these two types of community illustrate is that creating an immigrant community does not inhibit incorporation into the wider American society. It does, however, have important implications for the type of American society that results. The knowledge of marginalization and difference can lead immigrants to create spaces for religious practice and cultural expression that do not overlap with their new American commitments. Or it can lead immigrants to try to modify American society and culture so that it acknowledges what they bring as legitimate and valuable. In this chapter I explore some of the immigrant-centered characteristics—in particular, the roles of class and gender—that influence the types of adaptation immigrants choose. But it is also important to see that such choices are influenced by context—in this case, the types of changes over time in American society and in the world.

With America's response to the terrorist attacks of September 11, 2001, and the escalation of violence in the Middle East, pan-ethnic Arab and Muslim groups have become much more visible, and acts of discrimination against Muslims in the United States have received more publicity. Either could help these groups recruit—and then hold on to—a more diverse grass-roots base. Marches in solidarity with Palestinians, for instance, could bring out immigrants who could then be encouraged to participate in more sustained political action; fundraising for legal cases fighting discrimination might make people aware that collective action is possible.[5] Such events could also create new leadership and new organizations, some of which might be targeted specifically at second- and third-generation Muslim Americans and Arab Americans.

It is also important to realize that causes without concomitant forms of social organization are only partially effective in creating political power and social presence. The important role of women in creating and sustaining public forms of religious and ethnic community leaves open the question of how such groups will evolve as women, especially of the second and third generations, become as career-oriented as men. The fact that Islam is a noninstitutional religion means that shared faith, in and of itself, will not necessarily promote contact between Muslims, cooperative agendas, or organization. Muslims will need to create forms of religious worship and community that promote interaction in order to undergird effective social mobilization. The continued question of whether Arab and Muslim organizations will strengthen each other as coalition partners or, rather, compete for membership and agenda-setting power is particularly important if immigration from Muslim and Arab countries slows down in the wake of September 11 and any changes in American immigration policy.

NOTES

I thank Amaney Jamal, who collaborated in the research that led to this chapter, as well as in the larger project from which this is drawn.

1.   The deep roots of the African American community in Detroit also contribute to religious segregation; Muslim African Americans have long-established mosques, and they need not depend on immigrant institutions for worship.

2.   To protect our interviewees' privacy, all names are pseudonyms and some identifying details have been changed. Jamal and Lin conducted all of the interviews, using either Arabic or English, as the respondent preferred. Interviews were conducted privately, in person, at locations the respondents chose. Interviews lasted between one and two hours and followed a structured, open-ended questionnaire.

3.   There is one prominent exception to these observations. Organizing around Muslim or Arab issues could arise in response to particular acts of discrimination or harassment. For instance, one could imagine a class action suit against an employer for job discrimination against Arabs or Muslims, or violence spawned by tensions between Arab business owners and local, non-Arab patrons of their stores. We did not see evidence of such organizing in these interviews,

but obviously this kind of organizing would be event-specific and eusually does not translate into continued political involvement.

4.   These groups can also attract those who were politically active, or at least politically formed, in the Middle East. Some immigrants, for instance, carried ideas of Arab nationalism with them from the Middle East, ideas that were nurtured among the educated there in their formative yeours. Others, usually more recent immigrants, feel that their Islamic practices and beliefs were undeveloped, even restricted, in the Middle East by governments fearful of religious institutions and movements that they could not control. While these people are a minority of the group members we interviewed, they illustrate the general importance of understanding the development of political activity and affiliation over the life-course, especially for immigrants (Lin and Jamal, 1998).

5.   In our interviews, for example, many of the younger immigrants spoke of becoming aware of the work of Arab American groups through their efforts against the "secret evidence" provisions of the 1996 anti-terrorism legislation.

Part IV

||||||||||||||||||||||||||||||||||||||||||||||||||||

Religious Diversification among African American and Haitian Migrants

The juxtaposition of the cases of African American migration from the rural South to the urban North of the United States, roughly between 1910 and 1960, and Haitian immigration to Florida and New York, largely since 1980, is premised on the comparability of similarities and differences and on a history of interconnection and identification between the two populations stretching back into the early 19th century. Underlying these comparisons and connections is the two groups' shared African origin and history of enslavement.

That both African Americans and Haitians can trace their New World origins to Africa draws attention to their similar cultural heritages and formative experiences with slavery and racism, although a comparison points to significant differences as well. For the purposes of this introduction, considerations of commonality and difference are focused by their relevance to intersections between migration and religion.

As a condition of their histories of enslavement and postabolition racism, both African Americans and Haitians have suffered disempowerment and poverty relative to members of other races or nations. As a result, both groups' migrations have sought liberation from repressive regimes shaped by 18th-century and 19th-century slavery and plantation economies. Some middle-aged African Americans moving North in the early 20th century had themselves grown up in slavery and all had suffered inequality and injustice resulting from discrimination encoded in post-Reconstruction Jim Crow laws, including a wave of race riots and lynchings at the start of the first Great Migration (Marks, 1989). Similarly, many Haitians came to the United States as exiles, refugees, and labor migrants fleeing the repressive "kleptocratic" state that emerged out of French colonialism and was exploited by the dictatorships of the François and Jean-Claude Duvalier and military regimes (DeWind and Kinley, 1988; Lundahl, 1979).

There has been a long history of denial of contemporary cultural sur-
vivals of significance among descendents of enslaved Africans, but since
the ethnographic affirmations of African-origin traditions, including using religious ritual to sustain instrumental relations with spiritual powers
documented by Jean Price-Mars (1928) in Haiti and Melville J. Herskovitz (1990 [1941]) in the southern United States, scholarly debates have focused more over the extent and significance of such heritages than their
existence (Baker, 1998). Since the 1804 Haitian revolution overthrowing
French colonialism, Haitian practitioners of Vodou have kept alive and
developed their devotion of ancestral spirits, or *lwa*, whom they conceive
as residing across the sea in Ginen (Fr.: Guinée; Eng.: Guinea) but who
are capable of either beneficent or malign intervention into daily life.

In response to colonial and postcolonial efforts to supplant Vodou with
Catholicism, Haitians appropriated the Christian religion's spiritual powers, identifying the saints with the *lwa*. But a family's ritual securing of
the favor of their *lwa* places a heavy material burden on family members,
both at home and abroad. In the "land of progress," where Haitians face
a "contest for souls," as described in Karen Richman and Elizabeth McAlister's article (chapter 12), the migrants can choose to send home remittances and help their families continue to appease demands of the *lwa* or
they can turn to evangelical Protestantism and appropriate the spiritual
power of Jesus for both personal protection against the *lwa* and individual
enrichment. Regardless of where they seek spiritual power, in Vodou, Catholicism, or Protestantism, many Haitians seek spiritual powers to gain
greater control over a material world that is otherwise largely beyond
their individual or collective control.

In contrast, the different circumstances of slavery for African Americans—a relatively small importation of Africans enslaved among an equal
or larger European population and the rapid growth of an American-born
slave population—resulted in a greater suppression of African-derived
religions and greater adoption of Christianity. James Grossman and Albert J. Raboteau (chapter 11) suggest that African Americans employed a
distinctive interpretation of evangelical Protestantism instrumentally as a
means of their own realization of the biblical story of Exodus and entry
into the "Promised Land." To overcome barriers of racism in the North,
African Americans sought both spiritual strength and political leadership
through religion in their quest for equal rights in American society.

Whether the migrants have employed religion to sustain livelihoods
back home, as exemplified by Haitians sending remittances to support

familial rituals for the *lwa*, or to cut ties with the past and initiate new lives in destinations of migration, as do Haitians who embrace evangelical Protestantism and African Americans who shifted their affiliations among Christian churches or joined secular movements in the North, both groups, disadvantaged by a disempowerment derived from a history of slavery and racism, similarly used their religious devotions and practices to sustain their strength and power to attain material and social improvements in their lives.

The comparison of African American migration with Haitian immigration has a long historical prologue of movements that established contacts and identifications between peoples of African descent within the first two successful revolutionary states in the Americas. The 13-year-long struggle for freedom and citizenship for Haiti's African-descended majority was waged at the same time that plantation slavery was expanding in the new American nation to the north. The thoroughly "free" Haiti that emerged seemed to offer a direct threat to the stability of plantation slavery in the United States (Plummer, 1992: 18). In a response protective of its own slave economy, the emergent United States welcomed the fleeing French colonists and even provided funds to resettle them (Laguerre, 1998: 33). Many of these refugees arrived with their slaves. The U.S. government refused to recognize the revolutionary Haitian government for more than six decades, that is, until the emancipation of Black slaves within its own national borders.

The Haitian immigration is thus not entirely a post-1965 phenomenon. When the revolution started in St. Domingue, trading ships from the United States brought fleeing refugees to coastal commercial destinations (Laguerre, 1998: 23), notably Baltimore, New York, Philadelphia, and Charleston. In July of 1793 alone, for example, 53 vessels arrived in Baltimore carrying 1,000 colonists and 500 "slaves and free people of color" (33). Two black Haitian Americans, whose parents had settled in Charleston, even served in the state's House of Representatives between 1868 and 1875 (63). Louisiana was host to the largest community of the new Haitian diaspora in the United States. An early measure of its clout was the formation of a battalion of 500 freemen of color directed by a former French colonist that fought in the war of 1812 (65). At the end of the century, three decades after emancipation, Louisiana Haitians again made their mark on American society by forcing the nation-state to defend its denial of equal citizenship to Blacks. Homére Plessy, a member of the Haitian voluntary association, la Comité des Citoyens, dared to sit in a whites-only train cabin. The case of *Plessy vs. Ferguson* proceeded all the way to the Supreme Court, which issued its infamous "separate but equal" decision authorizing racial discrimination in 1896.

The Haitians' incorporation into American society, however irregular, partial, and unequal, coexisted with vital transnational allegiances. Refugees of the Haitian revolution maintained ties to the homeland and to other émigré locations through trade, visits, and exchanges of letters, money, gifts, news, and newspapers, three of which were published in Philadelphia alone. Others established subsidiaries of Haitian trading firms in East Coast cities, which, in turn, were used as mail and shipping services by transnationally dispersed families (Laguerre, 1998: 53). The Charleston congressional delegation introduced legislation "to establish an American line of steamships for direct trade with Haiti and for carrying the mails there" (Smith 1940; cited in Laguerre, 1998: 64).

Religion, and especially the Catholic Church, was particularly important for the Haitian immigrants. The church represented a locus of common interest and language and provided a place to gather and to assert immigrant identities. Thus Catholic affiliation was an important mode of ethnic incorporation. Yet the church also was the site for Haitian immigrants' challenges to the racial and gendered hegemonies of the church and the state (Laguerre, 1998: 38–39). Afro-Haitian women, barred from joining mainstream orders, founded a Black women's religious community, the Oblate Sisters of Providence, in Baltimore in 1828. Haitians' involvement as Catholics also advanced their transnational interests. For Haitians in Charleston, the Catholic Church linked them both to one another in their host society and to their homeland, even though it promoted European interests over Haitian ones. Their bishop, John England, was appointed to represent the pope in negotiating the reassertion of European domination of the Catholic Church in Haiti, which had been in local hands since the revolution. The return, in 1860, of this powerful institution to the control of Rome eventually provoked a counterreaction, a Black nationalist movement, which had better use for American and Anglican Protestantism. Thus while Catholicism played a key part in the incorporation of Haitian immigrants in early-nineteenth-century American society, Protestant influence moved in the opposite direction toward the end of the century, laying missionary claim to the southern, Caribbean frontier that had increasingly come under the purview of an expanding United States. Thus, the transnational ties of Haitians and the encounters of African Americans with Haiti, both real and imaginary, reach back more than two centuries.

Against this historical backdrop of common origins and connections, Elizabeth McAlister and Karen Richman (chapter 12) take up the intersecting themes of religion, race, labor, transnationalism, and identity in the experience of Haitians migrating to the United States. Their work within the plural and transnational religious landscape of Haitians in the United States focuses on the two largest Haitian American populations: New York City and South Florida. McAlister draws from her research among Haitians in New York City and in the Haitian capital of Port-au-Prince, the point of debarkation for many migrants headed to New York. Richman draws from her fieldwork in two locations of a single transnational community: a village in Léogane, Haiti, and in "Mayami" (South Florida), where the majority of its migrating members now reside.

Together they present evidence that transnational Haitians living in the United States have created a religious landscape that is at once American and diasporic. For Haitians in Haiti and in North America, the religious landscape consists of overlapping fields: (1) the indigenous Afro-Haitian religion called Vodou, (2) Haitian Roman Catholicism, and (3) the evangelical Protestant denominations such as Baptist and Pentecostal. Each of these religious fields is separate from, yet overlaps with, the others. Their religious frameworks and religious practices span transnational social spaces, interacting in complex and various ways with processes of migration. Each sphere is the site of a different dynamic of imagining, and entering into, American culture.

James Grossman and Albert Raboteau (chapter 11) examine the "great migration" of African Americans beginning roughly a decade after the *Plessy vs. Ferguson* decision of 1896, when unprecedented numbers of rural black laborers and their families left the land for the cities and the South for the North and West. The double process of migration and urbanization recast both the physical and social landscape for black migrants, creating new economic, educational, and civic opportunities while presenting new cultural challenges due to the pluralism characteristic of modernization. Various religious and secular voices offered narratives, some old and familiar, and some new, to guide the newcomers in their accommodation to an urbanizing America. They, like later Haitian immigrants, would make strategic choices among various religious options to better their status, buttress their dignity, and formulate identity in an often-hostile white world. The traditional numerical predominance of Baptist and Methodist churches did not deter the proliferation of different religious options of great variety made available and attractive by the concentration of black population in urban neighborhoods and the development of mass media, which served to transplant "down-home" southern rural religious practice and music and to spread the gospels of new "black messiahs." Old images of Exodus from slavery jostled with new visions of raceless "heavens," or with definitions of new racial/religious identities, as migrants chose among alternate maps of meaning to make sense of their experience and to carve out a position for themselves in American society (sometimes by opposition to American society).

These maps of meaning took form, as exemplified by Exodus, in religious narratives. For both Haitians and African Americans, migration opened the need and the possibility for "renarrativizing" their histories in terms of new religious options. For both groups, the explanatory power of evangelical Protestantism, especially in its Holiness-Pentecostal form, offered a set of values—honesty, thrift, and hard work: in a word, this-worldy asceticism—backed by powerful appeals to the Christian Bible, as a handbook of spiritual and temporal success. Emotionally expressive rituals of worship enacted the biblical miracles of healing and exorcism and applied them to the maladies that afflicted poor blacks in 20th-century America. The striking example of Protestant Haitian ministers exorcising the site of a Vodou ceremony that reputedly inaugurated the Haitian Revolution indicates the imaginative power of Evangelicalism to recast a people's history. Moreover, the very Pentecostalism that exerts such an appeal on Haitians today owes its origins in significant part to early-20th-century African American ministers such as William J. Seymour (leader of the 1906 Azusa Street Revival in Los Angeles) and C. H. Mason (founder of the Church of God in Christ, the largest black Pentecostal denomination).

While African American migrants had no "Bois Cayman" to exorcise, surely similar rejections of earlier mythologies occurred in the case of figures such as Fr. Divine, who offered a raceless heaven on earth, and various leaders of Black Judaism and Islam, who offered new racial-religious myths of origin and history. They explicitly rejected the traditional narratives of Christianity as lies or demonic illusions, which robbed Black people of their true history and identity.

The "roots" movement by which Haitian immigrants attempt to revalue their origins in Ginen has its analogues among those African Americans who, since at least the 1960s, reclaimed their African past as a crucial part of their history and identity, by renaming themselves with African names, wearing African-style clothes, learning African languages, and converting to such neo-African religions as Santería and Vodou. As for Haitians, Africa became a mythic land of origin and meaning for African Americans through acts of group and personal renarrativization.

Finally, the Roman Catholic Church appealed to African American migrants in the 20th century, as it has to Haitian immigrants, not only as a source of social capital and educational opportunity but also as a connection to a cosmopolitan, age-old, worldwide community of Christians, with claims to universality, a church, which a prominent 19th-century African American Catholic, Dan A. Rudd, proclaimed "has erased the color line" because it transcended the defining limits of Protestant "race churches," such as the Black Baptist and Black Methodist denominations of his day (quoted in Raboteau, 1995: 128–29). As Haitian immigrants emphasize their Catholicism, at least in part, to distinguish themselves from African Americans, who are largely Protestant, African American Catholics and black converts to Catholicism have emphasized the universality of the Church of Rome, with its history of honoring black saints, its wide expanse in Africa, and its current policy of "enculturation" (adapting to local cultures), as the embodiment of transcultural Christianity, a spiritual haven beyond the harsh and demeaning limitations of a racially defined society (Raboteau, 1995: 135–37).

Black Migration, Religion, and Civic Life

James Grossman and Albert J. Raboteau

For black and white Americans, the evolution of American culture has been shaped to a considerable extent by the transformation of rural cultures into urban ones. At the same time, these urban cultures have been reconfigured by a continued infusion of migrants from the countryside and small towns. For African Americans, this transformation has been underscored by the simultaneous movement from the proscriptions of the Jim Crow South to the apparent (and in many cases real) opportunity offered by the urban-industrial North. That perception of opportunity, and the successes achieved by many migrants, embodies a variety of themes central to American history and culture: landownership, independence, hard work, and the relationship between migration and the frontiers of human experience. "I dreamed of going north," recalled Richard Wright a decade after he left Mississippi headed toward Memphis and subsequently Chicago: "The North symbolized to me all that I had not felt and seen; it had no relation whatever to what actually existed. Yet by imagining a place where everything was possible, I kept hope alive in me" (1945: 147).

For most migrants, what they had not "felt and seen" encompassed both concrete and abstract elements. The concrete included the everyday opportunities and excitements of urban life that prospective migrants envisioned: factories with jobs, the bright lights of leisure districts, department stores, baseball stadiums. And if the reality for most bore at least some relation to the vision, in many ways the miles and miles of streets and alleys, the actual discipline of the factory, and the general scale of urban life could lie beyond the imagination of men and women from small towns and farms, whose images derived from letters, newspapers, and conversation with railroad workers and other mediators between country and city. This experience probably varied more according to hometown and previous travel experience than by race. It was the abstract imagination that set black migrants off from their white counterparts. For black southerners thinking about northern cities, the jettisoning of the dream of agricultural independence—coming to grips with the limitations of emancipation and the failure of Reconstruction—meant imagining a citizenship based on factory work. It meant trading the ethos of independence for the promise of the labor market, imagining a world where one's wage represented a ticket that could be cashed at the box office or ballot box. To imagine was to envision a world without Jim Crow, a world without the legacy of slavery—a world in which, as Wright believed, "everything was possible."

They found something else, and if it bore "no relation whatever to what actually existed," it was sufficiently foreign that most newcomers needed guides. They needed someone to tell them which lines they couldn't cross (in Chicago, Langston Hughes learned the hard way when nobody told him that Wentworth Avenue was a "dead line" that black people didn't cross except on well-traveled routes to workplaces; 1940: 33). They needed someone to help find homes and jobs.

There was no shortage of such resources. Like most migrants, black southerners tended to relocate where they had family or where men and women from their communities had gone before. There were Urban League branches, clubs, and other institutions all with a stake in making sure that migrants learned quickly so as not to embarrass. Most of all, there was religion and religious institutions. Some churches offered social services; others had links to employers. All offered fellowship. But religion also offered black migrants a symbolic and social system for mapping their location in a world changed by migration, just as migration itself changed and challenged the traditional institutions and ethos of African American religious life. Within a decade of the beginning of mass migration, northern black churches would become transformed, shaped in part by the religious culture of their new members and in part by their response to the spiritual and material needs of those members (Best, 2005; Gregory, 2005).

At the dawn of the 20th century, black America was mainly southern and largely rural and agricultural. Nine out of ten African Americans lived in the South, and three out of four lived in communities of fewer than 2,500 inhabitants. In the South, only one-fifth of the black population lived in communities that fulfilled the census bureau's generous definition of "urban." Half of all gainfully employed blacks in the United States worked in agriculture, with the proportion rising to three-fifths among men (U.S. Bureau of the Census, 1918: 32, 92, 504). For much of black America, time moved with seasons, the sunrises, and the sunsets more than the mechanical ticks of a clock. Black southerners worked when the cycles of agricultural production demanded their attention, and they worked still more when they could find short-term employment during slack time on the farm or plantation. They took their leisure and their rest when they could.

Rural churches, like rural life, offered few creature comforts. Just to attend church meetings, congregants had to travel miles by foot, by mule, or by wagon over dusty, muddy, or snowy roads until the coming of paved roads and automobiles made travel easier. The churches were typically small, frame structures of unpainted or whitewashed wood. Inside, rows of plain wooden benches faced a raised platform on which a pulpit and several chairs were set. Open windows and handheld fans provided a breeze in summer; wood-burning stoves radiated warmth in winter. Before electricity, light came from kerosene or coal oil lamps. Rural congregations rarely had enough money to support a full-time pastor. As a result, many rural ministers served several congregations on alternate Sundays and earned their living by other work during the week. Jesse Thomas recalled his turn-of-the-century church in Natalbany, Louisiana, a town of 5,000 (4,500 black), where "the pastor usually had two or three other churches which he was serving, so that he would get to us only once a month" (1967: 21–22).

These churches required the active participation of the congregation in a variety of roles: deacons, ushers, choir members, song leaders, Sunday-school teachers, and "mothers" (wise elders) of the church. Members were called on to lead prayers and hymns, read Scripture, collect offerings, host visitors, report spiritual experiences, and observe the customs and behavior that as children they had learned to associate with church. As a result, the church instilled in its members an intimate sense of place, as well as community, a sense of being comfortably at home, and an experience of rootedness that would stir the memories of people who had moved away, whenever they thought of "down home."

Seventy years later, black America encompassed worlds that were largely urban. One-half of all African Americans in 1970 lived in the North, nearly all in urban areas. Of those remaining in the South, two-thirds lived in cities. The transformation had begun in 1916, and in 64 years, 6 million black Southerners had moved to cities in the North and West. Known as the Great Migration, this unprecedented social movement reshaped the American cultural and political landscape. Since the 1970s, a much smaller—though still noticeable—shift has occurred away from central cities in the North, as African Americans began to move back to the South or to working-class and middle-class suburbs.

The first wave of the Great Migration occurred during World War I and the 1920s. Until 1916, black Southerners had generally moved within the South, searching for opportunity in the form of better land or more favorable terms of land tenure. They knew that the North promised relief from Jim Crow and other forms of racial oppression in the South, but it was difficult for African Americans to find employment outside the South. Northern industrialists were reluctant to hire blacks when they could draw on a seemingly unending supply of European immigrants. Occasional work, breaking strikes, was sometimes perilous and usually temporary. Soon after the start of World War I, however, northern employers turned their attention southward as immigration ceased and orders began pouring in to manufacturers eager to make profits from war production.

Although sparked by the opening of industrial jobs, the first Great Migration (1916–20s) drew on a broader impulse that led black southerners to leave their homes and start new lives in northern cities. For many, the decision to move involved a transformation of vision, a notion that industrial work in the North, rather than the promise of landownership in the South, represented the path to full participation in American society. Migrants used the term "bettering my condition" to at once describe economic disparities between regions and such opportunities as better schools, the right to vote, greater access to the legal system, and freedom from the fear of rape and other forms of violence.

To prospective migrants, the North seemed to offer a life graced with dignity and hope. Northern cities offered access to institutions—political, economic, cultural, social—that were off limits or unavailable in the South. And despite the considerable disappointments entailed by race riots, residential segregation, limits on advancement in the workplace, and new (although informal) forms of racial discrimination, migrants did generally enjoy considerable improvements in various aspects of life. Their homes were sturdier and better equipped; their children went to school for a full year and even had high schools available; adults could (and did) go to night school; political recognition implied a place at the table of city government; wages were adequate in good times to provide consumer goods unaffordable to most black Southerners; and indignity coupled with the threat of violence was present, but not ubiquitous.

Migration tailed off during the Great Depression of the 1930s as jobs disappeared and blacks were often the first to be laid off; in the rural South those able to stay on the land could at least grow some food. Industrial employment in the North boomed again during World War II as the military drained thousands of young men from the workforce. Family, church, and community networks linking northern cities to southern communities were already in place. The sources of information central to the first Great Migration—black newspapers (especially the *Chicago Defender*), letters, and visits—now operated even more powerfully. Moreover, with the introduction of the mechanical cotton picker after the war, migration during the following decades was less a choice than a necessity. What was once a decision to stay or leave had become a choice of alternative destinations for thousands of rural families who were no longer able to earn even a meager living in a rural economy in which they were largely superfluous. By the late 1940s, and especially in the 1950s, the Great Migration had become as much a movement of refugees as a venture toward new opportunities beyond the world of Jim Crow.

This "Second Great Migration" encompassed more people (at least 4 million between 1940 and 1970) than the first wave, and the black ghettoes that had begun to emerge during the earlier period now consolidated and grew. The renewed movement also produced virtually new, or dramatically expanded, black communities on the West Coast, as nearly 350,000 African Americans relocated to California between 1942 and 1945. Once again, migration provided African Americans with new opportunities, and once again the promise of those opportunities was partially fulfilled. Jobs in packinghouses, steel mills, automobile plants, shipyards, garment factories, and a variety of other industries provided well-paying and often unionized employment. Black political power began to emerge in many northern cities. Generally it remained more apparent than real, but nevertheless it was apparent. Chicago's South Side even boasted its own ritualized election for "mayor of Bronzeville." Pulsating with energy and self-confidence, vibrant black communities like New York's Harlem and Chicago's South Side became symbols of African American urban culture.

But the second Great Migration occurred under different circumstances in the North, as well as in the South. The schools by now were entirely segregated; slums were more evident, and there was less illusion about northern race relations being more benign. Although wartime conditions created plenty of jobs at first, the boom would become uneven by the 1950s. Contraction of labor markets in the late 1920s and 1930s had slowed migration in the earlier stage; but this time people displaced from rural employment kept coming, regardless of the vicissitudes of the urban economy. As migration continued into the 1950s and 1960s, a deindustrializing "Rust Belt" and the now infamous high-rise housing projects increasingly shaped the experiences of many newcomers and earlier migrants.

Yet the resources that had helped earlier newcomers to cities remained. By 1940, African American communities were well established in nearly all northern cities, and family and community networks linking North and South were in place. Migrants usually followed trails established by family members who had gone before (in some cases, this was an "irrational" economic choice but a logical approach to the anxieties of relocation). Church congregations sometimes relocated together, or in stages. Binding relationships between the migrants and the communities they left behind remain vital today.

The ongoing links between migrants and their home churches included the practice of requesting letters of recommendation (officially known as letters of dismissal) to northern ministers, indicating that the new arrival was a church member in good standing. A migrant to Pittsburgh wrote home to "dear Pastor and wife" in May 1917: "I hope you & sis Hayes are well & no you think I have forgotten you all but I never will how is ever body & how is the church getting along well I am in this great city & you no it cool here right now the trees are just peeping out." After describing the living conditions and work situation in the city, the letter concluded, "I hope you & your dear sweet wife will pray for me & all of my sisters & Bros & give Mrs. C. my love & sis Jennie & all the rest & except a barrelful for you and Hayes Pleas send me a letter of recommendation tell Dr., to sign & Mr. Oliver. I remain your friend" (Scott, 1919: 459–60). Requesting a letter of dismissal might seem like a poignant break with a treasured community connection. But some migrants maintained their connection by continuing to send financial contributions to their home churches. One letter, sent from Chicago, to a minister in Union Springs, Alabama, in July 1917, reveals the multiple ties binding new migrants to old congregations:

My dear Pastor: I find it my Duty to write you my whereabouts also family, I am glad to say Family and myself are enjoying fine health. Wish the same of you and your dear wife. Well I can say the people in my section are very much torn up about East St. Louis. Representative col men of Chicago was in conference with Governor he promise them that he would begin investigation at once tell Sister Hayes my wife Says She will write her in a few days. Dear Pastor I shall send my church some money in a few days. I am trying to influence our members here to do the same. I recd. Notice printed in a R.R. car (Get straight with God) O I had nothing so striking to me as the above mottoe. Let me know how is our church I am to anxious to no. My wife always talking about her seat in the church want to know who accupying it. Yours in Christ. (Scott, 1919: 463)

The Great Migration disrupted rural and urban congregations, transplanted southern religious customs north and west, strained the resources of urban churches, and generated new opportunities for religious creativity in black urban neighborhoods. At the same time, faced with an unfamiliar urban environment, rural migrants looked to churches to reaffirm the traditional values and community ties that had given them a sense of social location back home. In some instances, they joined already-established churches that antedated their arrival; in others, they founded new ones of their own. The sheer number of migrants enlarged the membership of existing churches and tested their capacity to absorb the newcomers. In the early years of the Great Migration, some churches were so overcrowded that they needed double services on Sundays to accommodate all comers.

As the migrant flood continued, pastors and church boards started extensive and expensive construction projects to increase the seating capacity of their buildings. Some churches took on the activities of welfare agencies, organizing for community service. Abyssinian Baptist of New York and Olivet Baptist of Chicago organized particularly extensive programs, which almost resembled settlement houses. But the sheer range of these programs suggests the variety of services that migrants might find at one church or another, including employment bureaus, day-care centers, kindergartens, adult education classes, drama groups, orchestras, social clubs, athletic events, outreach clubs, and various youth programs. In the 1920s, Olivet, led by Lacey Kirk Williams, had 42 departments and auxiliaries, 512 officers, 23 salaried workers, a congregation of 8,000–10,000 members (perhaps even 15,000 by 1929), a Sunday school enrollment of 3,100, two buildings, and five assistant pastors. St. Mark's Methodist Episcopal Church in Chicago, half the size of Olivet, employed five social workers during the 1920s, who visited parishioners in their homes (Redmond, 1935).

Church members in some cities met migrants as they arrived at train stations to offer them assistance and advice. Lessons in northern racial etiquette and in practical habits of thrift, punctuality, and respectability of appearance sometimes followed formal or informal instruction for rural southerners unfamiliar with life up north.

While some newcomers took pride in the size and prestige of the large urban churches, others missed the intimacy and the status they had enjoyed in the small churches "down home." Differences in levels of education and income and in styles of worship distinguished some migrants from some longtime residents, as well as from each other. The emotionalism and spontaneity of many rural southern services clashed with the decorum of some urban northern churches. These differences, as well as the usual divisiveness of church politics, multiplied the number of churches in urban black neighborhoods and led to complaints among ministers about "church tramps" (Sutherland, 1930: 84). Many of the newly formed congregations gathered initially in rented storefronts or private homes for worship. In time, many of these "missions" managed to grow and eventually purchased or constructed a church building. Others remained as storefront or home churches.

In addition to increasing the size and number of urban black churches, migration and urbanization enhanced the variety of black religious life by variegating the environment of religious choices. Accustomed to deciding among Baptist, Methodist, and perhaps Holiness-Pentecostal churches back home, migrants to the cities encountered in close proximity black Jews, black Muslims, black Catholics, and disciples of black charismatic religious figures like Daddy Grace and Father Divine, who believed that their leaders exercised divine power to heal their problems in this world as well as the next.

Migration brought many black Protestants into contact with Roman Catholicism for the first time. Initially, the contact was none too friendly, as ethnic fears and economic rivalry roused racial tension between the black migrants and Catholics of Irish, German, Italian, and Polish immigrant backgrounds. Blacks replaced immigrant Catholics in urban neighborhoods or settled into blocks adjacent to them. In addition, neither white Catholics nor Protestant black migrants from certain parts of the rural South had much experience with black Catholics, who came to northern and western cities from Louisiana and the Gulf Coast.

Occasionally, Catholic churches remained in the changing neighborhoods to accommodate old parishioners and to convert newcomers. As decades passed, the parochial school, which offered urban blacks an attractive alternative to public education, became an important source of black converts. The number of black Catholics increased due primarily to conversion. Between 1940 and 1975, the black Catholic population grew from roughly 297,000 to 917,000, an increase of 208 percent.

Of the new religious options, the most prominent might not seem religious at first glance. The Universal Negro Improvement Association (UNIA), led by an immigrant from Jamaica, Marcus Mosiah Garvey, has been generally regarded as a black nationalist movement. And so it was. But it was also offered black Americans a set of complex religious ideas, images, and rituals to support an alternative or at least complementary national identity. Settling in New York in 1916, Garvey lectured and organized on the necessity of "uniting all the Negro peoples of the world into one great body to establish a country and Government absolutely of their own" (Garvey, 1923). The organization mushroomed rapidly to 2,000 members in New York City alone. Through the UNIA journal, the *Negro World,* Garvey spread his philosophy of pan-Africanism far and wide. The UNIA served political, civic, social, economic, and religious needs.

Garveyites met in auditoriums called Liberty Halls and held a variety of programs, including Sunday morning services, afternoon Sunday schools, public meetings, dances, and concerts. The halls offered temporary housing, soup kitchens, and jobs for the unemployed. The UNIA had its own flag, its own national anthem, and, briefly, its own steamship line, all to create a sense of national identity and spiritual unity among its members—a "black civil religion," for those alienated from the dominant civil religion of the nation (Burkett, 1978). The UNIA also supplied a weekly Sunday service, a baptismal ritual, a hymnal, a creed, a catechism, and images of Jesus as a "Black Man of Sorrows" and the Virgin Mary as a "Black Madonna." In its heyday in the 1920s, the UNIA became the largest mass movement ever organized among African Americans. Garvey aroused the opposition of some black leaders, as well as the suspicion of the FBI. In 1927, he was arrested, tried for mail fraud, and imprisoned; in 1929, he was deported.

While Garvey encouraged African Americans to embrace their racial identity, other religious leaders claimed to have discovered the authentic identity of black people stolen from them by the experience of slavery. Several forms of indigenous black Judaism and black Islam conflated religious and racial identity by claiming that black people were Jews or, alternatively, Muslims. William S. Crowdy, who formed the first organization of black Jews in 1896, preached that black people descended from the 10 lost tribes of Israel. Timothy Drew, known to his followers as the Noble Drew Ali, the founder of the Moorish Science Temple in 1913, claimed that African Americans were not Negroes but "Asiatics." Their original homeland was Morocco; their true nationality was Moorish American. To symbolize the recovery of their true identity, neophytes received new names and identity cards issued by Noble Drew Ali. The Nation of Islam, founded in Detroit in 1930, likewise taught that black Americans were descendents of the lost found tribe of Shabbaz and that empowerment came with knowing one's true identity.

By rejecting Christianity as a religion for whites and by denying that American racial categories applied to them, black Jews and black Muslims imaginatively "emigrated," creating new racial, national, and religious myths of identity for themselves that contradicted racist myths of their inferiority. In some cases, these esoteric forms of Islam and Judaism served as bridges to conversion to "orthodox" Judaism and Islam. In other cases, African Americans converted directly to these faiths, as well as to Bahá'í, Buddhism, and other religions they encountered in the cities.

One of the most significant of the religious movements to attract blacks during the period of migration was in many ways a return to the emphasis on spiritual experience and emotional worship of the "old-time" religion. In the late 19th and early years of the 20th century, the Holiness-Pentecostal movement began to emphasize the ideal of sanctification and the experience of the gifts of the Holy Spirit, such as speaking in tongues and healing. The "sanctified" churches, as the Holiness and Pentecostal congregations were called, encouraged their members to express the gifts of the Spirit in ecstatic forms of religious worship. Ridiculed by outsiders as "holy rollers" because of the emotional expressiveness of their services, they introduced the use of "secular" instruments such as guitars, pianos, and drums into their religious services and made a major contribution to the development of black gospel music. Their style of religious music eventually influenced the tastes of churches that once banned such instruments as tools of the devil. The sanctified churches also required that their members abstain from tobacco, alcohol, drugs, gambling, dancing, makeup, and "worldly" entertainment. In effect, these congregations created little social worlds within the larger, often hostile white world. Members were trained to develop habits of honesty, thrift, hard work, and discipline. Eventually, they tended to move up economically and educationally, within the limits set by racial discrimination. One of the consequences of the sanctified practice of "this worldly asceticism" was upward mobility, a factor that would attract Haitian (as well as Hispanic) immigrants to Holiness and Pentecostal churches in increasing numbers.

In the later decades of the migration, Haitian, Cuban, and African immigration to the United States brought other religious options to African Americans. African and African-derived religious movements, such as Voudou from Haiti, Santería from Cuba, and the Aladura churches from Nigeria, brought unknown numbers of African American converts into membership with international networks of religious community and cultural exchange. Reclamations of African history and culture propagated by black consciousness movements in the late 1960s and 1970s may have helped to increase the visibility and appeal of these traditional religions for blacks in the United States.

The concentration of African Americans in cities and the development of new communication and entertainment media like radio and the phonograph spread black religious culture to a wide audience. Record companies produced race records specifically designed for black listeners. These included sermons, as well as blues and jazz. Radio stations featured black religious services and broadcast black preachers regularly to local listeners. One of the most popular was Elder Lucy Smith, a migrant to Chicago herself, who led the All Nations Pentecostal Church, a multiracial congregation, noted for its emotionally expressive worship. In 1933, Elder Smith began her radio ministry, broadcasting live services across the airwaves on Sunday evenings. For two decades, her "Glorious Church of the Air" program gained a huge audience. Many of those tuning in regularly were unlettered southern migrants attracted by the "southern religious style" with which Elder Smith delivered the gospel message, as well as her strong emphasis on faith healing and her promotion of gospel music. Gospel singers Mahalia Jackson, Sallie Martin, the Roberta Martin Singers, and the "father" of blues gospel, Thomas Dorsey, all appeared on her program (Best, 2005: 94–117, 145–80).

These and other religious leaders, with their access to a large audience and their influence over large congregations, attracted the attention of black and white politicians. To migrants from the South, this was a new phenomenon: because African Americans could vote in the North, their increasing numbers enabled community leaders—spiritual and otherwise—to claim roles in systems of political patronage. Newcomers, eager to exercise their newfound franchise, were often ready to at least initially look to religious leadership for guidance in matters of racial self-interest. More settled residents wanted their churches to have civic influence, and for African Americans the only route was generally through electoral politics. If they had nothing else, they increasingly had numbers. In some storefronts and other small churches that were unable to adequately support their minister, politicians were welcomed to the pulpit in return for a financial consideration (to the church or to the minister; in some cases this was one and the same). Other ministers traded access to their pulpits for access to political influence, thereby enhancing their position within the community (Williams, n.d. [1930s]). Reverend Archibald J. Carey, pastor at Chicago's venerable Quinn Chapel African Methodist Episcopal (AME) until 1909, and then successor to Reverdy Ransom at the innovative Institutional AME, used his clout in the black community to cultivate a relationship with the up-and-coming Republican William Hale Thompson. By the time Thompson was elected mayor in 1915, Carey was close enough to win patronage appointments for himself and his allies; Carey repaid the favor by publicly comparing Thompson with Abraham Lincoln (Gosnell, 1935: 49–51).

Southern black preachers, rural or urban, exercised secular power in large part because of the black church's distance from the white world and its relative autonomy from the relations of race and class that shaped the dynamics of African American place in southern society (Grossman, 1997). In the northern cities, a minister's role in public culture could be similarly focused inward toward the community, but it could also compete with newspapers, fraternal organizations, and other civic institutions that sought to represent black voters to white politicians. Although the church was still civic space for community building, it was also a venue for black and white politicians to reach captive Sunday audiences (Gosnell, 1935: 95–100).

The political role of religious institutions as gathering places, arenas for mobilization, and sources of leadership harked back to Reconstruction but, indeed, probably did not reach that earlier threshold of influence. Unlike recently emancipated slaves, black northerners had many other institutional resources, especially the political parties themselves, along with a matrix of fraternal organizations and a rapidly growing set of leisure institutions that provided sites of conversation and mobilization (Bachin, 2004; White and White, 1998: 220–47). In some northern black communities, a thriving underground economy provided black political leaders with financial resources, and ministers who decried gambling and other forms of vice were at once sending a moral message and attacking the competition. So were black newspapers in their frequent criticisms of politically active ministers for selling their church's soul—or at least its pulpit—for a mess of patronage. Far more than they had in the South, African Americans in northern cities had multiple sources of information and mobilization.

Religion had less competition in the realm of interpretation, especially if one considers some of the black nationalist movements as partially religious enterprises. From the beginning of the migration process, religion had given meaning to migration experiences. For some, the migration itself was cast into the imagery of Exodus, so familiar from slavery time, now applied to new and unfamiliar circumstances. Some spoke of the journey from the South to the North or the West as a new Exodus from Egypt to the Promised Land. But as this Promised Land, like emancipation, proved to be limited in its prospects for full equality, migrants turned to new religious options. Or, as their forebears had before them, they found in the tradition of African American Christianity the resources to wait and to struggle for full inclusion in the American promise.

Though the black population continued to migrate from the South until the 1970s and became more urban with passing decades, the rural churches remained the center of community life for those who stayed on the land, and these churches continued to influence the religious attitudes and customs of those urbanites long separated from their rural roots. Travel "down home," the custom of sending children to spend summers with southern relatives, and annual celebrations of "Homecoming," a day of special welcome to former members helped to renew the old ties. Sometimes migrants asked that their bodies be sent back home to the church of their baptism and the gravesite of their families for burial, even though they had moved away years before.

To understand the Great Migration from the perspective of participants who understood it as a transforming moment in their lives, we might reflect on T. S. Eliot's observation in *Four Quartets*: "We have had the experience, but missed the meaning." Scholars have explored the experience of the Great Migration, but perhaps we haven't listened carefully enough to discern the meaning. Certainly, part of that meaning consists in the perennial paradox of race in America. The image of movement to America as an Exodus, shared by Americans generally from at least colonial times, had an inverse meaning for African Americans, who viewed their experience as a journey into slavery in a new "Egyptland." This "abiding and tragic irony" (Harding, 1969: 829–40) took on paradigmatic meaning during slavery. Emancipation, however, did not solve the paradox, as African Americans found freedom less than complete and saw that the "promised land" still lay off somewhere in the future. For thousands of migrants, the physical journey of the Great Migration resonated with the old symbol as they prayed and hoped that finally they were "bound for the promised land." The symbol of Exodus, like a mirror, reflected both their disenchantment and their hope that this nation might someday be that "promised land." In this sense, the African American Exodus tradition was grounded in American civic values as a "prophetic" call to the nation to live those values by making them inclusive of all.

The Great Migration challenged religious life—and other aspects of civic culture—among African Americans by bringing them into an environment of much greater pluralism than most had experienced in the rural South and even many southern cities. The market place model of religious choice, and the separation of church and state, became real for African American migrants, just as the range of jobs (even if only of the unskilled variety) and the range of leisure opportunities widened. On the one hand, the sheer variety of religions created an opportunity to "try on" a variety of spiritual options for a variety of purposes—or even to participate in the creative process of eclectic blending of religious traditions and practices. On the other, the variety created a cacophony of different religious opinions that made real the opportunity to debate and decide among competing claims to truth. When Rev. C. L. Franklin, pastor of New Bethel Baptist Church in Detroit (and Aretha's father), invited Prophet Jones, a Holiness preacher into the pulpit to debate him, the congregation, which included a large number of immigrants, witnessed a very democratic exercise: the free discussion of religious difference in public space, based on a common agreement about the civic value of such exchanges (Salvatore, 2001, 2005; Glaude, 2003: 494–11).

Thus participation in church life itself provided an introduction to the activities of civic life. Voting, sitting on committees, writing and receiving reports, taking minutes, observing rules of order—all of these actions invoked the voluntary principle so fundamental to American public life. In the South, these voluntaristic behaviors generally were restricted to the church, but in the North, migrants had greater opportunity to exercise them in the larger political sphere as well.

Finally, the concentration of rural black southerners in cities, brought about by the Great Migration, led them to encounter to a much greater degree the ethnic pluralism of society, as their numbers also increased the ethnic variety of northern and western cities. This pluralism led sometimes to ethnic tension and strife. Sometimes, it also led to tension with black immigrants from elsewhere, such as the British West Indies and Haiti. But it also made possible the political, moral, and religious struggle for civic equality that remains paradigmatic for other groups.

During the early days of the first wave of the Great Migration, a group of 147 black migrants knelt in prayer as they reached the Ohio River, the old antebellum border between slavery and freedom. The men stopped their watches to mark the exact time. And both men and women joined in singing "I done come out of the Land of Egypt with the good news" (Sernett, 1997: 61). By this unique ritual act, they interpreted their migration as a second Exodus. Down the long years of successive migration and settlement, religious ritual, symbols, and institutions have continued to serve as sources of meaning, direction, and hope for black Americans in search of the Promised Land.

॥॥॥॥॥॥॥॥॥॥॥॥॥॥॥॥॥॥॥॥॥॥॥॥॥॥॥॥॥॥॥॥॥॥॥

Catholic, Vodou, and Protestant

Being Haitian, Becoming American—Religious Pluralism, Immigrant Incorporation, and Transnationalism

Elizabeth McAlister and Karen Richman

Just as religious congregation and ritual inspired African American migrants during the Great Migration with personal and communal strength to persevere against injustice and inequality, so, too, have Haitian migrants in the United States turned to religion as a buffer against the traumas of exile and the racial inequalities of American society. Like African Americans, some Haitian Protestants, whose numbers are relatively new yet growing, embrace the Exodus story of access to the Promised Land and concurrently invest in the classic myth of America as a nation chosen by God for a special destiny. But the majority of Haitian immigrants, who are practicing Catholics and Vodouists, seek through their religious practices to gain access to the power of saints and spirits, who can heal affliction and assure the protection of individuals and their families. For these Haitian migrants, migration and ritual have combined less to effect the escape from bondage and more to enable the fulfillment or renegotiation of spiritual and familial bonds that tie them back to their homelands.

African Americans and Haitians are similar in that both groups' origins in the Americas are located in the slave trade and chattel servitude. Dislocation, whether coerced or a "voluntary" escape from misery and oppression, has been a fact of life for African American and Haitian societies from their violent beginnings in the Americas until the present. Consciousness of violent displacement and loss of the African homeland remained a powerful metaphor for understanding subsequent and repeated experiences of migration and exile. For both groups, religious meaning-making, ritual, and social bonding have been the primary ways to cope with and struggle against the lasting effects of displacement, slavery, and racism.

Both groups have made subsequent migrations, which are the focus in this volume. For African Americans, religion facilitated the migration from the South to the North and was part of their long battle to establish their claims to full national membership and citizenship rights. Many looked "down home" with nostalgia and found ways to visit and remain connected to family who stayed. In their secondary migration, Haitians have come to the United States as citizens of a foreign nation, albeit a weakened one, often with a desire and many opportunities to sustain their national identities and homeland connections. Contemporary Haitian migration and settlement in the United States is distinctively transnational in character. Religion—in the form of Vodou, Catholicism, and Protestantism—has played a key role in both facilitating and renegotiating relations with Haiti but also in settling and adjusting to American society and realizing Haitians' own American dreams.

African Americans and Haitians also have in common hybrid religions forged on new soil out of diverse European and African traditions. Melville Herskovits (1990 [1941]) and subsequent scholars discovered in these religions African forms and styles of worship, including embodied or full performance, spirit possession, emotionalism, antiphonal singing, dance, and polyrhythmic percussion. Belief in the instrumental power and immediacy of spirits and ancestors, in divination and magic, and in spiritual affliction and ritual healing have also been attributed to African legacies, though some of these forms had European counterparts as well. Yet perhaps the most crucial resource for the African slaves and their long-suffering descendants was "a principle of disregard for outer form while retaining inner values" and openness to the "new and foreign" (Herskovits, 1990 [1941]: 141–42). In his analysis of African American slaves' religion, Albert Raboteau asserts that a pragmatic "respect for spiritual power wherever it originated" guided the development of a hybrid, practical, adaptive system of belief and practice in the one institution that slaves directly controlled (1978: 4). Through religion, slaves exerted control over a "world of practical power" (278) and so empowered themselves to contend with the violence of slavery, the suffering of poverty, and unremitting racial oppression.

The following exploration of the relations between migration and religion for Haitians begins with a historical account of their exile and flight to the United States as refugees and laborers. Next, we describe the transnational ties that Haitian migrants sustain with their homeland and the racial and class identities that they must negotiate in their ties with American society, to set the stage for our interpretation of their religious practices. African American migrants to the North engaged in similar negotiations of transregional and local identities and networks, with corresponding implications for religion, albeit within the same nation-state. After examining Haitian migrants' participation in rituals and practices of the Catholic Church and Vodou in New York City, our account turns to the intensive transnational relations of a Haitian migrant community bridging Léogane, Haiti, and Palm Beach County, Florida. This account examines the strains that transnational religious and social obligations to the *lwa* (spirits) and family impose on Haitian migrants and how such strains have led some to seek alternative spiritual powers and realize individualistic material success promised by evangelical Protestant churches. Finally, we examine how Haitian and American Protestants have made Protestantism's competition with Vodou and Catholicism a transnational project, establishing institutional transnational ties related to those of migrant family networks.

In our conclusion, we engage the essential fluidity and hybridity of religions born in the New World out of slavery, marginality, and racial oppression. Catholicism, Protestantism, and Vodou, the triad of faiths practiced by Haitians in the United States, as in Haiti, are not opposing religions but, rather, options in a fundamentally fluid and integrated continuum of flexible faith and practical power.

Migration History of Haiti

Ayiti (Haiti), the word the Taino Arawak people used to describe their mountainous home, is one of the few remnants of the people who inhabited the western islands of the Caribbean until the arrival of Spanish colonizers at the end of the 15th century. After these Native peoples were wiped out within a mere half-century of the Spaniard's arrival, Hispaniola, like the other islands of the Greater Antilles, was colonized as if its mountains and plains "were empty lands" (Mintz, 1971: 19). Some of the migrants from Europe arrived of their own free will to colonize St. Domingue, and others left Europe as indentured servants, but the vast majority of the "migrants" came from Africa in chains. The slaves' labor on sugar and coffee plantations made St. Domingue, France's colony on the western portion of the island, the richest "pearl of the Antilles" and the source of the majority of French wealth. About 800,000 Africans were enslaved by French planters in St. Domingue between 1687 and 1791. Because of the colonists' penchant for working their human capital to death, only about half a million slaves were alive in 1791, when the only successful slave revolution in the Americas began.

The overthrow of French colonial rule 13 violent years later led to the creation of independent Haiti, whose new name, harking back to the vanished Tainos, symbolized the new nation's defiance of the slave-based colonial economic system. In turn, that system would overwhelmingly reject and isolate the new, free African American nation-state. Fleeing French planters, slaves in tow, were welcomed generously into the United States, which refused to recognize Haiti until after the abolition of slavery.

The collapse of the colonial system and the destruction of plantation infrastructure provided openings for descendants of slaves in the newly independent nation of Haiti to reconstitute themselves as small, independent, land-holding farmers. The peasants resisted pressures to coerce them into plantation wage labor by the new state, beginning with the founding president and revolutionary leader, Jean-Jacques Dessalines. It took the economic and military might of a new 20th-century colonial power— the United States—to push the Haitian peasants into capitalist agriculture. Over the course of the 20th century, the Haitian peasant economy was transformed into one that produces unskilled, wage labor for export and increasingly consumes imported food. Haitian migrant laborers have thus followed and abetted the expansions and declines of North American capital by migrating to Cuba, other parts of Haiti, the Dominican Republic (the eastern side of the island), the Caribbean, and, ultimately, the United States and Canada as part of the broad "new" Caribbean migration feeding the restructuring and relocation of U.S. manufacturing (Bryce-Laporte, 1979).

The Immigration Act of 1965 liberalized entrance policies to allow large numbers of non-European peoples to immigrate legally to the United States. As service industries replaced manufacturing in center cities, low-paying, labor-intensive jobs pulled immigrant workers from the areas that were becoming attractive frontiers for the intensified "subcontracting" of phases of assembly-line production. New levels of capital penetrations into Caribbean and Central American economies, lured by their "comparative advantage" of rural decline, extreme poverty, and vast labor reserves, propelled the increased migration of people from the peripheries to the center (Wallerstein, 1974: 229–31; Sassen-Koob, 1982). During the 1970s, a higher proportion of the Caribbean population emigrated than did the peoples of any other world area (Barry, Wood, and Preusch, 1984: 13), with rates of outmigration ranging as high as 25 percent. Haiti fell in the middle with perhaps as many as 20 percent living "outside" (*deyò*) (Chaney, 1987; Segal, 1987). New York was Haitians' major destination, as it was for several other Caribbean and Latin populations, though migrants also settled in Montreal, Boston, Chicago, and Washington, D.C.

At the end of the 1970s, both the mode and the location of Haitian migration to the United States changed. A flotilla of boats, many of them tiny, open sailboats used for fishing, began leaving Haitian waters for the South Florida coast. These daring voyages designated South Florida as the new destination point and also transformed the character of Haitian migration to the United Statess, drawing from the poorest segments of the population.

Between 1979 and 1981, as many as 70,000 Haitians entered Florida by boat. The INS's policy was to deport the Haitian "economic migrants" while welcoming Cubans. After taking office in 1981, President Ronald Reagan moved to "regain control of the borders." The United States placed Coast Guard cutters in the windward passage between Cuba and Haiti to interdict and burn Haitian boats, determine passengers' valid claims for asylum, and repatriate those deemed ineligible for refugee status. Virtually all claims to political asylum were rejected. When tens of thousands of people tried to flee the violent coup d'état that ousted the eight-month-old government of Jean-Bertrand Aristide, Coast Guard cutters were again dispatched to prevent the Haitians from reaching the United States. In response to human rights protests of the practice of summarily returning them, the INS set up a detention camp in Guantanamo Bay to process their asylum claims. The INS found about 40,000 to have valid claims and permitted them to enter the United States. Fearful of the prospect of more Haitian refugees legally crossing U.S. borders, the government simply closed the camp in 1992 and resumed the earlier policy of interdicting boats and forcibly repatriating the refugees to Haiti. We can see that the United States has singled Haitians out for particularly exclusionary treatment.

Since the brief, intense wave of boat migrations from Haiti to South Florida, the movement of Haitians into and within the United States has continued. First is the stream coming from Haiti (primarily by airplane) comprised of family members of the immigrants. Second is the movement of Haitians within areas of settlement. In the New York area, successful Haitians move to more affluent urban and suburban neighborhoods. In Florida, those who arrived by boat and worked as migratory farm workers abandoned the poorly paid, irregular, and dangerous work on agribusiness farms as soon as they could and resettled in coastal cities to work in the lower levels of the burgeoning industries of tourism, service, health care, and construction. Third is the constant movement between these areas, especially that of Haitians who had achieved economic success in northern cities but then moved to South Florida. In addition to these circuits of movement to and within the United States, Haitians continue to travel to, and maintain family, business, political, and religious ties with the homeland. In this way, transnationalism structures much of Haitian life, both in Haiti and in the United States.

Everyday Transnationalism in Haitian Life

The theory of "transnationalism" describes a social field that extends across national boundaries and the encompassment of migrants (and their nonmigrant relations) by nation-building processes, which migrants and their relations exploit (Basch, Glick-Schiller, and Szanton-Blanc, 1994). While it is clear that transnationalism reaches back to the beginnings of the Haitian nation-state, it is only in the recent past that Haitian society has become thoroughly transnational. President Aristide in 1990 designated that Haitians living in the diaspora would constitute a "Tenth Province" of Haiti, which would in time be assigned a government ministry and come to wield significant political and economic power.

Migrants' kinship ties, economic relations, and religious maps and practices simultaneously involve them in home and diaspora communities. Families are often spread across several (three or more) national boundaries. Like other Caribbean migrants, Haitians often leave young children behind in the care of relatives, sending for them when they are in their early teens, believing that the moral practices of being home raised *Kretyen vivan* (moral persons; lit.: "living Christians") will serve them well in contending with the depravities of American life (Soto, 1987). Or, if children are born in the host society, parents sponsor the migration of a relative to help with child care. Meanwhile, men and women continue to establish new, transnational conjugal unions, where wife and husband live in different countries.

Migrants return to Haiti to seek help during periods of illness or unemployment; for vacations; for important family events like baptisms, marriages, and funerals; and for popular annual festivals, including patron saint pilgrimages, Carnival, and Rara (Lenten parades). Video and audio recordings allow those who cannot return to participate vicariously in the performances. After decades in the United States, the infirm and the elderly may return to spend their last years at home. Family roles shift over the span of two countries, so that children come of age and migrate north and old folks retire and return southward to home as both opportunity and tragedy occasion moves to *janbe dlo*, or "cross over the water."

It would not be an exaggeration to say that virtually every Haitian has a relative or friend who has emigrated to New York or Miami. Migration is so thoroughly normalized that children are raised with the expectation that they will migrate. Nor is it possible to talk about the Haitian economy, for instance, without considering the role of the money migrants send home. Their money has helped to finance entire families back in Haiti, with the eventual goal of reuniting families one by one, in the United States. Haitians have been honing this form of chain-migration for decades, as Susan Buchanan (1980) and Michel Laguerre (1998) documented in their studies of the migration strategies of Haitian families in New York. Transnational consciousness is also reproduced in everyday language. Children expect to one day grow up and leave, as it is said, in search of a livelihood for their (extended) family (*chache lavi pou fanmi yo*). Mundane references to members located "outside" (*deyò*) and "over there" (*lòt bò a*) further naturalize the reality of dispersal to South Florida, in particular.

Contemporary Haitian immigrants' transnational religious and social worlds resonate with the orientations of African Americans who migrated great distances within a single nation-state from about 1890 to 1970 and who still maintained ties to their home roots. Many young African American people, whose parents had headed North for jobs and freedom from overt racial hatred, grew up hearing nostalgic stories of the South from their elders or were sent "home" in the summers to stay with relatives. Occasional visits, along with mail and telephone communication, perpetuated contacts between the North and "down home." Near the end of the 20th century, as economic restructuring took its toll on urban African Americans in northern cities, in particular, their transregional consciousness fostered new strategies. Some of those born in the North, or who had migrated themselves, "returned home" (Stack, 1996).

Class, Race, Religion, and Identity among Haitians in the United States

In the United States, the Haitian population is engaged in a struggle over questions of identity and definition that are inseparable from Haitian and American processes of class formation in which race plays shifting and contradictory roles. This is true, of course, for all immigrant groups, whether they are ultimately perceived to be "White" or "African American." But for Haitians, who usually have melanin-rich complexions that are read as "African American," race and racism is an everyday issue in America. The struggle for a Haitian American identity is particularly charged because, like other Afro-Caribbean immigrants, Haitians are caught in a problematic position. As Black immigrants, they are offered the label and identity of "African American." But this is not the identity that they understand themselves to have. They understand themselves to be historically and culturally distinct from African Americans. Yet groups defined through race will have the least amount of choice toward self-identification; people of Black African descent will inevitably be labeled "African American." In contrast, "White ethnics" like Irish Americans and Italian Americans have a wider range of choice in the ways they may display their identity (Mittelberg and Waters, 1992, cited in McAlister, 1998).

Former slave-holding societies of Latin America, the West Indies, and the United States developed different racialized configurations. When Haitians arrive in the United States, they carry "cognitive maps" charting a complex sense of Caribbean racialization in which people are located along a color continuum, mitigated by class and family lineage. Race in the United States has been constructed along a "color line," making people either Black or White. Haitian Americans' identity and subjective positions of racialization must be seen as being "superimposed" onto their new experience of U.S. constructions of race. Part of the challenge facing African American immigrants is in assessing and renegotiating a newly found racial status in North America.

Unpacking the complexities of Haitian American identity, Carolle Charles (1990) argues that the categories of race, class, and ethnicity by which Haitians identify themselves are expressions of their social consciousness and are part of a process of rejection and redefinition of categories of race and ethnicity ascribed in the United States. Charles's work reveals Haitians' tendency to disaffiliate with African Americans. Haitians are acutely aware that African Americans have been assigned repeatedly to the lowest status position in the United States. Perceiving that African Americans represent "the bottom" of U.S. society, Haitians reject this placement and tend to dismiss U.S. meanings of Blackness, while affirming their own race and culture.

The paths that they chart reveal Haitians in the United States to be actors constructing their own identity as a population. They have now carved out a few alternative Black Haitian American identities. Language and religion are two important performative markers Haitians have available to use in producing their own identities. An early tactic exploited by Haitian immigrants, particularly those who arrived in New York during the 1960s and 1970s, has been to display, use, and value their Francophone (and Creolophone) abilities. By referring to themselves as "Frenchies" and speaking French in public, Haitians display a foreign-born status, which is also an upper-class marker in Haitian society (Charles, 1990; Mittelberg and Waters, 1992). By the same token, participating in Catholic congregations and public feasts became a way for Haitian Americans to distinguish themselves further from African Americans, whom they generally viewed as members of the African American Protestant Church establishment. This can be seen as "a self-constitution through the strategy of alterity within the broader context of American racial semiotics" (Orsi, 1992: 321). By maintaining Frenchness, Creoleness, and Catholicism, and by dressing in conservative, French-influenced fashions and hairstyles, Haitians can broadcast their difference from African Americans. Haitians can underscore to themselves, their children, and the larger society that they are fully Haitian, Afro-Caribbean, Catholic, immigrant—and not African American (McAlister, 1998).

Haitians in the United States do identify as African American, yet they link their Blackness through Haitian history to Africa and not through the United States. In the process of forging an ethnic identity, Haitian immigrants rediscover their nationalism. Their racial identity is closely connected to pride in the Haitian Revolution of 1791–1804, which created the first African American–ruled nation in the Americas. According to this nationalist discourse, the revolution was fought by slaves with the inspiration of Afro-Creole spirituality and magical weapons. Blackness and militarism became key tropes of Haitian nationalism, along with allusions to Afro-Creole spiritual power. Citizens of the Black nation that defeated Napoleon's army, Haitians carry a deep sense of national pride (Charles, 1990; McAlister, 2002). This nationalist ideology that links Blackness with Afro-Creole spirituality has yielded new forms of ethnic orientation among Haitians.

A figuring of a religious African American–Haitian American ethnicity that emerged as an alternative to the French-Catholic model became possible after the fall of Duvalier in 1986, when political shifts in Haiti opened cultural space in several spheres. For the first time, musicians could publicly perform popular music based on Vodou rhythms, a genre that tended to be critical of both the military juntas and North American hegemony. The resulting *mouvman rasin,* or "roots movement," became a popular mode of ethnic valorization from the late 1980s through the early 2000s. This popular ideology privileges (and sometimes romanticizes) Afro-Creole culture, including serving the spirits of Vodou, the *lakou* (family compound) system, the *konbit* (work party) system, and other forms of peasant life. Haitian migrants invested in this "roots" identity began to perform Rara, a parading Afro-Creole peasant festival, at political demonstrations and in public parks. Their ethnicity as Black Haitian Americans depended on ideas of "roots" to Africa, by way of Haiti. They actively learned Haitian Rara and Vodou music, dressed in stylized peasant clothes, and often dreadlocked their hair (as a reference to a category of Vodou mystic called *zing*) (McAlister, 2002).

Such formulations by Haitian immigrants—and by Haitians living in Haiti—link the Haitian nation with "blood ties" of primordial ethnicity and religion. Heightening homeland identity through "blood" and "roots" can also serve to work as a partial differentiation from African Americans (Glick Schiller and Fouron, 2002). Although many Haitian American youth in the 1970s and 1980s disavowed their Haitian identities to avoid stigma (Stepick, 1999: 1), the fall of Duvalier in 1986, and the rise of the "roots" movement have valorized Haitianness again. Despite being understood to be "African American," members of this younger generation underscore ethnic, homeland identities through revolution and "roots." In this way, both they and those oriented toward French-Catholic modes are comparable with other immigrant groups who have worked to distance themselves from African Americans and "become white" in America. Through the two distinct religious modalities of Catholicism and "roots," Haitian Americans can be said to be struggling to create a new African American ethnicity in the United States.

The Catholic Church: Institutional Mediator and Ethnic "Comfort Zone"

Haitians enter the United States as a majority Roman Catholic population (even though Haitian Catholicism is often creolized with Vodou, and although now, an estimated one-third of the Haitian population is Protestant). Of course, the Catholic Church has been a transnational institution for most of its long history. Although it is a minority religious institution in the United States, the Catholic Church is now both legitimate and powerful (Casanova, 1994: 168). Haitian Catholics entering the United States looked to the U.S. Catholic Church as an already-established religious institution, a possible refuge, a site of cultural affinity, and a place to network as well as to worship.

The Catholic Church in New York did respond to the new Haitian influx in the late 1960s and early 1970s (occasioned by the rise of the Duvalier dictatorship). The Church created a Haitian Apostolate, and various parishes organized events specifically for Haitians, such as French masses (and, later, Creole masses), and "welcoming centers" for Haitians in need of practical or spiritual help. They initiated Feast Day masses (to celebrate patron saint feasts in various Haitian towns); held special services; and published Scripture texts, hymnals, and newsletters in French and Creole (Buchanan, 1990). Churches also sponsored youth groups, discussion groups, singing groups, and even folkloric dance troupes, which, ironically, present the drumming and dances of Afro-Haitian religions in stylized form. As of 2006, there were at least 14 churches with French or Creole masses serving the Haitian community in Brooklyn and Queens, and another five in Manhattan and Rockland County.

Today, while some masses are spoken in French, in the conservative, European style, other masses are in Creole, with a Caribbean aesthetic. In these Creole services, young people dress in stylized Haitian peasant costumes and dance the offertory to the altar, accompanied by drum rhythms. They not only bring the wine and bread but also fruit, sugar cane, and other Haitian produce. Through reproducing these aspects of home-country religious institutions, Haitians both produce their ethnicity in the United States and simultaneously maintain ongoing ties to Haiti.

The church's ministry to Haitians was not always smooth, since the Haitian population has long been divided by class, language, and political differences. In the 1970s, the Creole mass was controversial among upper-class Francophone Haitians, who associated Creole with Vodou (Buchanan, 1990). In the 1980s, congregations were divided between the conservative stance of the Vatican, allied with the Duvaliers, and the liberation theology movement that was gaining momentum among Haiti's poor. Throughout the 1990s and into the early 2000s, the Haitian Apostolate struggled to maintain service centers for Haitian refugees and immigrants, many of whom were traumatized in various ways from their experiences of military repression and flight from Haiti. The legal issues that revolve around immigration status remain the populations' most pressing concerns. By providing cultural and religious space, as well as practical and legal services, the Catholic Church stands as a mediator institution in the civil incorporation of the New York Haitian population.

We can see that the Catholic Church's response to Haitian migration has followed its traditional pattern with other ethnic groups: it established separate ethnic congregations within the local parish. In this way, the Catholic Church has joined other institutions in encouraging ethnic group formation and ethnic identity (Glick, 1975; Buchanan, 1990) This process of ethnicity formation can also, in effect, be an Americanizing process, since many ethnic groups become American through the ironic process of heightening their homeland identities. Immigrants learn to become hyphenated Americans, since that is what is expected of them.

Part and parcel of creating Haitian ethnicity through Catholic practice involves distancing from African Americans. As we argue above, Haitians often underscore their differences from African American Americans through "everyday performances" of Haitianness. By continuing to participate in Catholic congregations, and by sending their children to Catholic schools, Haitian Americans can distinguish themselves from African Americans. In all of these ways, some New York Haitians can create their own American identities through their Catholicism, which, although a minority U.S. religion, is an accepted American identity.

Haitian Catholics also participate in transnational activities through Catholic institutions and spheres. During the rise of the ecclesiastical base communities in Haiti in the 1980s, transnational New York Catholics preached, prayed, and organized on behalf of the popular movement. They actively supported congregations, charities, priests, and media in Haiti such as Radio Soleil, an important Catholic radio news show openly opposed to Duvalierism. Catholics fleeing military repression were harbored by those in New York (Richman 1992b). Through Catholicism, then, Haitians find social space in the United States while simultaneously continuing cultural and religious citizenship in the homeland.

Despite the various controversies among Haitians, and despite a shortage of Haitian- and Creole-speaking priests, Haitian Catholics in New York have benefited from their reception in this powerful religious institution. Haitian migrants make sense of the confusing complexity of the New York ethnic landscape by locating the church as a center of spiritual and social power where they will be welcome. It is a space where Haitians can constitute themselves in the expanding religious landscape of transnational Haitian culture.

As spaces where other Haitians congregate, religious sites in diasporic locations become inflected with meanings that span both home and host nations. Thomas Tweed (1997) suggests that we can usefully understand diasporic religious communities as translocative (moving symbolically between the homeland and the new land) and transtemporal (relating to a constructed past and an imagined future). Public patron saint feasts sponsored by New York churches are translocative meaning-making events in the public sphere that enable transmigrants to reactualize memories of Haiti and reconnect with Haitian culture and Haitian compatriots. For example, since the early 1990s, thousands of Haitians have made the pilgrimage to the Church of Our Lady of Mount Carmel in East Harlem as the largest annual religious gathering of Haitians in North America. It takes place at the same moment when thousands in Haiti flock to a mountainside waterfall pilgrimage called Sodo, for the Fèt Vièj Mirak ("Feast of the Miracle Virgin").

While New Yorkers cannot possibly re-create the busy, celebratory atmosphere of the Sodo pilgrimage in the Haitian countryside, they can nevertheless find friends they know, reunite with long-lost neighbors, speak and sing in Creole and French, and perform devotions for the Vièj Mirak ("Miracle Virgin"). Our Lady of Mount Carmel is already a powerful nationalist symbol for Haitians, as she is said to have fought—in her guise as the spirit Ezili—alongside the slaves in the Haitian Revolution. Mount Carmel takes on poignant significance in the foreign New York setting. Temporarily relaxing class, color, and political boundaries during the liminality of pilgrimage, Mount Carmel the "Miracle Virgin" brings Haitian people in New York together for two days to pray, sing, socialize, and feast with one another in the comfort of the particularly Haitian style. Pilgrims are aware that at the same moment, others are celebrating the same feast back in Haiti. The feast becomes a transtemporal way to re-create a feeling of being at home (McAlister, 1998).

Vodou in New York: Ethnohistorical Enclave

In direct contrast with Roman Catholicism and Protestantism, the Afro-Haitian indigenous religion known as Vodou is not yet understood by most Americans. As a result, Haitians who "serve the spirits" in New York are reticent to share their religious views with others, and they approach worship with a restraint that would invite suspicion back home in Haiti. In order to continue everyday relationships with the spirits, many Haitians in New York—even those who are Catholic—maintain a private religious orientation, one centered on balancing relationships with the Afro-Creole spirits and on "working" the spirits for protection, healing, or luck. From their apartments in New York, *oungan* (priests) and *manbo* (priestesses) serve as healers and mediums. While clients seek help for a range of interpersonal and somatic disorders, job and money troubles are their major "dis-eases." For low-wage, African American, immigrant workers who may also be undocumented, these troubles are myriad: irregular work, low pay or underpayment, discrimination, sexual harassment, and threats by mafia or union-busters. There are relatively few official community service groups available to them for help, and the idea of making appointments with strangers and carrying out grievances may be a foreign one. Rather, they employ a familiar strategy: to seek the assistance of a mediator with the spirits.

The vast majority of ritual and prayer takes place in private homes, often in basements. The home is transformed into sacred space through rearranging the furniture, constructing an altar, and assembling a familial community in prayer. Drummers may be hired, and a long "feeding of the spirits" that might take days in Haiti will be condensed into one night-long ritual in New York. Importantly, the Haitian home altar is a religious space controlled primarily by women. It is they, as head of household, and not the (male) Catholic priest, who is in control of the prayer and its details (Brown, 1991).

Unlike the Catholic Church, which is a well-established and powerful American institution, Haitian Vodou—its congregations, its worship spaces, and its thought and practice—must all be re-created by migrants in the New York setting. But the United States is drastically different from

Haiti—especially rural Haiti. The differences in cultural constructions of time, in urban geography and architecture, and in culture and society force Vodou practitioners to adapt. Haitian ritual experts are the main agents in the re-creation and transformation of the religion in New York. Transnationally connected priests and priestesses form a loose network of Vodou congregations (called "societies") that practice the formal, temple rites of Port-au-Prince Vodou. (These rituals have specific liturgical songs, drum rhythms, dances, and ritual actions.) Members consist of large extended families in addition to initiates, seekers, and clients from outside the family. Haitian, Latino, Anglophone West Indian, and Black and White Americans of various backgrounds frequent or join these Vodou "Houses." Some members are in dialogue with other Afro-Creole religions such as La Regla de Ocha (Santería), and so Haitians reproduce Vodou while gaining exposure to other, similar traditions.

A Vodou society is, by definition, a congregation: a local religious body constituted by the group itself rather than by administrative or geographic definition. In this sense, Vodou shares its organizational structure with the Protestant Church (Warner and Wittner, 1998). However Vodou, with its emphasis on inherited spiritual entities and cyclical cosmology, stands outside of Christian thought and Christian institutions. For this reason, Americans are generally unsympathetic to Vodou practice. Most Americans are ignorant of the religious meanings of Vodou, since demonizing Vodou is normalized in mass media. Vodou is incorrectly represented in mainstream American culture as a criminal and evil magical practice. Hollywood films and television shows use "Voodoo" thematically, expanding colonialist images of African American people as nonrational, incapable of self-rule, feminized, and, most of all, inherently evil. Representations of "Voodoo" become a vehicle through which sentiment against people of color and immigrants becomes legitimate (McAlister, 1999).

Thus many Haitian migrants who rely on Vodou congregations and healers as their sole support network—and for building social capital—are at a disadvantage in incorporating into the American mainstream compared with their Catholic and Protestant compatriots. But established Vodou congregations do offer enormous spiritual and practical resources for their members and for visitors seeking assistance, and in this sense Vodou supports the process of incorporation with American culture. Vodou houses are particularly Haitian spheres that are enclaves of core Haitian cultural practice and sites for transmitting ethnohistorical knowledge.

In New York, "serving the spirits" of Vodou comprises a religious sphere geared toward practical survival for the most disadvantaged members of the Haitian immigrant population. Vodou houses operate as social support networks, and working healers become both spiritual and practical resources that are outside mainstream society, serving people who operate on the margins of that mainstream. Vodou buffers American culture for Haitians, who find "comfort zones" of core Haitian cultural practice and familiar ways to create community.

Also, as mentioned above, Vodou—and the *idea* of Vodou—becomes the basis for an alternative Black ethnic American identity. Those who adopt this form of Afrocentric Haitian identity are often from the middle class and are seeking to reconnect with their "roots" in order to find a comfortable identity. Ironically, these middle-class Haitians can better afford to openly display such alternative African American identities than their poorer, less-advantaged compatriots who might have been raised in Vodou-practicing families. Still, the open and active participation of middle-class and upper-class Haitians in Vodou circles in New York City opens networking opportunities and benefits the more vulnerable members of the community.

A very different relationship to Vodou emerges in another important poor and struggling community, to which we turn next: Haitians in South Florida and their ongoing ties with Léogane, Haiti.

Transnational Sacred Fields across Léogane and Palm Beach County

The transnational Haitian community discussed in this section is anchored in Ti Rivyè, a coastal hamlet in the Léogane Plain in Haiti. Though this impoverished, quasi-peasant economy involves fishing, farming (mainly sugar cane), and food commerce, its main activity seems to be producing low-cost labor for export, consuming migrants' wage remittances, and reabsorbing the migrant workers when they are spent (or deported). Though people from Ti Rivyè are spread across Haiti, the Caribbean, North America, and France, the vast majority of their expatriate members live in Palm Beach, Broward, and St. Lucie Counties, Florida. *Mayami* (Miami) is the term they use for this location, and they often refer to the nation-state as "the country of Miami" (*peyi Mayami*). (The majority of the emigrants sailed to Miami between 1979 and 1982 in their own tiny, motorless, fishing boats.) The imagined northern boundary of Mayami is New York, the other key U.S. destination point for Haitian migrants (Richman, 1992a).

Unlike Haitians in New York, those in Palm Beach County have not endeavored to serve or feed their spirits in the host society. Rather, the location of their ritual practice remains back home on the family land, reinforcing a transnational orientation, as transmigrants remain morally, somatically, and spiritually anchored there. Creative uses of cassette tape and video recorders have resulted in a reconfiguration of the boundaries of the ritual performance space, allowing migrants to continue to serve their spirits "back home." When migrants cannot personally attend the services, they participate indirectly by listening to cassette tapes of the rituals. On these tapes the migrants hear not only the sounds of the performance itself—drumming, singing, prayers, and chatter—but also the voices of narrators describing what the listener cannot see: the flow of possessions, offerings, sacrifices, prayers, conversations, and the like. Spirits possessing the bodies of ritual actors are not only aware of the recording devices, they often move to the recorder to personally address the absent migrant or migrants (Richman, 1990, 1992a).

Although they are characterized as ancient, immutable symbols of "African" tradition, the *lwa* have shown that they can be most adaptable to changing conditions of global reproduction. With so many of their "children" now living and working "over there," the *lwa* are busier than ever. The spirits' supervision of migrants' labor provided a rare opportunity for us to interview a female spirit. The female spirit was possessing a male ritual leader, who was conducting a healing rite for an absent migrant in the presence of the migrants' parents and the anthropologist. The spirit, whose name is Ezili Danto (and whose saintly manifestations are Our Lady of Lourdes and Our Lady of Mount Carmel) said, "Every three days I am in Miami. . . . I have to keep watch over everything that goes on. Miami is where the core is." (*Tou le twa jou m Mayami. F-m veye tout sa k pase. Se Mayami noyo a ye.*) Like all of the spirits, whose movements are said to be like the wind, Ezili Danto can instantly traverse these international boundaries (Richman, 1990).

Ezili Danto meant that, by "watching over" her peripatetic dependents, in return for "service" and "care," she would first of all safeguard life, prevent accidents, and divert sorcerers' aggressions. The *lwa* can also safeguard migrants' abilities to alienate their labor and to accumulate savings (to be remitted to Haiti). They are said to "protect" the migrant's productivity abroad. Consider how Ti Chini (Little Caterpillar), a Ti Rivyè migrant, used the term "protection" with regard to his patron *lwa*: "I have my protection here. My protection won't abandon me in anything I could achieve, in anything I could get, it's there with me." Pepe is a ritual specialist, or *gangan ason*, who is at once priest, healer, shaman, and sorcerer in Ti Rivyè; he explained how the *lwa* intervene in the lives of their emigrant "servitors." Rather than the term "protection," Pepe favored words deriving from contract: "guarantee" (*garanti*) and "de-guarantee" (*degaranti*). To illustrate the *lwa*'s guarantee, Pepe referred to the case of Lamersi, a resident immigrant of the United States who not only contributed to the rituals for her *lwa* but also returned each year to attend them:

> There are (migrant) people like Lamersi. She always returns to see how the annual service for the *lwa* is going. She sees how the work is going. It guarantees her. It supports her. It satisfies her. She knows that if she doesn't find anything today, tomorrow she'll find. She knows too that if she is employed, she won't be fired for any old reason. Instead of de-guaranteeing her, it always guarantees her little bonus even higher.

As long as Lamersi continues to "take care of" (*okipe*) her *lwa* in Haiti, they may reciprocate by guaranteeing her employment opportunities in the United States. The alternative, in Pepe's words, is the option of "de-guarantee." Pepe described how an emigrant might be de-guaranteed by a *lwa*:

> If the person is in a job that pays $200 or $300 (a week), the *lwa* can make you lose your job. The *lwa* can make you sick so you'll never find work and you'll spend everything you saved. The *lwa* can also make you get into a car accident, lose your job, and make you an alcoholic so that you can never guarantee anything in that country.

Thus spiritual affliction beliefs, ritual discourse, and performance symbolize and reinforce migrants' role as emissaries of their families' social, economic, and ritual interests. The social norms of generosity and giving to your capacity encompass migrants. Migrants are seen as the kinsmen with the "biggest wrists" (*ponyèt*) and are expected to contribute accordingly, not just to their own but to their extended family's ever-increasing obligations, ritual and secular alike. Haitian migrants seek the intervention of these peripatetic spirits to "protect" their *capacity* to produce in

"Miami" and to reproduce, in the Marxian sense of self-replacement of persons and things, through the consumption of remittances by kin and *lwa* alike back in Haiti. The *lwa* take revenge for migrants' neglect by "thwarting" (*anpeche*) and de-guaranteeing the same, by "holding" a recalcitrant migrant who can, but will not, take responsibility for his or her increased burden. Migrants are frequently the victims of vengeful spirits, which only an expiatory, healing rite performed by their home family, regardless of the migrant's absence, can assuage.

Some Ti Rivyè migrants attribute their gradual, if modest, success in the host society to the positive interdependence between their home kin, the *lwa,* and themselves. Dutiful deployment of their "bigger wrists" for ritual expenditures on the family land in Ti Rivyè has resulted in an enhanced "guarantee" and "protection" of their productivity in the host society. Regular demonstrations of generosity to the spirits of their descent group have solidified their social relations and reputations across their transnational community. But others have met disappointment as they struggle to survive in the lowest rungs of a hostile, discriminatory South Florida economy and, meanwhile, stay "healthy." In the background is the frustration of poverty. The migrants aren't as successful as they hoped: their home families are still poor, and remittances have been too meager to bring their families the mobility they had hoped for. The migrants' frustration is further linked to their perceptions that their families no longer look on them as people but see them, rather, as insensate beasts of burden. They slave away in hostile, foreign countries for the sake of people who resent them for ever having left. Many migrants feel that their home relatives are lazy and just eat up their remittances rather than investing them. Since many are still very poor here, and expect to recuperate or retire in Haiti, they are bitter and worried about their lack of economic security back home.

They have resisted their encompassment as migrant "mules" by converting to Protestantism. They have rejected their *lwa*, withdrawn from the system of family ritual obligations, and joined Pentecostal churches. They blame the *lwa* for being useless to them, for colluding with their families who exploit them, for turning a blind eye to migrants in need, even though those migrants have sent money for rituals. Resistance to ritual exploitation, rather than deep faith in a new, loftier religion, is the reason many convert (Richman, 2005a, 2005b).

The tactical use of conversion to contest relations with the *lwa* and people who serve them is described in the literature on Haitian ritual practice. Alfred Métraux (1953, 1972 [1959]) noted the use of conversion as an act of revolt against *lwa* more than half a century ago, before the post-war expansion of Pentecostals in the country. The act of conversion represented "a magic circle" of protection from attacks by *lwa* and sorcerers. He quoted what a Marbial person told him: "If you want the *lwa* to leave you in peace, become a Protestant" (1972 [1959]: 351–52). Roger Dorsainville, another early observer of the use of conversion as resistance, commented that a "true conviction and profound commitment to be saved" were "rarely" the reason people converted. Rather, he stated, "Protestantism is pursued as a superior magical power, the pastor is like a more powerful sorcerer" (quoted in Pressoir, 1942: 5).

The magic circle also protects the convert from the very real fear of sorcery, a social weapon long used by peasants throughout the world to limit individual greed and enforce reciprocity. Among this community, there is a widespread perception that those who dare to better themselves will inevitably be "killed for what they had." As economic emissaries, migrants are obvious targets for the envious. Indeed, some migrants avoid returning home for fear that they will be magically poisoned. Though they can be "hit" with poisonous powders anywhere in the world, and Ti Rivyè natives are believed to have been "hit" in Florida, the likelihood is believed to be far greater back home in Haiti. As one woman, who migrated to South Florida from Ti Rivyè said after her recent conversion, "as soon as you convert, nothing can harm you" (*depi ou konvèti, anyen pa ka fè ou*). After conversion, the healing powers of conviction are manifest in improved outlook and health, positive proof of the strength of the Protestant antidote (Richman, 2005b, 2005c).

Dorsainville's charge that the faith was frankly exploited as a superior magical power, and pastors acted as a more powerful sorcerer than the ritual leader (*gangan*), is echoed in sermons in South Florida Haitian churches today as preachers captivate parishioners with miraculous stories of persons who converted and the next day discovered checks for $100,000 in their mailboxes. A sermon by one pastor during an evening prayer service was a remarkably straightforward approbation of migrants' newfound liberation from this moral economy. The sermon, which he delivered in October 2000, had an indelible refrain. It was rendered in the oddly graceful mixture of Creole and English that typifies their speech: *Jezi set nou "free"* (Jesus sets you free).

What did he mean by freedom? If he implied spiritual freedom, it was only in an indirect sense, as he continued to explain in Creole English:

Free de pwoblem ou, free de soufrans ou, free de dèt ou dwe yo ("Free of your problems, free of your suffering, free of debts you owe"). Jesus liberates you from your obligations to send your wages back home. Jesus frees converts from the system of obligations tying them to their lineage, their spiritual legacy, and their inherited land. Fidelity to Jesus liberates migrants from obligations to contribute to rituals back home, which are major mechanisms for sharing and redistributing resources among members of the lineage. Paradoxically, the preacher's message validated the very tendencies toward individualism and greed, which the moral economy associated with the kin group and their Vodou spirits repudiates and seeks to contain. As migrants resist their perceived exploitation by kin and *lwa* by turning away from this moral economy, they reorient themselves determinately toward the acquisitive spirit of the Protestant American dream (Richman, 2005b, 2005c). Catholic Haitians' critique of the immorality of ambitious individualism and greed is graphically symbolized in the imagery of *dyab*, which means "devil" (*diable*). Like pre-capitalist European peasants, Haitians critique the immoral implications of capitalism through representations of the *dyab*. The *dyab* is as an illicit power that you buy from a sorcerer. You make a contract with it, and it works for you, making money fast, like wild interest, or pure capital (reaped from the surplus value of wage laborers). Though cloaked in modest robes, this puritan devil is the very essence of sorcery. An "uplifting" song intoned at prayer services captures this ethic. The first verse states, *Depi Jezi adopte mwen, mwen se yon milyonè* ("Since Jesus adopted me, I am a millionaire").

Contest for Souls in Palm Beach County, Florida

Among the Haitians of Palm Beach County today, self-identified Catholics and Protestants coexist in a fluid system of religious pluralism. This flexibility of religious practice and association, the Protestants' hardline stance notwithstanding, makes it difficult to measure their relative strength. Père Roland, who heads the Catholic parish in Delray Beach, home to the densest concentration of Haitians (about 17,000) in the county, estimated that, in 2001, Protestants slightly outnumbered Catholics. Alejandro Portes and Alex Stepick (1993) estimated that 40 percent of Haitians in the Little Haiti section of Miami were Protestant.

The early success of the Evangelicals among Haitian communities in Palm Beach County is in part due to the passivity of the Catholic Church.

While the thousands of Haitians who settled in Miami in the early 1990s were welcomed at the Creole masses and activities of the Haitian Catholic Center headed by Father Thomas Wenski, the charismatic, Creole-speaking priest (and presently bishop), those who settled directly in Belle Glade, Delray Beach, Fort Pierce, and Lake Worth had less access to a church in which they felt welcome, even though Father Wenski endeavored to set up satellite centers in these towns, and he and other Creole-speaking priests circulated to these communities. Lacking access to a Haitian Catholic church, many Catholics who wanted to attend Christian services and worship in their own language began going to Haitian Protestant churches. Though they originally attended in order only to attend a Christian service, some inevitably converted (Richman, 2005b).

The first Haitian priest, Père Roland, settled in the area in 1987 and established Notre Dame, the first Haitian Catholic Church in Delray Beach. A second Haitian church was established in the 1990s in Fort Pierce. The Catholic congregations in Belle Glade, Lake Worth, and West Palm Beach have recently hosted their own full-time Haitian Catholic priests, who use space in local Catholic churches. According to Père Roland, the belated establishment of a Haitian ethnic congregation has succeeded in "getting them back." The church, which is undergoing an enlargement and renovation, has added extra masses to accommodate the growing congregation of about 1,400 registered members (many representing nuclear families). Styles of worship that borrow from both Afro-Creole Vodou and Pentecostalism draw in members; drums beat during Creole mass; at small-scale prayer services, lay leaders in effect speak in tongues. The church hosts myriad religious and social clubs, as well as educational programs targeted at migrants' adjustment, some of which involve collaboration of local agencies.

In contrast, when the migrants began arriving around 1980, the evangelical churches responded swiftly to the new migrants' religious "needs." They quickly repatriated portions of North American missions, who were now thoroughly Haitianized, from the Haitian periphery back to the North American core. Haitian pastors were sent to seminaries in the United States and were then helped to establish mission churches in Palm Beach County (and elsewhere). The very qualities that propelled pastors' ascent in rural Haiti—literacy; a flexible, entrepreneurial bent; and a charismatic style—proved equally valuable in the rapidly changing immigrant communities.

There are many Protestant congregations in Palm Beach County, and they vary in size and autonomy. For the congregants of L'Eglise de Dieu, in particular, the church is the center of life outside of their (service) jobs. They spend long hours in church, including most evenings after work, part of Saturday, and most of Sunday. Those with young children take them along into the pews. The welcoming, friendly tone draws members in; the intimate, tactile contact of handshakes and blessings offer comfort and belonging. The Protestant congregations host myriad religious and musical groups but, unlike the Catholic church in Delray Beach, offer few programs aimed at migrants' adjustment. Nonetheless, respondents to our survey mentioned their relations with church members as their primary social networks, through which they exchange food, loans, help, rides, job referrals, child care, and other services. Their tightly knit Protestant social world separates them from both non-Haitians and unsaved Haitians. Their asceticism, prohibiting enjoyment of secular music, dance, drinking, and smoking, further estranges them from the unredeemed.

Through sermon, testimony, prayer, gesture, and song, the congregations represent their immigrant, ethnic, and national identities. The choice and positioning of linguistic register is an important way in which they symbolize who and where they are to themselves (Richman and Balan-Gaubert, 2000). In the service, they shift between Creole, the Haitian vernacular, French, the language of colonial conquest and the national Haitian elite, and English, the idiom of the 20th-century imperial power and of the Promised Land. Most of the communication is in Creole. By speaking Creole, rather than French, and singing hymns in Creole, they signify that they are from the lower rungs of Haitian society. They simultaneously reiterate their identification with popular Protestantism and the success of the churches of the third reform that adopted Creole early on.

French nonetheless proclaims its hegemonic voice in their discourse. The pastor highlights the rarity of his own competence in the higher status code by introducing his sermon in French, reading an inspirational line from the Bible, and then proceeding to interpret it for the others in Creole. Some of the hymns are sung in the prestige code, especially at formal points in the service, especially at the opening or the close. English is the third language that makes its way into the sermons. The sermons begin with a quote in French from the Bible, are conducted in Creole, and are strategically sprinkled with common American English argot. By speaking Creole publicly, they symbolize their identity as Haitians making it in the United States. The insertion of the English phrases demonstrates their competence in American culture and their incorporation into American society.

Their Creole, French, and English narrative remaps Haitian transnational space and demarcates their relationships to the nation-states of the United States and of Haiti. The sermons assert that their successful incorporation into American society is both inevitable and manifest.

It is important to note that even though they lay claim to the American dream, their discourse encourages estrangement from American society. Indeed, the term "American" (*Ameriken*) is often used pejoratively to refer to a pariah individual, lost to a life of drugs and violent crime. The church represents a refuge from the costs of becoming American. The sermons acknowledge that the adult members are in a struggle with "the street" for control of the moral lives of their children.

In spite of its internal contradictions, then, the separate-while-assimilationist model is the one that contrasts markedly with transnationalist orientation of migrants who arrived during the early 1980s and, of course, with the official discourse of the Tenth Province (Haitians living abroad). The utter absence of discussion of developing the home or retiring there is striking. Haiti is configured as a forlorn, backward place better abandoned to its own demise than resurrected. Neither is there talk of returning to Haiti to live out one's retirement. The message seems to be, "we are here to stay and to get ours." In the narratives of the preachers, Haiti often figures as a negative measure by which to gauge their increased self-worth and material fortune in the United States. In the evening sermons of one pastor, who employs an informal, playful speaking style, the living standards they once took for granted now seem so low they are implausible. He conveys the idea that in (hierarchical, caste-like) Haiti they were nothing, but here they are somebody. In Haiti, they couldn't even own a horse, but now they fly on airplanes. He pointed out his own experience when he arrived at the Miami airport and was delighted and shocked when he was greeted with deferential words he would only associate with the elite: "'What can I do for you, sir?' Can you imagine, Sir! Sir!"

Thus Haiti is configured as the place they were fortunate to leave, a fortune they attribute to their faith (and perhaps a fated encounter with an American missionary). Yet they cannot yet leave it entirely, since family members languish there as they await their visas to come to the United States, too. The preachers acknowledge the frequent comings and goings of the members to Haiti, and prayers for their safe passage are often included in the service. Preachers and church members also travel to New York, where similar dynamics are at play in its Haitian Evangelical community, which is involved in networks with churches in Florida and beyond.

Evangelical Protestantism and Americanist Narratives in New York

While mainline Protestantism has historically been a minority religion among Haitians, since the 1990s the Flatbush and Crown Heights sections of Brooklyn, as well as Jamaica, Queens, have increasingly seen the "planting" of hundreds of new Haitian evangelical Protestant churches, many of which are basements or small storefronts. Most of them are Baptist and Pentecostal denominations, and there are also Methodist, Episcopal, Lutheran, and others. Like Haitian Catholics and Vodouists, Haitian Protestants tend to worship in Creole-speaking congregations with other Haitians, producing religion along national-ethnic lines. Now, an estimated one-third of the population in Haiti identifies itself as *konvèti* (converted), and the figure is probably higher for the New York Haitian population.

As in Florida, the majority of the Haitian Protestant churches in New York are offshoots of congregations founded in Haiti by American missions. The churches are now returning to the United States along with the migrants in their number. Evangelical Protestants move within the eastern United States as well, as yearly most churches invite other Haitian Pentecostal congregations in Florida, New York, Boston, and Montreal for special Thanksgiving services.

Pentecostalism becomes an overarching identity that can include national identity but that makes issues of citizenship less problematic and traumatic, especially in the face of U.S. racism and anti-immigrant sentiment. Pentecostalism—with its global character, its new repertoires of images and narratives about "modernity," and its transnational social ties— both facilitates and enforces the experience of migration. Pentecostals join networks that extend from Haiti to the United States and beyond, opening up an extranational, international space, which strengthens individuals' sense of purpose and belonging in a global movement.

With its American historical underpinnings and its orientation toward the same principles of individuality and prosperity as the prevailing American civil religion, Haitian Protestant churches are religious spheres that articulate smoothly with many aspects of civic life. Haitian Protestants tend to be engaged church members, spending most entire Sundays and one or two other evenings at church events. Churches hold healing services, Bible study, children's classes, and homemaking and nutrition classes and sponsor visits to other churches. Members might also sing in the vibrant gospel music circuit that performs and records music in French and Creole throughout the Haitian diaspora. Several radio stations, like Radio Bonne Nouvelle ("Good News") broadcast Christian programming in French and Creole, and there are at least four weekly Haitian evangelical cable television shows. Churches sponsor tours to the Holy Lands, visiting Israel or Rome with other Creole-speaking Haitians in the diaspora. Haitian Protestant churches, like Vodou congregations, are often a crucial locus of social networking for new immigrants.

Haitian Evangelical Protestants in New York, as in Florida, are oriented to American society and culture in a contradictory way. On one hand, Protestants promote religious thought that enjoins them to be "in this world, but not of it" (Ammerman, 1987). They maintain a kind of cultural separatism common in American evangelicalism, which views much American media and mainstream culture as ungodly and dangerous. Haitian Protestants prefer to socialize and network with other Haitian Protestants, who hold similar values and whom they feel they can trust. They keep themselves and their children away from mainstream music and dance, away from drinking, smoking, gambling and engaging in other ungodly practices like participating in Vodou prayers or the summer Rara parades in Prospect Park. Through these social postures, Haitian Protestants produced "new public, visible persona" within the Haitian community (Brodwin, 2003).

On the other hand, Haitian Evangelical Protestants, coming out of the 30-year Duvalier dictatorship, wholeheartedly embrace American democracy. They form political opinions on current events and vote if they are naturalized. They also endorse entrepreneurship, public education, and others aspects of civil society such as military service. But their activities in the civic sphere are limited, and they direct most of their energies toward church activities. Haitian community activists criticize evangelicals for refusing to spend their energies on secular political and community-building projects, saying "they drag the community down."

Although they are embedded in transnational networks, Haitian evangelicals in New York, as in Florida, are also likely to cast Haiti as a negative place and a homeland to which they do not intend to return. The negative valence Haiti occupies for such Protestants is not surprising, since much of American Protestant missionizing has explicitly cast the worldview of the Haitian majority—Afro-Creole religion—as the enemy fighting against Christian redemption. The "African American Republic" as a whole was also cast as a "Magic Island" ruled by a diabolical army (Seabrook, 1989 [1929]). American Protestant missionaries have given themselves the task of saving Haiti's populace from the perceived evils of Vodou and its consequence: political instability. In the political logic of this "moral geography," Haiti's poverty, political turmoil, and structural disadvantage with regard to the United States are held up as proof of God's disfavor toward the Haitian nation. In sermons, White American missionaries in Haiti have interpreted the Blackness of Haitians' skin as the curse of Cain, demonizing Haitian identity further by racializing evil.

Receiving new stories about Christ's victorious army is complicated in the Haitian context, since national and martial tropes have also girded the structures of Vodou. According to Haitian national history, the revolutionary war was launched on the eve of a religious ceremony at a place in the north called Bwa Kayiman (Bois Caiman, in French). At that ceremony on August 14, 1791, an African slave named Boukman sacrificed a pig, and both Kongo and Creole spirits descended to possess the bodies of the participants, encouraging them and fortifying them for the upcoming revolutionary war. Despite deep ambivalence on the part of intellectuals, Catholics, and the moneyed classes, Vodou has always been linked with militarism and the war of independence and, through it, the pride of national sovereignty.

The Pentecostal Church demands active rejection of such Afro-Creole traditions and regards them as satanic practice. Sermons and literature about Haiti urges missions to "pull down strongholds" and aim efforts at destroying working Vodou temples in various ways. In group rituals of prayer and fasting, the Pentecostals marched through public space performing exorcisms at spots considered sacred in Vodou and recast as satanic for Pentecostals.

One such "crusade" ceremony has had a lasting resonance for Haitian evangelicals in New York. A group of Haitian Pentecostal pastors based near Port-au-Prince launched a serious critique of the Haitian government and indeed of Haitian nationalist mythology, when they marched on August 14, 1997, to the reputed site of the original religious ritual in 1791 when the slaves of St. Domingue vowed to fight for freedom. The pastors intended to exorcise the Vodou spirits who still governed the site and "win" the space "for Jesus." In a complicated view that blames the Catholic Church for blessing the slave market and racializing evil in terms of African's skin, the leaders of the "Bois Caiman for Jesus" crusade blamed slavery for causing Africans to turn to Satan as their divine protector. In invoking African and Creole spirits to possess the religious leaders who had attended, Boukman had made a "pact with the devil" and dedicated Haiti to serve Satan. It was this unholy alliance that had been responsible for Haiti's subsequent 200 years of misery. The idea of the crusade was to undo Boukman's pact with the devil and to halt Haiti's economic and political downward spiral by turning Haiti into a "favored nation" of God. Video crews and reporters captured the spectacle and relayed the news of the exorcism to Port-au-Prince and into the diaspora (McAlister, 2000).

The ritual exorcism was a direct challenge to the politics of national heritage and to the pro-"folklore" politics that had been at work since the Duvalier regime. The Pentecostal ceremony caused an uproar in the capital, and the Haitian government considered it an insult to national pride as it had in 1991 sponsored a bicentennial commemoration of Bwa Kayiman at the National Palace and the Haitian parliament had voted to make Boukman a national hero. By undoing that contract and claiming the birthplace of the Haitian nation for Jesus, however, some Pentecostals claimed they had symbolically "won Haiti for Jesus" and "converted" the entire nation to evangelicalism. When news of the crusade reached into the Haitian diaspora and to the Evangelical public sphere through radio and the internet, Protestant churches in New York celebrated the crusade and prayed for its lasting effect (McAlister, 2000).

Evangelical sermons in New York extended the symbolic action, collectively launching a new national narrative that repositioned Haiti in both time and space. Pastors taught that by undoing the contract with Satan, the Haitian nation could now dramatically enter millennial temporality and its citizens could join other evangelicals in their preparation for the end times. Advancing the notion of a "converted Haiti," evangelicals hoped to chart a new, Christian future. Like the ancient Israelites in exile, Haitians were now part of God's chosen people waiting to reenter Jerusalem. These themes of exile in scripture could be plainly understood by Haitians, as they had been by other African peoples throughout the Americas (Raboteau, 1994). In the new evangelical story of Haiti, it was now time for salvation and for belonging on a global, even cosmic, scale.

Other diasporic services continue and elaborate themes of redeeming Haiti and with it all Haitians. In perhaps the largest gathering of evangelical

Haitians to date, the Association of Evangelical Haitian Clergy organized a "jubilee celebration service" called "Vision 2000" in New York's Nassau Coliseum in January 2000. Thousands attended, and many (male) pastors flew in from Chicago, Boston, Florida, Haiti, and Côte d'Ivoire. Letters of support were read from Haitian Pentecostals in the Bahamas, France, and other parts of Africa, and "one hundred other pastors who wanted to come from Haiti could not get visas," and could not join. The aim of the conveners was to "achieve unity among Haitian Protestants."

The jubilee celebration was a distinct effort to simultaneously solidify transnational ties and address the problematic issue of Haitian national culture and heritage. Using military vocabularies and images from Vodou, the pastors continued to renarrate both the past and future for a new, Haitian American life and reimagine Haitian culture in evangelical terms. Becoming actors in this biblical story makes it possible for Haitians to enter the United States as a legitimate people instead of a denigrated people, a modern people instead of a "traditional" people, and it allows Haitians to forge connections with Evangelical networks in other places, both nationally and internationally (Peel, 1999; McAlister, 2000).

Pentecostal migrants have arrived in the United States, and they find security in the Americanness of Protestantism and the particularly American civil religious narrative of chosenness as "God's New Israel" (Cherry, 1998). The discourses that mediate the break with the past and the new future, Vodou and Protestantism, Haitian tradition and global modernity, also address the problematics of Haitian migration and the construction of a new American—or hyphenated American—identity. Weaving together Haitian, American, and Christian narratives, Haitians create a new form of religious mythmaking that announces and performs their unique religiosity.

Conclusion

For Haitians in the United States, religious ideologies and ritual practices are mediated by religious politics that span both home and host nations. The plural religious landscape of Haiti extends to the Tenth Province and back again to Haiti. Religious politics linking and dividing Catholicism, Vodou, and Protestantism in Haiti are transformed in the United States and vice versa, creating a fluid, plural religious world. The three religious possibilities co-define, mediate, and ultimately reproduce one another.

Each, in turn, articulates in a different dynamic process with American civil society. With few exceptions, Haitians demonstrate a preeminently immanent and pragmatic orientation toward religion. This orientation encompasses their interpretations of affliction and their choices of remedies for spiritual healing. Needless to say, the deep commitment to an instrumental view renders doctrinal boundaries porous. Even the assertive, separatist stance of the Protestants cannot disguise how firmly their congregants remain within this plural system of religious values and explanations of affliction and healing practices.

The pretended conflict between Haitian Protestants and those who "serve the devil" recapitulates African American Protestants' public repudiation of conjure. Analyzing slave religion, Albert Raboteau finds the conflict between "Christianity and conjure more theoretical than actual, . . . not so much antithetical as complementary" (1978: 288). The complementarity of Christianity and conjure made sense "in a world of practical power, [in which] good was power which worked for you, bad was power which turned against you. The primary categories were not good and evil but security and danger. Therefore an unequivocal rejection of conjure was not only unnecessary but foolhardy. To be safe, one kept on the right side of all spiritual power" (287).

In a similar vein, Catholicism, Protestantism, and Vodou ritual options offer a symbolic idiom for agents to control their incorporation in broader, more unequal, fully encompassing systems. Through their narratives of affliction and healing, actors can understand the structuring of their situations and the causes of their struggles. The ritual actions they take reiterate that they are not powerless. They can and do act positively to affect their fates. This instrumental view of religious choice and ritual action is a critical resource for migrants' struggling to succeed across the waters of the United States and Haiti.

The polymorphous religious world of Haitians offers alternative modes of understanding their insertion in a global system of labor migration and capital reproduction. Conceptions of the activities of the "superhuman" lwa reinforce the community's perception of its role as producers of migrants for export and the consumption of wage remittances back home. The spirits intervene in the migrant labor process by "protecting" migrants' capacity to produce "over there." Their primary power over migrants is to thwart their ability to work. Spirits also mediate the reproduction process, through threats to "hold" a recalcitrant or wayward migrant. The belief in their power to punish ensures that the home remains the valorized site for the consumption of migrants' wages, whether through wages remitted to pay for schooling, land, or visas or for rituals honoring the spirits of the kin group whose usual catalyst is affliction. Migrants are frequently the victims of vengeful spirits, which only an expiatory, healing rite performed by their home family, regardless of the migrant's absence, can assuage. Thus spiritual affliction beliefs, ritual discourse, and performance symbolize and reinforce migrants' role as transnational emissaries of their families' social, economic, and ritual interests.

Representations of the "superhuman" *lwa,* who live in far off Ginen and must cross waters to intervene in humans' lives, are, in addition, a mirror for understanding their experience as a mobile people for whom crossing the water (*janbe dlo*) and protracted separation are basic and recurrent historical conditions. The prayers and sacred songs intoned at rituals (and replayed on tapes of performances circulating in diaspora communities) imagine the difficult, long-distance bonds between people and their spirits, in which spirits complain about feeling neglected over in Ginen and threaten to punish those who ignore them. This imagery crystallizes the difficulties of family life that must be conducted across long distances (Richman, 1992a). As an ethnohistorical device, the movement of the spirits from their watery home in Ginen to ritual spaces, whether on Haitian soil or the basement floor of a New York row house, echoes the middle passage and reinforces the conception of Ginen as the moral center. It also reinforces the idea of places in Haiti as mediating points between Ginen and people, whether close to home or in diaspora.

In response to the conditions of transnational migration, these ritual practices have proven flexible and resilient. The huge exodus of young people from rural, coastal villages in the late 1970s and early 1980s did not disrupt service to the *lwa* but, rather, prompted a reconfiguration of the cosmography and the performance space. The sites where Haitian migrants worked were now crisscrossed by mobile, transnational spirits. Rituals taking place on the "inalienable" family land back home were reframed as recorded performances so that they could include and address absent migrants who were expected to hear the tape later. Ceremonies enacted in the home village unfold in a transnational ritual performance space. Those who cannot attend participate vicariously through audiotape or videotape, on which they hear or see themselves being addressed in song and prayer by the worshipers and even spirits possessing the bodies of participants. This complex set of practices—mobile, avenging spirits who send affliction across any national boundary and healing performance at the shrine on the family land back home—reinforces the meaning of the home as the anchor of migrants' transnational lives.

For Haitians in New York, a different migration history and relation to the home provides another set of the symbolic material for ritual performance. The earlier migrants to New York tended to have come from Port-au-Prince. They were urban migrants, some for over several generations. They were not peasants but urban workers. Many had become oriented to "temple Vodou," voluntary congregations under the direction of an *oungan* or *manbo,* rather than rooted in land-owning kin groups. The congregations appropriate the idiom of kinship to substantiate their relations as reconstituted families. Many no longer have rights to family lands and the shrines that sat upon them. Their sacred objects can be ritually reinstalled (through a rite of consecration) in the temple so that their patron spirits can be properly worshipped in the new and different abode.

Urban, temple Vodou practice is obviously adaptable to a larger city abroad—namely, New York. *Oungan* and *manbo,* having returned to Haiti to "take the *ason*" under the guidance of a prominent professional or having migrated with credentials in hand, set up performance spaces in their brownstone apartments. Yet, as Karen Brown (1991) describes, healers like Mama Lola remained tethered to Haiti through the same idiom of spiritual affliction and ritual therapy. They and their reconstituted Vodou families inevitably succumb to the pressure of the spirits' displeasure that they have too long delayed returning home. The only remedy is to return to worship the exacting, demanding spirits where they are most at ease—and easy to please.

Conversion to Protestantism is a strategy migrants have used to resist their roles as emissaries for kin, which are policed and reinforced by obligations to the spirits. By using conversion as a tactic of rebellion, they recapitulate an established Haitian practice (and also question the premise that conversion is motivated by deep, true faith in a loftier religion). Conversion also draws a "magic circle" of protection from spiritual affliction and sorcery—another attraction. Migrants gain defensive immunity from sorcery, a social weapon long used by peasants to limit individual greed and enforce reciprocity. This greed is crystallized in the nefarious Creole imagery of the devil (*dyab*). Conversion gives the Protestant new license to pursue the "devil," to frankly extol Jesus' route to pure capital. Yet this Puritan devil is cloaked in the modest robes of bodily restraint, savings, and abstinence.

Through conversion, migrants are asserting symbolic control over the terms of their relations with the home. Conversion offers them a cogent means of resistance to afflictions "sent" by jealous persons and unhappy *lwa* anchored in Haiti, and, as a result, freedom from the costs of treatment. The imagery, songs, and discourse associated with the *lwa* are symbolic ways of keeping migrants tied to their homes. They are also means of critiquing and containing individualism, which are graphically symbolized in the imagery of *dyab*. As migrants turn away from this ethic, they reorient themselves determinately toward the acquisitive spirit of the American dream.

Furthermore, conversion is itself a positive remedy to certain types of stubborn affliction, a power respected even by professional *oungan, gangan*, and *manbo* who, having failed to cure a patient, acquiesce or even suggest that they see a Protestant healer (and conversion is the prerequisite to the cure). More than one evangelical has attested to us that after conversion, the healing powers of conviction are manifest in improved outlook and health, positive proof of the strength of the Protestant antidote.

While some people convert to send a message of rebellion and "backslide" when the crisis ebbs, others are nonetheless appropriated by Protestant ideology and reoriented toward the Protestant ethic of individualism, saving, and abstinence. This ideology is reproduced in both subtle, metalinguistic ways, including an emphasis on the private relationships between an autonomous I (first person) and a solitary Jesus (in contrast to the crowded, heterogeneous, plural world[s] of the *lwa* and the saints) and rhetoric of progress through a proliferation of military metaphors of armies, fortresses, forces, and strength.

Protestant conversion signifies the culmination of a process of becoming American, the fruition of processes initiated long ago in Haiti that were inevitable religious corollaries of American-led "development." The mutual exploitation of missionaries and prospective pastors valorized the linkages between American imperialism, conversion, and passage to the United States. The remigration of these mission churches to the United States, as they follow the settlement of Haitian migrants in New York, Florida, and elsewhere, is the culmination of these processes linking American "development," missionization, and the structuring of Haitians as a mobile labor force that ultimately turned in the late 20th century toward the United States.

Haitian Protestants, like Haitian Catholics, have the advantage of arriving in the Unites States to join up with an already-existing institution. They need not re-create their religion completely in Florida or New York (Levitt, 2007). Catholic and Protestant churches offer steps to social legitimacy, and those that have set up "ethnic" Haitian services and social support systems can also be important mediators with civil society. Catholic and mainline Protestant churches offer comprehensive assistance, including English-language training, counseling, learning how to open bank accounts, family counseling, and voter registration. Pentecostal and other Haitian evangelical churches provide very few of these organized services, in part because of their lesser resources but also because of their belief that the spiritual support and comfort of the congregation are all the help they need (in order to help themselves). Nonetheless, even these congregations constitute vital informal networks for all sorts of exchange, including sharing food and finding jobs, loans, child care, rides, and the like.

Haitian immigrants' involvement as full members in Catholic, Vodou, and Protestant American congregations can also be used in their struggle to create an American identity that rejects hegemonic notions of race that would otherwise reduce them to two-dimensional racial stereotypes. As for garnering credentials of arrival in American society, Haitian Protestants appear to have the upper hand over the "undisciplined" Catholic Church and the marginalized Vodou societies. Thus while the Catholics evoked equivocal images of politics and practices of the Haitian "other," Protestant missions in Haiti unequivocally pointed to the "progress land." As testimonies by pastors heard in church services attest, the visa constituted the pastor's ultimate religious triumph. In their hard work, bodily restraint, and modest dress, Protestants symbolize their competence in American cultural values of entrepreneurship, temperance, and conservatism. In their public narratives, especially in those broadcast to a wider audience, they reaffirm their claim to being the ideal, modern, American individuals.

Integrated Bibliography

Abe, Frank. 2000. *Conscience and the Constitution* (VHS). Hohokus, NJ: Transit Media.

Abraham, Nabeel. 1977. "Detroit's Yemeni Workers." *MERIP Reports* 53: 3–9. .

_____. 1978. "National and Local Politics: A Study of Political Conflict in the Yemeni Immigrant Community of Detroit, Michigan." Ph. D. dissertation, University of Michigan.

Acuña, Rodolfo. 2006. *Occupied America: A History of Chicanos*. 6th ed. New York: Longman.

Alba, Richard. 1985. *Italian Americans: Into the Twilight of Ethnicity*. Englewood Cliffs, NJ: Prentice Hall.

_____. 1988. "Cohorts and the Dynamics of Ethnic Change." In *Social Structures and Human Lives,* edited by Matilda White Riley, Bettina Huber, and Beth Hess. Newbury Park, CA: Sage.

_____. 1990. *Ethnic Identity: The Transformation of White America*. New Haven: Yale University Press.

_____. 1995. "Assimilation's Quiet Tide." *Public Interest* 119: 1–18.

Alba, Richard, and Victor Nee. 1997. "Rethinking Assimilation Theory for a New Era of Immigration." *International Migration Review* 31: 826–74.

_____. 2003. *Remaking the American Mainstream: Assimilation and Contemporary Immigration*. Cambridge: Harvard University Press.

Alba, Richard, John Logan, and Kyle Crowder. 1997. "White Ethnic Neighborhoods and Spatial Assimilation: The Greater New York Region, 1980–1990." *Social Forces* 75: 883–912.

Alba, Richard, John Logan, Amy Lutz, and Brian Stults. 2002. "Only English by the Third Generation? Mother-Tongue Loss and Preservation among the Grandchildren of Contemporary Immigrants." *Demography* 39: 467–84.

Albanese, Catherine. 1992. "Civil Religion: Millennial Politics and History." In *American Religions and Religion*. 2nd ed. Belmont, CA: Belmont.

_____. 1996. "Religion and American Popular Culture." *Journal of the American Academy of Religion* 44: 733–42.

Allen, James Paul, and Eugene Turner. 1997. *The Ethnic Quilt: Population Diversity in Southern California.* Northridge: Center for Geopolitical Studies, California State University– Northridge.

al-Qazzaz, Ayad. 1975. "Images of the Arabs in American Social Science Textbooks." In *Arabs in America: Myths and Realities,* edited by Baha Abu Laban and Faith Ziadeh. Willmette, IL: Medina University Press.

_____. 1997. "The Arab Lobby: Toward an Arab-American Political Identity." *al-Jadid* 14: 10.

Ammerman, Nancy Tatom. 1987. *Bible Believers: Fundamentalists in the Modern World.* New Brunswick, N.J.: Rutgers University Press.

Arab American Institute. 2002. "Arab American Demographics." At http://www.aaiusa.org/demographics.htm.

Arab-American Institute. n.d. "Demographics." At http://www.aaiusa.org/arab-americans/22/demographics.

Aswad, Barbara. 1984. *Arabic-Speaking Communities in American Cities.* New York: Center for Migration Studies.

Bachin, Robin Faith. 2004. *Building the South Side: Urban Space and Civic Culture in Chicago, 1890–1919.* Chicago: University of Chicago Press.

Baker, Lee. 1998. *From Savage to Negro: Anthropology and the Construction of Race.* Berkeley: University of California Press.

Balderrama, Francisco, and Raymond Rodríguez. 2006. *Decade of Betrayal: Mexican Repatriation in the 1930s.* Albuquerque: University of New Mexico Press.

Banker, Mark. 1993. *Presbyterian Missions and Cultural Interaction in the Far Southwest, 1850–1950.* Urbana: University of Illinois Press.

Barkan, Elliott. 1995. "Race, Religion, and Nationality in American Society: A Model of Ethnicity—From Contact to Assimilation." *Journal of American Ethnic History* 14: 38–101.

Barrett, James, and David Roediger. 1997. "In Between Peoples: Race, Nationality and the 'New Immigrant' Working Class." *Journal of American Ethnic History* 16: 3–44.

Barry, Tom, Beth Wood, and Deb Preusch. 1984. *The Other Side of Paradise: Foreign Control in the Caribbean.* New York: Grove.

Basch, Linda, Nina Glick-Schiller, and Cristina Szanton-Blanc. 1994. *Nations Unbound: Transnational Projects and the Deterritorialized Nation-State.* New York: Gordon Breach.

Bassiouni, M.C. (ed.). 1974. *The Civil Rights of Arab-Americans: "The Special Measures."* Information paper no. 10. Belmont, MA: Association of Arab-American University Graduates.

Beal, Tarcisio. 1994. "Hispanics and the Roman Catholic Church in the United States." In *Hispanics in the Church: Up from the Cellar,* edited by Philip Lampe. San Francisco: Catholic Scholars.

Bean, Frank, Jorge Chapa, Ruth Berg, and Kathryn Edwards. 1994. "Educational and Sociodemographic Incorporation among Hispanic Immigrants to the

United States." In *Immigration and Ethnicity*, edited by Barry Edmonston and Jeffrey Passel. Washington, DC: Urban Institute.

Beechert, Edward. 1985. *Working in Hawai'i: A Labor History.* Honolulu: University of Hawai'i Press.

Bellah, Robert. 1967. "Civil Religion in America." *Daedalus* 96: 1–21.

____. 1975. *The Broken Covenant: American Civil Religion in Time of Trial.* 2nd ed. Chicago: University of Chicago Press.

Bellah, Robert N., Richard Madsen, William M. Sullivan, Ann Swidler, and Steven M. Tipton 1985. *Habits of the Heart: Individualism and Commitment in American Life.* New York: Harper and Row."Ben Hiroshi Tamashiro." 2004. *Honolulu Advertiser and Star-Bulletin* obituaries, January 1–December 31. Joseph F. Smith Library, Brigham Young University, Hawai'i. At http://w2.byuh.edu/library/Obituaries/2004/T.htm (accessed June 22, 2007).

"Ben Hiroshi Toma-Shiro," *Honolulu Advertiser and Star-Bulletin*, March 3, 2004

Berger, Joseph. 2002. "Well, the Ices Are Still Italian." *New York Times* (September 17): B1, B8.

____. 2003. "Ethnic Museums Abounding." *New York Times* (July 4): E2, E27.

Berman, Jerry. 1982. *A Public Policy Report.* Washington, DC: ACLU.

Best, Wallace. 2005. *Passionately Human, No Less Divine: Religion and Culture in Black Chicago, 1915–1952.* Princeton: Princeton University Press.

Billington, Ray Allen. 1938. *The Protestant Crusade, 1800–1860: A Study of the Origins of American Nativism.* New York: Macmillan.

Blau, Peter, and Otis Dudley Duncan. 1967. *The American Occupational Structure.* New York: Wiley.

Borowitz, Eugene. 1973. *The Mask Jews Wear.* New York: Simon and Schuster.

Bose, Christine. 1984. "Household Resources and U.S. Women's Work: Factors Affecting Gainful Employment at the Turn of the Century." *American Sociological Review* 49: 474–90.

Brodkin, Karen. 1998. *How Jews Became White Folks and What That Says about Race in America.* New Brunswick, NJ: Rutgers University Press.

Brodwin, Paul. 2003. "Pentecostalism in Translation: Religion and the Production of Community in the Haitian Diaspora." *American Ethnologist* 30/1: 85–101. At doi:10.1525/ae.2003.30.1.85.

Brown, Karen McCarthy. 1991. *Mama Lola: A Vodou Priestess in New York.* Berkeley: University of California Press.

____. 2003. "Making *Wanga*: Reality Constructions and the Magical Manipulation of Power." In *Transparency and Conspiracy*, edited by H. West and T. Sanders. Durham, NC: Duke University Press.

Bryce-Laporte, Roy. 1979. "The United States' Role in Caribbean Migration: Background to the Problem." In *Caribbean Immigration to the United States*, edited by Roy Bryce-Laporte and Delores Mortimer. Washington, DC: Smithsonian Institution, Research Institute on Immigration and Ethnic Studies.

_____. 1985. *Caribbean Immigrations and Their Implications for the United States.* Washington, DC: Woodrow Wilson International Center for Scholars.

Buchanan, Susan. 1990. "Scattered Seeds: The Meaning of the Migration for Haitians in New York City." Ph.D. dissertation, New York University.

Buddhist Churches of America. 1974. *75 Year History, 1899–1974.* 2 vols. Chicago: Norbart.

Burdick, John. 1993. *Looking for God in Brazil.* Berkeley: University of California Press.

Burkett, Randall. 1978. *Garveyism as a Religious Movement: The Institutionalization of a Black Civil Religion.* Metuchen, NJ: Scarecrow.

Burns, J. A. 1912. *The Growth and Development of the Catholic School System in the United States.* New York: Benziger Brothers.

Busto, Rudy. 2005. *King Tiger: The Religious Vision of Reies López Tijerina.* Albuquerque: University of New Mexico Press.

Camarillo, Albert. 1979. *Chicanos in a Changing Society: From Mexican Pueblos to American Barrios in Santa Barbara and Southern California, 1848–1930.* Cambridge: Harvard University Press.

Caroli, Betty Boyd. 1973. *Italian Repatriation from the United States, 1900–1914.* New York: Center for Migration Studies.

Casanova, Jose. 1994. *Public Religions in the Modern World.* Chicago: University of Chicago Press.

Chaney, Elsa. 1987. *Caribbean Life in New York City: Sociocultural Dimensions.* New York: Center for Migration Studies of New York.

Chang, Thelma. 1991. *I Can Never Forget: Men of the 100th/442nd.* Honolulu: Sigi Productions.

Charles, Carolle. 1990. "Distinct Meanings of Blackness: Haitian Migrants in New York City." *Cimarrón* 2: 129–38.

Chavez, Fray Angelico. 1974. *My Penitente Land: Reflections on Spanish New Mexico.* Albuquerque: University of New Mexico Press.

_____. 1981. *But Time and Chance: The Story of Padre Martinez of Taos, 1793–1867.* Santa Fe, NM: Sun Stone.

Cheng, Lucie, and Philip Yang. 1996. "The 'Model Minority' Deconstructed." In *Ethnic Los Angeles,* edited by Roger Waldinger and Mehdi Bozorgmehr. New York: Russell Sage Foundation.

Cherry, Conrad. 1998. *God's New Israel: Religious Interpretations of American Destiny.* Chapel Hill: University of North Carolina Press.

Cheung, King-Kok. 1993. *Articulate Silences: Hisaye Yamamoto, Maxine Hong Kingston, and Joy Kogawa.* Ithaca, N.Y.: Cornell University Press.

Chidester, David, and Edward Linenthal. 1995. "Introduction." In *American Sacred Space,* edited by David Chidester and Edward Linenthal. Bloomington: Indiana University Press.

Chiswick, Barry. 1991. "Jewish Immigrant Skill and Occupational Attainment at the Turn of the Century." *Explorations in Economic History* 28: 64–86.

Cho, David. 2002. "Evangelicals Help Pace U.S. Growth in Church Attendance: Tally of Muslims Rejected as Low by Islamic Groups." *Washington Post,* September 16. At http://www.washingtonpost.com .

Choy, Bong-youn. 1977. *Koreans in America.* Chicago: Nelson Hall.

"Church: A Faith Is Challenged." 2002. *Los Angeles Times* (September 1): 00.

Cinel, Dino. 1991. *The National Integration of Italian Return Migration, 1870–1929.* Cambridge: Cambridge University Press.

Clark, Peter Yuichi. 2002. "Compassion among Aging Nisei Japanese Americans." In *Revealing the Sacred in Asian and Pacific America,* edited by Jane Naomi Iwamura and Paul Spickard. New York: Routledge.

Clifford, James. 1994. "Diasporas." *Cultural Anthropology* 9(3): 302–38.

Cohen, Arthur. 1971. *The Myth of the Judeo-Christian Tradition.* New York: Schocken.

Cohen, Robin. 1997. *Global Diasporas.* Seattle: University of Washington Press.

Cohen, Steven. 2001. "Reflections and Update on *Jewish Continuity and Change.*" Paper presented at the Association of Jewish Studies meetings, Washington, DC.

Cohen, Steven, and Arnold Eisen. 2000. *The Jew Within: Self, Family and Community in America.* Bloomington: Indiana University Press.

Connor, John. 1977. *Tradition and Change in Three Generations of Japanese Americans.* Chicago: Nelson-Hall.

Conway, Frederick. 1978. "Pentecostalism in the Context of Haitian Religion and Health Practice." Ph.D. dissertation, American University.

Covello, Leonard. 1972. *The Social Background of the Italo-American School Child.* Totowa, NJ: Rowman and Littlefield.

Creef, Elena Tajima. 2004. *Imaging Japanese America: The Visual Construction of Citizenship, Nation, and the Body.* New York: New York University Press.

Crowder, Kyle, and Lucky Tedrow. 2001. "West Indians and the Residential Landscape of New York." In *Islands in the City: West Indian Migration to New York,* edited by Nancy Foner. Berkeley: University of California Press.

Dahbany-Miraglia, Dina. 1988. "American Yemenite Jewish Interethnic Strategies." In *Persistence and Flexibility: Anthropological Perspectives on the American Jewish Experience,* edited by Walter Zenner. Albany: State University of New York Press.

Daniel, Norman. 1993. *Islam and the West: The Making of an Image.* Oxford: One World.

Daniels, Roger. 1962. *The Politics of Prejudice: The Anti-Japanese Movement in California and the Struggle for Japanese Exclusion.* Berkeley: University of California Press.

———. 1995. *Prisoners without Trial.* New York: Hill and Wang.

———. 2002. "Incarceration of the Japanese Americans: A Sixty-Year Perspective." *History Teacher* 35: 297–310.

Daniels, Roger, Sandra C. Taylor, and Harry H. L. Kitano. 1992. *Japanese Americans: From Relocation to Redress.* Seattle: University of Washington Press.

David, Gary. 2000. "Behind the Bulletproof Glass: Iraqi Chaldean Store Ownership in Metropolitan Detroit." In *Arab Detroit: From Margin to Mainstream,* edited by Nabeel Abraham and Andrew Shryock. Detroit: Wayne State University Press.

Davidman, Lynn, and S. Tenenbaum. 1993. "Toward a Feminist Sociology of the American Jews." In *Feminist Perspectives on Jewish Studies,* edited by Lynn Davidman and S. Tenenbaum. New Haven: Yale University Press.

Davis, James, Tom Smith, and Peter Marsden. 2003. *The General Social Survey.* At http://www.icpsr.umich.edu:8080/GSS/homepage.htm.

de la Garza, Rodolfo, Louis Desipio, F. Chris Garcia, and John Garcia. 1992. *Latino Voices: Mexican, Puerto Rican, and Cuban Perspectives on American Politics.* Boulder, CO: Westview.

Del Castillo, Richard, Teresa McKenna, and Yvonne Yarbro-Bejarano. 1991. *Chicano Art: Resistance and Affirmation, 1965–1985.* Tucson: University of Arizona Press.

DeWind, Josh, and David Kinley III. 1988. *Aiding Migration: The Impact of International Development Assistance on Haiti.* Boulder, CO: Westview.

Doi, Joanne. 2002. "Tule Lake Pilgrimage: Dissonant Memories, Sacred Journey." In *Revealing the Sacred in Asian and Pacific America,* edited by Jane Naomi Iwamura and Paul Spickard. New York: Routledge.

―――. 2007. "Bridge to Compassion: Theological Pilgrimage to Tule Lake and Manzanar." Ph.D. dissertation, Graduate Theological Union, Berkeley, Calif.

Dolan, Jay. 1985. *The American Catholic Experience.* New York: Doubleday.

―――. 1987. *The American Catholic Parish: A History from 1850 to the Present,* Vol. 2. New York: Paulist.

―――. 1997. *Mexican Americans and the Catholic Church, 1900–1965.* South Bend, IN: University of Notre Dame Press.

Dolan, Jay, and Allan Figueroa Deck (eds.). 1994. *Hispanic Catholic Culture in the U.S.: Issues and Concerns.* South Bend, IN: University of Notre Dame Press.

Ebaugh, Helen Rose, and Janet Saltzman Chafetz. 2000. *Religion and the New Immigrants: Continuities and Adaptation in Immigrant Congregations.* Walnut Creek, CA: Altamira.

―――. 2002. *Religion across Borders: Transnational Immigrant Networks.* Walnut Creek, CA: Altamira.

Eck, Diana. 2001. *A New Religious America: How a "Christian Country" Has Become the World's Most Religiously Diverse Nation.* New York: HarperCollins.

Eisen, Arnold. 1983. *The Chosen People in America: A Study in Jewish Religious Ideology.* Bloomington: Indiana University Press.

―――. 1998. *Rethinking Modern Judaism: Ritual, Commandment, Community.* Chicago: University of Chicago Press.

Eisenhower, John. 2000. *So Far from God: The U.S. War with Mexico, 1846–1848.* Norman: University of Oklahoma Press.

Elkholy, Abdo. 1966. *The Arab Moslems in the United States: Religion and Assimilation.* New Haven, CT: College and University Press.

Embrey, Sue Kunitomi. 2004. "Speech at the National Park Service Opening of the Manzanar Interpretive Center, 4/24/04." Manzanar Committee Online. At http://www.manzanarcommittee.org/pilgrimages/manz2004/Speech-embrey. html (accessed June 22, 2007).

Embrey, Sue Kunitomi. 2005. "Press Release, 4/19/05." Manzanar Committee Online. At http://www.manzanarcommittee.org/pilgrimages/manz2005/PR-41905. html (accessed June 22, 2007).

Espinosa, Gastón, Virgilio Elizondo, and Jesse Miranda. 2003. *Hispanic Churches in American Public Life: Summary of Findings.* South Bend, Ind.: University of Notre Dame. At http://latinostudies.nd.edu/pubs/pubs/HispChurchesEnglish-WEB.pdf.

Espiritu, Yen Le. 1993. *Asian American Panethnicity.* Philadelphia: Temple University Press.

Fackenheim, Emil. 1970. *God's Presence in History.* New York: New York University Press.

Fessenden, Tracy. 2000. "The Sisters of the Holy Family and the Veil of Race." *Religion and American Culture: A Journal of Interpretation* 10: 187–224.

Findley, Paul. 1989. *They Dare Speak Out: People and Institutions Confront the Israeli Lobby.* Chicago: Lawrence Hill.

Finkelstein, Louis. 1938. *The Pharisees: The Sociological Background of Their Faith.* Philadelphia: Jewish Publication Society of America.

Fischbach, Michael. 1985. "Government Pressure against Arabs in the United States." *Journal of Palestine Studies* 14: 87–100.

Foley, Michael, and Dean Hoge. 2007. *Religion and the New Immigrants: How Faith Communities Form Our Newest Citizens.* New York: Oxford University Press.

Foner, Nancy. 2000. *From Ellis Island to JFK: New York's Two Great Waves of Immigration.* New Haven: Yale University Press.

Foner, Nancy, and Richard Alba. 2008. "Immigrant Religion in the U.S. and Western Europe: Bridge or Barrier to Inclusion?" *International Migration Review* 42: 360–92.

Form, William. 2000. "Italian Protestants: Religion, Ethnicity, and Assimilation." *Journal for the Scientific Study of Religion* 39: 307–20.

Fugita, Stephen, and Marilyn Fernandez. 2002. "Religion and Japanese Americans' Views of Their World War II Incarceration." *Journal of Asian American Studies* 5: 113–37.

Fugita, Stephen, and David O'Brien. 1991. *Japanese American Ethnicity: The Persistence of Community.* Seattle: University of Washington Press.

Fujitana, Takashi. 1997. "National Narratives and Minority Politics: The Japanese American National Museum's War Stories." *Museum Anthropology* 21: 99–112.

Gabaccia, Donna. 1984. *From Sicily to Elizabeth Street: Housing and Social Change among Italian Immigrants, 1880–1930.* Albany: State University of New York Press

Galarza, Ernesto. 1964. *Merchants of Labor: The Mexican Bracero Story.* Santa Barbara, CA: McNalley and Loftin.

Gambino, Richard. 1974. *Blood of My Blood.* New York: Doubleday.

Gamio, Miguel. 1930. *Mexican Immigration to the United States.* New York: Arno.

———. 1931. *The Mexican Immigrant: His Life Story.* Manchester, NH: Ayer.

Gamm, Gerald. 1999. *Urban Exodus: Why the Jews Left Boston and the Catholics Stayed.* Cambridge: Harvard University Press.

Gans, Herbert. 1979. "Symbolic Ethnicity: The Future of Ethnic Groups and Cultures in America." *Ethnic and Racial Studies* 2 (January): 1–20.

———. 1982 [1962]. *The Urban Villagers: Group and Class in the Life of Italian-Americans.* New York: Free Press.

Garvey, Marcus. 1923. "The Negro's Greatest Enemy." *Current History* 18/6 (September 1923).

Gill, Anthony. 1998. *Rendering unto Caesar: The Catholic Church and State in Latin America.* Chicago: University of Chicago Press.

Glaude, Eddie, Jr. 2003. "Babel in the North: Black Migration, Moral Community, and the Ethics of Racial Authenticity." In *A Companion to African American Studies,* edited by Lewis Gordon and Jane Anna Gordon. London: Blackwell.

Glazer, Nathan. 1972. *American Judaism.* Chicago: University of Chicago Press.

———. 1993. "Is Assimilation Dead?" *Annals of the American Academy of Social and Political Sciences* 530: 122–36.

Glick, Nina. 1975. "The Formation of a Haitian Ethnic Group." Ph.D. dissertation, Columbia University.

———. 1989. "Everywhere We Go We Are in Danger: Ti Manno." *American Ethnologist* 17: 329–47.

Glick Schiller, Nina, and Georges Fouron. 2001. *Georges Woke up Laughing.* Durham, NC: Duke University Press.

———. 2002. "'I Am Not a Problem without a Solution': Poverty and Transnational Migration." In *The New Poverty Studies: The Ethnography of Power, Politics, and Impoverished People in the United States,* edited by Judith Goode and Jeff Maskovsky. New York: New York University Press.

"A God-Centered Education." 1937. *Christian Century* (April 28): 542–44.

Goldscheider, Calvin. 1986. *Jewish Continuity and Change : Emerging Patterns in America.* Bloomington: Indiana University Press.

———. 1997a. "Measuring the Quality of American Jewish Life." In *American Jewry: Portrait and Prognosis,* edited by David Gordis and Dorit Gary. New York: Behrman House.

_____. 1997b. "Stratification and the Transformation of American Jews, 1910–1990: Have the Changes Resulted in Assimilation?" *Papers in Jewish Demography, Jewish Population Studies* 27: 259–76.

_____. 2001. "Ethnic Categorization in Censuses: Comparative Observations from Israel, Canada and the United States." In *Categorizing Citizens,* edited by David Kertzer and D. Arel. Cambridge: Cambridge University Press.

Goldscheider, Calvin, and Alan Zuckerman. 1986. *The Transformation of the Jews.* Chicago: University of Chicago Press.

Gomez, Michael. 1998. *Exchanging Our Country Marks: The Transformation of African Identities in the Colonial and Antebellum South.* Chapel Hill: University of North Carolina Press.

Gonzalez, Nancie. 1969. *The Spanish-Americans of New Mexico.* Albuquerque: University of New Mexico Press.

Gordon, Milton. 1964. *Assimilation in American Life.* New York: Oxford University Press.

Gorin, Gerald. 1992. *A Time for Building: The Third Migration, 1880–1920.* Baltimore: Johns Hopkins University Press.

Gosnell, Harold. 1935. *Black Politicians: The Rise of Negro Politics in Chicago.* Chicago: University of Chicago Press.

Granovetter, Mark. 1973. "The Strength of Weak Ties." *American Journal of Sociology* 78: 1360–80.

Grayson, James. 1989. *Korea: A Religious History.* Oxford: Clarendon.

Grebler, Leo, Joan Moore, and Ralph Guzman. 1970. *The Mexican-American People.* New York: Free Press.

Greeley, Andrew, and Peter Rossi. 1966. *The Education of Catholic Americans.* Chicago: Aldine.

Greenberg, Cheryl. 1998. "Pluralism and Its Discontents: The Case of Blacks and Jews." In *Insider/Outsider: American Jews and Multiculturalism,* edited by David Biale, Michael Galchinsky, and Susannah Heschel. Berkeley: University of California Press.

Greenberg, Simon. 1945. "Democracy in Post-Biblical Judaism." *CJ* (June): 1–9.

_____. 1966. "Judaism and the Democratic Ideal." In *Foundations of a Faith,* pp. 13–34. New York: Burning Bush Press.

_____. 1977. *The Ethical in the Jewish and American Heritage.* New York: Jewish Theological Seminary of Americal.

Gregory, James. 2005. *The Southern Diaspora: How the Great Migrations of Black and White Southerners Transformed America.* Chapel Hill: University of North Carolina Press.

Griswald, William. 1975. *The Image of the Middle East in Secondary School Textbooks.* New York: Middle East Studies Association of North America.

Grogger, Jeffrey, and Stephen Trejo. 2002. *Falling behind, or Moving Up? The*

Intergenerational Progress of Mexican Americans. San Francisco: Public Policy Institute of California.

Groot, Amy, and Steven Rosen (eds.). 1983. *The Campaign to Discredit Israel.* Washington, DC: American Israel Public Affairs Committee.

Grossman, James. 1997. "'Social Burden' or 'Amiable Peasantry': Constructing a Place for Black Southerners." In *American Exceptionalism? U.S. Working Class Formation in an International Context,* edited by Rick Halpern and Jonathan Morris. New York: St. Martin's.

Guglielmo, Thomas. 2003. *White on Arrival: Italians, Race, Color and Power in Chicago, 1890–1945.* New York: Oxford University Press.

Haddad, Yvonne Yazbeck, and Adair Lummis. 1987. *Islamic Values in the United States: A Comparative Study.* New York: Oxford University Press.

Hagopian, Elaine. 1975–76. "Minority Rights in a Nation State: The Nixon Administration's Campaign against Arab-Americans." *Journal of Palestine Studies* 5: 97–114.

Hagopian, Elaine, and A. Paden (eds.). 1969. *The Arab-Americans: Studies in Assimilation.* Wilmette, IL: Medina University Press.

Hansen, Arthur. 1995. "Oral History and the Japanese American Evacuation." *Journal of American History* 82: 625–39.

Harding, Vincent. 1969. "The Uses of the African-American Past." In *The Religious Situation 1969,* edited by Donald Cutler. Boston: Beacon.

Hashima, Lawrence. 2007. "Public Memories, Community Discord: The Battle over the 'Japanese American Creed.'" American Studies Association. At http://epsilon3.georgetown.edu/~coventrm/asa2001/pane111/hashima.html (accessed June 22, 2007).

Hatamiya, Leslie. 1993. *Righting a Wrong: Japanese Americans and the Passage of the Civil Liberties Act of 1988.* Stanford: Stanford University Press.

Hatem, Mervat. 2001. "How the Gulf War Changed the AAUG's Discourse on Arab Nationalism and Gender Politics." *Middle East Journal* 55: 277–96.

Hawai'i Hongpa Hongwanji Mission. 1989. *A Grateful Past, A Promising Future: Hongpa Hongwanji Mission of Hawai'i Hundred Year History, 1889–1989.* Honolulu: Hawai'i Hongpa Hongwanji Mission.

Hayashi, Brian Masaru. 1995. *"For the Sake of Our Japanese Brethren": Assimilation, Nationalism, and Protestantism among the Japanese of Los Angeles, 1895–1942.* Stanford: Stanford University Press.

Hayashi, Robert. 2003. "Transfigured Patterns: Contesting Memories at the Manzanar National Historic Site." *Public Historian* 25: 51–71.

Hazen-Hammond, Susan. 1988. *A Short History of Santa Fe.* San Francisco: Lexicos.

Herberg, Will. 1960 [1955]. *Protestant-Catholic-Jew.* New York: Anchor.

Herskovitz, Melville. 1990 [1941]. *Myth of the Negro Past.* Boston: Beacon.

Hertzberg, Arthur. 1964. "America Is Galut." *Jewish Frontier* July: 7–9.

_____. 1966. "Being Jewish in America." In *The Condition of Jewish Belief,* edited by Milton Himmelfarb. New York: Macmillan.

Heschel, Abraham. 1968. *God in Search of Man.* New York: Harper Torchbooks.

Higham, John. 1970. *Strangers in the Land: Patterns of American Nativism, 1860–1925.* New York: Atheneum.

Hirano, David. 1974. "Religious Values among Japanese Americans and Their Relationship to Counseling." D.M. dissertation, School of Theology at Claremont.

Hirschman, Charles. 2004. "The Role of Religion in the Origins and Adaptation of Immigrant Groups in the United States." *International Migration Review* 38: 1206–33.

Hirschman, Charles, and Morrison Wong. 1986. "The Extraordinary Educational Attainment of Asian Americans: A Search for Historical Evidence and Explanations." *Social Forces* 65: 1–27.

Hitti, Philip Khuri. 1924. *The Syrians in America.* New York: George H. Doran.

Hohri, William. 1988. *Repairing America: An Account of the Movement for Japanese-American Redress.* Pullman: Washington State University.

Honda, Ralph. 1941. "Honda Advocates Eightfold Path to YUBA Delegates." *Dobo.*

Hoogland, Eric (ed.). 1987. *Crossing the Waters: Arabic-Speaking Immigrants in the United States before 1940.* Washington, DC: Smithsonian Institution Press.

Horgan, Paul. 2003. *Lamy of Santa Fe.* Middletown, CT: Wesleyan University Press.

Horinouchi, Isao. 1973. "Americanized Buddhism: A Sociological Analysis of a Protestantized Japanese Religion." Ph.D. dissertation, University of California–Davis.

Howe, Irving (ed.). 1977. *Jewish-American Stories.* New York: New American Library.

Howlett, W. J. 1987. *The Life of Bishop Machebeuf.* Weston, MA: Regis College Press.

Hughes, Langston. 1940. *The Big Sea: An Autobiography.* New York: Knopf.

Hunter, Louise. 1971. *Buddhism in Hawai'i : Its Impact on a Yankee Community.* Honolulu: University of Hawai'i Press.

Hurh, Won Moo. 1998. *The Korean Americans.* Westport, CT: Greenwood.

Hurh, Won Moo, and Kwang Chung Kim. 1990. "Religious Participation of Korean Immigrants in the U.S." *Journal for the Scientific Study of Religion* 29: 19–34.

Hussaini, Hatem. 1974. "The Impact of the Arab-Israeli Conflict on Arab Communities in the United States." In *Settler Regimes in Africa and the Arab World: The Illusion of Endurance,* edited by Ibrahim Abu-Lughod and Baha Abu-Laban. Wilmette, IL: Medina University Press International.

Hyun, Peter. 1986. *Man Sei: The Making of a Korean American.* Honolulu: University of Hawai'i Press.

_____. 1991. *In the New World: The Making of a Korean American*. Honolulu: University of Hawai'i Press.

Ichioka, Yuji. 1988. *The Issei: The World of the First Generation Japanese Immigrants, 1885–1924*. New York: Free Press.

Imamura, Jane Michiko. 1998. *Kaikyo: Opening the Dharma*. Honolulu: Buddhist Study Center Press.

Imamura, Yemyo. 1918. *Democracy According to the Buddhist Viewpoint*. Honolulu: Publishing Bureau of Hongwanji Mission.

Ishizuka, Karen. 2006. *Lost and Found: Reclaiming the Japanese American Incarceration*. Urbana: University of Illinois Press.

Iwamura, Jane Naomi. 2003. "Altared States: Exploring the Legacy of Japanese American Butsudan Practice." *Pacific World: Journal of the Institute of Buddhist Studies* 3: 275–91.

Jabara, Abdeen. n.d. "The FBI and the Civil Rights of Arab-Americans." *ADC Issues* 5: 1.

Jackson, Kenneth. 1967. *The Ku Klux Klan in the City, 1915–1930*. New York: Oxford University Press.

Jacobs, Jerry, and M. Greene. 1990. "Race and Ethnicity, Social Class and Schooling in 1910." Paper presented at the annual meeting of the Population Association of America.

Jacobson, Matthew Frye. 1998. *Whiteness of a Different Color: European Immigrants and the Alchemy of Race*. Cambridge: Harvard University Press.

Janvier, Louis Joseph. 1883. *La République d'Haiti et ses visiteurs, 1840–1882*. Port-au-Prince: Fardin.

Japanese American National Museum (JANM). n.d. "Architectural Fact Sheet: Japanese American National Museum Phase II Pavilion." At http://www.janm.org/about/press/p_facts.html (accessed June 22, 2007).

Japanese American National Museum (JANM). n.d. "The Museum's Life History Program." At http://www.janm.org/lifehist/lhp.php/ (accessed June 22, 2007).

Japanese American National Museum (JANM). n.d. "Mission of the Japanese American National Museum." At http://www.janm.org/general/mission.html/ (accessed August 31, 2002).

Jarrar, Samir Ahmad. 1976. "Images of the Arabs in United States Secondary School Textbooks." Ph.D. dissertation, Florida State University.

Jeung, Russell. 2000. *Emerging Asian American Pan-ethnic Congregations: The Religious Construction of Symbolic Racial Identity*. Ann Arbor: University Microfilms.

_____. 2004. *Faithful Generations: Race and Asian American Churches*. New Brunswick, NJ: Rutgers University Press.

"The Jewish Problem." 1936. *Christian Century* (April 29): 625.

"Jewry and Democracy." 1937. *Christian Century* (June 9): 734–35.

Johannsen, Robert. 1988. *To the Halls of the Montezumas: The Mexican War in the American Imagination*. New York: Oxford University Press.

Jones, Arthur. 2000. "Pierre Toussaint, A Slave, Society Hairdresser, Philanthropist, May Become Nation's First Black Saint." *National Catholic Reporter* (August 25).

Juliani, Richard. 1998. *Building Little Italy: Philadelphia's Italians before Mass Migration.* University Park: Pennsylvania State University Press.

Jung, Leo. 1942. *Crumbs and Character: Sermons, Addresses, and Essays.* New York: Night and Day Press.

Kallen, Horace. 1970 [1924]. *Culture and Democracy in the United States.* New York: Arno.

Kaplan, Mordecai. 1934. *Judaism as a Civilization.* New York: Macmillan.

_____. 1948. *The Future of the American Jew.* New York: Macmillan.

Karim, Karim. 2000. *Islamic Peril: Media and Global Violence.* Montreal: Black Rose.

Kashima, Tetsuden. 1977. *Buddhism in America: The Social Organization of an Ethnic Religious Institution.* Westport, CT: Greenwood.

Katznelson, Ira. 2005. *When Affirmative Action Was White: An Untold History of Racial Inequality in Twentieth-Century America.* New York: Norton.

Kazal, Russell. 1995. "Revisiting Assimilation: The Rise, Fall, and Reappraisal of a Concept in American Ethnic History." *American Historical Review* 100: 437–72.

Kennedy, Ruby Jo Reeves. 1944. "Single or Triple Melting Pot? Intermarriage Trends in New Haven, 1870–1940." *American Journal of Sociology* 49: 331–39.

_____. 1952. "Single or Triple Melting Pot? Intermarriage in New Haven, 1870–1950." *American Journal of Sociology* 58: 56–59.

Kessner, Thomas. 1977. *The Golden Door: Italian and Jewish Immigrant Mobility in New York City, 1880–1915.* New York: Oxford University Press.

Kibria, Nazli. 2002. *Becoming Asian American: Second Generation Chinese and Korean American Identities.* Baltimore: Johns Hopkins University Press.

Kiernan, V. G. 1972. *The Lords of Human Kind: European Attitudes to the Outside World in the Imperial Age.* London: Pelican.

Kikuchi, Shigeo, 1991. *Memoirs of a Buddhist Woman Missionary in Hawai'i.* Honolulu: Buddhist Study Center Press.

Kikumura-Yano, Akemi, Lane Ryo Hirabayashi, and James A. Hirabayashi (eds.). 2005. *Common Ground: The Japanese American National Museum and the Cultures of Collaboration.* Boulder: University of Colorado Press.

Kim, Ai Ra. 1996 *Women Struggling for a New Life: The Role of Religion in the Passage from Korea to America.* Albany: State University of New York Press.

Kim, Bernice. 1937. "The Koreans in Hawaii." M.A. thesis, University of Hawai'i at Mānoa.

Kim, Hyung-Chan. 1977. *The Korean Diaspora: Historical and Sociological Studies of Korean Immigration and Assimilation to North America.* Santa Barbara, CA: ABC-Clio.

Kim, Jung Ha. 1997. *Bridge-Makers and Cross–Bearers: Korean American Women and the Church.* Atlanta: Scholars.

_____. 2002. "Cartography of Korean American Protestant Faith Communities in the United States." In *Religions in Asian America: Building Faith Communities,* edited by Pyong Gap Min and Jung Ha Kim. Walnut Creek, CA: Altamira.

Kim, Warren. 1971. *Koreans in America.* Seoul: Po Chin.

Kimura, Gibun. 1976. *Why Pursue the Buddha.* Los Angeles: Nembutsu.

Kondo, Dorinne. 1990. *Crafting Selves: Power, Gender, and Discourses of Identity in a Japanese Workplace.* Chicago: University of Chicago Press.

Kramer, Martin. 1993. "Islam vs. Democracy." *Commentary* (January): 35–42.

Kurashige, Lon. 2002. *Japanese American Celebration and Conflict: A History of Ethnic Identity and Festival in Los Angeles, 1934–1990.* Berkeley: University of California Press.

Kurien, Prema. 1998. "Becoming American by Becoming Hindu: Indian Americans Take Their Place at the Multicultural Table." In *Gatherings in Diaspora: Religious Communities and the New Immigration,* edited by R. Stephen Warner and Judith Wittner. Philadelphia: Temple University Press.

Kuznets, Simon S. 1960. "Economic Structure and Life of the Jews." In *The Jews: Their History, Culture and Religion,* edited by L. Finkelstein, Vol. 2, pp. 1597–1666. New York: Harper.

Kwon, Ho-Youn, Kwang Chung Kim, and Stephen Warner (eds.). 2001. *Korean Americans and Their Religions: Pilgrims and Missionaries from a Different Shore.* University Park: Pennsylvania State University Press.

Kwon, Victoria Hyonchu. 1997. *Entrepreneurship and Religion: Korean Immigrants in Houston.* New York: Garland.

Laguerre, Michel. 1998. *Diasporic Citizenship, American Odyssey: Haitians in New York City.* New York: St. Martin's.

Laremont, Ricardo René. 2001. "Jewish and Japanese American Reparations: Political Lessons for the Africana Community." *Journal of Asian American Studies* 4: 235–50.

Lee, Hannah Farnham Sawyer. 1854. *Memoir of Pierre Toussaint, Born a Slave in St. Domingo.* Boston: Crosby, Nichols.

Lee, Robert. 2001. *Orientals: Asian Americans in Popular Culture.* Philadelphia: Temple University Press.

Lee, Sharon, and Marilyn Fernandez. 1998. "Patterns in Asian American Racial/Ethnic Intermarriage." *Sociological Perspectives* 216: 323–42.

Lee-Sung, Audrey. 2005. "Community Building through Fund-raising." In *Common Ground: The Japanese American National Museum and the Cultures of Collaboration,* edited by Akemi Kikumura-Yano, Lane Ryo Hirabayashi, and James A. Hirabayashi. Boulder: University of Colorado Press.

Lemann, Nicholas. 1992. *The Promised Land: The Great Black Migration and How It Changed America.* New York: Vintage.

Leonard, Karen Isaksen. 2003. *Muslims in the United States: The State of Research.* New York: Russell Sage Foundation.

Levine, Gene, and Colbert Rhodes. 1981. *The Japanese American Community.* New York: Praeger.

Levitt, Peggy. 2002. "Two Nations under God? Latino Religious Life in the United States." In *Latinos: Remaking America,* edited by Marcelo Suarez-Orozco and Mariela Paez. Berkeley: University of California Press.

———. 2007. *God Needs No Passport.* New York: New Press.

Lieberson, Stanley. 1963. *Ethnic Patterns in American Cities.* New York: Free Press.

———. 1980. *A Piece of the Pie: Black and White Immigrants since 1880.* Berkeley: University of California Press.

Lieberson, Stanley, and Mary Waters. 1988. *From Many Strands: Ethnic and Racial Groups in Contemporary America.* New York: Russell Sage Foundation.

Lin, Ann Chih, and Amaney Jamal. 1998. "Ties of Memory and Experience: Arab Immigrant Political Socialization and Activity." Paper presented at the MESA Annual Meeting, Chicago. Also presented at the APSA Annual Meeting, Boston, Mass.

Lin, Ann Chih, Alana Hackshaw, and Amaney Jamal. 2001. "When Does Discrimination Count as Discrimination? Images of Arab Immigrants to Detroit." Paper presented at the Annual Meeting of the American Political Science Association, San Francisco.

Logan, John. 2001. "Something Old, Something New." Paper presented at the annual meeting of the American Sociological Association.

Lopez, David. 1996. "Language: Diversity and Assimilation." In *Ethnic Los Angeles,* edited by Roger Waldinger and Mehdi Bozorgmehr. New York: Russell Sage Foundation.

———. 2002. "Bilinguisme et changement ethnique en Californie." In *La Politique de Babel: Du monolinguisme d'Etat au plurilinguisme des peuples,* edited by Denis Lacorne and Tony Judt. Paris: Editions Karthala.

Lopez, David, and Ricardo Stanton-Salazar. 2001. "Mexican Americans: A Second Generation at Risk." In *Ethnicities: Children of Immigrants in America,* edited by Rubén Rumbaut and Alejandro Portes. Berkeley: University of California Press.

Loyola Marymount University. n.d. "MAAA." At http://www.lmu.edu/Page38470.aspx.

Lowe, Lisa. 1996. *Immigrant Acts: On Asian American Cultural Politics.* Durham, NC: Duke University Press.

Luconi, Stefano. 2001. *From Paesani to White Ethnics: The Italian Experience in Philadelphia.* Albany: State University of New York Press.

Lundahl, Mats. 1979. *Peasants and Poverty: A Study of Haiti.* London: Croon Helm.

Magagnini, Stephen. 2001. "A Nation's Apology: Formal Gesture Erases a Half Century of Shame." *Sacramento Bee* (October 8).

Maki, Mitchell, Harry Kitano, and S. Megan Berthold. 1999. *Achieving the Impossible Dream: How Japanese Americans Obtained Redress*. Urbana: University of Illinois Press.

Malek, Abbas. 1996. *Newsmedia and Foreign Relations: A Multi-faceted Perspective*. Norwood, NJ: Ablex.

Manzanar Committee. n.d. "Manzanar History." Manzanar Committee Online. At http://www.manzanarcommittee.org/manzhistory.html (accessed June 22, 2007).

Marks, Carole. 1989. *Farewell—We're Good and Gone: The Great Black Migration*. Bloomington: Indiana University Press.

Marshall-Fratani, Ruth. 1998. "Mediating the Global and Local in Nigerian Pentecostalism." *Journal of Religion in Africa* 28.

Martinez, Richard. 2005. *PADRES: The National Chicano Priest Movement*. Austin: University of Texas Press.

Massey, Douglas, and Katherine Bartley. 2002. "The Creation of Ascriptive Effects in the U.S. Labor Market." Paper presented at the American Sociological Association meeting.

Massey, Douglas, Rafael Alarcon, Jorge Durand, and Humberto Gonzalez. 1987. *Return to Aztlan: The Social Process of International Migration from Western Mexico*. Berkeley: University of California Press.

Massey, Douglas, Jorge Durand, and Nolan Malone. 2003. *Beyond Smoke and Mirrors: Mexican Immigration in an Era of Economic Integration*. New York: Russell Sage Foundation.

Matsuura, Shinobu. 1986. *Higan: Compassionate Vow*. Berkeley: Privately Published.

McAlister, Elizabeth. 1992–93. "Sacred Stories from the Haitian Diaspora: A Collective Biography of Seven Vodou Priestesses in New York City." *Journal of Caribbean Studies* 9: 10–27.

_____. 1995. "A Sorcerer's Bottle: The Art of Magic in Haiti." In *Sacred Arts of Haitian Vodou*, edited by Donald Cosentino. Los Angeles: UCLA Fowler Museum of Cultural History.

_____. 1998. "Vodou and Catholicism in the Age of Transnationalism: The Madonna of 115th Street Revisited." In *Gatherings in Diaspora: Religious Communities and the New Immigration*, edited by R. Stephen Warner and Judith Wittner. Philadelphia: Temple University Press.

_____. 1999. "Cellulose Spirits and White Racism: White Fear and Black Gods in Film." Paper presented at the conference on the Globalization of Yoruba Religious Culture, International Florida University, Miami.

_____. 2000. "African Ginen and American Zion: United States Diffusions and the Rise of Pentecostalism in the Haitian Context." Paper presented at the Pew

Program in Religion and American History Conference at Yale University, New Haven.

———. 2002. *Rara! Vodou: Power and Performance in Haiti and Its Diaspora.* Berkeley: University of California Press.

———. Forthcoming. "Haitian Transnational Religioscapes in New York City, Immigrant Incorporation and American Civil Religion." In *Religion and Immigrant Incorporation in New York,* edited by Jose Casanova and Aristide Zolberg.

McGloin, John Bernard. 1966. *California's First Archbishop.* New York: Herder and Herder.

McGreevy, John. 1996. *Parish Boundaries: The Catholic Encounter with Race in the Twentieth-Century Urban North.* Chicago: University of Chicago Press.

McLellan, Jeffrey. 2000. "Rise, Fall and Reasons Why: U.S. Catholic Elementary Education, 1940–1995." In *Catholic Schools at the Crossroads,* edited by James Youniss and John Convey. New York: Teachers College Press.

McWilliams, Carey. 1968 [1948]. *North from Mexico: The Spanish-Speaking People of the United States.* New York: Greenwood.

Meir, Matt, and Feliciano Ribera. 1993. *Mexican Americans/American Mexicans: From Conquistadors to Chicanos.* New York: HarperCollins.

Métraux, Alfred. 1953. "Vodou et Protestantisme." *Revue de L'histoire des Religions* 144: 198–216.

———. 1972 [1959]. *Voodoo in Haiti.* New York: Schocken.

Meyer, B. 1998. "'Make a Complete Break with the Past.' Memory and Post-Colonial Modernity in Ghanaian Pentecostal Discourse." *Journal of Religion in Africa* 28.

Miller, Robert. 1989. *Shamrock and Sword: The Saint Patrick's Battalion in the U.S.-Mexican War.* Norman: University Oklahoma Press.

Min, Pyong Gap, and Jung Ha Kim. 2002. *Building Faith Communities: Religions in Asian America.* Walnut Creek, CA: Altamira.

Min, Pyong Gap, and Dae Young Kim. 2005. "Intergenerational Transmission of Religion and Culture: Korean Protestants in the US." *Sociology of Religion* 66: 263–82.

Mintz, Sidney. 1960. *Worker in the Cane.* New Haven: Yale University Press.

———. 1971. "The Caribbean as a Socio-Cultural Area." In *Peoples and Cultures of the Caribbean,* edited by Michael Horowitz. Garden City, NY: Natural History Press.

———. 1973. "A Note on the Definition of Peasantries." *Journal of Peasant Studies* 1: 91–106.

———. 1974. "The Rural Proletariat and the Problem of Rural Proletarian Consciousness." *Journal of Peasant Studies* 1: 291–325.

Mittelbach, Frank, and Joan Moore. 1968. "Ethnic Endogamy: The Case of Mexican Americans." *American Journal of Sociology* 74: 50–62.

Mittelberg, David, and Mary Waters. 1992. "The Process of Ethnogenesis among Haitian and Israeli Immigrants in the United States." *Ethnic and Racial Studies* 15: 412–35.

Moffat, Susan. 1993. "Museum to Link Japanese, U.S. Cultures Architecture." *Los Angeles Times* (February 16): B1.

Mokarzel, Salloum. 1928. "Can We Retain Our Heritage: A Call to Form a Federation of Syrian Societies." *Syrian World* (November): 36–40.

Monroy, Douglas. 1993. *Thrown among Strangers: The Making of Mexican Culture in Frontier California*. Berkeley: University of California Press.

_____. 1999. *Rebirth: Mexican Los Angeles from the Great Migration to the Great Depression*. Berkeley: University of California Press.

Montero, Darrel. 1975. "The Japanese American Community: Generational Changes in Ethnic Affiliation." Ph.D. dissertation, University of California–Los Angeles.

_____. 1980. *Japanese Americans: Changing Patterns of Ethnic Affiliation over Three Generations*. Boulder, CO: Westview.

_____. 1981. "The Japanese American: Changing Patterns of Assimilation over Three Generations." *American Sociological Review* 46: 829–39.

Moore, Kathleen. 1995. *Al-Mughtaribun: American Law and the Transformation of Muslim Life in the United States*. Albany: State University of New York Press.

Morawska, Ewa. 1994. "In Defense of the Assimilation Model." *Journal of American Ethnic History* 13: 76–87.

Morgenstern, Julian. 1943. *Nation, People, Religion: What Are We?* Cincinnati: Union of American Hebrew Congregations.

_____. 1945. *Unity in American Judaism: How and When?* Cincinnati: Union of American Hebrew Congregations.

Morikawa, Hazel. 1990. *Footprints: One Man's Pilgrimage—A Biography of Jitsuo Morikawa*. Berkeley: Jennings Associates.

Muller, Eric. 2001. *Free to Die for Their Country: The Story of the Japanese American Draft Resisters in World War II*. Chicago: University of Chicago Press.

Murguia, Edward, and Edward Telles. 1996. "Phenotype and Schooling among Mexican Americans." *Sociology of Education* 69: 276–89.

Murphy, Joseph. 1988. *Santeria: An African Religion in America*. Boston: Beacon.

Naber, Nadine. 2002. "So Our History Doesn't Become Your Future: The Local and Global Politics of Coalition Building Post September 11th." *Journal for Asian American Studies* 5: 226–27.

Nagano, Paul, and William Malcomson (eds.). 2000. *Jitsuo Morikawa: A Prophet for the 21st Century*. Richmond, CA: Council for Pacific Asian Theology.

Nagata, Donna. 1993. *Legacy of Injustice: Exploring the Cross-Generational Impact of the Japanese American Internment*. New York: Plenum.

Nakamura, Tadashi H. Director. 2006. *Pilgrimage*. Digital video. Los Angeles: Center for Ethno Communications, UCLA Asian American Studies Center.

National Asian American Telecommunications Association (NAATA). n.d. "Postwar and Impact Today: Exploring the Japanese American Internment through the Internet and Film." At http://www.jainternment.org/postwar/ongoing.html (accessed June 22, 2007).

National Catholic Educational Association. n.d. "Parental Choice in Education: A Statement by the National Catholic Educational Association (NCEA)." At http://www.ncea.org/about/NCEAPolicyStatements.asp.

National Center for the Preservation of Democracy. n.d. "Fighting for Democracy Exhibition." At http://www.ncdemocracy.org/node/1097 (accessed June 22, 2007).

National Center for the Preservation of Democracy. n.d. "Vision and Mission." At http://www.ncdemocracy.org/node/1126 (accessed June 22, 2007).

Neff, Alixa. 1985. *Becoming American: The Early Arab Immigrant Experience.* Carbondale: Southern Illinois University Press.

Nelli, Humbert. 1983. *From Immigrants to Ethnics: The Italian Americans.* New York: Oxford University Press.

Neusner, Jacob. 1979. "The Tasks of Theology in Judaism: A Humanistic Program." *Journal of Religion* 59(1): 71–82.

Ngai, Mae. 2004. *Impossible Subjects: Illegal Aliens and the Making of Modern America.* Princeton: Princeton University Press.

Nichols, David. 1970. "Politics and Religion in Haiti." *Canadian Journal of Political Science* 3: 400–414.

_____. 1979. *From Dessalines to Duvalier: Race, Colour, and National Independence in Haiti.* Cambridge: Cambridge University Press.

Nishime, Leilani. 2004/5. "Communities on Display: Museums and the Creation of the (Asian) American Citizen." *Amerasia Journal* 30: 41–60.

Ogura, Kosei. 1932. "A Sociological Study of the Buddhist Churches in North America, with a Case Study of Gardena, California Congregation. M.A. thesis, University of Southern California.

Okihiro, Gary. 1984. "Religion and Resistance in America's Concentration Camps." *Phylon* 45: 220–33.

_____. 1991. *Cane Fires: The Anti-Japanese Movement in Hawai'i, 1865–1945.* Philadelphia: Temple University Press.

Omi, Michael, and Howard Winant. 1994. *Racial Formation in the United States: From the 1960s to the 1990s.* 2nd ed. New York: Routledge.

O'Neill, Carolyn. n.d. "L.A. Museum Shares Japanese-American Struggles, Triumphs." CNN.com. At http://www.cnn.com/2000/TRAVEL/DESTINATIONS/06/30/japanese.museum/ (accessed June 22, 2007).

Onishi, Katsumi. 1937. "The Second Generation Japanese and the Hongwanji." *Social Process in Hawai'i* 3: 43–48.

Orfalea, Gregory. 1989. "Sifting the Ashes: Arab-American Activism during the 1982 Invasion of Lebanon." *Arab Studies Quarterly* 11: 207–26.

Orsi, Robert. 1985. *The Madonna of 115th Street: Faith and Community in Italian Harlem.* New Haven: Yale University Press.

_____. 1992. "The Religious Boundaries of an Inbetween People: Street Feste and the Problem of the Dark-Skinned Other in Italian Harlem, 1920–1990." *American Quarterly* 44: 313–41.

_____. 2004. *Between Heaven and Earth: The Religious Worlds People Make and the Scholars Who Study Them.* Princeton: Princeton University Press.

Ortiz, Vilma. 1996. "The Mexican-Origin Population: Permanent Working Class or Emerging Middle Class?" In *Ethnic Los Angeles,* edited by Roger Waldinger and Mehdi Bozorgmehr. New York: Russell Sage Foundation.

Park, Kyeyoung. 1997. *The Korean American Dream.* Ithaca, NY: Cornell University Press.

Park, Robert E. 1950. *Race and Culture.* Glencoe, IL: Free Press.

Park, Soyoung. 2001. "The Intersection of Religion, Race, Gender, and Ethnicity in the Identity Formation of Korean American Evangelical Women." In *Korean Americans and Their Religions: Pilgrims and Missionaries from a Different Shore,* edited by Ho-Youn Kwon, Chung Kim Kwang, and R. Stephen Warner. University Park: Pennsylvania State University Press.

Patterson, Wayne. 2000. *The Ilse: First-Generation Korean Immigrants in Hawai'i, 1903–1973.* Honolulu: University of Hawai'i Press.

Peel, J. D. Y. 1999. "Looking Back: Christianity in the Trajectory of Yoruba History over the Past 150 Years." Paper presented at the conference on the Globalization of Yoruba Religious Culture, International Florida University, Miami.

Perlmann, Joel. 1988. *Ethnic Differences: Schooling and Social Structure among the Irish, Italians, Jews and Blacks in an American City, 1880–1935.* Cambridge: Cambridge University Press.

_____. 2005. *Italians Then, Mexicans Now: Immigrant Origins and Second-Generation Progress, 1890 to 2000.* New York: Russell Sage Foundation.

Perlmann, Joel, and Roger Waldinger. 1997. "Second Generation Decline? Children of Immigrants, Past and Present—A Reconsideration." *International Migration Review* 31: 893–922.

Perry, Glenn. 1975. "Treatment of the Middle East in American High School Textbooks." *Journal of Palestine Studies* 4: 46–58.

Petersen, William. 1966. "Success Story Japanese-American Style." *New York Times Magazine* (January 6): 180.

_____. 1977. *Japanese Americans: Oppression and Success.* New York: Random House.

Pew Forum on Religion and Public Life. n.d. "God Bless America: Reflections on Civil Religion after September 11, 2/06/02." At http://pewforum.org/events/index.php?EventID=R22.

Pew Hispanic Center. 2007. *Changing Faiths: Latinos and the Transformation of American Religion.* At http://pewhispanic.org/reports/report.php?ReportID=75.

Pierce, Lori Anne. 2000. "Constructing American Buddhisms: Discourses of Race and Religion in Territorial Hawaiʻi." Ph.D. dissertation, University of Hawaiʻi at Mānoa.

Pierre-Louis Jr., Francois. 2006. *Haitians in New York City: Transnationalism and Hometown Associations.* Gainesville: University Press of Florida.

Pipes, Daniel. 1990. "The Muslims Are Coming! The Muslims Are Coming!" *National Review* (November 19): 28–31.

Plate, S. Brent (ed.). 2002. *Religion, Art, and Visual Culture.* New York: Palgrave.

Plummer, Brenda Gayle. 1992. *Haiti and the United States: The Psychological Moment.* Athens: University of Georgia Press.

"Pluralism: National Menace." 1951. *Christian Century* (June 13): 701–2.

Portes, Alejandro, and Rubén Rumbaut. 2001. *Legacies: the Story of the Immigrant Second Generation.* Berkeley: University of California Press.

_____. 2006. *Immigrant America.* 3rd ed. Berkeley: University of California Press.

Portes, Alejandro, and Alex Stepick. 1993. *City on the Edge: The Social Transformation of Miami.* Berkeley: University of California Press.

Pressoir, Catts. 1942. "L'Etat actuel des missions protestantes en Haïti." Paper presented at L'Eglise St. Paul, December 13.

Price-Mars, Jean. 1928. *Ainsi parla l'oncle: Essais d'ethnographie.* Port-au-Prince: Imprimeur de Compiègne.

Pye, Michael. 1994. "Religion: Shape and Shadow." *Numen* 41: 51–75.

Qian, Zhenchao. 1997. "Breaking the Racial Barriers: Variations in Interracial Marriages between 1980 and 1990." *Demography* 34: 263–76.

Raboteau, Albert J. 1978. *Slave Religion: The Invisible Institution in the Antebellum South.* New York: Oxford University Press.

_____. 1994. "African Americans, Exodus, and the American Israel." In *African American Christianity: Essays in History,* edited by Paul Johnson. Berkeley: University of California Press.

_____. 1995. *A Fire in the Bones: Reflections on African-American Religious History.* Boston: Beacon.

Redmond, J. B. 1935. Interview Typescript, Folder 1, Box 133, Section IV (Others' Work). Ernest Burgess Papers, Regenstein Library, University of Chicago.

Richman, Karen. 1990. "Guarantying Migrants in the Core: Commissions of Gods, Descent Groups, and Ritual Leaders in a Transnational Haitian Community." *Cimarrón: New Perspectives on the Caribbean* 2: 114–28.

_____. 1992a "'A *Lavalas* at Home/A *Lavalas* for Home': Inflections of Transnationalism in the Discourse of Haitian President Aristide." In *Towards a Transnational Perspective on Migration,* edited by Nina Glick-Schiller, Linda Basch, and Cristina Szanton-Blanc. New York: New York Academy of Sciences.

_____. 1992b. "'They Will Remember Me in the House': The Pwen of Haitian Transnational Migration." Ph.D. dissertation, University of Virginia.

_____. 2005a. *Migration and Vodou.* Gainesville: University Press of Florida.

_____. 2005b. "The Protestant Ethic and the Dis-spirit of Vodou." In *Immigrant Faiths: Transforming Religious Life in America*, edited by Karen Leonard with Alex Stepick, Manuel A Vasquez, and Jennifer Holdaway, pp. 165–87. Lanham, Md.: AltaMira Press.

_____. 2005c. "A More Powerful Sorcerer: Conversion and Capitalism in the Haitian spora." Paper presented to the Chicago Area Group for the Study of Religious Communities, Loyola University.

Richman, Karen, and William Balan-Gaubert. 2000. "A Democracy of Words." *Journal of the Haitian Studies Association* 7/1: 90–103.

Roediger, David. 1991. *The Wages of Whiteness: Race and the Making of the American Working Class*. London: Verso.

_____. 2005. *Working toward Whiteness: How America's Immigrants Became White; The Strange Journey from Ellis Island to the Suburbs*. New York: Basic Books.

Romain, Charles-Poisset. 1986. *Le Protestantisme dans la Société Haïtienne*. Port-au-Prince: Deschamps.Roman Catholic Archbishop of Los Angeles. n.d. "Our Heritage. At http://www.archdiocese.la/about/heritage/index.html.

Roof, Wade Clark. 1993. *Generation of Seekers: The Spiritual Journeys of the Baby Boom Generation*. San Francisco: HarperSanFrancisco.

_____. 1999. *Spiritual Marketplace: Baby Boomers and the Remaking of American Religion*. Princeton: Princeton University Press.

Rosales, Francisco (ed.). 2000. *Testimonio: A Documentary History of the Mexican-American Struggle for Civil Rights*. Houston: Arte Publico.

Roth, Philip. 1963. "The Jewish Intellectual and Jewish Identity." *Congress Bi-Weekly* (September 16).

_____. 1994. *Goodbye, Columbus: And Five Short Stories*. New York: Vintage.

Rouse, Roger. 1991. "Mexican Migration and the Social Space of Postmodernism." *Diaspora* 1: 8–23.

Russo, Nicholas John. 1969. "Three Generations of Italians in New York City: Their Religious Acculturation." *International Migration Review* 3: 3–17.

Said, Edward. 1997. *Covering Islam: How the Media and the Experts Determine How We See the Rest of the World*. New York: Vantage.

Sakamoto, Arthur, J. Liu, and J. M. Tzeng. 1998. "The Declining Significance of Race among Chinese and Japanese American Men." *Research in Social Stratification and Mobility* 16: 225–46.

Salvatore, Nick. 2001. Paper presented at the Shelby Cullom Davis Seminar, October, Princeton, NJ.

_____. 2005. *Singing in a Strange Land: C. L. Franklin, the Black Church, and the Transformation of America*. New York: Little, Brown.

Samhan, Helen Hatab. 1987. "Politics and Exclusion: The Arab American Experience." *Journal of Palestine Studies* 16: 11–28.

Sánchez, George. 1993. *Becoming Mexican American: Ethnicity, Culture and Identity in Chicano Los Angeles, 1900–1945*. New York: Oxford University Press.

Sandoval, Moises. 1990. *On the Move: A History of the Hispanic Church in the United States.* Maryknoll, NY: Orbis.

_____. 1994. "The Organization of a Hispanic Church." In *Hispanic Catholic Culture in the U.S.: Issues and Concerns,* edited by Jay Dolan and Allan Figueroa Deck. Notre Dame, IN: University of Notre Dame Press.

Sassen-Koob, Saskia. 1982. "Recomposition and Peripherialization at the Core." *Contemporary Marxism* 5: 88–100.

Schmitt, Robert. 1973. "Religious Statistics of Hawai'i, 1825–1972." *Hawaiian Journal of History* 7: 41–47.

Schnall, Nina. 1998. "'Agimal': Syncretism and Disavowal in Haitian Conversions to Evangelical Christianity." Paper presented at the annual meeting of the American Anthropological Association.

Schopmeyer, Kim. 2000. "A Demographic Portrait of Arab Detroit." In *Arab Detroit: From Margin to Mainstream,* edited by Nabeel Abraham and Andrew Shryock. Detroit: Wayne State University Press.

Sciorra, Joseph. 1999. "'We Go Where the Italians Live': Religioius Processions as Ethnic and Territorial Markers in a Multi-Ethnic Brooklyn Neighborhood." In *The Gods of the City: Religion and the Contemporary American Urban Landscape,* ed. Robert A. Orsi. Bloomington: Indiana University Press.

Scott, David. 2004. "Modernity That Predated the Modern: Sidney Mintz's Caribbean." *History Workshop Journal* 58: 191–210.

Scott, Emmett. 1919. "More Letters of Negro Migrants of 1916–1918." *Journal of Negro History* 4: 290–340.

Scult, Mel (ed.). 2001. *Communings of the Spirit: The Journals of Mordecai M. Kaplan.* Vol. I: *1912–1934.* Detroit: Wayne State University Press.

Seabrook, W. B. 1989 [1929]. *The Magic Island.* New York: Paragon House.

Segal, Aaron. 1987. "The Caribbean Exodus in a Global Context: Comparative Migration Experiences." In *The Caribbean Exodus,* edited by Barry Levine. New York: Praeger.

Sephardic Archives. 1986. *The Spirit of Aleppo Syrian Jewish Immigrant Life in New York, 1890–1939.* New York: Sephardic Archives.

Sernett, Milton C. 1997. *Bound for the Promised Land: African American Religion and the Great Migration.* Durham, NC: Duke University Press.

Servin, Manuel. 1970 [1965]. "The Post-World War II Mexican-American, 1925–1965: A Non-Achieving Minority." In *The Mexican Americans: An Awakening Minority,* edited by Manuel Servin. Beverly Hills, CA: Glencoe.

Shaheen, Jack. 1980. *ABSCAM: Arabophobia in America.* Washington, DC: American-Arab Anti-Discrimination Committee.

Shimabukuro, Robert Sadamu. 2001. *Born in Seattle: The Campaign for Japanese American Redress.* Seattle: University of Washington Press.

Shin, Eui-Hang, and Han Park. 1988. "An Analysis of Causes of Schisms in Ethnic

Churches: The Case of Korean-American Churches." *Sociological Analysis* 49/3 (Fall): 234–48.

Shryock, Andrew. 2000. "Family Resemblances: Kinship and Community in Arab Detroit." In *Arab Detroit: From Margin to Mainstream,* edited by Nabeel Abraham and Andrew Shryock. Detroit: Wayne State University Press.

Sklare, Marshall, and Joseph Greenblum. 1967. *Jewish Identity on the Suburban Frontier: A Study of Group Survival in the Open Society.* New York: Basic Books.

Smith, Charles D. 2004. *Palestine and the Arab-Israeli Conflict: A History with Documents.* 5th ed. Boston: Bedford/St.Martins.

Smith, James. 2003. "Assimilation across the Latino Generations." *AEA Papers and Proceedings* 93: 315–19.

Smith, Robert Courtney. 2006. *Mexican New York: Transnational Lives of New Immigrants.* Berkeley: University of California Press.

Smith, Timothy. 1978. "Religion and Ethnicity in America." *American Historical Review* 83: 1155–85.

Smith, William C. 1923. "Anti-Japanese Agitation in Hollywood." Papers of the Survey of Race Relations, Box 23, Major Documents. Stanford, CA: Hoover Institution.

Soto, Isa. 1987. "West Indian Child Fostering." In *Caribbean Life in New York City: Sociocultural Dimensions,* edited by Constance Sutton and Elsa Chaney. New York: Center for Migration Studies.

Spencer, Robert F. 1946. "Japanese Buddhism in the United States, 1940–1946: A Study in Acculturation." Ph.D. dissertation, University of California–Berkeley.

———. 1948. "Social Structure of a Contemporary Japanese American Buddhist Church." *Social Forces* 26: 281–87.

Spickard, Paul. 1983. "The Nisei Assume Power: The Japanese American Citizens League, 1941–42." *Pacific Historical Review* 52: 147–74.

———. 1996. *Japanese Americans: The Formation and Transformations of an Ethnic Group.* New York: Twayne.

———. 1999. "Not Just the Quiet People: The Nisei Underclass." *Pacific Historical Review* 68: 78–94.

———. 2002. "Pacific Diaspora?" In *Pacific Diaspora: Island Peoples in the United States and across the Pacific,* edited by Paul Spickard, Joanne Rondilla, and Debbie Hippolite Wright. Honolulu: University of Hawai'i Press at Mānoa.

Stack, Carol. 1996. *Call to Home: African Americans Reclaim the Rural South.* New York: Basic Books.

Steinberg, Milton. 1955 [1934]. *The Making of the Modern Jew.* New York: Behman's Jewish Book House.

Steinberg, Steven. 1974. *The Academic Melting Pot.* New York: McGraw-Hill.

———. 1989. *The Ethnic Myth: Race, Ethnicity and Class in America.* Boston: Beacon.

Steinfels, Peter. 2003. *A People Adrift: The Crisis of the Roman Catholic Church in America.* New York: Simon and Schuster.

Stepick, Alex. 1999. *Pride against Prejudice: Haitians in the United States.* Boston: Allyn and Bacon.

Stevens-Arroyo, Anthony. 1998. "The Latino Religious Resurgence." *Annals of the American Academy of Political and Social Science* 558: 163–76.

Stoll, David. 1990. *Is Latin America Turning Protestant?* Berkeley: University of California Press.

Suh, Sharon Ann. 2000. *Finding/Knowing One's Mind in Koreatown, Los Angeles: Buddhism, Gender and Subjectivity.* Ann Arbor, MI: University Microfilms.

Suleiman, Michael. 1987. "Early Arab-Americans: The Search for Identity." In *Crossing the Waters: Arabic-Speaking Immigrants to the United States before 1940,* edited by Eric Hoogland. Washington, DC: Smithsonian Institution Press.

———. 1999. "Introduction: The Arab Immigrant Experience." In *Arabs in America: Building a New Future,* edited by Michael Suleiman. Philadelphia: Temple University Press.

Sumner, Margaret. 1970. "Mexican-American Minority Churches, U.S.A." In *Mexican-Americans in the United States,* edited by John Burma. Cambridge: Schenkman.

Sutherland, Robert Lee. 1930. "An Analysis of Negro Churches in Chicago." Ph.D. dissertation, University of Chicago.

Takahashi, Jere. 1997. *Nisei/Sansei: Shifting Japanese American Identities and Politics.* Philadelphia: Temple University Press.

Takaki, Ronald. 1998. *Strangers from a Different Shore: A History of Asian Americans.* Rev. ed. Boston: Backbay.

Takezawa, Yasuko. 1995. *Breaking the Silence: Redress and Japanese American Ethnicity.* Ithaca, NY: Cornell University Press.

Tamura, Eileen. 1994. *Americanization, Acculturation, and Ethnic Identity: The Nisei Generation in Hawai'i.* Urbana: University of Illinois Press.

Thomas, Jesse. 1967. *My Story in Black and White: The Autobiography of Jesse O. Thomas.* New York: Exposition.

Thomas, W. I., and Florian Znaniecki. 1918–20. *The Polish Peasant in Europe and America.* Boston: Richard Badger.

Tolan, John. 2002. *Saracen: Islam in the Medieval European Imagination.* New York: Columbia University Press.

Trouillot, Michel-Rolph. 1990. *Haiti, State against Nation: The Origins and Legacy of Duvalierism.* New York: Monthly Review.

Tuan, Mia. 1999. *Forever Foreigners or Honorary Whites? The Asian Ethnic Experience Today.* New Brunswick, NJ: Rutgers University Press.

Tweed, Thomas. 1997. *Our Lady of the Exile: Diasporic Religion at a Cuban Catholic Shrine in Miami.* New York: Oxford University Press.

U.S. Bureau of the Census. 1918. *Negro Population, 1790–1915.* Washington, D.C.: Government Printing Office.

———. 2001. "Profiles of General Demographic Characteristics." 2000 Census of Population and Housing: United States. At http://www.census.gov/prod/cen2000/dp1/2khoo.pdf.

U.S. Commission on Wartime Relocation and Internment of Civilians (USCWRIC) and Tetsuden Kashima. 1997. *Personal Justice Denied: Report of the Commission on Wartime Relocation and Internment of Civilians.* Seattle: University of Washington Press.

U.S. Conference of Catholic Bishops. 1987. "National Pastoral Plan for the Hispanic Minority." At http://www.usccb.org/hispanicaffairs/plan.shtml.

U.S. Department of State. 2002. "Muslim Life in America." Office of International Information Programs. At http://usinfo.state.gov/products/pubs/muslimlife.

Vanderwood, Paul. 2004. *Juan Soldado: Rapist, Murderer, Martyr, Saint.* Durham, NC: Duke University Press.

Vecoli, Rudolph. 1978. "The Coming of Age of the Italian Americans, 1945–1974." *Ethnicity* 5: 119–47.

Waldinger, Roger. 1986. "Changing Ladders and Musical Chairs: Ethnicity and Opportunity in Postindustrial New York." *Politics and Society* 15: 369–410.

———. 2007. "Did Manufacturing Matter? The Experience of Yesterday's Second Generation: A Reassessment." *International Migration Review* 41: 3–39. Available at: http://works.bepress.com/roger_waldinger/21.

Waldinger, Roger, and Michael Lichter. 1996. "Anglos: Beyond Ethnicity?" In *Ethnic Los Angeles,* edited by Roger Waldinger and Mehdi Bozorgmehr. New York: Russell Sage Foundation.

Waldron, Jeremy. 1995. "Minority Cultures and the Cosmopolitan Alternative." In *The Rights of Minority Cultures,* edited by Will Kymlicka. Oxford: Oxford University Press.

Walker, Randi Jones. 1991. *Protestantism in the Sangre de Cristos 1850–1920.* Albuquerque: University of New Mexico Press.

Wallerstein, Immanuel. 1974. *The Modern World-System.* New York: Academic Press.

Walzer, Michael. 1992. *What It Means to Be an American: Essays on the American Experience.* New York: Marsilio.

———. 1997. *On Toleration.* New Haven: Yale University Press.

Warner, R. Stephen. 1993. "Work in Progress toward a New Paradigm for the Sociological Study of Religion in the United States." *American Journal of Sociology* 98: 1044–93.

Warner, R. Stephen, and Judith Wittner (eds.). 1998. *Gatherings in Diaspora: Religious Communities and the New Immigration.* Philadelphia: Temple University Press.

Warner, W. Lloyd. 1941. "Introduction." In *Deep South: A Social Anthropological*

Study of Caste and Class, edited by Allison Davis, Burleigh Bradford Gardner, and Mary R. Gardner. Chicago: University of Chicago Press.

Warner, W. Lloyd, and Leo Srole. 1945. *The Social Systems of American Ethnic Groups.* New Haven: Yale University Press.

Watanabe, Teresa 2002. "Ethnicity Colors Views of Scandal." *Los Angeles Times* (June 10): B1.

_____. 2003. "Déjà Vu." *Los Angeles Times Magazine* (June 8): I16.

Waters, Mary. 1990. *Ethnic Options: Choosing Identities in America.* Berkeley: University of California Press.

_____. 1999. *Black Identities.* Cambridge: Harvard University Press.

Weber, David. 1994. *The Spanish Frontier in North America.* New Haven: Yale University Press.

Weber, Max. [1904–1905] 1958. *The Protestant Ethic and the Spirit of Capitalism.* New York: Scribner's.

Wei, William. 1992. *The Asian American Movement.* Philadelphia: Temple University Press.

Weigle, Marta. 1976. *Brothers of Light, Brothers of Blood: The Penitentes of the Southwest.* Albuquerque: University of New Mexico Press.

White, Shane, and Graham White. 1998. *Stylin': African American Expressive Culture from Its Beginnings to the Zoot Suit.* Ithaca, NY: Cornell University Press.

"Why Is Anti-Semitism?" 1937. *Christian Century* (July 1): 862–64.

Whyte, William Foote. 1955 [1943]. *Street Corner Society: The Social Structure of an Italian Slum.* Chicago: University of Chicago Press.

Wilder, Esther, 1996. "Socioeconomic Attainment and Expressions of Jewish Identification: 1970 and 1990." *Journal for the Scientific Study of Religion* 35: 109–27.

Williams, A. n.d. [1930s] "The People's Community Church of Christ." Typescript, Box 23 ("Churches") Illinois Writers Project, " The Negro In Illinois." Vivian Harsh Collection, Woodson Regional Library, Chicago.

Williams, Duncan Ryûken. 2006. "From Pearl Harbor to 9/11: Lessons from the Internment of Japanese American Buddhists." In *A Nation of Religions: The Politics of Pluralism in Multireligious America,* edited by Stephen Prothero. Chapel Hill: University of North Carolina Press.

Wojtkiewicz, Roger, and Katharine Donato. 1995. "Hispanic Educational Attainment: The Effects of Family Background and Nativity." *Social Forces* 74: 559–74.

Woocher, Jonathan. 1986. *Sacred Survival: The Civil Religion of American Jews.* Bloomington: Indiana University Press.

Woodrum, Eric. 1981. "An Assessment of Japanese American Assimilation, Pluralism, and Subordination." *American Journal of Sociology* 87: 157–69.

Wright, Richard. 1945. *Black Boy: A Record of Childhood and Youth.* New York: Harper and Brothers.

Wuthnow, Robert. 1998a. *After Heaven: Spirituality in America since the 1950's.* Berkeley: University of California Press.

_____. 1998b. "Divided We Fall: America's Two Civil Religions." *Christian Century* (April 20): 395–99.

_____. 1999. *Growing up Religious: Christians and Jews and Their Journeys of Faith.* Boston: Beacon.

_____. 2005. *America and the Challenges of Religious Diversity.* Princeton: Princeton University Press.

Yamamoto, Traise. 1999. *Masking Selves, Making Subjects: Japanese American Women, Identity, and the Body.* Berkeley: University of California Press.

Yang, Fenggang. 1999. *Chinese Christians in America: Conversion, Assimilation, and Adhesive Identities.* University Park: Pennsylvania State University Press.

Yans-McLaughlin, Virginia. 1977. *Family and Community: Italian Immigrants in Buffalo, 1880–1930.* Ithaca, NY: Cornell University Press.

Yih, Y.-M. D. 1995. "Music and Dance of Haitian Vodou: Diversity and Unity in Regional Repertoires." Ph.D. dissertation, Wesleyan University.

Yoo, David. 1996. "Captivating Memories: Museology, Concentration Camps, and Japanese American History." *American Quarterly* 48: 680–99.

_____. 2000. *Growing up Nisei: Race, Generation and Culture among Japanese Americans in California, 1924–1949.* Chicago: University of Illinois Press.

Young, Lawrence. 1997. *Rational Choice Theory and Religion: Summary and Assessment.* New York: Routledge.

Young, Robert. 1990. *White Mythologies: Writing History and the West.* London: Routledge.

Youniss, James, and John Convey (eds.). 2000. *Catholic Schools at the Crossroads.* New York: Teachers College Press.

Yu, Eui Yong. 1982. "Koreans in America, 1903–1945." In *Koreans in LA: Promises and Prospects,* edited by Eui Yong Yu, Earl Phillips, and Eun Sik Yang. Los Angeles: Koryo Research Institute, Center for Korean and Korean American Studies.

_____. 1988. "The Growth of Korean Buddhism in the United States, with Special Reference to Southern California." *Pacific World: Journal of the Institute of Buddhist Studies* 4: 82–93.

Yu, Henry. 2001. *Thinking Orientals: Migration, Contact, and Exoticism in Modern America.* New York: Oxford University Press.

Zeitlin, Joseph. 1945. *Disciples of the Wise: The Religious and Social Opinions of American Rabbis.* New York: Teachers College Press.

Zenner, Walter. 2002. "The Syrian Jews of Brooklyn." In *A Community of Many Worlds: Arab Americans in New York City,* edited by Kathleen Benson and Philip Kayal. Syracuse, NY: Syracuse University Press.

Zhou, Min, and Carl Bankston. 1998. *Growing up American: The Adaptation of Vietnamese Adolescents in the United States.* New York: Russell Sage Foundation.

About the Contributors

RICHARD ALBA is Distinguished Professor of Sociology at the Graduate Center of the City University of New York and the author of many books including (with Victor Nee) *Remaking the American Mainstream: Assimilation and Contemporary Immigration* and *Ethnic Identity: The Transformation of White America.*

JOSH DEWIND is Director of the Migration Program of the Social Science Research Council. He is the co-editor of *The Handbook of International Migration: The American Experience.*

ARNOLD EISEN is Chancellor of the Jewish Theological Seminary. He is coauthor (with Stephen Cohen) of *The Jew Within: Self, Family, and Community in America.*

CALVIN GOLDSCHEIDER is Professor of Sociology and Ungerleider Professor of Judaic Studies at Brown University. He is the author of *Israel's Changing Society.*

JAMES GROSSMAN is Vice President for Research and Education at Newberry Library in Chicago.

YVONNE YAZBECK HADDAD is Professor of the History of Islam and of Christian-Muslim Relations at Georgetown University. She is the author of *A Vanishing Minority: Christians in the Middle East* and coeditor of *Islam and the West Post 9/11.*

JANE NAOMI IWAMURA is Assistant Professor of Religion and of American Studies and Ethnicity at the University of Southern California. She is the coeditor (with Paul Spickard) of *Revealing the Sacred in Asian and Pacific America.*

ANN CHIH LIN is Associate Professor of Political Science at the University of Michigan. She is the author of *Reform in the Making: The Implementation of Social Policy in Prison.*

ROBERTO LINT SAGARENA is Assistant Professor of Religion and American Studies and Ethnicity at the University of Southern California.

DAVID LOPEZ is Professor of Sociology at University of California Los Angeles.

ELIZABETH MCALISTER is Associate Professor of Religion at Wesleyan University. She is the author of *Rara! Vodou, Power, and Performance in Haiti and Its Diaspora.*

ROBERT ORSI is the Grace Craddock Nagle Chair in Catholic Studies at Northwestern University. He is the author of *Between Heaven and Earth: The Religious Worlds People Make and the Scholars Who Study Them.*

LORI PIERCE is Assistant Professor in the American Studies Program at DePaul University.

ALBERT J. RABOTEAU is the Henry W. Putnam Professor of Religion at Princeton University and the author of *Slave Religion: The "Invisible Insitution" in the Antebellum South* and *Canaan Land: A Religious History of African Americans.*

KAREN RICHMAN is Assistant Professor of Anthropology at the University of Notre Dame. *She is the author of Migration and Voudou (New World Diasporas).*

PAUL SPICKARD is Professor of History at University of California, Santa Barbara. His books include *Race and Nation: Ethnic Systems in the Modern World* and *Racial Thinking in the United States.*

SHARON A. SUH is Associate Professor of Religious Studies at Seattle University.

DAVID YOO is Associate Professor of History at Claremont McKenna College.

Index

1.5 generation, 100. *See also* first generation; second generation; third generation; fourth generation; fifth generation
100th Infantry Battalion, 147
442nd Regimental Combat Team, 108, 147
"614th commandment," 237

A Piece of the Pie (Lieberson), 44
Abraham, Spencer, 282
ABSCAM investigation, 262
Aburezk, James, 263
Abyssinian Baptist Church (New York), 310
acculturation: Arab Muslim immigrants, 254; Japanese immigrants, 138; Korean immigrants, 167; spatial/outward mobility, 55; without assimilation, 86. *See also* Americanization; assimilation; integration into American society; religious incorporation
Addams, Jane, 42
African Americans: in 1970, 306–307; African religions, 22; Catholic schools, 90; Catholicism, 22; civil religion, 163, 312; Detroit, Michigan, 295n1; ghettos, consolidation of, 308; Haitian immigrants' distancing from, 20, 303, 326–328, 330, 334; hybrid religions, 320; Islam, 312–313; Judaism, 312–313; political power, 308; Protestantism, 303; Protestantism, evangelical, 298; "roots" movement, 302–303
African Americans of the Great Migration, 304–318; 1916-1920s (first wave), 307–311, 318; 1930s (Great Depression), 308; 1940-1970 (second wave), 308–314; African-origin traditions, 298, 320; "bettering my condition," 307; black newspapers, 308; Catholic Church, 303, 311–312; Catholicism, conversion to, 312; "church tramps," 311; communication, entertainment media, 314; deindustrialization, 309; disempowerment, 297; Exodus narrative, 20, 316–317, 318; ghettos, consolidation of, 308; Haitian immigrants compared to, 12, 19–21, 297–303, 319–321, 325, 348; improvements in life, 307–308; land ownership, 307; letters of recommendation (letters of dismissal), 309–310; minister's role, 315; North's appeal, 304–305, 307; Pentecostalism, 313–314; political power, 314–316; poverty, 297; Promised Land narrative, 20, 316–317, 318;

African Americans of the Great Migration (*Continued*) Protestantism, evangelical, 302; religious options, proliferation of, 8, 21, 302, 311–312, 314, 317, 318; remittances to home churches, 309; "renarrativising" their history, 302; rural congregations, 306; social networks, 309; in the South, 305–306; ties to communities left behind, 309–310, 316; transformation of rural into urban culture, 304–305; urban churches, 310–311, 314; urbanization, 301, 316; West Coast, 308
African religions, 20, 22
Afro-Creole culture, 328, 345
Ahn, Chang-ho, 119, 126
'Alawi immigrants, 251
Alba, Richard, 75, 86, 89, 242
Alemany, Joseph Sadoc, 62
All Nations Pentecostal Church, 314
Alta California (territory), 57, 59
al-Alwani, Taha Jaber, 293
Amat, Thaddeus, 81
American-Arab Anti-Discrimination Committee (ADC): founder, 263; high socioeconomic status, 289; model for, 263; organizational allies, 276n8; president, 269; religious involvement, 292–293
American Catholic Parish (Dolan), 59
American Israel Public Affairs Committee, 263
American Jewish Committee, 248
American mainstream: Arab Muslim immigrants, 272–273; Asian immigrants, 101; Catholic Church, 15, 29; Catholicism, 11; changes in, 26; charter religions, 10–11, 191; exclusion from, 13, 101–102, 272; generation-by-generation progression into, 28–29, 33; Haitian immigrants, 333; interpretations of World War II experience, 33; Italian immigrants, 26, 28–29, 48; Japanese immigrants, 105, 138; Judaism, 11, 15; Korean immigrants, 101–102, 105; Mexican immigrants, 13, 15; Muslim immigrants, 15; Protestantism, 11; religious incorporation, 28–29; whiteness, 101
American Muslim Alliance (AMA), 266
American Muslim Council (AMC), 266, 289, 292
Americanization: Arab Muslim immigrants, 253–257; Christianity, 113; ethnicity formation, 330; Issei Christians, 113–114; of Jewishness, 204; Korean immigrants, 167; Muslim women, 256–257. *See also* acculturation; assimilation; integration into American society; religious incorporation
Amida Buddha, 160, 164n7
anti-Arab sentiments, 258, 262–263, 272–273, 277–278
anti-Catholic nativism, 58
Anti-Defamation League (ADL), 263
anti-immigrant politics, 78
anti-Italian sentiments, 32
anti-Japanese sentiments, 107–108, 114, 129–130, 132
anti-Mexican sentiments, 63
anti-Muslim sentiments, 258, 273, 294
anti-Saracen heritage, 258–259, 273
anti-Semitism, 232–233
"Arab," 258, 267
"Arab-American," 261, 267
Arab American Chamber of Commerce, 284
Arab American identity, 267
Arab American Institute (AAI), 263, 282, 289

Arab Christians, 249, 260, 272–273, 275n1
Arab Community Center for Economic and Social Services, 276n8
Arab Muslim immigrants, 191–197, 246–296; acculturation, 254; 'Alawis, 251; American mainstream, 272–273; Americanization, 253–257; anti-Arab sentiments, 258, 262–263, 272–273, 277–278; anti-Muslim sentiments, 258, 273, 294; anti-Saracen heritage, 258–259, 273; Arab American identity, 267; Arab nationalist identity, 261; assimilability of, doubts about, 193, 196; assimilation, 250, 253, 254; civil religion, 163; coalition building, 271–272, 274, 288, 292, 293; common language, 252; Dearborn, Michigan, 255, 256, 278; detention, 269–270; Detroit, Michigan, 194, 253–254, 255, 260, 278–279, 292; discrimination, perception of, 289; diversity, 251–252, 279; Druze, 251; eastern European Jewish immigrants compared to, 10, 15–17, 191–197; educational attainments, 192, 255; Egyptians, 252; events overseas, influence of, 191–192, 260–261, 273–274, 285–286; first generation, 194, 274, 278; first wave, 249–250; freedom of thought, 272; gender segregation, 256; governmental scrutiny of, 269–271; Gulf Arabs, 252; Gulf War (1990–1991), 252; identities, 247–248; identity, self-, 267, 291; iman, role of, 255; Immigration and Nationality Act (1965), 250–251; immigration waves, 249–253; individualism, 241; institutions, 279–280, 286; integration into American society, 250; intermarriage, 251, 293–294; Iraqis, 251, 260; Islamic identity, 260–261; Islamic schools, 287, 288; Islamism, 261; Isma'ilis, 251; isolation, 264, 285, 293; Israel, 196–197, 259–264; Israelis, 251; Ithna 'Asharis (Ja'faris), 251; Jewish immigrants as model for, 192, 197, 263; Jordanians, 252; *jum'a* (Friday communal prayers), 257; Lebanese, 251, 260, 264; Los Angeles, 278; Maghrebis (North Africans), 252; marginalization of, 262; marriage, 255–256; Mashreqis (Levant and Arabian Peninsula), 252; minority and ethnic communities, 251–252; Moroccans, 252; mosque attendance, 257, 282–283, 287; national identities, attachment to, 252; National Origin Act (1924), 249; networks, personal, 277–278, 281, 283, 285, 288; number, 250; occupations, 253, 283; Operation Boulder (FBI), 262; organizations, 193, 259–260, 261, 263–264, 276n8, 277–278, 283, 284, 287–293, 294–295; Palestinians, 251, 252; pan-ethnic identity, 285–286, 290, 291, 293, 294; as percentage of Muslim immigrants, 249; political activism, 262, 263–264, 268, 271–272, 273, 283, 286, 296n4; post 9/11 era, 267–272, 277; professional attainments, 192, 255; relationship between mosqued and un-mosqued, 271; sample studied, 280; second generation, 263, 274; second wave, 250–251; self-censorship, 271; settlement patterns, 248–249, 264; Shi'ites, 251; "sisters" groups, 257, 271; small businesses, 284; Sunnis, 251; Syrians, 249–250, 251, 252, 260, 264; temporary residents, 252; third generation, 263; as threat to United States, 261–262, 268; Toledo, Ohio, 253–254, 255; Tunisians, 252;

Arab Muslim immigrants (*Continued*)
United States foreign policy, 197,
252, 281–282, 294; veiling, 256, 271;
virtual communities, 294; visibility,
294; whiteness, 272; women, 256–
257, 270, 283, 284–285, 287–291, 295;
Yemenis, 251, 256, 260; Zaidis, 251;
Zionism, 259–264
Arab nationalist identity, 258, 261
Aristide, Jean-Bertrand, 323, 324
Asian American congregations, 18,
102–103
Asian immigrants: 1965, 99–100;
American mainstream, 101; assimilability of, doubts about, 107;
educational attainments, 92–95;
Immigration and Nationality Act
(1965), 250; Kumon cram schools,
94; Latino immigrants compared
to, 92–94; Lowe on, Lisa, 140; Muslim immigrants, 251; organization
of religious youth activities, 93–94;
pan-ethnic identity, 102, 109; post-
immigrant generations, 140–141;
Protestantism, 94; religious diversity, 11; stereotypes of, 101; upward
mobility, 93–94
assimilation: acculturation without, 86;
Arab Muslim immigrants, 193, 250,
253, 254; Asian immigrants, 107;
correlation between age and generational distance from immigration, 27; doubts about assimilability,
13, 25, 62, 107, 193, 196; eastern
European Jewish immigrants, 193,
198–199, 200, 204, 211, 214, 237–238;
Haitian immigrants, 20; intermarriage, 10, 220; Islam, practice of,
253, 254; Italian immigrants, 13, 25;
Japanese immigrants, 101, 104, 109,
115, 138–139; Mexican immigrants,
13, 25, 62, 72–73; religion, 279;

"segmented assimilation," 43; time,
222; Triple Melting Pot thesis, 10,
29. *See also* acculturation; Americanization; integration into American society; religious incorporation
Association of Arab-American University Graduates (AAUG), 261, 289
Association of Evangelical Haitian
Clergy, 347

Bankston, Carl, 93
Barrett, James, 32
"Becoming American by Becoming
Hindu" (Kurien), 103
Beecher, Lyman, 58
Bellah, Robert, 143, 144, 163, 239–240
Black Identities (Waters), 12
"Bois Caiman for Jesus" crusade,
345–346
Bokser, Ben Zion, 228
Borowitz, Eugene, 235, 236
Boukman (a slave), 345, 346
Braceros, 64
Bridge Refugee and Sponsorship Ser-
vice, 276n8
Brown, Karen McCarthy, 2, 350
Buchanan, Susan, 325
Buddhism, 166–190; American values,
5, 19, 105, 128, 169, 172, 178, 184;
Amida Buddha, 160, 164n7; at-
tendance, 186, 190n4; California,
110; changes before being brought
to United States, 129; community
organizing, 111–112; conversion
to Christianity, 166, 170, 175, 177,
179, 180–183, 185, 187–189; democracy, compatibility with, 104, 130,
133n9, 167, 168, 183; discrimination
against Buddhists, 178; equality of
believers, 130; freedom, 183; fund-
raising, 110–111; girls, 176; growth,
110–111; Hawai'i, 109–110, 111, 116,

130; hiding Buddhist identity, 169, 182, 186; independence, 169, 172, 183; individualism, 5, 19, 130, 188; intellectual challenge, 187; Japanese immigrants, 100, 107, 109–112, 116, 128–130, 138, 141; Jodo Shinshu, 109, 128–129, 130, 133n9; *karma*, 172–173, 174; Korean immigrants, 104–105, 118, 124, 166–190; Los Angeles, 171; monks, dissatisfaction with, 172, 175, 179, 183, 186; monks, English-speaking, 172; Nichiren, 109; Nishi Hongwanji, 109, 149–151, 156; open-mindedness, 169, 172; outreach to immigrants, 172, 179–180, 189; *pogyo*, 171; Pure Land, 160; recruitment campaign, 170–171; religious marginalization, response to, 169; self-agency, 172–173, 178, 184; self-awakening, 174; self-enlightenment, 168, 187; self-esteem, 169, 170, 190; self-knowledge, 169, 172; self-reliance, 5, 19, 167, 178, 183, 184, 190; Shingon, 109; Soto Zen, 109; survival of, 176, 185; *Tanko* (coal miner's dance), 155; temple administration, responsibilities for, 183; temple membership, 131, 138; Tendai, 109; young adult socialization, 174, 190n4; young people, 172, 176
Buddhist Churches of America (BCA), 138
Buddhist Mission of North America (North American Buddhist Mission), 110, 131
Bush, George W.: Arab Muslim immigrants, 263, 268; post-9/11 appeal for tolerance, 155, 192; war on terrorism, 272
Bush administration, George W., 270
Bwa Kayiman, Haiti, 345

Cabrini, St. Frances Xavier, 41
California: Alien Land Acts, 17; Alta California (territory), 57, 59; anti-immigrant politics, 78; anti-Mexican sentiments, 63; Bracero program, 64; Buddhism, 110; Catholic Church, 30, 62, 81, 82–83; Japanese immigrants, 108, 116, 117t; Los Angeles (*see* Los Angeles); Mexican immigrants, 61–62, 64, 77, 78; population growth, 77; Proposition 187, 5, 78
California Gold Rush (1849), 61, 62
Cantwell, John, 81–82
Carey, Archibald J., 315
Caribbean emigrants, 323
Casanova, Jose, 22
Catholic charismatic movement (Catholic Pentecostalism), 42, 52
Catholic Church, 56–61, 80–88; African Americans of the Great Migration, 303, 311–312; Afro-Haitian women, 300; in Alta California, 57; American mainstream, 15, 29; Americanization campaign, 30, 63, 64; anti-Catholic nativism, 58; attitudes toward Mexican American Catholics, 14; black saints, 303; California, 30, 62, 81, 82–83; catechism, study of, 94; Católicos por la Raza, 56; central authority of the episcopacy, 60–61; church attendance, 36, 37, 53, 63; civil rights movement, 65–66; clergy, 41, 56, 63; clerical prerogative, 61; colleges and universities, 33, 97; competitors worldwide, 79; "congregationalism" within, 86–88; contributions to, 39; Cristero revolt (1926-1929), 68; Cursillo movement (*Cursillos de Cristianidad*), 52, 64–65, 83; devotional groups, 81–82;

Catholic Church (*Continued*) Division (later Secretariat) for Hispanic affairs, 83; East Coast, 14; elementary, high schools (*see* Catholic schools); "enculturation" policy, 303; episcopal tithes, 61; ethnic community building, 5–6; ethnic/national parishes, 5–6, 7–8, 28, 36, 39, 54, 82, 84, 85–88, 330, 340; Euro-American clergy, 30; European American ethnics, 15, 30–31; family chapels on private property, 40–41; *festa* societies, 39–40; Franciscans, 41, 59; French clergy, 61; French or Creole masses, 329–330; growth in, 24; Guadalupanas, 64; Haitian Apostolate, 330; Haitian immigrants, 300–301, 329–332, 339–340; Hermanidad de Penitentes (the Penitentes), 59–60, 70n1; institutional survival, 97; institutional weakness, 79; integration of immigration communities in United States, 87–88, 95–96, 191; Irish American priests, superiors, 46, 82–83, 86; Italian immigrants, 13, 28–29; "Italian problem," 28, 41–42, 49–50; Jesuits (Society of Jesus), 61; Latino immigrants, 24, 31, 56, 71–72, 79–80, 84, 97–98; Latino priests, 83–84; lay religious traditions, 57, 60; Los Angeles archdiocese, 84–85; Mexican immigrants, 13, 30–31, 56, 64–66, 67, 72, 75, 76, 80–85; Midwest, 14, 30; Missionary Sisters of the Sacred Heart of Jesus, 41; multiethnic, territorially based parishes, 33, 45, 49; "National Pastoral Plan for the Hispanic Minority," 83; New Mexico, 57, 58–61, 81, 82–83; New York City, 329–331; Northeast, 30; Oblate Sisters of Providence, 300; Padres Asociados para Derechos Religiosos, Educativos y Sociales (PADRES), 66; Pious Society of St. Charles (Scalabrini Fathers), 39, 41; priest-centered approach, 75, 96; progressive priests, nuns, 84; Protestantism, evangelical, 79–80; protests against, 56; religious orders, 41; representation in church hierarchy, 76; representation of immigrants, ethnic peoples, 29; rites of, 58; saints, patronal, 38, 68, 331–332; Second Vatican Council (*see* Vatican II); Sisters of Charity, 61; Sisters of Loretto, 61; Sisters of Mercy, 61; social mobility, 29; social services, 94; Southwest, 30, 57, 63, 80–81, 82, 84; Spanish-speaking clerics, parishes, 30, 66, 81, 82, 83–84, 86; stole fees, 61; success of Protestant proselytizers, 8; Texas, 82–83; transnational ethnic parishes, 69; transnationalism, 303; U. S. Conference of Catholic Bishops, 5, 76, 83; Virgin of Guadalupe (*see* Virgin of Guadalupe); vocations to the religious life, 45–46, 50; West Coast, 14

Catholic Pentecostalism (Catholic charismatic movement), 42, 52

Catholic schools, 88–92; African Americans, 90; enrollment, 89, 90; Euro-American Catholics, 30–31; financial aid, 90, 98n4; Italian immigrants, 14, 29, 45, 89; Latino immigrants, 75, 90–91, 96; Los Angeles, 91; Mexican immigrants, 15, 75–76, 82; selectivity, 88; tuition, 89–90; upward mobility, 91

Catholic Youth Organization, 45

Catholicism: African Americans, 22; American mainstream, 11; as charter religion, 10–11; Haitian immigrants, 21, 303, 327, 328; Italian immigrants, 10, 36–37, 49, 53; Korean immigrants, 94, 118; Mexican immigrants, 10, 13; Protestant nativists, 58; syncretic Catholicism, 13; as threat to United States, 58; transnationalism, 20; Vietnamese immigrants, 93

Católicos por la Raza, 56

cemetery customs, Italian immigrants, 51–52

Central American immigrants, 73, 77

Chafetz, Janet Saltzman, 4

chain migration, 202–203, 325

Charles, Carolle, 326–327

Charleston, South Carolina, 300

charter religions, 10–11, 191

Chávez, César, 65, 163

Cheney, Dick, 268

Chicago Defender (newspaper), 308

Chidester, David, 162

Chin, Mi Young, 178–179

chosenness doctrine, 224–232; American civil religion, 347; Conservative Judaism, 228, 229; democracy, 233; eastern European Jewish immigrant reinterpretation of, 8, 16, 23, 224–229, 235, 245; Japanese immigrants, 115; Kaplan and, Mordecai, 228, 229–232; Orthodox Judaism, 228, 229; Reform Judaism, 227, 229

Christian Century (magazine), 232–233, 245n2

Christian fundamentalists, 268–269

Christianity: Americanization, 113; Arab Christians, 249, 260, 272–273, 275n1; business connections, 177–178, 182–183; community building, 188–189; conjure and, 348; conversion to, 17, 18; dependence on authority agents, 183–184; dependence on others for support, 189; dependence on outside agents, 178;

Japanese immigrants, 17, 112–116; Korean immigrants, 17, 18, 100, 102, 166, 171–172; modernity, 168; outreach to immigrants, 179–182, 189; ritual and administrative positions, 183

Church of God in Christ, 302

Church of Our Lady of Mount Carmel (East Harlem), 40, 331

"church tramps," 311

CIA, 270, 273

City College of New York (CCNY), 203

Civil Liberties Act (1988), 137, 144–146, 148, 149

civil religion, 141–148, 156–164; African Americans, 163, 312; American chosenness doctrine, 347; appeals to tolerance, 163; Arab Muslim immigrants, 163; Bellah on, Robert, 143, 144, 163; integrative function, 143; Japanese immigrants, 137, 141–148, 153, 156–164, 162–164; Mexican immigrants, 162–163; Sikhs, 163; "times of trial," 144. *See also* Days of Remembrance; Japanese American National Museum; Manzanar Annual Pilgrimage

civil rights movement, 65–66

Cline, Edgar, 150

Clinton, Bill, 266

Clinton, Hillary, 263, 266

Cohen, Arthur, 235

Cohen, Steven, 239, 241

"color," 25

Columbia University, 203–204

Commission on Wartime Relocation and Internment of Civilians (CWRIC) hearings, 146, 148–149, 161

community building: Christianity, 188–189; ethnicity, 5–6; Haitian immigrants, 344; Japanese immigrants, 107, 111–112; religion, 5–6

Comprehensive Antiterrorism Act
(1995), 269–270
Confucianism, 99
Conservative Judaism, 228, 229, 238
conversion: African Americans of
the Great Migration, 312; to Catholicism, 312; to Christianity, 17, 18,
103–104, 112–113, 166, 170, 175, 177,
179, 180–183, 185, 187–189; Haitian
immigrants, 337–339, 343, 350–352;
Italian immigrants, 28, 41–42, 50;
Japanese immigrants, 17, 112–113; to
Judaism, 219; Korean immigrants,
17, 18, 166, 170, 175, 177, 179, 180–183,
185, 187–189; in Latin America, 80;
Mexican immigrants, 63, 67, 83;
modernity, 352; to Presbyterianism,
60; to Protestantism, 28, 41–42, 50,
63, 67, 80, 337–339, 343, 350–352; to
Protestantism, evangelical, 4, 20
Council of Masajid, 253
Council on American-Islamic Relations
(CAIR), 248, 266, 276n8, 289, 292
Covello, Leonard, 44
Cristero revolt (1926-1929), 68
critical faith, 144, 146, 153, 159
Crowdy, William S., 313
Cuban immigrants, 94–95
Cuomo, Mario, 29
Cursillo movement (*Cursillos de Cris-
tianidad*), 52, 64–65, 83

Daddy Grace (Charles M. Grace), 311
Daniels, Roger, 141
Day of Remembrance, 159–160, 164n6
Days of Remembrance, 153
Dearborn, Michigan, 255, 256, 278
democracy: Buddhism, 104, 130, 133n9,
167, 168, 183; Catholicism as threat
to, 58; chosenness doctrine, 233;
Judaism, 227; religion, compatibility
with, 104

*Democracy according to the Buddhist
Viewpoint* (Imamura), 133n9
deportation of Mexican immigrants
(1930s), 27, 54, 63–64
Dessalines, Jean-Jacques, 322
detention: Haitian immigrants, 323;
Japanese during World War II,
101, 108, 134n10, 136, 137, 141, 143,
144–149, 156, 158, 162; Muslim im-
migrants, 269–270
Detroit, Michigan: African Americans,
295n1; Arab Muslim immigrants,
194, 253–254, 255, 260, 278–279, 292;
New Bethel Baptist Church, 317
discrimination against: Buddhists, 178;
Italian immigrants, 43; Mexican im-
migrants, 31; Muslims, 289
Divine, Father (George Baker), 8, 302,
311
Doi, Joanne, 136–137, 153
Dolan, Jay, 2, 59
Dorsainville, Roger, 338
Dorsey, Thomas, 314
Drew, Timothy (Noble Drew Ali), 313
Druze immigrants, 251
Duvalier, François, 297, 330
Duvalier, Jean-Claude, 297, 328, 330

eastern European Jewish immigrants,
191–245; "614th commandment,"
237; Americanization of Jewishness,
204; anti-Semitism, 232–233; Arab
Muslim immigrants compared to,
10, 15–17, 191–197; assimilability of,
doubts about, 193; assimilation, 193,
198–199, 200, 204, 211, 214, 237–238;
capitalist goal, 201; chain migration,
202–203; chosenness doctrine, reinterpretation of, 8, 16, 23, 224–225,
235, 245; communal cohesion,
204–205, 211, 223; communal continuity, 199, 210–211, 213, 217, 220;

communal institutions, 199, 200, 220, 223; contemporary communities, 221–222; disengagement from Jewish community, 220; distinctiveness, 193, 199, 213, 224, 226, 228, 229, 233, 237, 239, 244; educational attainments, 203–204, 205–207, 209, 210–216, 212, 213; factory work, 207–208; family- and community-based immigration, 201–202; family life, 240–241; fear of "decline," 196; first generation, 201, 203–204; fourth generation, 237–242; Great Depression, 226; help from earlier Jewish immigrants, 202; Holocaust, 237, 240; hyphenated identity, 224, 225, 227, 231, 232, 237, 242, 243–244; integration into American society, 244; intergenerational conflict, 206, 215–216; intermarriage, 8, 15, 216–221, 236, 240; intragroup and intergroup interactions, 200, 210–211; Israel, 196–197, 221, 237–238, 240; Jewish identification, Jewishness, 214, 217, 219–221; Jewish theology, disinterest in, 236–237; *landsmanschaften* (benevolent societies), 35, 203, 204; literacy, 206–207; "living in two civilizations," 230–233, 242; networks, occupational, 204; networks, social and family, 199, 200, 210–211, 220, 223; number, 201; occupational concentration, 209–210, 212, 213, 214; occupations, 207–213; professionals/managers, 207, 208, 209, 213; racial redefinition, 192; religious leaders, 202; ritual observance, 236, 240–241; sales jobs, 207–208, 209; second generation, 192, 204, 225, 226–234; secularism, 16, 201, 202; selectivity of immigration, 202; self-employment, 208–209, 212; semiskilled workers, 207, 209; settlement patterns, 201, 203, 205, 213; skilled workers, 202, 203, 207, 209; social mobility, 203, 205, 209, 211; synagogue membership, attendance, 236, 241; third generation, 205, 234–237; ties to communities of origin, 203; transformation of, 199–200, 225; United States foreign policy, 197; upward mobility, 15; women, 206–207, 209, 210, 241; Yiddish, 204

Ebaugh, Helen Rose, 4
Eck, Diana, 2
educational attainments, 92–95, 210–216; Americanization, 215; Arab Muslim immigrants, 192, 255; Asian immigrants, 92–95; Central American immigrants, 73; community-based programs focused on education, 96; Cuban immigrants, 94–95; disaffection from ethnic community, 212; eastern European Jewish immigrants, 203–204, 205–207, 209, 210–216, 212, 213; ethnic-language study and maintenance, 95; intergenerational conflict, 215–216; Italian immigrants, 25, 44; Jewish immigrants, 87; Korean immigrants, 101; Kumon cram schools, 94; Mexican immigrants, 25, 30, 73, 75; organization of religious youth activities, 93–94. *See also* schools
Egyptian immigrants, 252
Eisenhower, Dwight D., 264
"Eli the Fanatic" (Roth), 234, 235
Elkholy, Abdo, 250, 253–254, 255–256, 260
Embrey, Sue, 156
England, John, 300
Enlightenment, 225
Episcopalians, 124

ethnicity: Americanization, 330;
"color," 25; community building,
5–6; difference between religiosity
and, 242; disaffection from ethnic
community, 212; ethnic identity,
222–223; expression of ethnic difference, 22–23; formation of, 330;
generational replacement, 216
evangelical Protestantism, 339–347;
African Americans, 298; African
Americans of the Great Migration, 302; "Bois Caiman for Jesus"
crusade, 345–346; Catholic Church,
79–80; conversion to, 4, 20, 84;
Creole, 341–342; cultural separatism, 344; Haitian immigrants, 7, 20,
21, 298, 302, 321, 339–347; Korean
immigrants, 17, 100; Mexican immigrants, 30, 84; New York City, 343–
347; Vatican II, 79; "Vision 2000"
service, 347. *See also* Pentecostalism
Executive Order 9066, 144–146, 164n6
Exodus narrative, 20, 316–317, 318, 319
Ezili, 331
Ezili Danto, 7, 335–336

Fackenheim, Emil, 235, 237
Father Divine (George Baker), 8, 302, 311
FBI, 262, 273, 312
Federation of Islamic Associations
(FIA), 264, 265
feminism and Judaism, 238
Ferraro, Geraldine, 29
Fèt Vièj Mirak ("Feast of the Miracle
Virgin"), 331–332
fifth generation of Japanese immi-
grants (Gosei), 145
Filipino immigrants, 133n1
Finkelstein, Louis, 227, 228
First Amendment, 9
first generation: Arab Muslim im-
migrants, 194, 274, 278; eastern

European Jewish immigrants, 201,
203–204; Italian immigrants, 34–43;
Japanese immigrants (Issei), 99,
107–108, 112–114, 116, 117t, 145, 158;
Korean immigrants, 18, 100; Mexi-
can immigrants, 59, 73, 75
Florida. *See* South Florida
foreign policy. *See* United States for-
eign policy
Four Quartets (Eliot), 316
fourth generation: eastern European
Jewish immigrants, 237–242; Italian
immigrants, 29, 33, 52–53; Japanese
immigrants (Yonsei), 99, 104, 145
Fox, Vincente, 67
Franciscans, 41, 59
Franklin, C. L., 317
freedom of thought, 272
Fulbright, J. William, 262
Furuya, Magojiro, 115

Gaceta de Sante Fe (newspaper), 60–61
Gans, Herbert, 89, 226
Garvey, Marcus, 312
Gatherings in Diaspora (Warner and
Wittner), 2–3
General Social Survey, 50, 53
generation-by-generation ascent, 33.
See also first generation; second
generation; third generation; fourth
generation; fifth generation; inter-
generational conflict
generational replacement, 216
Gentlemen's Agreement (1907-1908), 107
geographic dispersion. *See* settlement
patterns
Giambastini, Luigi, 41
Gila River Relocation Center (Ari-
zona), 157, 162
Gill, Anthony, 72, 80
Glazer, Nathan, 234–235
Go for Broke Monument, 164n4

Gonzalez, Nancie, 83
Goode, Wilson, 263
Gordon, Milton, 86
Gore, Al, 263, 268
Grace, Daddy (Charles M. Grace), 311
Great Depression, 63, 76, 226
Great Migration, meaning of, 316–317.
  See also African Americans of the
  Great Migration
Greenberg, Simon, 227
Greenblum, Joseph, 234
Guadalupanas, 64
Gulf Arab immigrants, 252
Gulf War (1990-1991), 252, 265

Haddad, Yvonne, 253, 254–255, 256
Haiti: to Haitian immigrants, 342–343,
  344–345; Liberation Theology, 330;
  Sodo pilgrimage, 331; "Tenth Province," 324, 342; Vodou (*see* Vodou)
Haitian immigrants, 319–352; access
  to power of saints and spirits,
  319; African Americans, distancing from, 20, 303, 326–328, 330,
  334; African Americans of the
  Great Migration compared to, 12,
  19–21, 297–303, 319–321, 325, 348;
  African-origin traditions, 298, 320;
  Afro-Creole culture, 328; American
  mainstream, 333; assimilation, 20;
  boat people, 323; "Bois Caiman for
  Jesus" crusade, 345–346; Catholic
  Church, 300–301, 329–332, 339–340;
  Catholicism, 21, 303, 327, 328; chain
  migration, 325; Charleston, South
  Carolina, 300; community building,
  344; Creole, 330, 341–342; Creoleness, 327; cultural separatism, 344;
  detention, 323; disempowerment,
  297; *dyab* (devil), 339, 350; English
  language, 341–342; Exodus narrative, 319; expectations of migration,
  325; Frenchness, 327, 341–342; Haiti
  to, 342–343, 344–345; home altars,
  332; hybrid religions, 320; Immigration and Nationality Act (1965), 322;
  integration into American society,
  300, 342; *konbit* (work party system), 328; *lakou* (family compound
  system), 328; Louisiana, 299–300;
  Mayami (Miami), 334–335; middle-
  class, 334; migrant laborers, 322, 350;
  national pride, 327–328; New York
  City, 301, 323, 324, 327, 343–347, 350;
  Pentecostalism, 20, 21–22; perception that those bettering themselves
  will be killed, 338; political activism, 344; political asylum, 323; from
  Port-au-Prince, Haiti, 350; poverty,
  297; Promised Land narrative, 319;
  Protestantism, 329, 339–340; Protestantism, conversion to, 337–339, 343,
  350–352; Protestantism, evangelical,
  7, 20, 21, 298, 302, 321, 339–347; race,
  326–327, 352; racism, 326; Rara, 328,
  344; refugees of the Haitian revolution, 299–300; religious affiliations,
  21, 247–348, 301, 321, 352; religious
  choice, instrumental view of, 348;
  remittances, 298, 337; "renarrativising" their history, 302; "roots"
  movement *(mouvman rasin)*, 302–
  303, 328; saints, patronal, 331–332;
  settlement patterns, 323–324; social
  support networks, 334, 341, 344,
  352; sorcery, fear of, 338–339; South
  Florida, 301, 323, 324, 334–343; from
  Ti Rivyè, Haiti, 334–335, 337; ties to
  communities left behind, 337, 351;
  transnationalism, 20, 300–301, 320,
  324–325, 330–331, 335, 342, 349–350;
  upper-class Francophone, 329–330;
  upward mobility, 21; Vodou (*see*
  Vodou); women, 332

Haitian Revolution (1791-1804): African Americans, Haitians' distancing from, 20; beginning, 322, 345–346; Our Lady of Mount Carmel, 331; pride in, 327; Vodou, 345

Handlin, Oscar, 33

Hanna, Edward Joseph, 81

Hansen, Arthur, 236

Hawai'i: Buddhism, 109–110, 111, 116, 130; Japanese immigrants, 107–108, 108–109, 112, 116; Korean immigrants, 118, 119, 123, 171

Hawai'i Mission of Hongpa Hongwanji, 109

Hayashi, Brian Masaru, 113–116, 128

Herberg, Will: importance of religious institutions, 33; *Protestant-Catholic-Jew*, 1, 102–103, 233; third generation, 236

Hermanidad de Penitentes (the Penitentes), 59–60, 70n1

Herskovits, Melville J., 233, 298, 320

Hertzberg, Arthur, 235

Heschel, Abraham, 235

Higa, Karin, 150

Hinduism, 103

Hirano, David, 142

Hirschman, Charles, 92–93

Hitti, Philip, *Syrians in America,* 250

Holocaust, 237, 240

home-centered religion, 36–37, 63, 332

Honda, Eryu, 110

Honda, Ralph, 130

Hong, Mr. (Korean immigrant), 184–185

Howe, Irving, 235

Hughes, Langston, 305

Hull House, 42

Hunter College, 203

Hurh, Won Moo, 166–167, 190n2

Hussein, Saddam, 252, 274

hybrid religions, 320

Hyun, Peter, 122–123

Hyun, Soon, 123

Ichioka, Yuji, 127

identity: Arab American identity, 267; Arab Muslim immigrants, 247–248, 267, 291; Arab Muslim pan-ethnic identity, 285–286, 290, 291, 293, 294; Arab nationalist identity, 258, 261; Asian pan-ethnic identity, 102, 109; ethnic identity, 222–223; fragmented selves, 243; hiding Buddhist identity, 169, 182, 186; hyphenated identity, 224, 225, 227, 231, 232, 237, 242, 243–244; Italian American identity, 36; Japanese impact on American identity, 139; Japanese racial-ethnic identity, 104, 137; Korean identity, 167–168, 189; multicultural selves, 243; Muslim immigrants, 267, 291; reinforcement of, 4; as temporary alliances, 243

Imamura, Yemyo, 130, 133n9

"immigrant," 140

"immigrant community," 140

immigrant congregations, 23

immigrants: generation, immigrant (*see* first generation); generation 1.5, 100; generations, post-immigrant (*see* second generation; third generation; fourth generation; fifth generation); geographic dispersion (*see* settlement patterns); with religions related to charter religions in United States, 10–11; with religions unrelated to charter religions in United States, 11; with religions well-established in the United Sates, 10, 25; religious pluralism in United States, 7–8; salvific role in United States, 6; success of, 92–95

immigration: concentration in time, 27, 34; linkages to home country, 126;

race, 131–133; religion-immigration nexus, 103; religion in studies of, 1–4; religious diversity of contemporary immigration, 11

Immigration Act (1924), 114, 121, 131. *See also* National Origin Act

Immigration and Nationality Act (1965), 12, 250, 322

Immigration and Naturalization Service (INS), 248, 249–250, 273, 323

Immigration Reform and Control Act (1986), 77

Indian immigrants, 6, 103

individualism: Arab Muslim immigrants, 241; Buddhism, 5, 19, 130, 188; Islam, 241; Judaism, 239–240, 241

Ingram, Abdullah, 264

integration into American society: Arab Muslim immigrants, 250; Catholic Church, 87–88, 95–96, 191; civil religion's integrative function, 143; eastern European Jewish immigrants, 244; Haitian immigrants, 300, 342; Japanese immigrants, 138; Mexican immigrants, 31, 73, 87–88, 95–96; Vodou, 333. *See also* acculturation; Americanization; assimilation; religious incorporation

intergenerational conflict: eastern European Jewish immigrants, 206, 215–216; educational attainments, 215–216; Italian immigrants, 46–47

intermarriage: Arab Muslim immigrants, 251, 293–294; assimilation, 10, 220; eastern European Jewish immigrants, 8, 15, 216–221, 236, 240; generational context, 216; Italian immigrants, 26, 29, 33, 45, 49–50, 53, 54, 55; Japanese immigrants, 101, 109; Korean immigrants, 101; Mexican immigrants, 74; Triple Melting Pot thesis, 10, 29

International Migration Program, 4

internment. *See* detention

Iraqi immigrants, 251, 260

Irish Catholics, 36, 45, 46, 58

Ishizuka, Karen, 162

Islam: African Americans, 312–313; assimilation, 253, 254; Christian fundamentalists, 268–269; individualism, 241; internal structures (families, networks, etc.), 194–195; as noninstitutional religion, 295; orthodoxy, debates over, 195–196; reinterpretation of traditional symbols, verities, 195–196; religious organization, 194; teachers and scholars, 195; *zakat,* 270

Islamic Center of Portland, 276n8

Islamic Horizon (journal), 265

Islamism, 261

Isma'ili immigrants, 251

ISNA (Islamic Society of North America), 265–266

Israel: Arab Muslim immigrants, 196–197, 259–264; Cohen on, Arthur, 235; eastern European Jewish immigrants, 196–197, 221, 237–238, 240; support for, 240

Israeli immigrants, 251

"Italian Americans," 47

Italian immigrants, 32–55; 1900-1914 period, 27, 34; American mainstream, 26, 28–29, 48; anti-Italian sentiments, 32; assimilability of, doubts about, 13, 25; *campanilismo* (parochialism), 35, 36; Catholic charismatic movement, 42; Catholic Church, attachment to, 13, 28–29; Catholic Church, attendance, 36, 37, 53; Catholic Church, contributions to, 39; Catholic Church, representation in church hierarchy, 76; Catholic clergy, attitudes toward, 41;

Italian immigrants (*Continued*)
Catholic devotional groups, 81–82;
Catholic identification, 50; Catholic religious orders, 41; Catholic schools, 14, 29, 45, 89; Catholicism, 10, 36–37, 49, 53; cemetery customs, 51–52; citizenship rights, 54; "color," 25; concentration of immigration in time, 27, 34; correlation between age and generational distance from immigration, 27; Cursillo movement, 52; discrimination against, 43; educational attainments, 25, 44; epithets for, 43; family chapels on private property, 40–41; family reunification, 34; *feste* (street festivals), 37–41, 46–48, 49, 51; first generation, 34–43; fourth generation, 29, 33, 52–53; generation-by-generation ascent, 33; goals, 26; healing tradition, 37; heterogeneity, 44; home-centered religion, 36–37; hospitals, fear of, 37; human-capital levels, 34, 43; intergenerational conflict, 46–47; intermarriage, 26, 29, 33, 45, 49–50, 53, 54, 55; Italian American identity, 36; Italian-language parishes, 28, 36, 39, 54; "Italian problem," 28, 41–42, 49–50; labor force participation, 44; low-wage migrants, 13, 25, 75; loyalty to Italy, Italian state, 35; Mexican immigrants compared to, 9–10, 13–15, 25–31, 49, 54, 78, 92; from the Mezzogiorno, 32, 34; mixed ancestry, 53; multiethnic, territorially based parishes, 45, 49; no religious affiliation, 50; from northern Italy, 34; organizational life, 35; in Philadelphia, 34; political power, 48, 51, 54; prayer, 53; Protestantism, conversion to, 28, 41–42, 50; public schools, 14, 44; racial "in-betweenness," 32; regional differences in intergenerational trajectories, 34; religious incorporation, 33; remittances, 34; return migration, 26, 34; saints, patronal, 38; seasonal migrants, 34; second generation, 14, 40, 41, 43–48, 89; "segmented assimilation," 43; settlement house workers, 42–43; settlement patterns, 35, 44, 49, 50–51; social mobility, 45, 54; socioeconomic distribution, 48–49; from southern Italy, 34–35, 36, 38, 41, 46, 49; spatial/outward mobility, 14, 33, 45, 54, 55; suburbanization, 50–51; syncretic Catholicism, 13; third generation, 14, 29, 33, 41, 48–52, 54, 76, 89; unskilled laborers, 35; upward mobility, 10, 14, 33, 35; urban renewal, 51; Vatican II, 52; vocations to the religious life, 45–46, 50; women, 35, 36–37, 41, 46
Ithna 'Ashari immigrants (Ja'faris), 251

Jackson, Jesse, 263
Jackson, Mahalia, 314
Jaisohn, Philip, 126
Jamal, Amaney, 280
Jang, James, 188–189
Japanese American Citizens League, 143, 148
"Japanese American Creed," 143, 164n3
Japanese American National Museum (JANM), 149–153; critical faith, 146, 153; cultural memory, 104, 137; history of, 149–153; Japanese spiritual ethos, 161; Life History Program, 152; photograph of, *150*; sister institution, 156
Japanese immigrants, 106–117, 135–165; 1885-1920, 106; 1888-1910, 107;

acculturation, 138; Alien Land Acts (California), 17; American mainstream, 101–102, 105, 138; ancestors, homage to, 159–161; anti-Japanese sentiments, 107–108, 114, 129–130, 132; assimilability of, doubts about, 107; assimilation, 101, 104, 109, 115, 138–139; boundary between religion, politics, culture, 142; Buddhism, 100, 107, 109–112, 116, 128–130, 138, 141; California, 108, 116, 117t; chosenness doctrine, 115; Christianity, 112–116; Christianity, conversion to, 17, 112–113; civil religion, 137, 142–148, 153, 156–160, 162–164; Commission on Wartime Relocation and Internment of Civilians (CWRIC) hearings, 146, 148–149, 161; community building, 107, 111–112; Confucianism, 99; critical faith, 144, 146, 153, 159; cultural memory, 104, 137, 153; detention of other immigrants, 155; fifth generation (Gosei), 145; first generation (Issei), 99, 107–108, 112–114, 116, 117t, 145, 158; fourth generation (Yonsei), 99, 104, 145; Gentlemen's Agreement (1907–1908), 107; "group orientation" of, 161; Hawai'i, 107–108, 108–109, 112, 116; homeland orientation of Japanese Christian churches, 18–19; impact on American identity and experience, 139; institutionalization of memory, 148 (*see also* Days of Remembrance; Japanese American National Museum; Manzanar Annual Pilgrimage); integration into American society, 138; intermarriage, 101, 109; internment during World War II, 101, 108, 134n10, 136, 137, 141, 143, 144–149, 156, 158, 162;

Japanese nationalist sentiment, 114, 115–116; Kibei, 127; Korean immigrants compared to, 12, 17–19, 99, 125, 126–127; Los Angeles, 117t; as "model minority," 138, 143; Naturalization Act (1790), 125; Nikkei, 164n1; Northwest, 108, 116, 117t; number, 106, 134n10; oral history, 152, 156, 160, 161; pan-ethnic identity, 109; patriotism, 143; political visibility, 106; Protestantism, 19, 107, 113–116, 117t, 128; Protestantism, conversion to, 100; racial-ethnic identity, 104, 137; racism, 147; racism against, 131; religious affiliations before immigrating, 100; religious affiliations in United States, 116–117, 139–140, 158, 161–162; religious beliefs, fundamental, 158; religious institutions as a refuge, 18; return migration, 108, 114; Seattle, 117t; second generation (Nisei), 99, 108–109, 112, 115, 116, 117t, 127, 128, 130, 145, 147–148, 149, 153–154, 158; segregated schools, 107; *senzo kuyô* (ancestral memorial rites), 159; settlement patterns, 108; *shikata ga nai* ("it cannot be helped now"), 146–147, 164; Shinto, 116, 117t; socioeconomic attainments, 101; spiritual culture, 159–162; *Tanko* (coal miner's dance), 155; third generation (Sansei), 99, 109, 142, 145, 147, 153; ultra-Americanness, 19; United States-Japan relations, 127; *Yamato damashii* ("Japanese spirit"), 159
Japanese Methodist Church, 113
Japanese Union Church, 113
Jesuits (Society of Jesus), 61
Jew Within (Cohen and Eisen), 241–242

Jewish immigrants: attractiveness to others, 216; from eastern Europe (*see* eastern European Jewish immigrants); educational attainments, 87; Jewish identification, Jewishness, 214, 217, 219–221; as model for Muslim immigrants, 11, 15, 192, 197, 263; salvific role in United States, 6; study habits, 87

Jin, Dr. (Korean immigrant), 185–187

Jin, Mrs. (Korean immigrant), 174–176

job skills: Central American immigrants, 73; Mexican immigrants, 73

Jodo Shinshu Buddhism, 109, 128–129, 130, 133n9

John Paul II, Pope, 68, 79

Jordanian immigrants, 252

Judaism: "614th commandment," 237; African Americans, 312–313; American mainstream, 11, 15; Americanness, 195; appeal of ancestors, 239; arguments about Jewish past, 222–223; as charter religion, 10–11, 191; Christian fundamentalists, 268–269; as a civilization, 229–233; communal commitment, 239–240; Conservative Judaism, 228, 229, 238; conversions to, 219; democracy and, 227; demographic continuity, 220; disengagement from Jewish community, 220; explanation of particularist practices in universal terms, 239; feminism, 238; Hanukkah, 229; individualism, 239–240, 241; internal structures (families, networks, etc.), 194–195; Jewish identification, Jewishness, 214, 217, 219–221; Jewish religion, 230; Jewish theology, disinterest in, 236–237; "maximalist Judaism," 231; ordination of women as rabbis, 238; Orthodox Judaism, 228, 229, 238, 239; orthodoxy, debates over, 195–196; Passover, 229; "public Judaism," 240; rabbinic teachings and Puritan ideals, 227; Reconstructionism, 238; Reform Judaism, 227, 229, 238; reinterpretation of traditional symbols, verities, 195–196; religious organization, 194; ritual observance, 236, 240–241; search for authority, 239; secularization, 222–223; *struggle with* God, 239; synagogue membership, attendance, 236, 241

Judaism as a Civilization (Kaplan), 232

Juliani, Richard, 34

Jung, Leo, "Sinai and Washington," 227

Kadowaki, Kakichi, 162

Kagahi, Soryu, 109–110

Kaji, Bruce, 151

Kallen, Horace, 233, 244

Kaplan, Mordecai: boundary between self and group, 245; chosenness doctrine, 228, 229–232; "living in two civilizations," 230–233, 242; "maximalist Judaism," 231; tolerance of cultural differences, 243

Kashima, Tetsuden, 131

Katayama, Sen, 113

Kennedy, John F., 9

Kennedy, Joseph, 263

Kennedy, Ruby Jo Reeves, 10, 33

Kibei, 127

Kim, Bernice, 118

Kim, Jung Ha, 120

Kim, Young Oak, 151

King, Martin Luther, Jr., 163

Kondo, Dorinne, 160

Korean Christian Church (KCC), 123–124

Korean Delegation of America, 120

Korean Evangelical Society, 123, 124

Korean immigrants, 118–128, 166–190; 1.5 generation, 100; 1903-1945 (early years), 119–120; 1945-1965 (aftermath of war), 120–121; 1965-present (recent arrivals), 121–122; acculturation, 167; American mainstream, 101–102, 105; Americanization, 167; Asian American congregations, 18; Buddhism, 104–105, 118, 124, 166–190; business connections, 177–178, 182–183; Catholicism, 94, 118; *chaesa* (ancestor memorial rites), 176; *chondo sa* (evangelizing woman), 181–182; Christianity, 100, 102, 171–172; Christianity, conversion to, 17, 18, 166, 170, 175, 177, 179, 180–183, 185, 187–189; Confucianism, 99; discrimination against Buddhists, 178; educational attainments, 101; English classes, 181–182, 184; Episcopalians, 124; first generation, 18, 100; girls, 176; growth of Korean American churches, 171–172; Hawai'i, 118, 119, 123, 171; hiding Buddhist identity, 169, 182, 186; independence movement against Japanese colonialism, 126; intermarriage, 101; Japanese immigrants compared to, 12, 17–19, 99, 125, 126–127; Korean identity, 167–168, 189; in Los Angeles, 171; Los Angeles riots (1992), 122; Methodist Church, 123–124; Naturalization Act (1790), 125; number, 119, 121; professional attainments, 101; Protestantism, 94, 118, 119, 121, 124, 126–127, 128; Protestantism, evangelical, 17, 100; race, 131–132; religion in life of, 118–120, 121–122; religious affiliations before immigrating, 100; religious affiliations in United States, 124; religious institutions as a refuge, 18; return migration, 120; rotating credit clubs *(kye)*, 172; salvific role in United States, 6; second generation, 18, 100, 173, 185–186; self-evaluation through high-status positions, 183; Seventh-Day Adventists, 124; small business successes, 172; social acceptance, 102; students, 121; war orphans, brides, 120–121; workers, 121; young adult socialization, 174, 190n4

Korean Methodist Church (Honolulu), 123–124

Korean United Church News (newspaper), 124

Ku Klux Klan, 1

Kumon, 88, 94, 98n2

Kwak, Soo Young, 179–180

Laguerre, Michel, 325

Lamersi (Haitian immigrant), 336

Lamy, Jean Baptiste, 60–61

Lana (housewife), 284–285

Latino immigrants: Asian immigrants compared to, 92–94; Catholic Church, 24, 31, 56, 71–72, 79–80, 84, 97–98; Catholic schools, 75, 90–91, 96; Latino priests, 83–84; no religious affiliation, 50; Protestantism, 80; upward mobility, 72, 91

Lazio, Rick, 263

Lebanese immigrants, 251, 260, 264

Lee-Sung, Audrey, 165n8

Leila (real estate broker), 290–291

Liberation Theology, 79, 84, 85, 330

Lieberman, Joe, 266

Lieberson, Stanley, *A Piece of the Pie*, 44

Lim, Dr. (Korean immigrant), 177–178

Linenthal, Edward, 162

Logan, John, 44

Lopez, David, 27–28

Los Angeles: Arab-origin population, 278; Buddhism, 171; Catholic
archdiocese, 84–85; Go for Broke
Monument, 164n4; Japanese immigrants, 117t; Korean immigrants,
171; Mexican-born population, 62;
Our Lady of the Angels, 68–69;
riots (1992), 122; Sa Chal temple,
167; St. Basil's Cathedral, 56, 69; St.
Vibiana's Cathedral, 68; schools,
Catholic, 91; schools, Spanish-language, 95; study habits, 95
Los Angeles Holiness Church, 113
Louisiana, Haitian immigrants in,
299–300
low-wage migrants, 13, 25, 75
Lowe, Lisa, 140
Lummis, Adair T., 253, 254–255, 256

Maeda, Sentoku, 136
Maghrebi immigrants (North Afri-
cans), 252
Mahmoud (restaurant owner), 286
Mahoney, Roger: cathedral project
(Our Lady of the Angels), 31, 80, 85,
97–98; positions on issues, 84–85
mainstream. *See* American mainstream
Mamiya, Y. B., 151
Manning, Timothy, 81
Manzanar Annual Pilgrimage, 136–137,
153–155, *154*, 159–160
Manzanar Committee, 155, 156
Manzanar National Historic Site, 156,
163
Manzanar National historic Site,
135–136
Martin, Sallie, 314
Martínez, Antonio José, 60–61
Masaoka, Mike, 143
Mashreqi immigrants (Levant and
Arabian Peninsula), 252
Masjid as-Sabir of Portland, 276n8

Mason, C. H., 302
Massey, Douglas, 77
McCarthy, Joseph, 15
McGovern, George, 263
McIntyre, James, 81
McVeigh, Timothy, 269
Mercy International, 288–289
mestizidad, 27–28
Methodist Church, 123
Métraux, Alfred, 338
Mexican immigrants, 56–98; 1910 to
1930, 73, 76; 1910s, 62; 1920s, 62–63;
1980s, 67; American mainstream,
13, 15; Anglo attitudes toward, 27;
anti-Mexican sentiments, 63; assimilability of, doubts about, 13,
25, 62; assimilation, 72–73; Blessing of the Animals, 82; Bracero
program, 64; California, 77, 78;
in California, 61–62, 64; Catholic Church, 56, 64–66, 67, 72, 75,
76, 80–85; Catholic Church, attachment to, 13, 30–31; Catholic
Church, attendance, 63; Catholic
Church, representation in church
hierarchy, 76; Catholic Church's attitude toward, 14; Catholic clergy,
56, 63; Catholic schools, 15, 75–76,
82; Catholicism, 10, 13; Católicos
por la Raza, 56; citizenship rights,
54; civil religion, 162–163; civil
rights movement, 65–66; "color,"
25; Cursillo movement (*Cursillos
de Cristianidad*), 64–65; deportations (1930s), 27, 54, 63–64; dual
nationality, 67; educational attainments, 25, 30, 73, 75; ethnic ascription, shift in, 62; first generation,
59, 73, 75; folk religious practices,
56; goals, 26; Great Depression, 76;
historical relation to United States,
25, 27, 57; home-centered religion,

63; institutional discrimination against, 31; integration, economic, 73; integration into American society, 31, 87–88, 95–96; intermarriage, 74; Italian immigrants compared to, 9–10, 13–15, 25–31, 49, 54, 78, 92; job skills, 73; lay practitioners, 57; lay societies, 30; legal immigrants, 67; in Los Angeles, 62; low-wage migrants, 13, 25, 75; *mestizidad,* 27–28; occupational segregation, 78; political activism, 65; political power, 54; population growth in United States, 77; Protestantism, 74, 82, 84; Protestantism, conversion to, 63, 67, 83; Protestantism, evangelical, 30, 84; protests at St. Basil's Cathedral, 56; public schools, 31; racism against, 27–28, 74; saints, patronal, 68; second generation, 28, 73; "segmented assimilation," 43; segregated schools, 27; settlement patterns, 77–78, 82; social acceptance, 78; social mobility, 30; Spanish-speaking clerics, parishes, 30, 66, 81, 82, 83–84, 86; syncretic Catholicism, 13; Tejanos, 62; in Texas, 78; third generation, 28, 49, 54, 73, 78–79; transnationalism, 67; undocumented immigrants, 27, 67, 68, 76–77; upward mobility, 10, 72–74, 75, 78, 93–94
Mexican Revolution (1910), 62–63
Mexican War of Independence (1810-1821), 59
Missionary Sisters of the Sacred Heart of Jesus, 41
Miyama, Kan'ichi, 113–114
Miyamoto, Ejun, 110
"model minority," Japanese immigrants as, 138, 143
Mondale, Walter, 263

Monroy, Douglas, 82
Moorish Science Temple, 313
Morales, Juan Castillo (Juan Soldado), 68
Morgenstern, Julian, 227–228
Morikawa, Jitsuo, 142
Moroccan immigrants, 252
Morse, Samuel, 58
Muhammed, Warith Deen, 248
Muslim American Society (MAS), 248
Muslim Brotherhood, 260
Muslim Community Association of Ann Arbor, 276n8
Muslim immigrants, 264–273; 1970-1990, 265; American mainstream, 15; anti-Muslim sentiments, 258, 273, 294; Arab Muslim immigrants as percentage of, 249 (*see also* Arab Muslim immigrants); Asian immigrants, 251; coalition building, 271–272, 274, 288, 292, 293; detention, 269–270; discrimination, perception of, 289; diversity among, 193; emphasis on differences with American culture, religion, 265; freedom of thought, 272; governmental scrutiny of, 269–271; Gulf War (1990-1991), 265; identity, self-, 267, 291; institutions, 279–280, 286; "Islamic dress," 256–257, 265; Jewish immigrants as model for, 11, 15, 192, 197, 263; *juma* (Friday communal prayers), 257; leadership, 265; mosque attendance, 257, 282–283, 287; Muslim women, 256–257, 265, 270, 283, 295; networks, personal, 277–278, 281, 283, 285, 288; number, 248; organizations, 265–267, 283, 284, 287–293, 294–295; political activism, 268, 271–272; post 9/11 era, 267–272, 277; relationship between mosqued and un-mosqued, 271;

Muslim immigrants (*Continued*) salvific role in United States, 6; secular Muslims, 267; self-censorship, 271; "sisters" groups, 257, 271; as threat to United States, 268; veiling, 256, 271; visibility, 294

Muslim Public Affairs Council (MPAC), 266

Muslim World League (MWL), 252–253, 255

Najwa (teacher), 287–290, 292

Nasser, Gamal Abdel-, 260

Nation of Islam, 313

National Association of Arab Americans (NAAA), 263

National Association of Federations, 259

National Association of Syrian and Lebanese-American Organizations, 259

National Catholic Education Association (NCEA), 90

National Center for the Preservation of Democracy, 156–157

National Coalition for Redress/Reparations (NCRR), 148

National Council for Japanese American Redress (NCJAR), 148

National Japanese American Monument to Patriotism, 145, 164n3, 164n4

National Jewish Population Surveys, 206, 208

National Origin Act (1924), 249

Naturalization Act (1790), 125

Near East Report (weekly publication), 261–262

Negro World (journal), 312

Neusner, Jacob, 237

New Bethel Baptist Church (Detroit), 317

New Ethnic and Immigrant Congregations Project, 2

New Mexico, 57, 58–61, 81, 82–83

New Religious America (Eck), 2

New York City: Catholic Church, 329–331; Haitian immigrants, 301, 323, 324, 327, 343–347, 350; Protestantism, evangelical, 343–347; Vodou, 332–334, 350

Nichiren Buddhism, 109

Niisata, Kan'ichi, 114

Nishi Hongwanji sect, 109, 149–151, 156

Nishijima, Kakuryo, 110

Nixon, Richard, 262

North American Buddhist Mission (Buddhist Mission of North America), 110, 131

Oakar, Mary Rose, 269

Oblate Sisters of Providence, 300

occupational mobility and disaffection from ethnic community, 212

Ogura, Kosei, 131

Oh, Mrs. (Korean immigrant), 168–169

Okihiro, Gary, 141, 158

Olivet Baptist Church (Chicago), 310

Omar (autoworker), 280–282, 286, 287

Operation Boulder (FBI), 262

Organization of Arab Students (OAS), 261

Organization of Islamic Conference (OIC), 252–253

Orsi, Robert: Catholic schools, 89; ethnicity of Catholic priests, 86; framework for comparing Italian and Mexican immigrants, 75; history of Catholics, 163; religion and immigration, 2

Orthodox Judaism, 228, 229, 238, 239

Outb, Sayyid, 260

outward mobility. *See* spatial/outward mobility

Padres Asociados para Derechos Religiosos, Educativos y Sociales (PADRES), 66

Pak, Yong-man, 119, 126

Pakistani immigrants, 255

Palestinian immigrants, 251, 252

Palmieri, Aurelio, 41

Park, Kyeyoung, 172, 190n2

Patterson, Wayne, 119, 123

Penisulares, 59

Penitentes (Hermanidad de Penitentes), 59–60, 70n1

Pentecostalism: African Americans of the Great Migration, 313–314; Afro-Creole culture, 345; American chosenness doctrine, 347; attractiveness to immigrants, 42; Catholic charismatic movement (Catholic Pentecostalism), 42, 52; Haitian immigrants, 20, 21–22; transnationalism, 343; upward mobility, 21, 314; Vodou, 345–346. *See also* evangelical Protestantism

Pepe (Haitian immigrant), 336

Percy, Charles H., 262

Petersen, William, 138

Pew Charitable Trusts, 3, 4

Pharisees (Finkelstein), 227

Pious Society of St. Charles (Scalabrini Fathers), 39, 41

Plate, S. Brent, 153

Plessy, Homére, 299–300

Plessy v. Ferguson, 300

Polish Peasant in Europe and America (Thomas and Znaniecki), 1–2

political activism: Arab Muslim immigrants, 262, 263–264, 268, 271–272, 273, 283, 286, 296n4; Haitian immigrants, 344; Mexican immigrants, 65; Muslim immigrants, 268, 271–272

political asylum and Haitian immigrants, 323

political power: African Americans, 308; African Americans of the Great Migration, 314–316; Italian immigrants, 48, 51, 54; Mexican immigrants, 54

Portes, Alejandro, 93, 339

Price-Mars, Jean, 298

professional attainments: Arab Muslim immigrants, 192, 255; eastern European Jewish immigrants, 207, 208, 209, 213; Korean immigrants, 101

Promised Land narrative, 20, 316–317, 318, 319

Protestant-Catholic-Jew (Herberg), 1, 102–103, 233

Protestant Ethic and the Spirit of Capitalism (Weber), 2

Protestantism: African Americans, 303; American mainstream, 11; Anglo-Saxonism, 8–9; Asian immigrants, 94; attitudes toward Mexican American Catholics, 14; as charter religion, 10–11; conversion to, 28, 41–42, 50, 63, 67, 80, 100; evangelical forms (*see* evangelical Protestantism); Haitian immigrants, 329, 339–340; home missionary outreach programs, 42; Italian immigrants, 28, 41–42, 50; Japanese immigrants, 19, 100, 107, 113–116, 117t, 128; Korean immigrants, 94, 118, 119, 121, 124, 126–127, 128; Latin America, 79; Latino immigrants, 80; Liberation Theology, 85; Mexican immigrants, 63, 67, 74, 82, 83, 84; proselytizers among Catholics, 8

public schools, 14, 31, 44

Puerto Ricans, 48

Pure Land Buddhism, 160, 164n7

Quinn Chapel African Methodist Episcopal (AME), 315

Raboteau, Albert, 320, 348
race: "color," 25; eastern European Jewish immigrants, 192; Haitian immigrants, 326–327, 352; immigration, 131–133; "in-between," 32; Italian immigrants, 32; Korean immigrants, 131–132; religion, 12; religion-immigration nexus, 103; religious incorporation, 17
racism: Haitian immigrants, 326; Japanese immigrants, 131, 147; Mexican immigrants, 27–28, 74; religion, 19–20; religious incorporation, 12
Radio Bonne Nouvelle, 344
Radio Soleil, 330
Ransom, Reverdy, 315
Reagan, Ronald, 145, 323
Reform Judaism, 227, 229, 238
religion: as an institution, 3–4; assimilation, 279; charter religions, 10–11, 191; compatibility with democracy, 104; connections to the homeland, 6–7; conversion from one religion to another (*see* conversion); economic significance, 2; ethnic community building, 5–6; expression of ethnic difference, 22–23; hybrid religions, 320; identity, reinforcement of, 4; immigrant congregations, 23; pluralism, 244; race, 12; racism, 19–20; religion-immigration nexus, 103; religious diversity of contemporary immigration, 11; religious pluralism in United States, 7–8; return to religion of grandparents, 236; self-esteem, support for, 4; social services, 4; in studies of immigration, 1–4; success of immigrants, 92–95; as a system of meaning, 3–4; as transnational institutions, 7. *See also* civil religion; critical faith

Religion across Borders (Ebaugh and Chafetz), 4
"Religion and Ethnicity in America" (Smith), 162
"Religion and Resistance in America's Concentration Camps" (Okihiro), 158
Religion and the New Immigrants (Ebaugh and Chafetz), 4
"religious competition," 72, 97
religious incorporation: American mainstream, 28–29; Italian immigrants, 33; race, 17; racism, 12
Religious Pluralism Project, 2
remittances: African Americans of the Great Migration, 309; Haitian immigrants, 298, 337; Italian immigrants, 34
Republican Party, 78
residential distribution. *See* settlement patterns
return migration: Italian immigrants, 26, 34; Japanese immigrants, 108, 114; Korean immigrants, 120
Rhee, Syngman, 119, 123, 126
Roberta Martin Singers, 314
Roediger, David, 32
Roland, Père, 339, 340
Roman Catholic Church. *See* Catholic Church
Roman Catholicism. *See* Catholicism
Romo, Toribio, 68
Roof, Wade Clark, 239
Roosevelt, Franklin, 114, 144–145, 164n6
"roots" movement, 302–303, 328
Roth, Philip, "Eli the Fanatic," 234, 235
Rudd, Dan A., 303
Rumbaut, Rubén, 93
Ryang, Ju-sam, 124

Saeed, Agha, 266
St. Dominique island, 321–322

St. Mark's Methodist Episcopal Church (Chicago), 310–311
St. Patrick's Battalion, 58
Santería, 22
Scalabrini, Giovanni Battista, 41
Scalabrini Fathers (Pious Society of St. Charles), 39, 41
schools: Catholic schools (*see* Catholic schools); Islamic, 287, 288; Kumon cram schools, 94; Los Angeles, 91, 95; public schools, 14, 31, 44. *See also* educational attainments
seasonal migrants, 34
second generation: Arab Muslim immigrants, 263, 274, 279; eastern European Jewish immigrants, 192, 204, 225, 226–234; Italian immigrants, 14, 40, 41, 43–48, 89; Japanese immigrants (Nisei), 99, 108–109, 112, 115, 116, 117t, 127, 128, 130, 145, 147–148, 149, 153–154, 158; Korean immigrants, 18, 100, 173, 185–186; Mexican immigrants, 28, 73
Second Vatican Council. *See* Vatican II
Servin, Manuel, 83
Servites, 41
settlement house workers, 42–43
settlement patterns: Arab Muslim immigrants, 248–249, 264; eastern European Jewish immigrants, 201, 203, 205, 213; Haitian immigrants, 323–324; Italian immigrants, 35, 44, 49, 50–51; Japanese immigrants, 108; Mexican immigrants, 77–78, 82
Seventh-Day Adventists, 124
Seymour, William J., 302
Sheil, Bernard, 44
Shi'ite immigrants, 251
Shin, Jae Woo, 184
Shingon Buddhism, 109
Shinto, 116, 117t

Sikh immigrants, 163
"Sinai and Washington" (Jung), 227
Sisters of Charity, 61
Sisters of Loretto, 61
Sisters of Mercy, 61
Sklare, Marshall, 234
Smith, Al, 9
Smith, Lucy, 314
Smith, Timothy, "Religion and Ethnicity in America," 162
Smith, William C., 132
social mobility: Catholic educational institutions, 29; eastern European Jewish immigrants, 203, 205, 209, 211; Italian immigrants, 45, 54; Mexican immigrants, 30; occupational mobility, 212. *See also* upward mobility
Social Science Research Council, 4
Soldada, Juan (Juan Castillo Morales), 68
Song, In Soon, 180–182
Sonoda, Shuye, 110
Soto Zen Buddhism, 109
South Florida, Haitian immigrants in, 301, 323, 324, 334–343
Southern California Japanese Christian Church Federation, 115
spatial/outward mobility: acculturation, 55; Italian immigrants, 14, 33, 45, 54, 55
Stanton-Salazar, Ricardo, 27–28
Steinberg, Milton, 226
Steinberg, Steven, 87, 93
Stepick, Alex, 339
Street-Corner Society (Whyte), 44
Sunni immigrants, 251
Survey of Race Relations (1924), 132
Syrian and Lebanese American Federation of the Eastern States, 259
Syrian immigrants, 251, 252, 260, 264
Syrians in America (Hitti), 250

Takei, George, 143
Tamashiro, Ben, 164n5
Tejanos, 62
Tejas (territory), 59
Tendai Buddhism, 109
Texas, 78, 82–83
third generation: Arab Muslim immigrants, 263; eastern European Jewish immigrants, 205, 234–237; Herberg on, Will, 236; Italian immigrants, 14, 29, 33, 41, 48–52, 54, 76, 89; Japanese immigrants (Sansei), 99, 109, 142, 145, 147, 153; Mexican immigrants, 28, 49, 54, 73, 78–79; return to religion of grandparents, 236
Thomas, Jesse, 306
Thomas, W. I., *Polish Peasant in Europe and America* (with Znaniecki), 1–2
Thompson, William Hale, 315
Ti Chini (Haitian immigrant), 336
Ti Rivyè, Haiti, migrants from, 334–335, 337
Tijerina, Reies, 65
Toledo, Ohio, 253–254, 255
Tonantzin, 67
transnationalism: Catholic Church, 303; Catholicism, 20; Haitian immigrants, 20, 300–301, 320, 324–325, 330–331, 335, 342, 349–350; linkages to home country, 126; Mexican immigrants, 67; Pentecostalism, 343; religions as transnational institutions, 7; Vodou, 20
Triple Melting Pot thesis, 29
Tule Lake Pilgrimage, 153
Tunisian immigrants, 252
Tweed, Thomas, 331
Tydings-McDuffie Act (1924), 133n1

undocumented immigrants: Central American immigrants, 77; Mexican immigrants, 27, 67, 68, 76–77

United Auto Workers (UAW), 283
United Farm Workers (UFW), 65
U. S. Conference of Catholic Bishops, 5, 76, 83
United States foreign policy: Arab Muslim immigrants, 197, 252, 281–282, 294; eastern European Jewish immigrants, 197
U. S.-Mexico War (1846-1848), 57
U. S. Supreme Court, 101
Universal Negro Improvement Association (UNIA), 312
upward mobility: Asian immigrants, 93–94; Catholic schools, 91; community spirit, 94; Cuban immigrants, 95; eastern European Jewish immigrants, 15; empowerment of local congregations, 94; Haitian immigrants, 21; Italian immigrants, 10, 14, 33, 35; Latino immigrants, 72, 91; Mexican immigrants, 10, 72–74, 75, 78, 93–94; Pentecostalism, 21, 314. *See also* social mobility
urban renewal, 51
USA PATRIOT Act (2001), 269

Vatican II (Second Vatican Council, 1962-1965): Italian immigrants, 52; Liberation Theology, 84; Protestantism, evangelical, 79; secular left, 79; Spanish in the mass, 30, 66; vocations to the religious life, 50
Vietnamese immigrants, 93, 94
Virgin of Guadalupe: Guadalupanas, 64; procession honoring, 82; at St. Basil's Cathedral, 69; as symbol of protest, 65, 66–67; United Farm Workers (UFW), 65
Vodou, 332–339; African Americans, distancing from, 334; African religions, 20, 22; cassette tapes of rituals, 335; conversion to

Protestantism, 337–339, 350–352; Creole, 330; economic responsibilities, 7; Ginen, 349; Haitian Revolution (1791-1804), 345; integration into American society, 333; *Iwa* (ancestral spirits), 298; *Iwa*, obligations to, 321, 335–339, 348–349; *manbo* (priestesses), 332, 350; middle-class Haitians, 334; New York City, 332–334, 350; *oungan* (priests), 332, 350; Pentecostalism, 345–346; pride in national sovereignty, 345; resistance to ritual exploitation, 337, 351; social support networks, 334; transnationalism, 20; upper-class Haitians, 334

Wakahiro, Soichi, 136
Waldinger, Roger, 87
Waldron, Jeremy, 243
Walzer, Michael, 243–244
Warner, Stephen, 2–3
Wartime Relocation Authority, 159
Waters, Mary, *Black Identities*, 12
Weber, Max, *Protestant Ethic and the Spirit of Capitalism*, 2
Weigle, Martha, 70n1
Wenski, Thomas, 340
Whyte, William Foote, *Street-Corner Society*, 44
Williams, Duncan, 141
Williams, Lacey Kirk, 310
Wittner, Judith, *Gatherings in Diaspora* (with Warner), 2–3
women: Afro-Haitian, 300; eastern

European Jewish immigrants, 206–207, 209, 210, 241; Haitian immigrants, 332; healing tradition, 37; "Islamic dress," 256–257, 265; Italian immigrants, 35, 36–37, 41, 46; Jewish immigrants, 217; Muslim immigrants, 256–257, 265, 270, 283, 284–285, 287–291, 295; ordination as rabbis, 238; religious orders of, 41; settlement house workers, 42–43
Wong, Flo Oy, 152
Wong, Morrison, 92–93
Woocher, Jonathan, 157–158
World War II, 108, 141, 156
Wright, Richard, 304
Wuthnow, Robert, 239

Yamada, Shoi, 110
Yemeni immigrants, 251, 256, 260
YMCA, 113, 126, 129
Yoo, David, 112
Young Buddhists Association, 129, 130
Young Men's and Women's Buddhist Associations (YBAs), 111–112
Young Men's Buddhist Association, 110

Zaidi immigrants, 251
Zhou, Min, 93
Zionism, 229, 235, 259–264
Znaniecki, Florian, *Polish Peasant in Europe and America* (with Thomas), 1–2
Zogby, James, 263, 282
Zubria, Bishop, 59–60